BRENTWOOD

LORD GODDARD

The Lord Chief Justice upon his appointment to office, the
photograph signed and dated by Lord Goddard and given to his
grandson, Richard Sachs

Goddard
L.C.J.
21/1/46.

LORD GODDARD

A Biography of Rayner Goddard
Lord Chief Justice of England

FENTON BRESLER

With a Foreword by Lord Denning

Harrap  London

To My Wife Gina—in love and tribute

First published in Great Britain 1977
by GEORGE G. HARRAP & CO. LTD
182–184 High Holborn, London WC1V 7AX

ISBN 0 245 50955 0

Designed by Michael R. Carter

Text set in 11/13 pt Photon Baskerville, printed by photolithography,
and bound in Great Britain at The Pitman Press, Bath

Foreword

by The Right Honourable Lord Denning
Master of the Rolls

This book tells the story of a great man. There are still a few living who knew him well. Their recollections have formed the source of much that is written here. So the author has been able to give us a portrait of the man as he truly was—of his upbringing, his home, his family and his work, both at the Bar, on the Bench, and as Lord Chief Justice of England. Many biographies of lawyers are little more than a recitation of the cases in which they have been engaged. This biography is different. In it the reader does get to know the man as he was. There are some cases in it. But they serve to show the man at work: and they are fascinating in themselves. The author does not suffer from hero-worship. He gives a true rendering of his subject. He has remembered the request which Oliver Cromwell made to Mr Lely: "I desire you would use all your skill to paint my picture truly like me and not flatter me at all; but remark all these roughnesses, pimples, warts and everything as you see me, otherwise I will never pay a farthing for it." Just such words as Rayner Goddard himself would have used.

Rayner Goddard was the very embodiment of the common law. He seemed to have it in his very bones. He knew all about the relics of medieval lore, such as "praying a tales" or "puts himself upon his country". He knew by heart the oath taken by the Grand Jury. He used to say that it was the finest piece of prose in the language. He got all this knowledge, not from reading books on legal history, but from tradition handed down on the Western Circuit. He used to speak of Cockburn, Coleridge and Foote as if they were only of yesterday. Yet, although he had all this knowledge of ancient practice, he had a firm grasp of principle. He delighted in legal argument. He often said that, of all his time on the Bench, he enjoyed most his time in the Court of Appeal on the civil side. He was only there six years—not long enough to preside in that Court, but he liked the variety of the cases—on every subject of law there ever was. He liked the pressure of work and the companionship of minds as quick and alert as his own. In contrast, he did not like the slow pace of the House of Lords. There was not enough scope for his abundant vitality and energy. It was a stroke of genius that, after only two years there, he was brought back to be Lord Chief Justice. It was there that he achieved his greatness. What was the secret of it?

First, I would put his quickness of perception. He rarely read the papers beforehand. But, as Counsel opened the case, he grasped the point with extraordinary rapidity. Like the runner, quick off the mark. If Counsel was fumbling his way, he would say sharply: "Come to the point. Is it this?" As soon as the point emerged, he could dart at once to its solution. Like a sprinter, in a flash. Almost too quick. Counsel would sometimes be left gasping. The case would be on and over in no time. A young man would go away crestfallen. For some it was rather frightening. The formidable Chief Justice put them in fear. But if the young man had a good answer—and made it—the great man would listen and give effect to it. Many a time I have known him come round—resiling from his first initial leap. It was a lesson which many learnt. "Stick to your guns. If you are right, you will win."

Next, his despatch of business. He brooked no delay. Every case had to be ready when it was called on. Otherwise he said firmly—"Strike it out. Call the next." His list of cases had to be full for the day so that no time of the Court was left spare. He disposed of the cases so rapidly that Mr Justice Cassels—beloved 'Jimmy'—made a little fun about it. As the Chief went into the near door into the Court—and Jimmy had to go further to the far door—he would say: "I must hurry or the case will be on and over before I get there". The Chief, too, had a good way of reducing the number of appeals in criminal cases. The Court then had the power to increase the sentence. He let that be known. That disposed of many frivolous appeals.

Besides this, he dominated the Court. He was so much in command that his colleagues on either side did not venture to take much part in the discussion. At any rate, not too much part. Only an experienced and wise old hand like Mr Justice Humphreys—'Travers', as we called him. Even the Chief would listen respectfully to anything that Travers said, and would follow his line of thought. Apart from those rare occasions, the Chief would, as often as not, whisper to his colleagues: "There's nothing in this, is there?" Then, on getting their murmured assents, he would straightway give judgment. I have known him not to bother to ask them, but to take their assent for granted and deliver judgment forthwith.

Important as well was that he was forthright in speech. He was not an orator to sway a crowd. He was not eloquent to charm an audience. But he was clear and forceful. Never long-winded. No long or confused sentences. No parenthesis. No shilly-shallying. Simple sentences in words which everyone in Court would understand—straight to the point—such that all would at once feel—"That's sound common-sense".

He usually gave judgment extempore—straight off the reel. Occasionally in a difficult case he would take time to consider it. But he did not do a great deal of research himself. He expected Counsel to have drawn attention to all the relevant authorities. He was so well-versed in the law that he would reach the right result almost by instinct. And, when he came to prepare his judgments, he did not cite many cases, or rely on long quotations from others. He stated his propositions or conclusions simply and clearly. That is why they command such respect.

He looked the part, too. His keen brown eyes, his rugged features, his firm mouth and strong chin showed the character of the man. It showed that he was one who would uphold the law. He would "clear the innocent and convict and punish the guilty". He would stand no nonsense from anyone. He would pronounce the sentence. He would see that it was carried out. All respected him. Some feared him. None dare scorn him.

There were some of us who were privileged to see the other part of his life. At home with his wife whom he adored, and three charming daughters; or on holiday by the sea in Dorset. Their welfare was his dearest concern. At the Bar-mess on Circuit or in the Lodgings. He was excellent company, telling his stories with zest; reciting "Albert and the Lion"; showing his knowledge of port and his taste for it. At a sip he could tell the very year of its vintage, and always correctly. He was ever thoughtful for others, helping those in need, sharing their troubles, and rejoicing in their joys. It is strange how one who was stern in the public estimation should kindle such affection in those close to him. But he did so. It is well to have this recorded. This book is a true record of one of the foremost men of his time. It is well worth reading, not only by lawyers, but by all.

Preface

This is the story of a man's life. It was a long life, lived entirely within the confines of his chosen profession: the Law. Rayner Goddard had few outside interests, very little involvement with anything else other than his work, his family and his friends.

He lived for just over ninety-four years. This book is not, and does not purport to be, a record of that near-century of history. It does not attempt to assess the legal validity of his judgments from the Bench, the precise nature of his achievements as Lord Chief Justice of England or his effect upon the evolution of English law: that task is left to other, more academic, minds to weigh and assert.

This is an official biography. But it is a portrait of a man, bull-dog of face and stout of heart, told without fear or favour: independent of influence from friend and foe alike.

Rayner Goddard needs no apology, whitewash was never a form of colouring acceptable to him. If anyone wants to know what manner of man was the most controversial Lord Chief Justice of this century, what were the mainsprings of his being, the cases that provided the full, rich back-drop to his remarkable career—then it is hoped they will read on, and feel that they have come into the presence of a personality whose imprint on all those who came into contact with him, whether privately or as fellow-judge, counsel, defendant in the dock, litigant, witness or juror remains undimmed by time. Greatness is not a catching disease, and people remember it when they meet it.

I must express my sincere gratitude to the following persons, whose co-operation and helpfulness alone made it possible for this book to be written:

Family: Sir Eric and Lady Sachs, Mrs Pamela Maurice, Mrs Prue Clayton, Mr Richard Sachs.

Judges and Lawyers: the late Lord Parker of Waddington, Lord Denning, Lord Dilhorne, Lord Edmund-Davies, Lord Hodson, Lord Shawcross, Lord Stow Hill, Lord Justice Cairns, Sir Norman Skelhorn, Q.C., Sir Albert Napier, Sir Joseph Molony, Q.C., Sir George Coldstream, Sir Peter Rawlinson, Q.C., M.P., Judge Peter Mason, the late Judge Clifford Cohen, Mr Eric Crowther, Mr Edward Grayson, Mr Philip Panto, Mr Quintin Iwi, Mr Anthony Samuelson, Mr Edward Birch, Mrs Irving Gradwell, Mr Phillip Levy, Sir Anthony Highmore King, Q.C., Sir Fred Pritchard, Judge Ifor Lloyd, Q.C., the late Sir Kenneth Younger, Sir Gordon Willmer, Mr Timothy Daniell.

Others: Mr Sidney Newland, J.P., Lord Cudlipp, Major Cyril Tolley, Lord Adeane, Lord Arran, Mr Bernard Levin, Dowager Countess de la Warr, Mrs Frida Laski, Mrs Nellie Walpole, Mrs Joan Weston, Mrs Naomi Lloyd, Mr H. N. Kent, Mr Tom Ashworth, Mr Reginald Jennings, Sir John Masterman, Mr William Miller, Professor Paul Thompson, Mr Peter Stephenson, Mr William Fell, Mr Frederick Fairfax, Dr David Haler, Mr Joseph Gaute and Mr Roy Minton for his Index.

During the text, when any of these persons are quoted, without any specific source being cited, they have, in fact, spoken or written direct to me; and I must also state my special indebtedness to Weidenfeld and Nicolson, publishers of *Lord Goddard*, a book of reminiscences by the late Arthur Smith, Lord Goddard's former clerk, for the quotations from Mr Smith, and to the Director of Public Prosecutions for his kind permission to quote from the official transcript of the Craig and Bentley trial.

Contents

Illustrations

"Lord Goddard? You mean Lord God-damn!"
— Winston Churchill

1 The Start of the Story

Rayner Goddard, who, as judge and Lord Chief Justice, was to embody all the traditional characteristics of the Englishman, pugnacious, outspoken, bulldog of appearance and of temperament, came of stock as English as ancient oak. His very name would indicate that his roots lie deep in the history of our nation.

The Norsemen of Norway and Denmark acknowledged the divine right of the descendants of Odin. To that man-god their kings invariably traced their origin. He whose descent was undoubted was a Godr—one of the sacred race—able to make sacrifice in his double office of priest and king. When the land became too crowded, or the spirit of adventure stirred, a member of that sacred race—a Godr—stepped on board his nailed bark and, followed by a small band of warriors, sailed away across the seas to seek a new land.

Arrived, he ran his ship ashore, took possession of the soil and, consecrating a spot to Odin, became the Godord or priest-king.

So late as the mid-eleventh century, only a few weeks before William of Normandy embarked from France, came the last invasion of England by Norsemen in their long, dark, menacing boats. They were repulsed by Harold at Stamford Bridge in Yorkshire a bare three weeks before Harold met his death at Hastings. Many of the Northern invaders were killed, some escaped back across the North Sea—and others scattered, to settle and build their lives afresh in the alien land. Only a century or so later, documentary evidence already shows the existence of a local family bearing the name of Godardville—the 'ville' a Norman-French addition.

By the early thirteenth century, they had gravitated down to the

Swindon region of North Wiltshire, and ever since, soon jettisoning the 'ville' suffix, the Goddards have been one of the leading families of the area. Writing in 1873, with all the confident assurance of mid-Victorian prosperity and only four years before Rayner Goddard's birth, Richard Jefferies in his privately published memoir *The Goddards of North Wilts* asserted, "The history of England is the history of great families; and, following the same general rule, the history of Swindon, since it became a place, is, in fact, the history of the family of Goddard".

But it would be a mistake to confuse ancient lineage with material wealth. One can still see in St Michael's Church, Aldbourne—the Wiltshire village which Rayner Goddard later took as part of his title as Baron Goddard of Aldbourne—a large stone monument with kneeling effigies of Thomas Goddard, who died in 1597, his second wife and their four children. But Rayner's was a collateral branch of the family; the large country houses, the splendid memorials in the local churches, were not theirs.

Rayner's grandfather, Charles Goddard, born in 1807, was a doctor in Stroud, Gloucestershire. He married an Uxbridge girl called Maria Catherine Rayner, and 'Rayner' has since frequently been a Christian name for a Goddard. Not that the two families got on very well: writing to Lady Pickthorn, a great-great-niece of his grandmother, in February 1969, during his ninety-second year, Lord Goddard wrote, "I never really knew anything about my Rayner relations except that I was once taken by my father to see three old ladies who lived at Uxbridge with their brother who had a very small medical practice—his qualification was that of L.S.A. only. I did see the old ladies very occasionally after I had gone into practice at the Bar.

"But my aunts, my father's sisters, would never tell me anything about the Rayners—I gathered there had been some family quarrel which I suppose involved my grandmother in some way—my father said it was all great nonsense, but he was the only one of his family who would have anything to do with his mother's family."

Rayner's father, also a Charles Goddard, was born in 1842. One of a family of eight children, he was brought up by two maiden aunts in a small house near Newbury that is now an antique shop on the road from Marlborough. "They used to maltreat him," says Mrs Pamela Maurice, Rayner's eldest daughter and a repository of much family history.

He was articled to a firm of solicitors at Stroud; but as soon as he could he moved away from the country and came to live and practise in London. In December 1870, aged twenty-eight, he founded with Henry Peacock the firm of Peacock & Goddard at 3 South Side, Gray's Inn. It proved a highly successful practice and Charles Goddard's portrait as an old man—looking remarkably like his famous son in later life—still hangs on the wall of the downstairs waiting-room in the firm's present offices at Raymond Buildings, Gray's Inn, to which they moved after bomb damage in the Second World War.

Since Charles Goddard's third son Ernest, Rayner's younger brother, died in 1956, no member of the family has been associated with the practice, and in 1975 it changed its name to Turner Peacock.

In 1872 Charles Goddard married Janet Gertrude Jobson, a very pretty girl from Derbyshire who was known as "the Belle of Derby". They had three sons and two daughters: "a nice, well-planned Victorian family" comments Lady (Peggy) Sachs, Rayner's second daughter.

"My grandfather was very much the family solicitor," says Lady Sachs. "He would not ever do, or be seen or be thought to be seen doing, anything to promote his own personal family interest. He doted on Rayner, who was appallingly spoiled—but I don't think he ever gave him a brief!

"He was very much of the old school. He would never have a typewriter, telephone or woman worker in his office.

"Rayner was very close to his father. 'It was Rayner, Rayner all the way,' said my Aunt Maud, his younger sister. He had everything he wanted from the day he was born, nothing was too good for him. Uncle Harry, the eldest son, had infantile paralysis—and no one realized it: so he was a little retarded. All the family hopes and fears went to Rayner, the No. 2. There was a very great affection between Rayner and his father. They used to go for walks together on Sundays. He was very, very sad when, in May 1922, just ten days after his Golden Wedding, the old man died at the age of eighty."

Charles Goddard's obituary in *The Times* could, almost word for word, have been written with equal appositeness for his son Rayner: "He devoted his life to his profession and had few outside interests, but in his profession he found ample scope for his energies. By his integrity, high character and practical common sense, he won the respect of all and, though the last thing he sought was popularity, there were few men more popular among lawyers. He was a very clear-headed man of rapid decision, with power of incisive statement which commanded conviction." The father was the mould of

3

the future Lord Chief Justice.

Janet Goddard did not have so powerful an impact upon her son. "It was not a special relationship in any sense," says Lady Sachs. "He was fond of her—she was very proud and fond of him, though Uncle Ernest, the baby of the family, was her pet. He was a weakly child, the apple of her eye. She was slightly in awe of Rayner. She had five children to share herself between, including a full-time involvement with two unmarried daughters."

She was a delightful person—but not likely to leave a deep imprint on an already strong character. "Peggy, will you please remember if you sit in the Park after dark, be sure and wear a flannel petticoat!" she once advised her granddaughter.

It was to this couple, stern Charles Goddard and the gentle Janet, that Rayner was born on 10 April 1877, at 53 Bassett Road, near Ladbroke Grove in London's Notting Hill. Over ninety years later, Sir Arthur Bryant, the historian, was to write of a dinner which he attended and at which Sir Winston Churchill and Lord Goddard were the principal guests: "I remember thinking afterwards that in the statesman and the lawyer who had been born in the same half-decade—that during which Lord Beaconsfield had presided over an imperial Britain's destinies and Gilbert and Sullivan produced their first operas—I had encountered that evening two of a kind, each possessed of a certain indomitable and rock-like quality which only the long and stable civilization of our island country could have produced in men who happened also, by the accident of birth, to be invested with genius." Not inappropriately, Churchill himself used to refer to Lord Goddard as "Lord God-damn".

It is perhaps a strange paradox that, although the countryside and its joys were to mean so much to Rayner Goddard during his long life—its walks, its quiet beauty, its villages, its ancient history—he was both born, and lived most of his life, in London. He was a product of the city who yet never lost a feeling of belonging to the country.

His family connections were with Berkshire and, farther afield, Wiltshire; and from a very early age the western counties of this isle exerted most influence upon him.

At the age of eleven he was sent to a boarding preparatory school near Reading. "He hated it," says Lady Sachs. "The food was so ghastly he could not eat it when he got it." That early experience etched itself deeply into his gastronomic subconsciousness. He was always an excellent trencherman in later life, and thought a lot about his food (and wine). He never drank spirits, except a small whisky in the evening during his very last years when it was medically essential; but of port he was a lover and a connoisseur—perhaps one of the foremost authorities in the country. He preferred no-nonsense English cooking in ample proportions, and the one rule that was sacrosanct in his house was that meals had to start on time.

But if it was his prep school that affected for ever after his concern for food, it was his public school that had the one single greatest effect of his formative years upon his later life. Only the English seem so to worship their school days and, generally speaking, only those who went to public school. Few middle-aged or elderly eyes mist with tears when recalling long-past mornings in grammar-school classrooms or halcyon hours in the playground of some State secondary school. But with English boarding public schools it has always been different; the school—whether directly or indirectly through provoking an opposite reaction—has often played a greater role in the pupil's life than his parents; its atmosphere, fearsome or benign, has been more important in the child's development than the atmosphere at home.

So it was with Rayner Goddard. He was a boarder at Marlborough College, the establishment founded in 1843 and straddling the old Bath Road leading out of the Wiltshire town of Marlborough, for only four years out of a total lifetime of ninety-four years: from September 1891 to July 1895. But its mark upon him never faded. "He enjoyed Oxford, but not so much as Marlborough. It never meant to him what Marlborough did. I don't know why. He loved Marlborough," says Lady Sachs.

No one can seek to understand Lord Goddard, the forthright, controversial Lord Chief Justice of the mid-twentieth century, with his outspoken views on corporal punishment, hanging and the rest, without taking into account that he was born and lived the first twenty-four years of his life as a Victorian—and that he went to a school like Marlborough as it was during the twenty-seven-year rule of one of its most famous Masters, Canon G. C. Bell, of whom two ex-pupils wrote in the school magazine, in 1913, when he died:

"In his daily lessons with the Sixth Form, Bell's instinct led him to foster the excellent virtues of clear thinking and precision of statement. Towards original composition and the subtler forms of critical scholarship he had no strong bent, though he valued and studied these. He aimed rather at wholesome discipline than inspiration. . . .

"If I had to describe in one word the result of his influence upon character and intellect, I think I should choose to call it 'bracing'; perhaps sometimes the premature flower of the precocious may have been nipped, but he was helping to strengthen in us the quality of moral and mental fibre."

To modern eyes the words read chilly upon the printed page: "He aimed rather at wholesome discipline than inspiration" sounds almost like a grim parody of a late-Victorian headmaster. But the stamp of the school that Bell ruled remained upon his pupil Rayner Goddard for the rest of his long life: over fifty years later, when Lord Chief Justice, Rayner was delighted to travel down to the College to attend a royal visit in March 1948 when, on a unique occasion, the Archbishop of Canterbury (Lord Fisher), the Lord Chancellor (Lord Jowitt) and the Lord Chief Justice were all present, and all Old Marlburians.

In 1958, while still Lord Chief Justice, he came down again to referee the 1st VI Schools Meeting on the newly opened racing tracks. In 1959–60, when retired from office, he was President of the Old Marlburian Club. In June 1969, in a wheel-chair and in his ninety-third year, he came to luncheon in the Lodge given by the Acting Master.

There is a path down to the Bath Road used by the boys— generally running to be in time for Chapel or School. On one of his visits Lord Goddard told Reginald Jennings, then Housemaster of his old house, Littlefield: "Put a large brass plate on the gate at the bottom with the inscription: 'In 1893 Rayner Goddard, later Lord Chief Justice, broke his nose on this gate, damn it!'"

Was there ever such a love affair with one's old school?

During his last fifteen months at Marlborough, from the time of his seventeenth birthday, Rayner Goddard blossomed. Athletically he had already developed as a sprinter—at Rugby he was never more prominent than as a useful centre three-quarter for his house. In his last year he took the Champion Cup for athletics by winning the 100 yards in $10^2/_5$ seconds, the 200 yards in $19^3/_5$ seconds, the quarter-mile in 55 seconds, and taking second place in the 120 yards hurdles. He showed even more astonishing speed in his advancement within the Rifle Volunteer Corps.

This was at that time a functional training body in the national militia, and it had a particular significance at Marlborough since it came occasionally under the bright eye of the Quartermaster-General to the Forces, Sir Evelyn Wood, V.C., himself an Old Marlburian. In March 1894 Rayner Goddard was promoted corporal in the Rifle Corps. By October he had gone through every rank to acting-captain, and in January 1895 he was appointed to command the corps as Captain Goddard. He was never a good shot—far from leading the eight at Bisley, he merely scraped into the shooting efficiency tables with one mark over the minimum. But he excelled at command, tactical drill and morale-building. No doubt there was a comic *Stalky & Co.* aspect to the frequent Field Days which were then indulged in, often with a thousand public-school boys diluting Regular detachments of infantry and hussars: "Captain Goddard, probing with his cyclist scouts, divined a gap and threw forward three sections which did excellent work and rapidly got in touch with the enemy." But to control 140 adolescents uncertain whether they were engaged in a lark or a battle, to use their weight in concerted manoeuvres, to drill them under the gaze of Regular officers—this was no mean feat, and amply merited the recognition bestowed at the end of the long Wiltshire day, when the Marlborough Town Band paraded at the railway station to swell the band of the corps; and Captain Goddard marched his men to College in the June twilight to the sound of brass and cymbal and the sincere huzzas of the citizenry.

As Captain of the Rifle Corps at Marlborough, Rayner Goddard was recognized as a leader, "smart, correct, energetic in raising the standard of efficiency". His leadership was singled out for more than formal praise when, in a review of the corps over a twenty-year period, he was named with three others as 'one of those fellows who have thrown their heart and soul into it, fellows who will make their marks wherever they go; fellows who, if ever a great national crisis comes, will show that they have learned something worth learning in their cadet corps". He never neglected his homage to arms. Writing in 1942 at the age of sixty-five as Lord Justice Goddard in a series of regular cheery correspondence with a prisoner of war—Lieutenant Clifford Cohen, a junior barrister on the North-Eastern Circuit who had been captured at Dunkirk, and later a county court judge—he requested, after some paragraphs of circuit gossip: "Please don't address me as My Lord if you write again. Judge is quite enough from a member of the Bar; nor subscribe yourself as 'yours respectfully'—respect is and ought to be paid nowadays for the men like yourself who went at the instant and thank God you are still alive and I hope we shall meet again before very long, yours v. sincerely, Rayner Goddard."

In the academic sphere at Marlborough Rayner took the Bowen

History prize in the Vth form and the School's Cotton English Essay prize in the VIth. Towards the end of his school career he contributed effectively sombre prose readings to the concert held every term at Marlborough, and known as the Penny Reading—though at that time Goddard was the first soloist actually to read anything. The funereal choice for his first performance may have started a disconcerting legend. Lord Goddard in later years vigorously denied the anecdote persistently told in public by Earl Jowitt, who as Lord Chancellor from 1945 to 1951 played an ambivalent role (as we shall see) in Rayner's early years as Lord Chief Justice. Jowitt declared that during new boys' dormitory initiation rites at Marlborough young Goddard, instead of the customary singing or reciting, declaimed the formal judicial death sentence in its full horrific terminology. Lord Goddard declared that this account was 'utter nonsense from start to finish', and since Jowitt did not go to Marlborough until Goddard had left Oxford his evidence can at best be termed hearsay. "My father assured me there was not a word of truth in the story," says Lady Sachs. "He was always very upset by it."

What is true is that Rayner Goddard chose for his first Penny Reading a passage called 'The Revenge of the Soul', on which a contemporary critic commented: 'We understood it to describe the supposed sensations of a soul when its concomitant body is buried. A humorous piece would have been rather more in keeping with the character of the programme.' Next term Rayner presented 'My First and Last Appearance', about which the critic was more enthusiastic: 'We are sure the title of the reading will not hold true of the reader, who is certain to be heard again in a like capacity—and the sooner the better.' Possibly, through his long life, the reader responded to this current of appreciation. He became famous at Bar Mess dinners for rendering a somewhat earthy version of the comic recitation 'Albert and the Lion'. If he sang at these evenings he often committed himself to 'Two Little Eyes of Blue, Dear'.

But Rayner Goddard's great inspiration during his last four terms at Marlborough was the revival of the school Debating Society. It came when he was at a formative stage in opinion and expression, and he spoke at every debate. It is perhaps not surprising to see from the records that the young R. Goddard (Littlefield) spoke vigorously in favour of competitive examinations for the Army, compulsory games at school, the fagging system, the Rifle Corps, and the Tory Party as against the Liberal Government. He spoke with equal energy against reform of the House of Lords, Welsh

Disestablishment, total abstinence, the evacuation of Egypt (then a topical fancy, though Sir Evelyn Wood was about to undertake the Nile Expedition), and he 'strongly condemned' the New Woman—a very vivid chimera even at a time fifteen years before H. G. Wells's *Ann Veronica*.

"I am not here", R. Goddard (Littlefield) told a select audience in the Bradleian hall at Marlborough, "to argue against the type of New Woman we read of in books or see on the stage: a sort of neuter creature—though personally I should prefer one who could translate flour into paste, rather than Herodotus into English. I am here to argue against her who professes contempt for love, and marriage, and everything which makes the world what it is."

In his oratory the future advocate and judge did not escape perceptive criticism. In his summing up of the case against Welsh Disestablishment, an observer noted: "Goddard adopted the patriotic and loud-mouthed style that suits him well, hitting off the various speakers with apt and concise remarks. At the same time, we feel it our duty to remind him that contradictions should be tempered with politeness." When the debating society escalated its activities into a mock trial, on 20 June 1895, the school scribe reported: "A formidable array of legal talent was retained. For the prosection Mr Goddard, Q.C., led Mr Dobbs, a rising junior in criminal practice. Mr Goddard made a powerful opening speech"—prosecuting a man for murderous assault. At the end of a long trial counsel for the defence, Mr A. S. MacDowall, "addressed the jury on the evidence in a calm and well-reasoned speech, commenting on the weak points in the case of the prosecution, and rising in eloquence when in pathetic terms he spoke of the fresh young face of the poor lad in the dock. Mr Goddard, replying in a rattling Old Bailey speech, ridiculed any such sentimental appeals, pointed to his bruised and battered client, and pressed strongly for a conviction." He succeeded. He secured fifteen years for the fresh-faced lad in the dock and, already discriminating between the action of the court-room and the theatre, or even the Penny Reading, did not bow to acknowledge the accompanying applause.

2 The Old Western Circuit

Goddard left Marlborough as a Victor Ludorum and captain of the Rifle Corps. In October 1895 he went up to Trinity College, Oxford, to read law and to practise athletics. By a sheer freak of the weather, the two pursuits clashed damagingly in his final year.

In the Hilary term of 1898 Goddard was awarded a full Blue for athletics, after winning the 100 yards race in the University sports. This was an achievement that beat the betting book, since the short-framed Goddard had after rigorous training thrashed into second place a far more fancied sprinter, C. R. Thomas of Jesus, and had won in the then respectable time of $10^3/_5$ seconds.

He remained inordinately proud of his feat throughout his long life. He kept few letters or private papers, but tucked away among his effects Lady Sachs found after his death the official printed card from the Oxford University Athletic Club telling him that at a Committee Meeting of the Club held on 9 March 1898 he had been awarded his full Blue for the 100 yards. When lying close to death in the last two weeks of his life, aged ninety-four, he overheard a visitor to his bedside talking about his race and getting the time wrong. One eye opened—"No, it was $10^3/_5$ seconds!" he growled.

Whatever the timing, Goddard and C. R. Thomas were nominated for the annual championship meeting against Cambridge—with Goddard, as the first representative in the event, glorying in his full Blue while Thomas had to be content with only a half-Blue. But "the whirligig of time brings in his revenges", as we shall see.

The Oxford v. Cambridge athletics meeting was fixed for

25 March 1898, the day before the University boat-race. Unprecedented gales and snowfall caused the field contest—but not the boat-race—to be postponed until 29 June, the day before the University cricket match. It was an appalling decision as it affected Goddard, for he was in his last term of study for his final examinations. The demand for a good degree had to be matched against the pressure of training. Goddard never bragged that he could have got a first in either event, but it was a certainty that he could not win both exercises. On the morning of 29 June 1898 the Oxford class lists announced that R. Goddard, Trinity, had been awarded second-class honours in the Final School of Jurisprudence. In the afternoon of the same day the University athletics contest was decided at the Queen's Club. In the hundred yards event R. Goddard, Trinity, Oxford, finished fourth out of four. Ahead of him were two Cambridge men. Leading them all by two yards was C. R. Thomas, Jesus, Oxford, who ran out an easy winner in $10^2/_5$ seconds.

No one could claim that Rayner Goddard was a brilliant scholar at Oxford. He enjoyed his time there, he got a fair degree—but he probably learnt as much law in those early days from his solicitor father as he did from his amiable university tutors. Sir Harold Morris, Q.C., was a contemporary of Rayner's at the university. In his biography *Back View* he recounts: "Rayner Goddard's father initiated him into the mysteries of the law when he was still a boy at school. He was in consequence well ahead of his contemporaries at Oxford, speaking with easy assurance of such unknown things to us as demurrer, replevin, estoppel, liquidated damages and Order XIV."

But not all his teachers were equally impressed. When Rayner came down from Oxford he went to say goodbye to Sir William Anson, the Warden of All Souls and author of two leading books on the law of the Constitution and the law of contract. Rayner had attended his lectures. "Goodbye, Goddard," said Sir William. "I hope you will get on well. You will make an income at the Bar, but you will never make a lawyer!"

Rayner had already joined the Inner Temple as a student member, and had nearly finished his three years' ritual of Dining in Hall. He passed his Bar Final Examinations with ease, if no great distinction; and on the evening of Thursday, 26 January 1899, he presented himself in dress clothes in Hall at six o'clock. Twenty-seven young men were in Hall similarly attired that night; and in Rayner's 'mess' of four were John Simon, also just down from

Oxford and later, as Lord Simon, to be Lord Chancellor when Rayner was a Lord Justice of Appeal, Harold Morris, another Oxford friend and later Sir Harold Morris, Q.C., and the Hon. Victor Russell, later a leading junior at the Divorce Bar.

After dinner the Benchers—the 'elders' of the Inn—retired, and the Sub-Treasurer of the Inn marshalled the new recruits and led them in order of seniority into the Inn's Parliament chamber where the Benchers were seated at a long table with the Treasurer in the centre.

The young men stood in a semicircle in front of the table and the panniers—an old Inner Temple word for waiters, now fallen out of use—came round with trays on which were glasses of port, madeira and sherry, of which they were offered a choice. It is, alas, not recorded of which wine Rayner partook, but it would be pleasant to think it was port, of which later he was to be such a devotee.

The Treasurer was T. H. Baylis, Judge of the Court of Crown Passage at Liverpool. He told the assembled young men that they were now members of a great and honourable profession, as their calls to the Bar had been moved at a Parliament (the governing body of the Inn) before dinner and had been accepted. His speech was, perhaps mercifully, a short one, consisting mainly of an appeal to take great care of their health and not to tax it too severely, as the Bar was an exacting and arduous profession. The Benchers then rose and drank a toast to the fledgling barristers' health. John Simon, as the senior of their number, made, to use Sir Harold Morris's words, "a commendably brief speech" in reply. The young men drank the old men's health. And that was it!—Rayner Goddard, along with his twenty-six companions of that night, was qualified to wear wig and gown.

Professional life was much more of a 'closed shop' in those days than now. Numbers were much fewer, the class basis was tighter and more selective, members of the Bar really *were* an élite—socially, if not necessarily intellectually. Queen Victoria still had two years to reign. The 'old order' was still very much in command.

Nowadays practitioners at the Bar are still divided up into Circuits, depending on which part of the country they will substantially devote themselves to. But the Circuits have lost much of their former close-knit unity. In the young Rayner Goddard's time—and for over sixty years thereafter—one had to join one's selected Circuit promptly within two years of Call and one could not accept a brief on another Circuit without the client having to pay a special fee for the privilege, *and* brief a barrister regularly on the Circuit in addition. The young barrister at the turn of the century went from one close, all-male preserve to another—from his boarding public school to his university to his Circuit.

And no Circuit had a more highly developed sense of 'belonging', of superiority, of being apart from the rest, than had the Western Circuit. Exposed on the westernmost tip of England, it felt itself virtually a state within a state. The new-fangled train connection from Paddington pressing ever further westward over past years had to some extent shattered its remoteness and sense of isolation. But a golden glow of affection seems to permeate every reference to the old Western Circuit by its reminiscing members. Perhaps this is true of the other old Circuits as well, but the Western seems to have had the better raconteurs, the keener scribes and seers, the finer harpists in nostalgia and a total lien on Avalon.

"In truth, it is a goodly land and fair, through which His Majesty's Judges follow those well-worn ways. Fairest, without doubt, in summer, when the southward uplands are bathed in sunshine, and the lanes are starred in wild roses and guarded by nodding fox-glove; but still fair in misty autumn or chilly winter, with the solemn beauty of time-worn stones and everlasting hills," a devotee, styling himself "A Circuit Tramp", wrote as late as 1911.

Through his family's links with the West Country, there could be little doubt which Circuit the 22-year-old Rayner Goddard would elect to join. He went straight from Call into Western Circuit chambers at 1 Mitre Court Buildings in the Temple. His pupil-master and the head of the Chambers was A. Clavell Salter, later a Member of Parliament and High Court Judge, whose nickname of "Dry Salter" was grandly acknowledged when he was made a member of the Worshipful Company of Drysalters. Thirty-three years later, when the Western Circuit held a dinner in Inner Temple Hall to congratulate Rayner on his own High Court Judgeship, Rayner was to call Clavell Salter his "father in the law".

Anyone who has known the terse expressiveness of Rayner Goddard's own judgments on the Bench may realize what he owed to Clavell Salter when they read this assessment of his mentor by Professor H. G. Hanbury: "His brain was of the highest calibre and he displayed an almost uncanny power of illuminating the dark recesses of a complicated case, and separating the vital from the non-essential. His judgments contain no unnecessary word, and no word out of place. He saw no useful purpose in the elaborate enumeration of a chain of authorities; reserving his speech for the results, rather than the process of his thought."

Salter's chambers handled a lot of civil, mainly commercial, litigation in London, but the bulk of their practice when Rayner joined them (he stayed on as a full member of Chambers after serving his year's pupillage) consisted of the rough-and-tumble of Circuit criminal and civil briefs on the three annual pilgrimages to the Assize towns from Winchester westward.

Rayner's formal election as a member of the Circuit took place at Bristol, and by one of those coincidences that could easily occur in the closed ranks of the Bar of those days the other new boy with him on that occasion was the young Thomas Inskip, later to be Lord Caldecote and Rayner's immediate predecessor as Lord Chief Justice.

Rayner's first actual appearance as a barrister in court was on the Western Circuit: at Salisbury in June 1899. He travelled down from Paddington in the same train as the judge. Now all is 'low-profile' and 'under-play' in the rituals of the law: one sometimes wonders for how long even wigs and gowns will remain permitted in the age of the common man. But in that era pageantry was accepted as a valid extension of reality—in the Law, if not in the Church. The judge donned his full-bottomed wig and scarlet and ermine robes on the train and stepped forth on to the platform at Salisbury station in full regalia to personify the majesty of the law, receive the trumpet fanfares and homage of the Mayor and Corporation, acknowledge the guard of honour and process in high state, pike-guarded, to the Judge's Lodging.

Rayner Goddard was there. He recalled the occasion from the Bench at Salisbury in June 1933, when he was charging the last Grand Jury in Wiltshire before the abolition of that inquisition of first instance:

"Thirty-four years ago this week, in a very white wig and with a very blue bag, I joined the Western Circuit at Salisbury. I well remember that Mr Justice Phillimore was the judge. I remember going home to my lodgings the first night and finding that which no barrister ever forgets—my first brief—to prosecute a man for breaking into the North Wiltshire Brewery at Wootton Bassett, for which offence he was acquitted, and I thought it a grave miscarriage of justice. From that time I became a very faithful attendant at the Assizes. I was a member of the delightful Wiltshire Bar and Bench Mess, which I hope still flourishes, and I hope its port is as good as it used to be."

His Circuit meant a very great deal to Rayner Goddard. On becoming a High Court Judge in 1932 after thirty-three years' loyal, assiduous membership, he could thenceforth only be an honorary member, but he assured those gathered to do him honour at the congratulatory dinner "I hope I will still be *with* you, if not *of* you". In March 1949 when, as Lord Chief Justice, he attended a dinner to congratulate fellow-Circuiteer Patrick Devlin on his appointment to the High Court Bench, he toasted the Circuit with these words: "This is not a toast of 'our noble selves' but of something that lives, no matter who are the members. It is the one Circuit which remains as it originally was since the time of the Bloody Assize". It never seems to have occurred to him that that may not necessarily have been such a marvellous thing.

In 1903 a fourteen-year-old boy named Arthur Smith first came into the Temple as a junior barristers' clerk. He went to work in Clavell Salter's chambers, and in his book on Rayner Goddard he gives a graphic account of the future Lord Chief's chambers in those far-off days:

"I read the names painted on the board by the door: one above the other, Chinese fashion:

A. CLAVELL SALTER
W. H. DUCKWORTH
JOHN H. HARRIS
RAYNER GODDARD

"I had never heard of any of them and they meant nothing to me. . . . There was a step behind me and the sound of a key in the lock. I turned. Newman had arrived. Newman, the Senior Clerk, with an expression as severe as the cut of his clothes. He did not look to me as though he much liked boys. We went in.

"There were two rooms for the barristers and one for the boys. They seemed dreadfully dingy to me. Each had sad-coloured walls, unpapered, and was furnished with a dark mahogany table and a number of straight-backed chairs. There was also a basement room, almost a cellar, where were kept the brushes and pails and firewood, and, so it appeared, the barristers' pupils."

On that very first day young Arthur was to encounter the remarkable generosity of Rayner Goddard. Those who only know of him by repute, as the stern old man of the law, the believer in corporal punishment, hanging and resolute methods of dealing with criminals, will learn, perhaps with surprise, that throughout his life, when he was a young man making his own way at the Bar or as a venerable judge full of distinction, he would make sudden spontaneous gestures of warmth and concern for his fellow human

15

beings that completely belied his later outward image of bulldog severity.

It was Arthur Smith's job to stay in Chambers, take in papers and write down messages, learn where speedily to lay his hands upon a particular law report and answer the telephone. He had never used a telephone before. As was then the custom, it was fixed to a bracket high up the wall; and Arthur was very small. He looked at it unhappily.

"At that moment, someone entered the room," he relates. " 'Who is this?' he asked. 'Oh, this is the new boy, sir,' said Newman. 'He is so small he can't reach the telephone.' 'Well, then, let him run up to Fetter Lane and buy a sugar-box to stand on,' said the newcomer." And Rayner handed the lad a sixpence.

It was not a time of over-thoughtfulness on the part of the haves for the have-nots of this world. Lord Justice Vaughan Williams would grandly drive to the Law Courts every day in his carriage with Lady Vaughan Williams beside him. Mr Justice Grantham, magnificent in mutton-chop whiskers, used to ride up the Strand on horseback, followed by a resplendent groom dressed in a top hat, white breeches and shining leather boots with yellow tops. Mr Justice Darling wore a powdered wig in court, and before entering would stand for some while before the looking-glass in his private room to ensure he looked suitably patrician.

Likewise, in the clerks' room at Mitre Court Buildings, Newman, the austere senior clerk, delighted in exerting his authority over the hapless, hard-pressed boy of fourteen. "It was at these times that Mr Goddard, noticing the long hours I worked and that I often had no lunch, started to give me 3d. a day and instructions to buy a glass and a couple of buns from the dairy at Fetter Lane," records Mr Smith. When summer came, and Rayner heard that young Arthur could only afford to spend his holiday at home, "telling me that I needed a change, he sent me off at his own expense for a fortnight by the sea".

"It is easy for a rich man to be generous," you may say; although others may counter that those with most money are the most loath to part with it. But even so, Rayner Goddard was never throughout his long life a wealthy man: few judges in this century have been. He had family connections in the right places, he had no difficulty in getting into 'good' Chambers or joining probably the most socially acceptable Circuit: all that is true. But he built up his practice—a young man's rag-bag of Common Law county court and minor criminal work—by his own industry and his own efforts. Arthur

Smith, writing in 1959, commented on "his voracious appetite for work. Then, as now, he detested having too little to do, and he used to seize and read each set of papers as it arrived in chambers irrespective of for whom it was intended. Newman would rebuke me for allowing this to happen (he never allowed any papers to leave his table until they had been entered in the records, a perfectly reasonable rule) and I would plead that I, the boy, could hardly dictate to R.G., as we all called him."

"My impression is that it was quite tough going for Rayner in those early days," says Lady Sachs. "He had his own way to make. There was no helping hand from his father. He had to succeed by his own ability."

Plus his own brand of integrity. Says Sir John Masterman, former Provost of Worcester College, Oxford University, "I cherish one story which he told me of an early brief which he was offered. The solicitor, apparently cautious about his youth, had said in describing one of the witnesses: 'Deal cautiously with this witnesss, for he is firmly resolved to tell the truth.' Rayner told me that he refused the brief!"

But there is more to life than work, or even a burgeoning appreciation of good port. In 1904 the balance of Clavell Salter's chambers changed when Salter took silk and became a K.C., and Rayner left to join other Western Circuit chambers at 1 Paper Buildings in the Temple. In that year also he met the girl who was to become his wife.

3 Marriage and Family Life

It is surely something of a paradox, and not generally known, that Rayner Goddard, of pure English stock with entirely Christian forebears for as far back as records can tell, should have met, fallen in love with and married a highly strung, sensitive and artistic girl of mixed German and Jewish parentage.

Few who think of Goddard as the arch-embodiment of all things English realize his involvement with, and sympathy for, people of Jewish race. It was his warmth and his compassion that spanned the chasm between the austere, chill late-Victorian Christianity of his upbringing and the more emotional, demonstrative nature of the ancient creed that Adolf Hitler—and others—have wished to destroy. Not that this proclivity was shared by all his Christian friends in the law: "Rayner was curiously disposed to express friendship for Jews," comments one of his former judicial colleagues. "He had a definite pro-Semitic tendency. He had a lot to do with Neville Laski's appointment as the first permanent Recorder of Liverpool."

In the nineteen-thirties, shortly before becoming a High Court Judge, he resigned in protest from the Garrick Club—the same club that was later to blackball his posthumous (and Jewish) detractor Bernard Levin—because a barrister friend of his, of Jewish origin, was rejected as a member. When Rayner was Lord Chief Justice he was hearing a case which surprisingly—bearing in mind that Goddard was the judge!—was lasting longer than expected, and a Jewish Q.C. asked if Rayner would see him in his private room. Embarrassedly, he explained that he would not wish to make an

Rayner Goddard, three years old in 1880, and already adopting a commanding pose between his elder brother Harry, then aged six, and sister Mary, five

Charles and Janet Goddard, Rayner's parents, on the day of their Golden Wedding in 1922

The only remaining photograph of Rayner Goddard robed as a young barrister, dating from 1911

Rayner in 1909 with Pamela, his eldest daughter

application in open court for a day's adjournment to suit his own personal convenience, but he was an Orthodox believer and—well, the morrow was the Day of Atonement. "Good Lord, my boy, Yom Kippur—I quite forgot!" said the Chief, and gave him his adjournment without demur.

The name of the girl that the young Rayner Goddard met at a Society dance in 1904 was Marie Linda Schuster—known as "Mollie". She was the daughter of Felix Schuster, an extremely wealthy German-Jewish banker who had emigrated to England with his father and two brothers from their native Frankfurt after that city had been annexed by Prussia in 1866. Felix had, like other German-Jewish émigrés of that time, officially converted to Christianity, and married a Christian girl. Marie was brought up a passionate believer in her parents' faith.

"She was a great churchgoer," says her daughter, Lady Sachs. "She lived by her religion. She believed in God and her duty towards her neighbour. She had a much stronger religious feeling than Rayner. 'I do wish your father would not deride missionaries so much,' she used to say. 'He is always quoting rude rhymes about them!'

"Every Sunday morning, she would read a story from the Bible to us; and there would be hymns around the piano in the nursery."

The same robust attitude to conventional religious faith by a man who at his death decreed there should be no memorial service for him is related by Mrs Pamela Maurice, the Goddards' eldest daughter: "When he accompanied us to church, usually during our seaside summer holidays, he would occupy the sermon time by going through the small print at the beginning of the Book of Common Prayer with me, and explaining the Act of Uniformity and so on to me—much to the disgust of my mother. When remonstrated with, he would say then that sermons were illegal except at Holy Communion (when they were seldom given): so what? To which my mother had no answer!"

The wedding took place at St Jude's Church, South Kensington, on 31 May 1906. Rayner was then aged twenty-nine, his bride was twenty-two. Their first married home was at 98 Palace Gardens Terrace, London, W.8. The house still stands: a narrow, terraced building—a good solid house for a young barrister at the start of his career.

But it was no mansion. Rayner may have married into a remarkably rich family, but none of their wealth rubbed off on to him. It was a marriage of love, not of ambition. Although his father-in-law was granted a baronetcy by the Liberal Government in July 1906, two months after the wedding, Rayner never benefited materially from the advantageous position of his wife's family. They were, as he often told his daughter Peggy, "a very funny family". In the nineteen-twenties, when his practice had blossomed to its greatest and he was doing primarily commercial work with almost certainly the biggest banking practice at the Bar, the only one of the 'Big Five' national banks that did *not* brief him was that on which his father-in-law was on the board, the National Provincial!

But then they were "a very funny family" to their own daughter. "She was very intelligent and a highly accomplished musician with a beautiful singing voice and an accomplished touch at the piano", says Mrs Pamela Maurice. "But she had a tremendous inferiority complex because she felt she was unwanted by her parents, the third daughter of a baronet who already had a male heir. She was cruelly treated by her parents in many ways."

Lady Sachs is even more outspoken: "The Schusters were very rich, but Grandmother Schuster was just plain mean. When my parents were courting my mother's eldest sister got engaged but she could not do so at the same time, because there was only one coat and skirt between them! It never occurred to my mother that she was a rich woman—or should have been. There was only one walking-out costume between them. She had to wear her sister's hand-me-down shoes.

"When Grandfather Schuster died in 1936 he left a quarter of a million pounds—but not to us! He said to Rayner that Rayner wanted for nothing; all his daughters made such excellent marriages, they needed nothing too—so we only got what was left in some family trust!"

Yet Rayner and his wife were happy, and reasonably prosperous, without financial help. Pamela was born in 1908, Janet Margaret (Peggy) followed in 1909 and Ruth Evelyn (Prue) brought up the tail in 1912. The Goddards had no son—which was a disappointment to both of them: "I think he was awfully grieved he did not have a son," says Lady Sachs. "But it *embittered* her life that she had no son. We were three grievances: we were always being told by her what we would have been called if we had been boys."

Of the two parents, it seems abundantly clear that it was the father who made most impact—and a loving, warm, open-hearted impact—upon the three girls.

Mrs Pamela Maurice, the eldest, gives her own impressions of

'Life with Father' in those early years. Her words deserve to be quoted in full: "It has always seemed to me that he was a wonderful father to us, encouraging our interests and stimulating our imaginations, and spending so much time with us as his work as an extremely busy junior counsel allowed.

"Nearly every Saturday during the years of the First World War he would take us to see some place of interest, chiefly in the City of London, which he knew and loved well, and indeed he once took my own two children during a period of lull in the bombing of London in the second war on a wonderful bus ride through the City, visiting the Tower of London, St Paul's and other places, and ending up with a cinema show and a tea as large as the rigours of those days allowed. I know they have never forgotten it.

"My father started me off in my love of books and reading which has been a lifelong joy to me, by reading aloud to us, very beautifully, and explaining what he read as we went along. I remember starting with Grimm's *Fairy Tales* and progressing through *Lamb's Tales from Shakespeare* to *Kidnapped* and *Catriona* (which I fear I never liked). Every year from my third birthday onward he and my mother gave me a book, and I am glad to say I still have every one of them—a collection of well over sixty volumes!

"Curiously enough, though in most ways my father and I were very alike, our tastes in reading differed markedly. His preferences were all for the Victorians—Dickens, Trollope, Thomas Hardy (whom he adored this side idolatry). He confessed that he could not read Jane Austen, who is a constant joy for me, whereas I find the Victorian novelists sententious and boring. Be that as it may, he gave us the opportunity and the chance to become acquainted with the best in English literature, and there were always many books in our house on which constantly to browse.

"Though never having the opportunity to take up any country pursuits, my father loved the country, and I think that the summer holidays we spent in Dorset during my mother's lifetime—in a summer home at Lulworth—were among his happiest days. He taught us all to swim before the age of eight, and to manage a rowing-boat, and I well remember his teaching me to ride a bicycle during the summer of 1916, which we spent in a small house in Sussex belonging to my maternal grandparents. I would count the days until he could join us at weekends and take me for bicycle rides with him.

"Until quite late in his life, he would enjoy long walks in the country, during most of which I would accompany him, and which he would enjoy working out with maps and timetables. We would discuss every subject under the sun, and I was always encouraged to express my own views."

What about Lord Goddard, the believer in corporal punishment? Did he practise what he preached? "In our nursery days, Father was a disciplinarian, and stood no nonsense. He particularly disliked too much noise consequent upon our sisterly quarrels, and somehow I managed to attract more of his wrath than my sisters—possibly because I was the eldest.

"Many a time did I have to bend over and receive six of the best from his hands on that portion of my anatomy which, so I was advised by him and implicitly believed, was specially designed for the purpose. In spite of what modern psychologists assert, I never found this altered my very close and loving relationship with him.

"I have so many reasons to be grateful to him. He it was who taught me to appreciate good wine; more especially his own love of vintage port was inculcated in me. Possibly in some ways I took the place of the son he never had."

Lady Sachs's version of those early years is substantially similar: "I was very frightened of my mother. She could be perfectly charming—but she was partially deaf, inheritedly, and it was getting worse. She was liable to go off into violent hysterical rages about nothing at all. Looking back on it, I think my father put up with a great deal at one time.

"It was a marriage of opposites—even his best friend would not have called him musical, though he sang quite nicely. She was a lover of classical music, and no mean pianist. He could not have cared less!

"Of the years before my mother died I cannot write. Children take their parents so much for granted—or they did in those days—that we just accepted things as they were. The only outstanding memory is that she allowed her life to be embittered by the fact of having no son, and rather too frequently reproached the three of us for being girls, which, even from a very tender age, I thought distinctly unfair. Rayner never did this, though we knew he was equally disappointed.

"I am sure that basically Rayner was fond of all three of us—he certainly was of Pamela—but he belonged spiritually to a generation which held women in condescending contempt, tempered with almost pathological fear and distrust of what he, to the end of his days, would describe as 'a designing harpy'."

But it was for his courtroom defence of a woman on a murder

charge that, in the summer of 1909, Rayner Goddard's name first became known outside the narrow confines of the law. And the case occurred on his beloved Western Circuit.

4 More Western Circuit and the Haskell Murder

Throughout his life Rayner Goddard was always a hard worker. Even when a junior barrister of many years' standing, and later a K.C., he would always come into Chambers every Saturday morning when most other barristers were at home with their families, out on the golf course or otherwise at strictly non-work pursuits. "He was always in on a Saturday morning," says Mr Sidney Newland, who became Rayner's junior clerk in September 1919 at the age of sixteen and after a working span of fifty-six years retired from the Temple only in the summer of 1975. "There would always be an excuse, but he would always be there. He had a passion for his work."

As a young man at the Bar, this exploding enthusiasm enabled him to build up a practice—mainly of a good deal of small work—that other more languid young practitioners did not even bother to emulate. "I had many a gay and gory fight against Rayner in the salubrious surroundings of Edmonton, Shoreditch and Whitechapel County Courts," records Sir Harold Morris, Q.C. "He was a doughty opponent, and a good clean fighter."

But it was not merely in the London county courts, in countless minor civil disputes, that Rayner earned his courtroom spurs. Although in later life his practice was substantially civil and commercial, his first years at the Bar—like those of many young men, both then and since—were spent in the hurly-burly of the criminal courts; and, in his case, mostly on Circuit.

Because of his Wiltshire family connection, he had attached himself immediately to the Wiltshire Quarter Sessions—the local courts trying secondary offences, generally a week ahead of the

Assizes—and claimed that he did not miss a single session before the First World War. Future Lord Chief Justices generally do not have the solid 'grass-roots' training that Rayner was able to enjoy: their early days at the Bar are often spent in more rarified spheres than humble police courts, Quarter Sessions and ancient Assize courts spread out over hundreds of miles of English countryside.

Although for many years before his High Court Judgeship in 1932 Rayner hardly entered a criminal court—other than to sit as judge as the local Recorder—his solid apprenticeship in criminal work on Circuit in his early days (plus his father's table-talk at home) gave him a bedrock of fundamental knowledge that no other twentieth-century judge has surpassed. When later on the Bench counsel would seek to persuade him to follow such and such a late-Victorian or Edwardian judgment he would often say, "But Mr Justice So-and-So was notoriously weak on that point" or "Yes, Mr Justice Such-and-Such was always very sound on these matters." In several of his own judgments to be found in the Law Reports one will find glowing references to Mr Justice Channell, for example, whose decisions he was always ready to follow, since Channell was in his view the best criminal judge of the first decade of this century.

Again, unlike many other future Lord Chief Justices, his criminal experience was not virtually one-sided. A criticism that at one time could be made with some force of English judicial appointments, and can still be made to a lesser extent today, is that our judges all too often in their own days at the Bar only prosecuted: they seldom if ever defended. "Once a prosecutor, always a prosecutor" could sometimes be said with accuracy of some of the older generation of judges.

But that was never true in Rayner's case. As a young man in the criminal courts he did both: he prosecuted *and* he defended. Staunchly independent as a judge, he was nobody's creature as a practising barrister. Not that this meant he was anybody's man: he trimmed his cloth to suit no one. David Lloyd George once supposedly said of John Simon, Rayner's contemporary at Oxford and fellow-celebrant on Call Night, that "he had sat for so long on the fence the iron had entered into his soul". That could never be said of Goddard.

An extended account of part of one Winter Assize on the Western Circuit in 1909 may serve to portray Rayner Goddard (whom most people remember as a venerable, gnarled old man) in the full vigour of his youth—effortlessly switching roles from prosecution to defence. The account may also present something of the unique flavour of provincial England before the First World War, a period beyond which in one sense he never progressed during the rest of his life. His own daughter, Lady Sachs, says with loving candour, "I think it is true to say that his views on life remained static after 1914—he never really adjusted to the changed *mores* of the post-First War society, nor I think did my mother, and we three girls were frankly often stunned at his rigid and reactionary strictures on con-temporary behaviour. It did make communication difficult sometimes—we were so conscious of a barrier between us, though I knew it sprang from no lack of affection on either side. This in no way affected his sense of fun and the immense pleasure we all derived from his company and companionship."

Mr Justice Ridley and his retinue entrained at Waterloo on Thursday, 11 February 1909, to open the Wiltshire Winter Assizes at Devizes. The trumpeters announced his arrival at 4.51 p.m. He was greeted by the High Sheriff and the Sheriff's Chaplain. A body of divisional police escorted the carriage procession to the Judge's Lodging. Mr Rayner Goddard, with a dozen other counsel, detached themselves and were driven to the Bear, which was the Bar hotel, and relaxed before dining in mess. Divine service was attended in the parish church next morning. The judge took his seat in the Assize Court at eleven.

The first prisoner literally stumbled into the dock. He was a local Baptist minister who pleaded guilty to attempted suicide by cutting his throat with a razor. He gave as his reason that he had done wrong in respect to a lady, and he had not obeyed the call which he had previously recognized as from God. Mr Justice Ridley vainly sought someone who would offer to take care of him; but his wife, who was an invalid, would have nothing to do with him, and another minister declined to take responsibility for his brother pastor, saying that he was still suicidal. "If we cannot get anyone to look after him", said the judge, "he must be put in a place where he can be taken care of." He spoke directly to the man who sought oblivion: "I shall sentence you to six months' imprisonment in the second division. There you will be taken care of, and I hope you will then be able to look after yourself, and that you will not make another wicked attempt on your own life. I am passing this sentence upon you not by way of a punishment, but in order that you may be taken care of."

The man was guided down to the cells and a woman of forty-six was put up. She pleaded guilty to bigamy. Mr Parr prosecuted, Mr

Goddard defended. Rayner said that over the last thirteen years the woman had supported the four children of her valid marriage while her husband had paid nothing towards their upbringing. "I ask your Lordship to deal leniently with her. She bears a good character, and I can call a witness." "I will assume that she has a good character," said the judge. "But she has broken the law. People must not commit bigamy. I will sentence her to three months' hard labour."

Rayner bowed, and crossed to the right of the court. Edith Bourton was put up. She pleaded not guilty to a charge of attempting to administer poison in the shape of phosphorus to her mistress Kate Large at Little Hinton with intent to kill and murder her. Mr Goddard prosecuted, Mr Seaton defended. Rayner outlined the facts. The 17-year-old maidservant undoubtedly bore a grievance against her mistress, a farmer's wife, after having been accused, apparently with justification, of pilfering. She put some rat poison into some bread and milk which her mistress was to take at bedtime. When the saucepan was being heated on the fire a flame overlapped the rim and the phosphorus in the rat poison flared up. The farmer's wife sensibly declined to consume the bread and milk. The charge against Edith Bourton could therefore only be of attempting to administer poison. But, since the hearing before the magistrates, an official analyst had reported that there had not been sufficient phosphorus in the milk to constitute a fatal dose. So a charge of attempted murder would be difficult to sustain. Mr Seaton, for the defence, promptly rose and submitted that therefore there could also be no case to go to the jury on the poisoning with intent to kill charge. The judge concurred. The girl was found not guilty and discharged.

Swiftly the prisoners succeeded each other in the dock. Malicious wounding; ticket-of-leave man not reporting to the police; maidservant concealing the birth of her child—bound over on consenting to accept a situation offered her by a well-wisher.

Josiah Saunders, sixty-eight, painter, a member of the Salisbury Town Council, was indicted for indecently assaulting Mary Louisa Coombs, a child. Mr Ratcliffe Cousins to prosecute, Mr Goddard to defend. The case for the defence, otherwise commonplace enough, had two features: the child might have been unreasonably nervous because of the recent notorious murder of little Teddy Haskell, in which Goddard had been briefed to defend later at these Assizes; and the accused had admitted "tweaking" the girl's leg, besides kissing her. The word *tweaking* had in the 1900s, like the word goosing in the 1970s, a wide range of meaning. In a court of law defence counsel would need to make it seem as innocent as possible—especially as Mr Justice Ridley ruled at the end of the prosecution case that it *could* amount to an indecent assault.

Mr Cousins, prosecuting, said the prisoner Saunders had gone to carry out minor repairs on the house occupied by the child's family. Part of his task was to mend a bedroom window. The girl and her brother showed him upstairs, the staircase was dark and the prisoner touched the girl's leg as he went up. When they got to the bedroom the girl removed the curtain from the window. While she was standing on a box to do so the prisoner caught hold of her leg and tickled her. He then gave the girl's brother a penny to get some sweets, and the boy went downstairs. The little girl was about to follow when the prisoner called her back and gave her a penny. He offered her sixpence and made "an improper suggestion". He then put his arm round her neck, kissed her and behaved indecently. The child gave evidence and said that she struggled when the prisoner caught hold of her; she was frightened through thinking of little Teddy Haskell who had been murdered in a bedroom. Saunders went into the box and denied any indecency. He admitted that he had tweaked the girl on the knee and afterwards kissed her, and he expressed his regret if it had caused the mother any annoyance. Rayner rose to his feet to do the best he could with a difficult case.

"I should like to remind you", he told the jury, "of the seriousness of the charge against this man. He is a member of the Salisbury Town Council, he has been four times re-elected to that office, he has been for over thirty years a public man in Salisbury, serving on one of the most important public bodies in the town, the education authority. He is a man sixty-eight years of age, with great-grandchildren. If this offence is proved it makes him unfit not only for all the many public positions he has held, but unfit for decent society at all.

"I beg of you to bear with me while I point out to you exactly the defence which has been put up from first to last since this charge was brought against this old gentleman. He has never denied that he did touch the little girl, but what he has denied is that he touched her in any indecent way at all. What he did amounted really to nothing more than a harmless little joke—although perhaps it was not the wisest thing to do—and it has been exaggerated by this little girl, quite innocently, no doubt, into a case of indecent assault.

"I am sure my Lord will allow me to submit to you that whether or no it is indecent for a man to tweak a girl on the knee must depend very much on the circumstance in which it was done, and on the respective ages of the parties. What a man may do to a grown-up woman and what he may do to a little girl are surely two very different things. It may perhaps be a silly thing for this man to jokingly tweak little girls' legs, but it is a very different thing to say that it is indecent to do it.

"I am not saying that it was wise or polite in this man's case, but I do say that it was not indecent. I am sure that if a grandfather were to tweak the legs of his grandchildren it would never enter the minds of any of you, gentlemen of the jury, that it was indecent to do so."

Rayner made a slight grimace.

"When I came into court", he continued, 'I did not think I should have to concern myself with the question of *tweaking* the girl's leg, which my client has admitted. But, from my Lord's remarks, apparently I was wrong, and such a thing may be construed into an indecent assault. No doubt if this man deliberately with indecent intention committed the other act which is complained of, then you will be justified in finding him guilty. But can you not picture to yourselves what happened?

"The girl was in the bedroom alone with a strange man. She has told you that she had often thought, when she had been in the bedroom, of the little boy Teddy Haskell who was murdered at Salisbury. Her mind was rather ripe to put a wrong construction upon an act which, I submit, was a perfectly innocent one.

"Everyone who has anything to do with courts knows that these charges of indecent assault are exceedingly easy to make, but very difficult to disprove, because any girl can come and say an assault has taken place, and the only thing a man can do is to say 'I didn't do it'. I do not say that this girl has come here deliberately to tell an untrue story, but with her mind full of the horrors of a murder her mind was ripe for putting a wrong construction on an innocent act.

"On account of the ease with which these charges can be made, and the difficulty of repelling them, it is a well-worn rule, well understood and invariably acted upon by juries, that they should not convict a man in a case of this sort unless there is real corroboration of the girl's story. Now, in this case, there is not an atom of corroboration of this girl's story."

Mr Justice Ridley summed up very strongly against Mr Goddard's defence. But the jury brought in a verdict of not guilty, and the man was discharged. Thirteen cases had been cleared from the calendar in the first day, and the stage was set, after the weekend, for the most sensational murder trial to be heard in Wiltshire for well over a decade—in which counsel leading for the defence was Rayner Goddard, aged thirty-two.

The victim was Edwin Richard Haskell, aged 12, a winning boy better known than most youngsters in Salisbury, and always called Teddy Haskell. He was conspicuous because he always walked—and as often as not ran—with crutches, having had his right leg amputated below the knee as the result of bone disease; but he was a very cheerful lad, remarkably agile and a notably skilful footballer, whether in the streets or in the field. His father had died of consumption six years previously, just before the boy's operation. His mother, Flora Fanny Haskell, aged thirty-four, made a living by taking in washing and going out to upper-class homes as a laundress. By every account she was devoted to Teddy. Mother and son lived in a two-storey cottage in Meadow Road, Fisherton, Salisbury, in a district where everybody knew each other and members of Mrs Haskell's family lived in the same street.

At a time—confirmed by unchallenged evidence—between 10.20 and 10.30 on the night of Saturday, 31 October 1908, the sleeping Teddy was murdered in his bed by having his throat cut with one long stroke of a household knife. The knife was drawn through the jugular vein and the windpipe at a point below the vocal cords, so that the boy could not have made even an involuntary cry. Death was virtually instantaneous, certainly occurring within less than a minute.

There was a remarkably precise succession of timed sightings of Mrs Haskell before 10.20 that night, and after 10.30, when the crime was discovered. In the earlier part of the evening she had been seen shopping in Salisbury, chatting with acquaintances and a relative. She came home at 8.30, collected Teddy from his uncle's house next door, and they went together to the corner shop, where Teddy bought a ha'penny comic, *The Butterfly*. They were back in their home by 8.45. During the next hour, Mrs Haskell said—and no one disputed it—she gave her son his supper, washed him, gave him a footbath for his good left leg, and put him to bed.

At five past ten, as the Co-operative Stores in Winchester were shutting, the manager asked a boy assistant, John Wyatt, to deliver a parcel to a Mrs Manning in Meadow Road. Not entirely pleased to be given an extra task so late in the evening, Wyatt went on his bicycle and, arriving in Meadow Road, had to inquire where Mrs Manning lived, for he had been given no house-number. He was told, "No. 42". He knocked at 42 but could get no answer. Eventually he knocked at No. 40. He heard the door being unlocked from the inside, and Mrs Haskell opened it. He asked about Mrs Manning and was told she was out, but Mrs Haskell agreed to take the parcel in for her. Mrs Haskell spoke absolutely normally, and Wyatt saw nothing extraordinary about her appearance. The time was then 10.20.

At 10.30, or possibly a few minutes earlier, Mrs Haskell's nephew Percy Noble, who lived next door at No. 38, decided to repay a shilling he had borrowed from his aunt, and went to the back door of No. 40. Finding that it was fastened, he knocked. He heard his aunt say "All right" in a normal voice. He heard what he recognized as a chair scraping, the ordinary sound of a kitchen chair being pushed back from a kitchen table. He then heard, a few seconds afterwards, a noise which he described as a "jump"—the sort of sound made by someone taking the last steps of a flight of stairs in one bound. Immediately, he heard a scream. Mrs Haskell then came to the door. Her hair was half down and she was shrieking. Between her piercing cries she said, at intervals, "Go and stop that man! He has killed my poor Teddy! Go for a doctor quick!"

Percy Noble rushed down a passage from the back door, but could see no man in the street outside—he ran on to the doctor's. Mrs Haskell, still screaming, went through her house to the front door. Outside it she was met by Walter Steer, a neighbour who came running in answer to her shrieks. Mrs Haskell gasped, "That man!" Walter Steer ran to the corner of the street, but saw no one except two men talking in the road outside the local pub. He spoke to both, and recognized one but not the other, who had meandered into a corner of the pub yard for an understandable purpose. (Both men were speedily traced and cleared.)

Mrs Chivers, a widow who lived with the Steers, was left with the distraught mother, who asked her to go back into the house with her. Mrs Haskell said, "Someone has killed my Teddy!" Mrs Chivers said, "Oh, don't think that." Mrs Haskell said, "I think someone has killed him. He is so quiet and I can't hear him. Would you go upstairs?" Mrs Haskell then pointed to an object near the foot of the stairs, and Mrs Chivers saw that it was a bloodstained knife.

Mrs Haskell said, "There is the knife. I fancied I heard footsteps upstairs. Someone came down the stairs and threw the knife at me. Look, there is blood on my sleeve!" In the yellow light of the naked gas-jet in the kitchen Mrs Chivers noticed a few spots of blood on the right sleeve of Mrs Haskell's blouse.

Mrs Haskell was still screaming hysterically, and more neighbours were arriving. With these sounds of terror in his ears, Walter Steer came back from his encounter with the two men outside the pub, and went upstairs. By the light of the street lamp shining through the window, he saw that there was no man in the front bedroom. The other two rooms upstairs were in total darkness. He went down and called for a lamp, which his son brought from their own house. He went upstairs again quickly, and in the middle bedroom found Teddy Haskell lying on his back with his throat cut, and the bedclothes saturated with blood.

A doctor, called by Percy Noble, was already on his way, and this doctor, H. L. E. Wilks, was never contradicted on the three judicial occasions when he said on oath that he had been summoned from his house in Wilton Road at 10.30 p.m. At 10.20, when the Co-op bicycle boy John Wyatt was having his conversation at her front door with a perfectly calm Mrs Haskell, not even the prosecution seriously believed that the murder had been already committed. By 10.30 a doctor some distance away was being called by a messenger from a frantic mother. In those ten minutes a child died.

Dr Wilks, according to his undisputed timing, arrived at 10.35, went up immediately to the body of the boy; and deduced that death would have taken place within the previous fifteen minutes. Air was still escaping through the blood in the wound. The body was lying peacefully, his hands unclenched as if he had died in his sleep. Because of the position of the bed, the body could be approached only from the right, and there was a wound on the right side of the neck, about $2\frac{1}{2}$ inches long, beginning at the left side of the windpipe and continuing in a transverse and slightly downward direction. (That is, a deep-plunged knife was drawn towards the person who wielded it, and more pressure was used at the end of the stroke than at the beginning.)

Dr Wilks removed the mass of blood and air covering the wound, and found that the windpipe and the main artery were divided. The double severance had caused an immediate massive spurt of blood from the artery, travelling over a yard as it was projected, and the parallel sucking of blood into the lungs by the act of breathing. The reflex action from the lungs had caused a secondary air spray pumping blood froth from the open wound. There were signs of this spray on the bedclothes, but the bedding was principally saturated by the seepage of arterial blood from the wound after the initial spurt. This first spouting had, however, gushed strongly enough to hit a chest of drawers near the bed.

The first policeman appeared, a sergeant named Golding. One of the many neighbours already crowded into the tiny house told him dramatically, "There is the knife which was thrown at Mrs Haskell!" A bloodstained knife was lying at the foot of the stairs and project-ing through the open door two inches into the kitchen. "Don't touch it!" cried Sergeant Golding, and gingerly edged some brown paper under it, picked it up and rolled it in his pocket; before going off to telephone for police reinforcements.

Meanwhile the men of the district were arming themselves with sticks and lanterns. They split into search-parties and scoured the neighbourhood and the countryside beyond Salisbury for a somewhat vaguely described man. The police had no more precise description. Mrs Haskell told them that there was no light in the passage of her house when the stranger had appeared down the stairs, and she could offer no description of him. Nevertheless, the police somehow had a note of a man between thirty and forty years old, five feet six or seven inches high, dressed in a dark suit of clothes but wearing no collar or tie. The Chief Constable of Salisbury, who was on the scene as quickly as possible, called out all available city police to search the town; Wiltshire county police were sent out on bicycle patrols to post road-blocks and search the lanes; and on the next day bloodhounds were brought in. But no assailant was ever found.

No one had had the courage to answer in direct terms Mrs Haskell's continued questions about the fate of her son. When Dr Wilks came downstairs he asked the women sitting with her, "Doesn't she know?" Someone said, "We haven't told her." Wilks said, "I might as well tell her. She will have to know." Mrs Haskell said, "Do tell me, Dr Wilks." Wilks said, "Well, Mrs Haskell, I'm afraid it's a sad case. Someone has taken Teddy's life." But he gave no details, and went back to his house to prepare a sedative for Mrs Haskell. When he returned both Mrs Haskell and her widowed mother (called from her home in the district almshouse) asked if they could see Teddy. It was now about 11.30 p.m. Dr Wilks said he wanted a little time. He went upstairs with some helpers and they washed the body, arranged a handkerchief around the neck, rolled away the bloodstained bedclothes and laid fresh linen. Dr Wilks went downstairs and brought up Mrs Haskell and her mother. Mrs Carter went into the room first and kissed her grandson's face. Mrs Haskell came into the room and burst into fresh tears. She kissed her son and went away.

The Chief Constable of Salisbury had been unable to get a coherent story from Mrs Haskell during the first hours following the tragedy, and he posted Sergeant Golding to stay at the house all night, instructing him that Mrs Haskell and Mrs Carter were to rest downstairs. At about 3.30 in the morning Mrs Haskell asked the sergeant, "Is the money all right?" She explained that in the top drawer of the chest in Teddy's room there were eight pounds in gold and a two-shilling piece. It was money which Teddy had saved, from dribs and drabs given him by his grandmother, towards buying an artificial cork leg to be fitted as soon as he had stopped growing. Golding went upstairs and brought down a drawer, the lock of which had been wrenched off. Inside the drawer were three sovereigns and a half-sovereign. Mrs Haskell said that £4 12s. was missing.

The night passed. At six o'clock Mrs Carter said she was going to wash the hall. With a bucket of water and a cloth she scoured the passage and removed the bloodstain at the foot of the stairs where the knife—which Golding had already recovered—had lain. Criticized by the trial judge later for allowing this, and "by such a piece of folly losing the one piece of evidence in this case", Sergeant Golding said that his instructions had been to allow no one to go upstairs but to let the women do as they liked downstairs. The unfortunate sergeant admitted he had made an error of judgment.

When daylight came the Chief Constable knew that the all-night manhunt had been abortive. He telephoned Scotland Yard, and Chief Inspector Dew of the Criminal Investigation Department was sent down immediately. Dew was to achieve much greater fame two years later as the detective whose assiduous inquiries panicked Dr Crippen into his give-away flight with Ethel le Neve, and who subsequently arrested the couple at sea off the coast of Canada after a wireless message from the captain of their liner, the *Montrose*.

At Salisbury Dew, leaving any search for a supposed assailant to the city and county police, concentrated his investigation within the house and neighbourhood of 40 Meadow Road. But he had to wait a further day to get any fluent statement from Mrs Haskell, who was still in a state of shock. She conceded that a knife was missing from her kitchen, and she was unable to trace it. Dew would have been surprised if she had found it, since this was the knife being held by the police as the murder weapon—though the forensic science of that day could not isolate any fingerprints or other indications as to its handling.

Dew questioned Mrs Haskell closely about the man she said she had seen leaving the house. He asked if she had any idea who he was. She said that on the night before the murder a man had called at the house and, addressing her by name, had asked for lodgings, saying that he had been recommended to her. She had told him that she never let out a room for lodgings, and after some pressure he went away. She added that, two days before the call, a man had approached Teddy in the street. He had asked for the boy's name and address, for which he gave the lad twopence, had asked what his mother did, and inquired whether Teddy had any brothers or sisters. Mrs Haskell said that she thought the man who came downstairs and threw the knife at her on the night of the murder might well have been the man who called the previous night for lodgings, and she again described the Friday-night caller, as best she could.

Searching the house, Dew had found some freshly washed man's clothing in a drawer. He had already encouraged discreet inquiries among Mrs Haskell's neighbours, and had heard gossip that she was contemplating another marriage. He asked Mrs Haskell if she had a young man. "No," she said. He asked if any man had slept in her house recently. She said, "I have never let lodgings to male or female, and the only male person who has slept in this house is my eldest brother, Richard Carter." What about the fresh clothing found in a drawer? She said, "They belong to Mr Alfred Mold, who is a steward on the *Adriatic,* which sails between Southampton and New York, and he has slept in this house twice within the last three months, once about three months ago and once last Saturday week, and I do his laundrywork for him, which he leaves behind when he is going on a voyage. He left here for Southampton a fortnight today [that is, Monday 19 October] but he did not sail until the following Wednesday. He slept here on these occasions because his mother was full up."

Dew questioned Mrs Haskell about the money she said was missing from the drawer in Teddy's room. She said she had last seen it in the drawer on the previous Thursday, and it had been made up of seven sovereigns, two half-sovereigns and a two-shilling piece. After the murder there were only three and a half sovereigns in the drawer. She said that no one but herself, her mother and little Teddy knew about the money. Chief Inspector Dew told Mrs Haskell that, as she knew, he had found in her possession a purse containing eight sovereigns. She had an answer for this: it was her mother's purse, and she was keeping it for her. Mrs Carter confirmed this, and the money was handed back to her.

Mrs Haskell remained in the house with the body of her son, under police escort, through the following Sunday, Monday and

Tuesday. She did not attend the inquest, which was opened on the Tuesday afternoon. But she had to endure the arrival at her house of the coroner's jury, who had been brought in a brake to view the body. When the jury returned to the court Mrs Carter gave evidence of identification of her grandson, and the inquest was adjourned.

At 10.30 that night, a hired motor car brought Chief Inspector Dew and senior officers of the local police to 40 Meadow Road. The Chief Constable carried a warrant, and told Mrs Haskell that she was under arrest. She clutched her throat and said, "No! No!" Before the magistrates next morning, she was charged "that you did feloniously, wilfully and of your malice aforethought kill and murder Edwin Richard Haskell, aged twelve years, at 40 Meadow Road in this city on Saturday October 31st 1908, by cutting his throat". After formal evidence of arrest, she was remanded and sent to Devizes Prison.

The boy's funeral was held in the afternoon, and it was an elaborate local occasion. Twelve of Teddy's schoolfellows walked behind the mourning coach carrying white chrysanthemums. Among the many wreaths from local gentry, political organizations, and even the Salisbury Football Club, was a tribute of white flowers inscribed "In loving memory of darling little Teddy from his loving Mother and Grandma." Immediately after the funeral it was announced that a defence fund was being set up.

Eight days after Mrs Haskell's arrest a letter was delivered at her home. Chief Inspector Dew opened it. It read:

> *Pier 48,*
> *North River,*
> *New York,*
> *November 4th.*

DEAR FLO,
I shall try and get home on Friday evening November 13th. I hope you are well and Mother improved. Thanks very much, dear, for looking after her. I am very well and looking forward to seeing you again. I am sending this by the Lusitania so that you ought to get this on Thursday.

> Much love

> yours sincerely,
> ALF

The letter had in fact been delivered a day earlier than Mr Mold had expected. Dew, with a flair that would not have shamed James

Bond, consulted timetables, caught a train to Plymouth with the Chief Constable of Salisbury, and sailed out by tender to the White Star liner *Adriatic*, which was then discharging passengers and mails two miles out to sea. Before they could interview Mr Mold the ship sailed, and they had to travel to Cherbourg, and then Southampton. After talking with Mr Mold, however, Dew told him that it would be unnecessary to involve him any further in the case and he disappears from the story.

The evidence at the coroner's inquest took eight days to present. Mrs Haskell, looking dazed and extremely haggard, was present at every sitting; but time after time, when reference was made to the mutual devotion of mother and son, and to the reiterated details of the state of Teddy's body, she broke down in tears or into screaming fits which left her unconscious; and she was out of the court under medical care for much of the proceedings. But at the end of the proceedings the verdict was one of murder against Flora Fanny Haskell.

She was then brought before the magistrates for a hearing which lasted six days. Again there were painful scenes as she reacted to the evidence, and it was at one time considered that she should be committed to a hospital rather than sent back to prison on remand. But finally she was committed for trial at the next Assizes.

T. H. Parr, who had acted at the inquest and the preliminary hearings, was now led for the prosecution by J. Alderson Foote, K.C. At the previous hearings Parr had elicited evidence that Mrs Haskell had talked of a possible marriage with the steward Alfred Mold, and had used the relationship between Mrs Haskell and Mold to advance the prosecution's only imputation of a valid motive for Mrs Haskell's having committed the murder: that she thought her remarriage would be more likely if Teddy was out of the way.

But Alderson Foote, in his opening speech for the prosecution, caused a sensation when he swept aside every suggestion of this sort, and frankly confessed that the Crown could show no reason why the prisoner should have murdered her child. "The only theory which the Crown are able to present", he said, "is that this woman committed this act in one of those extraordinary abnormal conditions of mind which overtake human beings sometimes, and which it is impossible for medical men or legal experts to give any adequate explanation of. During her stay in prison the accused has been under the observation of the prison doctor, and he is of the opinion that she is perfectly sane."

The evidence given at the trial duplicated the colourful and extremely detailed accounts which had been given before the coroner and the magistrates, and which were now very familiar to almost everyone in the court, not excluding the jury. Forensic interest lay, therefore, in how the defence counsel (leading, although he was still a junior barrister, his wife's kinsman, Alfred Felix Schuster) would deal with it. In fact, Rayner's cross-examination of the lay witnesses was remarkably spare. None of the timings given by the neighbours and the errand-boy were in his view adverse to his client, and he merely emphasized them. But he did not fail to elicit from the neighbours their opinion of the relations between mother and son; and the response was always favourable. "Describe what Mrs Haskell was as a mother," Rayner said to Walter Steer. "Everything a mother ought to be, she was," came the reply.

Dr Pepper, a Home Office consultant and the main prosecution 'expert', gave the evidence on which the Crown was principally relying, which was to attribute the bloodstains on Mrs Haskell's clothing to her having been the murderess, and not to her having had a bloody knife thrown at her. (Mr Justice Ridley at one point inquired whether two people might not have been present at the murder, but was resolutely steered away from this theory by the prosecution.)

Dr Pepper was precise in his testimony. He said that there were twenty-eight spots of blood on the right side of the body of the blouse and about fifty on the sleeve. The spots on the body of the blouse were widely scattered over at least ten inches. The marks on the sleeve were also widely scattered, and extended from the wrist to within an inch of the yoke. There was a mark at the top of the sleeve which tailed in an upward direction, and there were two linear bloodmarks above it. These were caused by the blood going upward. However, all these bloodstains were either sprinkled or sprayed on, and could have been caused by a spray of blood projected by air from the open windpipe of the boy in bed. Such a spray of air-activated blood might well carry for two yards. The stains of blood both on the blouse and on the skirt could *not* have been caused from a knife such as that exhibited striking the fabric after being thrown at it, or spraying the fabric as it passed in its fall. The stains were entirely consistent with the effects of blood spraying from a cut throat.

Rayner Goddard, in cross-examination, asked a disingenuous question: "I suppose", he speculated to the witness, "I am right in assuming that you have never seen a human throat cut?"

"I hope not!" interjected the judge. But Dr Pepper thought his reputation was being slighted.

"As a surgeon, yes," he said.

Rayner asked, "Do you mean dead people?"

"No. Living people," the expert insisted.

"The windpipe?"

"Not the windpipe. But transverse cuts. I don't mean for the purpose of killing," the surgeon added somewhat lamely.

Rayner let the matter rest there for the moment.

The only entirely new evidence, which had not been available at the previous hearing, was offered in the closing minutes of the case for the prosecution. Alderson Foote called the police matron at Salisbury. The witness stated that after her committal for trial from the Police Court Mrs Haskell said to her, among other remarks, as she came down to the cells, "Oh, Mrs Shepherd, if I did it, I don't remember it."

The trial entered its closing stages. At last Rayner rose to address the jury of twelve men on behalf of the accused woman in the dock. "Edwin Richard Haskell was murdered on the night of October the 31st," he began quietly. "The prisoner, his mother, was arrested and charged with the crime on the 3rd of November, and this is the first occasion during all those months which have elapsed—which must have seemed as many centuries to this unhappy woman—that any opportunity has offered for evidence to be criticized, and remarks to be made, and a defence to be put forward on behalf of this woman.

"I should like at the outset of my remarks to pay a tribute of thanks to the prosecution for the way in which this case has been presented from start to finish, and the exemplary fairness with which, from the first time my client was suspected of this crime down to this moment, she has been treated.

"Gentlemen, I should like to ask you most earnestly to bear one question in mind. The question you have to try is not: Who committed the murder? The issue which you have to try is a much narrower one than that. It is this: Have the prosecution proved that this woman committed the murder?

"I cannot help feeling that in any case where the prisoner is the only person known to have been in the house at the time of the murder, there must inevitably be the temptation to put the question to oneself: 'If the prisoner did not do it, who did?'

"I venture to think that that is a most dangerous speculation. But, whether it is a dangerous speculation or not, it is not the question that you are here to try. The question you are here to try is *Aye* or *Nay*—beyond the shadow of doubt or possibility of mistake, is it proved that this woman slew her only child upon that night?

"That is the point which the prosecution have attempted to prove, and it is for them to prove it. I hope before I conclude my remarks to show that the only evidence against this woman is the fact that there were stains on her clothing. The only other evidence has been the theories and conjectures which medical men of eminence and fairness have drawn from these facts. I think that, before we come to the end of this case, the matter really comes down to this: Are you content to condemn a fellow-creature to death on the evidence of the theories of doctors?"

At this point Mrs Haskell was weeping bitterly in the dock; and this served as no discouragement to others in the court.

"You will not forget", counsel reminded the jury, "that remark by Mr Steer, when I asked him what sort of a mother she was to Teddy, and he said, "She was all that a mother should be." I wonder how many women there are in this world of whom that can be said." He looked around the court. "And I wonder how many mothers there are who would give *anything* to feel that that can be said of them. . . .

"This prosecution has been put forward from first to last as against a sane woman. I have met the prosecution upon that ground, and no theory or suggestion of insanity has been raised. Now, gentlemen, the Crown have put forward the case as one of premeditated crime.

"If this was a premeditated murder, as the Crown has put forward, there must have been some overwhelming motive which induced this woman to do it. . . . The Crown has all along been unable, so they say, to suggest a motive. But at the same time they have not eliminated from the case evidence which can have been put forward for no other reason than to suggest a motive. You have heard letters read which passed between Mrs Haskell and Mold, although the prosecution have expressly disclaimed the view that the motive for murder could be this marriage.

"I think that they probably feel they did well to drop that suggestion, for a more hideously inadequate suggestion, I should think, could not possibly be put forward. Especially when you remember that it was in evidence before you that Mold used to make this little lad his playfellow, give him money occasionally, and go about with the little lad as a companion. If Mold were some fiend, some man who, it could be suggested, said, 'Get rid of the cripple, and I will marry you', would he make this little lad his companion and playfellow when he was at home on leave in Salisbury?"

"If a sane person commits murder in cold blood there must be some motive. . . . Gentlemen, there is no motive in this case against this woman, and no motive is put forward by the Crown."

It is ironic to contemplate that on many occasions later, when on the Bench, Rayner was to point out forcibly to juries that—as is, indeed, the case—the prosecution does not have to prove a motive in order to obtain a conviction for murder.

But now he continued: "I am going to come at once to the most difficult part of the case, and to the part which, I am well aware, conveys most suspicion against my client. That is the evidence which deals with the stains on this woman's clothing and the medical theories therefrom. I do not care how eminent a gentleman may be in his profession, or how fairly he gives his evidence. Human judgement is always fallible. Because he is eminent in his profession, that is no more reason why Dr Pepper should not have made a mistake than with anyone else. And I can't help feeling that you will require something very much stronger than has been adduced in this case before you can possibly accept theories, however plausible they may be, as sufficient to find a verdict in a case of life and death.

"Now, gentlemen, the prosecution are inviting you to find that the stains on this woman's clothing are proof that she is a murderess. I am going to invite you to say that her story is by no means impossible. And I believe I am not overstating my case when I say that unless you find that these circumstances could not have come about by any other conceivable means, you will not be entitled to return a verdict of murder against her.

"The suggestion is, gentlemen, that the blood got on to the blouse as a result of the spray from the larynx. You have seen the pillows. It was a horrid task, but I had to bring them out. You have heard a description of the room. Can you believe that if this woman cut the boy's throat she could have got so little blood on her as there is on this blouse? You have seen the blouse, and the amount of blood on it is infinitesimal. Can you believe that if that blood got on the blouse by the accused cutting the boy's throat, it would not be infinitely more?

"Dr Pepper has said in his evidence that the whole thing depends on the position, as to whether she was in the line of spray, whether she moved or whether she did not. What is it more than the purest conjecture? On that conjecture you are asked to find a verdict of guilty.

"But there is another matter. How is it, accepting the theories of the doctors, that there is no blood on the left side of the blouse? If it all depends on position, and the woman came into the line of spray, I can conceive that you might be able to frame a theory. But does that fit in with the facts of the case?"

Rayner looked hard towards the jury. "You must pardon me if I uncover this pillow once more," he said. He arranged the pillows from the dead boy's bed on the table before him, and put his hands down almost as if he were strangling something on the pillow.

"We know, because there is undoubted evidence of it, that the boy's head was lying *there*, and as I stand here I should be looking straight in the boy's face. We know there is blood on the wall and we know there is blood on the chair. We know there is blood on the chest of drawers *which would be on my left side as I stand here*."

Rayner did not change his position, but bent his neck to give the jury his full regard as he spoke most emphatically. "Does it not occur to you as a most astonishing thing that whichever way the woman stood she had not got any blood on her left side?" It was a bull point, made by an able—if still somewhat inexperienced—courtroom lawyer.

Rayner straightened himself, and covered up the fearful-looking pillow on the table. "Gentlemen, there is not a trace or mark of blood anywhere other than on the right front of this blouse, and I venture to think you will pause before you draw an unfavourable inference against this woman on that account.

"Let us see", he said, "whether or not the explanation which this woman has given fits in. She has said that as a man came downstairs she looked out of the kitchen, that he threw a knife at her and it splashed her. Dr Pepper has agreed with me that with a knife thrown and hitting some firm inanimate object, blood might spray from it. A point in Dr Pepper's evidence of the first importance is that, coming downstairs, there is a mark on the right-hand side of the wall as if blood had been projected."

Good for Rayner! But Mr Justice Ridley does not seem to have pointed out in his subsequent summing up to the jury the fairly obvious point that the blood-mark could possibly have got on the wall through Mrs Haskell rushing downstairs immediately after the murder and brushing against the wall.

Be that as it may, Rayner continued, "I put it to Dr Pepper as to whether he had ever seen a throat cut in this way, and it caused some amusement. But my point is this: that no one has ever seen such a thing, and one has to speculate about it, and there is no certainty. No doctor has ever said that these stains on the woman's clothes *must* have been caused by a spray from that boy's throat. The most they have said is that they *could* have been caused, or *might* have been caused. I suggest that nothing short of certainty, beyond any doubt, *must* and not *may*, will entitle you to find a verdict of guilty."

Rayner then dealt with another telling point: "Where did this woman cleanse her hands? You will not consider it possible that she could have committed this murder and not got a considerable quantity of blood on her right hand. Is it conceivable that she could have got it out of her nails in the time? Blood does not come off all that easily. And yet we know it has never been suspected from first to last that she had any blood on her hands. If she had not any blood on her hands, she must have washed it off somewhere. There is no trace of blood on the sink, on the tap, or on the door which she opened to Percy Noble. . . .

"A great deal has been made of the fact that she did not go upstairs at once. But how can anyone say what inference can be drawn from what anyone does in a moment of panic? She may have had time to recover, but she knew that some man had come down from the place where the only person who was there was her only child, and that he had come downstairs and he threw something at her which splashed her. What inference can anyone draw from the ghastly tragedy enacted there? She is seized with panic. She feels the shrinking which people always have from a terrible thing, from a thing she feared to come to grips with, fearing the worst."

As he neared the end of his speech his style became more histrionic—and bear in mind that Sir Henry Irving was only three years dead. He turned towards Mrs Haskell in the dock:

"Remember that she is not a man, but a woman. The person you have to deal with is a woman, a mother, a loving mother, a weak woman. You see this poor thing in the dock, and you can judge for yourself whether you think she has the bravery and the resolution which is needed to come to grips with the worst, to come to grips with that which she feared, and must have feared, and must have known had taken place. Is any inference at all unfavourable to her to be drawn from what she did when she knew some disaster had happened to her boy?

"Do you remember that Dr Wilks told you how, when she did go up to the bedroom to see the child, she controlled herself, she went into the room, and she kissed that boy?" Here Mrs Haskell sobbed bitterly.

"If that woman is a guilty woman, what would you say of that kiss? Gentlemen, it is the most infamous kiss ever recorded. It shows that she is not only one of the worst criminals, but one of the greatest actresses that ever lived."

Rayner let his gaze rest on the weeping woman in the dock, and slowly shook his head.

"This woman is a humble woman of the people. She is not trained by the arts of society to restrain and repress her feelings in this way. Do you think it possible she could have proved herself such a consummate actress as she must have been if the story of the prosecution is true?"

"I would ask you to remember that it is not for me to draw aside the mantle of the night which hides this deed. But it is for the Crown to prove by evidence cogent and conclusive that the prisoner slew that boy and that she is guilty of his death. If this evidence, with its inconsistencies and improbabilities and with its theories, causes that woman's guilt to stand out red before you, you will convict her as your duty and your oath compels.

"But if there is in the mind of any one of you a lingering doubt"—and here a watching newspaperman reported that Rayner's voice faltered, then recovered—"a lingering doubt as to whether this awful deed was done by that poor creature, if you can find anything in the case which does not bring home that proof with that certainty which alone can justify you in passing a verdict fatal to a fellow-creature, then you will return that verdict which I believe will be hailed with a sigh of thankfulness and relief by every person in this court and country—of relief that this poor creature's sufferings are at an end, and of thankfulness that the sweet name of motherhood is not stained with so foul a crime." It was a passionate performance, totally geared to the standards of his time—and totally at variance with the pithy terseness of his later years.

Mr Justice Ridley summed up—lamely, as was usual with that lacklustre judge. He said the absence of motive was the best topic that could be urged on the prisoner's behalf, together with the prosecution's admission that the prisoner had been a good mother to this crippled boy. He declared that Mr Goddard had dealt with the evidence in an able manner, but he disagreed with him when he said it was theoretical. There was no theory about it that he could see, except that Dr Pepper had been called to give evidence for the prosecution, but that did not make it theoretical. Circumstantial evidence it was, because there was no direct evidence of any kind at all from anyone who saw the deed done. Circumstances properly judged could not lie, and it was from these circumstances that the jury were asked to come to a conclusion. If there was any reasonable doubt the prisoner must have the benefit of it. If they did not find that reasonable doubt they must find her guilty.

The jury retired. After three hours the judge sent and asked them if they had arrived at a verdict. They said they were unable to arrive at a conclusion in the case, and they were unlikely to do so. After further efforts the judge accepted this, and the jury were discharged. The judge said the case would have to be retried at the next Assizes, and fixed a date some fifteen weeks forward, at Salisbury on 5 June. But a wave of local protest that Mrs Haskell should have to wait so long in suspense, which was reflected in a Parliamentary question, coincided with the Home Office's desire to get the case finished—and preferably not in Salisbury, where the issues were extremely well known, and minds securely made up. It was announced that when Mr Justice Ridley had completed his Circuit for the current Western Assizes Mr Justice Darling would come down to Devizes to retry the case *R.* v. *Haskell,* and the date was set for the first week in April, 1909. Rayner therefore rode the Circuit longer that term.

The evidence offered at the second trial was no different from the first. Alderson Foote, for the prosecution, was as fair as before. Rayner's speech second time round for the defence was almost a verbatim copy of his first—like an actor on the second night of a play.

Even so, it created a profound impression in court, and Mr Justice Darling warmly complimented Rayner upon it. But that did not mean that Darling, a far more astute judge than Ridley, was going to let him off the hook so easily as his predecessor for his wise decision not to put Mrs Haskell in the witness-box.

"It must be a certain satisfaction to you all", Darling told the jury, "that counsel for the defence has spoken of the fairness with which the prosecution has been conducted, and it must be an even greater satisfaction that the prisoner has been defended with such remarkable ability and such good judgment displayed throughout the whole of the trial by Mr Goddard.

"But if Mr Goddard asks the members of the jury to uphold any lingering doubt which they may have in their minds, it becomes my duty to tell you that any such doubt must be of a reasonable nature. You must not judge the case on any different standard than you would adopt in regard to your own affairs."

He continued in a manner which did not favour the prisoner: "Although the defence argue that there is no motive for the woman's guilt," he said, "it is altogether difficult to see why a man should have come to the house to murder the boy. It has not been shown that there is a man who had any ill will against the lad. Mr

Rayner Goddard argued that if the prisoner had committed the crime she would have got more blood on her clothing. But you must apply that argument to the man who, it is suggested, murdered this boy. If he got such a large quantity of blood upon him, how is it that he got away undetected?"

The judge commented that the only person who could explain how bloodstains came on her clothing was the prisoner herself, but her counsel had not called her. "There are various hypotheses and suppositions in this case upon which explanations might have been offered. You must not convict a defendant because they have not been explained. But if there is something that admits of explanation, and that explanation is not given, it must gravely weaken the supposition that is put before you."

The judge summed up for two hours: longer than the defence counsel's speech, and long enough to let its impact grow dim. Nevertheless, the jury took only ten minutes over their deliberation, and when they filed back into court the foreman was able to report: "We find her not guilty on the ground of insufficient evidence".

There was a deep stillness in the court. Mrs Haskell smiled at her three brothers, who had supported her near the dock in both trials, and then she burst into a torrent of tears. The warder and wardress with her in the dock passed some paper bags of her belongings over to her, and she signed for them and left the dock. At that moment there was an outburst of cheering and clapping from the gallery of the court. Mrs Haskell passed from the building, and out of the sight of Rayner Goddard for ever.

Rex v. *Haskell* is the only murder case in which Rayner defended while he was at the Bar of which any substantial trace remains. In later years he conducted a few routine prosecutions for the Crown in 'low-profile' murder trials on Circuit, but few were exceptional: one might describe them as the 'normal' run-of-the-mill country murder where passions ignite, a blow is struck or a shotgun fired and, although, in human terms, the cost is appalling, in legal terms the playing out of the machinery of detection and calling to account for guilt requires no great display of intellectual or forensic power.

Rayner's 'triumph' in the defence of Mrs Haskell—for such it seemed to the outside world—certainly did him no harm in cementing an already bustling and prodigious Circuit practice, and as the nation advanced unsuspectingly towards the holocaust of the First World War he continued to ride the Circuit with ever-increasing success. Life was, indeed, pleasant for the young barrister and his growing family in those last dying years of the old order. Interesting work, congenial companions, an attractive wife, three small children whom he adored, a comfortable London house, a delightful summer home at Lulworth Cove, devoted parents, an assured confidence about the future—what could possibly go wrong?

5 Gentle Progress–
Towards Tragedy

The War at first made little impact on the somewhat routine progress of Rayner's career. Circuit work tailed off, but there was now enough in London to keep him reasonably busy. From 1912 to 1917 he was Honorary Secretary of the Barristers' Benevolent Association. In 1913 he had been elected to the General Council of the Bar, the governing body of his profession. He changed Chambers yet again—to those of George Wallace, K.C., a man *not* on the Western Circuit, and with a predominantly civil practice, based solidly on London.

It was all low-key, but suffused with the warmth of his personality and the strength of his bustling energy. James Tucker, later Lord Tucker, a Lord of Appeal in Ordinary, was one of his pupils at that time, and stayed on in Chambers as a full member. He became a close friend of his ex pupil-master, and shared his enthusiasm for the plight of their less fortunate colleagues and their families succoured by the Barristers' Benevolent Association: "I remember the early days when the B.B.A. functioned in the basement of Harcourt Buildings without a typewriter. Goddard wrote all the correspondence himself, and even when in some practice as a junior he used always to go down after lunch and attend to anything that needed to be done. He also frequently visited the applicants or their widows on Sunday afternoons." Rayner never learned to drive a car—"I several times drove him down to Sussex where several of our 'cases' lived."

At home his wife's health was beginning to fade. Their youngest daughter, Prue, born in 1913, had been an exceptionally large baby.

"My mother was never quite the same afterwards," says Mrs Pamela Maurice. "Her partial deafness, caused by hereditary disease of the middle ear, got appreciably worse, and eventually she had to give up singing. Her joy in music was an essential part of her life. It heightened her tendency to be nervy and on edge."

But there was a contentment between Rayner and Mollie Goddard in those years. Sir Harold Morris tells us of an evening when he and his wife dined with the Goddards and "after dinner he and I and another guest finished the last bottle of port from a bin. It was Dow 1881, which his dear old father always referred to as a summer wine. It was in perfect condition and a really good bottle. Mollie Goddard, who had just come back from a weekend at a girls' school, said, 'I'm so sick of the sight of food after what I had there that I can't look a mutton in the neck!' " They all laughed, and not least Rayner.

Even so, he found that he needed to play to the full a father's role in the lives of his daughters; and he did so in his own characteristic fashion. "I shall never forget one occasion, on a Sunday morning," says Mrs Maurice. "My two sisters and I were then sharing a large night nursery and, on this particular Sunday morning, we were, to use my father's own words, 'kicking up Hell's delight' and hurling wet sponges and mutual abuse at each other indiscriminately.

"Suddenly the door opened and in stalked Papa in his pyjamas and dressing gown. He never said a word, but removed his slipper, dealt each one of us a resounding whack on that part of our anatomy best fitted to receive it, and stalked out again—still without uttering. I think we all shut up after that!"

The girls looked to Rayner more and more as the dominant influence in their lives. He realized the burden cast upon him. Perhaps that is why he never felt free to volunteer for service abroad in one of the Armed Forces. Instead he joined the Special Constabulary, and Mrs Maurice still remembers his telling her one day of the old lady who summoned his assistance while he was on duty because "a young man was watching her dress through the window". "Better than watching you *un*dress!" was the retort of this somewhat unconventional 'Special'.

Eventually he won promotion to the rank of sergeant; and the future Lord Chief Justice more than once did wartime duty patrolling outside Buckingham Palace.

But by 1917 Rayner felt he could not longer continue in practice—"He did not like the idea of taking other people's briefs, who were away fighting in the trenches." So he joined the Civil Service for the rest of the War, and became Temporary Legal Assistant for War Work at the Board of Trade.

He did not sever all links with the Bar. In October 1917 his old pupil-master, Clavell Salter, now an M.P. and Recorder of Poole, was appointed a High Court Judge. That left a vacancy at Poole where a new Recorder was required to preside over the local Quarter Sessions. Mrs Maurice remembers coming downstairs for breakfast one morning in November 1917 and her father announcing to his assembled family at the breakfast table, "Children, I've been made Recorder of Poole!" "He was very pleased with himself," says Mrs Maurice.

All the family went down to Poole to see him sworn in, including 5-year-old Prue. "It was the first time we had ever stayed in a hotel. It was a tremendous occasion!"

That same year the Zeppelin raids on London made Mr and Mrs Goddard anxious for the safety of their family. They moved from their home at Durham Villas (now Phillimore Place) in Kensington to the calm of West Byfleet in Surrey. But in November 1918, with the end of hostilities, they at once returned to the capital—to 32 Argyll Road, again in Kensington—and as soon as possible Rayner gave up his Board of Trade post and came back to the Temple.

But it was not at all easy to pick up again the even tenor of his practice. Other barristers had not felt the same need to deprive themselves of wartime pickings, and those returning from active service understandably had a certain call on solicitors' loyalties. At this stage occurred an incident described in several books about the Temple but so apparently apocryphal that one would have been loath to believe it if Lady Sachs and Mr Sidney Newland (who as a boy of sixteen had just joined Rayner's chambers as junior clerk) did not both earnestly proclaim it to be true.

One Friday morning Rayner arrived in Chambers to find an empty day ahead of him. No briefs, no conferences, no sets of papers to read: nothing. As usual he could not bear wasting time. What to do? He paced up and down, took a Law Report from the shelf and idly began reading it. Suddenly he became interested in one particular case. It was on some abstruse aspect of banking law. Despite the Schuster connection, he only knew about the laws of banking in the most general terms: this specific point fascinated him. He read through the report from first to last.

Next morning was a Saturday, and of course Rayner was in Chambers—although he had nothing really to do. A senior representative of a well-known firm of City solicitors (Mr Newland

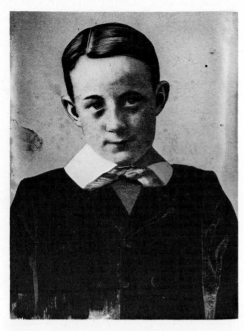

The Haskell Murder

Teddy Haskell, the murdered boy
Photo Radio Times Hulton Picture Library

Bottom left
Mr Justice Ridley, who conducted the first
Haskell Trial
Photo Radio Times Hulton Picture Library

Bottom right
Mr Justice Darling, who presided over the
second Haskell Trial
Photo Radio Times Hulton Picture Library

Mrs Marie Linda ('Mollie') Goddard, as she was in 1927, the year before her prematurely early death following an operation

Sir Rayner Goddard, as he was in 1932, five years later, upon his appointment to the High Court Bench

says it was Coward Hawksley, Sons & Chance, now Coward Chance & Co.) came into the almost deserted Temple seeking urgently advice of counsel on a difficult point of banking law. He and his companion went to their usual counsel in these matters, but he was otherwise engaged on more congenial affairs on a Saturday morning. "Let's try Mr Goddard," said the solicitor. "He does some civil work for us. Perhaps he'll be available." They knocked at the door of Rayner's chambers in 3 Plowden Buildings, Sidney Newland ushered them into Rayner's room—and it turned out that the point on which they were needing such immediate advice was precisely that covered by the Law Report that Goddard had by chance been reading only the previous morning.

As the *Law Times* in one account of this famous story has it, "He was able to refer, casually, as it were, to the year and the report, and even the name of the case; and taking down the volume found that his memory was not at fault." The solicitor and his client were most impressed, and within a short while Rayner had become one of the foremost practitioners in banking law—briefed on behalf of all the leading banks, save for (as we have already seen) the one in which his father-in-law had a commanding voice.

The link that Rayner Goddard forged with his clerk Sidney Newland has to be known in order to judge the full flavour of the man. Mr Newland is himself no run-of-the-mill character. By the time he retired in 1975 after fifty-six years in the Temple he had become the doyen of barristers' clerks, a Justice of the Peace, the holder of the M.B.E. and, in his private life, a singularly successful Mayor of Wembley.

"It is almost impossible to describe how grateful I was to Mr Goddard when I first came into Chambers. I was only a lad of sixteen, and remember in those days barristers were wondrous creatures to the likes of us. Yet from the very first he had no 'side' or pretensions whatsoever.

"I remember that soon after joining I had to go out with him on Circuit to Exeter Assizes. He insisted firmly on the old rule that his clerk must accompany a barrister when going on Circuit. So off we went together, but instead of just leaving me to my own devices—as most other barristers would have done—when it came to getting a bite to eat, he took me with him into the refreshment room at St David's Station at Exeter and we had lunch together. Perhaps it does not sound very much these days, but then it was out of the world for me!

"He was a very, very generous man. I went in to see him when my

first baby was born, it was a boy. It was about 4 o'clock in the afternoon, just the time when a barrister's Chambers get especially busy
coping with the next day's fixtures. 'Good, go home, at once,' he
said, 'and see your son'. I was making towards the door, and he
called me back. 'Wait a moment, you'll have lots of expenses'—and
he pulled £25 out of his wallet, and gave it to me. That was a fortune
in those days!

"Then when our second baby was coming along, he said to me
once, 'When is the baby due?' I said, 'In April', and he said, 'Right!
If the baby's born on my birthday, I'll be the godfather!' The baby,
a girl, *was* born on his birthday, April 10th, and he *did* become my
daughter's godfather.

"When I was Mayor of Wembley he came out to my mayoral
reception with Lord Tucker. When he celebrated his fifty years since
his Call to the Bar in 1949, we clerks in the Temple got together a
collection between ourselves and bought him a magnificent bound
volume of Harold Nicolson's *Life of George V*. We knew he would like
that. So a small deputation of the Barristers' Clerks' Association
went over to his private room, by appointment, after court at 4.30 in
the afternoon and made the formal presentation. I made a short
speech, and he just sat there at his desk with the tears streaming
down his face.

"And *that* is the man whom Bernard Levin and the rest would
have us believe was a cruel, bloodthirsty old ogre! It makes me so
angry.

"He never failed on the Sunday before Christmas to be driven out
to my home in Kenton to have tea with us, and he did that right up
till the end. You can never forget a man like that. He will be part of
my life until I die."

In February 1923 Rayner Goddard 'took silk' and became a K.C.,
a senior member of his profession. With the sixteen other new silks
of that year, he made his formal bow to the judges of the High
Court on Wednesday, 14 February; on the following Saturday the
senior clerk to his chambers died and young Sidney Newland, aged
twenty, became the new senior clerk. "I had the pleasure of writing
thirty-nine letters to applicants for the post telling them all it had
been filled."

As a leader Rayner Goddard, had a good, solid, busy practice.
His work was primarily commercial, and he was never anything less
than competent. His clients were usually banks, insurance com-
panies, great trading-houses; seldom popular personalities from the
theatre or the world of fashion—or alleged criminals. His earnings

were substantial, his publicity generally meagre.

Vignettes contributed by his contemporaries are difficult to find for this period.

But: "He was called 'Doggie' at the Bar, and indeed on the Bench, because of his bulldog countenance," says Mr J. E. S. Ricardo, a veteran junior on the Western Circuit. "As a silk, he led me once on an appeal to the High Court to set aside an arbitration award in a case where the arbitrator was an engineer and the father of the self-same young man whose company had installed an early oil-fired central heating system in a house in Pont Street. I am pleased to recall that we won handsomely."

"He was brought in once to lead me in a case before the Official Referee," says Mr Justice Melford Stevenson. "It was a case to do with architects' copyright. We were for an architect. A building developer had made use of plans he had employed the architect to prepare for a building development in the Hounslow area, but then without permission he had used them for a further development elsewhere. The question was whether the developer had acquired copyright in the plans. I think we won, but I remember distinctly that in the middle of what was a very long case some point arose on the pleading, which, of course, as the junior I had settled, and I had to make a somewhat difficult amendment overnight during the adjournment. I went off back to my chambers to start grappling with the thing, when my clerk suddenly opened my door to say that 'Mr Goddard' was there. He had come round to see if he could be of any help. It was a charming thought. Leaders don't usually bother themselves with juniors' problems with their pleadings. I cannot think of anyone else who would have done that."

"As a silk, we did quite a lot of medical work," says Mr Newland, "briefed by Hempson's, the solicitors acting for the Medical Defence Union. I remember one case where a woman sued a surgeon named Miles because she had a pair of Spencer Wells forceps in her after an operation. She had had an operation by Miles, then gone off to France and had a second operation—in which they found the forceps, allegedly left over from the first one. It was said that they must have been left there by Miles, and not by the surgeon in the second, French, operation because they didn't use Spencer Wells forceps in France. But Rayner Goddard took the point, and called evidence to support it, that after the Great War quite a few British hospitals in France sold up, and the French surgeon could easily have got hold of Spencer Wells forceps that way. The lady lost her case!"

"In 1927 my father, R. C. Tuckett of Bristol, briefed Mr Goddard, K.C., in a right-of-way case situated in Walton-in-Gordano," says Mrs Irving Gradwell. "My father was a specialist in such cases; and in the 1880s he had had an extremely interesting case in Gordano, which included the right of recreation over Walton Common. When over forty years later a case arose in the same area in which the plaintiff was a son of one of his old freeholder witnesses my father decided that I should handle it. At that time I was not out of my articles, and was the first woman law student in Bristol.

"I interviewed all the seventy or eighty witnesses and drew the brief, which my father read through, but would not comment upon. When the Assizes came on he said he would not come into court: 'It's your case, get on with it!' I did. I had consultation with the junior, Mr Nils Moller, but not with the silk.

"On the opening day Goddard had not appeared, and Moller had just begun to open in his stead when Goddard came in—very irritable, nervous and cross, his train having been held up by fog. He looked round the court and glowered, and muttered to Moller, 'Where's Tuckett?' Moller gestured towards me and said, *'Miss* Tuckett is instructing us.' Goddard turned, glared at me, rolled his eyes and exclaimed—I thought all too audibly—'Christ! A Woman! It needed only that!'

"The case lasted several days, and I had a wonderful opportunity to study closely his quite brilliant powers of cross-examination. At the same time I studied him personally, because I was determined to make him change his attitude. Of course, with so many witnesses I was bound to know far more about the facts than counsel could. At each consultation I picked a suitable moment to say, 'If I may mention it, sir, I thought the point you made yesterday which comes out most strongly in Mary Smith's or George Jones's evidence is particularly telling in that connection.' To which he would reply, 'Did I say that . . .? Well, yes, of course! It's self-evident, isn't it?' Moller kept a very straight face, and by the fourth day I hardly needed to do it, and he had about 'rumbled' me—except that my face remained poker-straight throughout.

"We won handsomely; and I was distinctly pleased when he wrote to my father saying, 'Your articled clerk clearly knew every word of the case', and congratulating him on me. In the circumstances, I thought it was somewhat graceful on his part; he needn't have done it. I was twenty-one at the time."

The strain running throughout Rayner Goddard's long life, as much in his years at the Bar as later in the richness of his experience on the Bench, was his concern for, and kindness to, youth. Writes his ex-pupil, the late Lord Tucker: "When a busy junior, he never had more than two pupils and one of them always sat in his room and was present when solicitors called for conferences. Contrast this with the Chambers where six or seven pupils were accepted and rarely sat in during a conference." Sir Joseph Molony, Q.C., was in turn a pupil of Lord Tucker's: "Rayner knew my father when he was Lord Chief Justice of Ireland and later when he became chairman of one of the leading London banks. When I came to the Bar in 1930 and Rayner was already a silk, he very kindly and easily arranged for me to come as a first pupil to James Tucker. He was very kind and generous to me, even though I was one of the most lowly members of Chambers. He was a little gruff, a little rough perhaps on certain mornings, one must say. Brusque in speech, but thoroughly kind and courteous underneath. Once he made up his mind he liked you, you could always come to him as a friend."

"I knew him on the Circuit in the nineteen-twenties", says a present holder of high judicial rank. "I was a very young man at the time. I used to go to dances with his daughters, and used to go down and spend the summer with them all in their summerhouse near Wyke Regis. It was a very cheery, delightful household for a youngster in those days."

The picture culled from his contemporaries is that of a good Circuiteer—a good Circuit silk, doing some crime and a great deal of civil work and banking cases. But he would not seem to have been pre-eminent. Few remember him as an impressive advocate, as such. He eschewed any of the flamboyance of the more flowery advocates of those days—Marshall Hall, Pat Hastings, Birkett and the rest. He was not of that mould. He was not usually eloquent or dramatic. He was a good, competent all-rounder.

Yet, just as in later life he expected barristers on their feet in front of him to stand up to him and give the judge as good as they got, so had he been courageous himself when he was at the Bar. One afternoon, thirty years later, when he was presiding as Lord Chief Justice over the Court of Criminal Appeal, counsel said to him, "M'lord, I humbly submit—" "Mr—, when I was at the Bar I never humbly submitted to anybody," growled the Lord Chief. "I bet you bloody didn't!" was the stage whisper that emerged from counsel's benches, and brought a smile to "Doggie's" countenance.

In 1925 he was translated to the somewhat grander Recordership of Bath from the quieter stretches of Poole, and three years later, in March 1928, following in the footsteps of another old Western Circuit friend, J. A. Hawke, K.C. (later Mr Justice Hawke), he was appointed to the even more splendid Recordership of Plymouth. In the light of his later reputation for savagery in his sentences, it is interesting to record the local Bath newspaper's comment on his departure: "Those who know him will regret to learn that Mr Rayner Goddard, K.C., is severing his connection with Bath. . . . He has held the position of Recorder for only just over three years, but in that time he has displayed outstanding ability for the office, and shown that he is one of those who view the law and its punishments in quite a new light as a means to preventing crime and, where committed, to a reformation of the criminals."

They were comfortable years, not brimful of adventure or turbulent seeking after some compelling inner happiness, but pleasant enough, in all conscience.

The three girls were growing up. Sadly, his wife's health was not improving—for some years she had been in almost continual pain with a distressing gall-bladder condition. Mollie Goddard, never the most equable of women, was going through an early change of life, and Rayner's daughters today candidly admit she must have been rather trying for her husband at that time. But he was very much 'a man's man': he had his clubs, his Circuit dinners, his other professional social engagements. He sincerely loved his wife, he had his other interests, life was agreeable.

His Kensington home was ample and commodious. No less than five domestic servants—a cook, kitchen-maid, parlourmaid, housemaid and between-maid—attended to his own and his family's needs. He was fifty-one, assured in his profession, solid and accomplished.

Ernest Charles, K.C., another Western Circuit colleague, had just been appointed a High Court Judge. Charles's old chambers at 1 Mitre Court Buildings, where Rayner had started as a pupil twenty-nine years earlier, were on the point of breaking up. Overtures were made, the delicate niceties of Temple protocol complied with: Rayner Goddard, taking with him the young James Tucker and the loyal Sidney Newland, went back to his old Western Circuit 'stables' to take over as head of chambers.

All seemed set for an acceptably roseate future—with perhaps even in a few years' time the prospect of a High Court Judge's scarlet and ermine robes adorning his shoulders, as already they were those of several of his contemporaries.

Then suddenly tragedy struck—at just the moment when Rayner

could have expected to sail calmly and assuredly into warm, late-summer waters, without even a ripple or wavelet to disturb the soft-swelling calm.

6 Widowhood and the South Kensington Election

In May 1928 Mollie Goddard went into a London nursing-home for an operation for the removal of gall-stones. She had the operation on a Monday, and that evening her husband told their daughters, "She has come through it well, don't go and see her tomorrow—wait until Wednesday." But on the Wednesday morning, as the family was sitting down to breakfast, Rayner received a telephone call from the nursing-home: Mollie was dying—she had suffered a pulmonary embolism as an after-effect of the operation.

"She should never have died from that operation," says Mrs Pamela Maurice. "Operation successful—the patient died," says Lady Sachs, with even after all these years a trace of bitterness in her voice.

"Rayner was very, very sad and distracted by his wife's death," says Mrs Joan Conway, now a Q.C.'s widow and long-standing friend of the family. "He would always refer to her afterwards in a rather sweet old-fashioned way as 'my dear wife'."

"It is only after years of hindsight that one realizes what an appalling situation it must have been for Rayner to find himself saddled with three daughters, aged twenty, eighteen and fifteen, and no female relative to take the responsibility from his shoulders," says Lady Sachs. "This apart from the fact that he was then at the height of a large and increasingly busy practice at the Bar; though possibly that may have been his salvation, as it gave him little time to think of the pitfalls ahead.

"He had, in fact, two unmarried sisters—our Aunts Mary and Maud Goddard—living at home and squabbling, and my own sisters and I have often wondered whether they expected him to ask one of them to undertake the task of hostess/housekeeper and chaperone. She would (one hopes) most certainly have refused, and one shudders at the thought of what horrors acceptance would have meant—but all the same I think they'd have liked to be asked.

"We lived in a large, comfortable, fairly ugly old house in Campden Hill. Nasty little snob that I was, I resented living in what was then an unfashionable neighbourhood, and was bitterly conscious of the scarcely concealed dismay of any male escort who volunteered to take me home from parties in Mayfair or Belgravia when faced with paying large taxi fares. (Not to mention the prospect of being confronted in the hall by Rayner in his Jaeger pyjamas demanding what I thought the time was—but I soon learned exactly which floor-boards creaked, and which door needed oiling, and to take action accordingly.)

"At the time of our mother's death we were unbelievably lucky in having a dearly loved companion/governess, 'Nicky', for whose loving loyalty my sisters and I can never be sufficiently grateful, and who in fact stayed on as housekeeper to Rayner for years after we were all married."

"Nicky" used to dine with Rayner and his daughters—except for formal dinner-parties. She lived as one of the family; "but", says Lady Sachs, "from the first, Rayner was quite positive that one of his daughters should run his household, and since the eldest was happily engaged in working in Slaughter and May's, the well-known solicitors (where her godfather W. E. Mortimer, Rayner's oldest and closest friend, was senior partner) and was likewise showing signs of becoming engaged to be married, and the youngest was still at school, it seemed obvious that the lot should fall on me. Which it did, and I never had six happier years till I married in 1934.

"At the time of Rayner's retirement in 1958, when a great deal about him—of varying accuracy—appeared in the Press, one enterprising journalist wrote a few paragraphs regarding his relationships with his daughters that were so wide of the mark as to reduce us to helpless laughter.

"He was portrayed as a stern Victorian paterfamilias who supervised our every action, and to whom we had to account for every penny of our personal spending. In fact, he never—or almost never—questioned our activities at all, not even my depredations of the very generous housekeeping allowance of which I had control, and of which a shamingly large proportion went in taxi fares and dress bills.

"He frequently, to my intense embarrassment, referred to his gratitude to me for, as he put it, 'giving up my life to him'—an aspect of the situation that would never have occurred to me, because I was having a ball!!!! The only rigorous proviso that I can recall was that he should never have to dine in the house alone—so one of the three of us was always there to accompany him, albeit it not seldom sparked off some pretty acrimonious discussion between ourselves as to which should sacrifice her evening assignment—if any!"

"I think he was a shy man in a lot of ways," says Mrs Joan Conway. "He was essentially a family man—devoted to his three daughters: worried a lot about them when they were ill or whether they would marry the right man. In later life, if they were going to have a baby, he would be worried if they would come out alive. In due course, he was devoted to his grandchildren—especially Richard Sachs, Peggy's son.

"But I think he was very lonely in a way. He did not like being alone."

Rayner never remarried. He lived as a widower for forty-three years. "He was—I am sure—genuinely frightened of women, though easily influenced by, and strongly attracted to, them," says Lady Sachs. "My sisters and I always greatly regretted that he never remarried. His last years could have been so much happier and more comfortable had he done so, but it was not to be."

In fact, in extreme old age, Rayner once told Mrs Naomi Lloyd, wife of Judge Ifor Lloyd, two staunch family friends, that he did not marry again because of his three daughters—"I didn't want to upset them!" he claimed. It sounds like an excuse, but he was always a realist: "Anyway, I should have been a widower again by now!"

It is perhaps in the temporary unsettling of a life that had always until then flowed so equably that the explanation is to be found of the extraordinary error of judgment that, in the aftermath of Mollie Goddard's death, made Rayner throw away the constraints of three decades of professional life and plunge into an ill-starred political venture that attracted more publicity to his name than all his years of practice—and for a brief while made him virtually a public laughing-stock.

In the spring of 1929 it became clear that a general election was imminent, although Stanley Baldwin, the Conservative Prime Minister, could have kept his Government in office until the

November of that year. The election was to be governed by a new factor, the so-called "Flapper Vote" consequent on the passing of the Representation of the People (Equal Franchise) Act of 1928. This gave the vote to women at the age of twenty-one, rather than at thirty, as the law had stood since 1918.

In South Kensington, where Rayner and his family had long lived, there was an additional consideration. The sitting Conservative member, Sir William Davison, a barrister, had recently had his marriage dissolved. A proportion of the local Conservative Party thought that this made him unsuitable as a parliamentary candidate, although he had held the seat for ten years. An Emergency Committee was formed under the chairmanship of another barrister, Sir Miles Mattinson, K.C., and it issued a circular advocating that a new candidate "agreeable to all sections of the party" should be sought. "The opinion is widely held", said the committee, "that the Conservative Party will be severely handicapped at the coming election if its representative is exposed to all the criticisms which, in the heat of an election, are likely to be directed against someone who has just passed through the divorce courts."

Common-sense logic might have suggested that the 1929 flappers, a formidably permissive section of society according to the standards of the time, would not be in the least fazed by the fact that they were being asked to vote for a divorced man. Noël Coward had already presented *Easy Virtue* and *Fallen Angels,* and was then writing *Private Lives.* However, the old ladies of both sexes in Kensington, led by a bishop's daughter, decided that an Independent Conservative candidate should stand against Sir William Davison, and they approached Rayner Goddard. In an ill-considered moment he agreed.

He was immediately dubbed "the Purity Candidate". The flappers, as he might have anticipated, flocked to his meetings only to barrack him: "Have you ever committed adultery?" they demanded. Kensington church unity was split from St Barnabas to St Mary Abbots. On the day that Parliament was dissolved the Liberals announced that they were putting up a candidate. Rayner Goddard, who had previously thought that this was a private fight in a Conservative stronghold, took extra-emergency measures. He wrote to the Press suggesting a third, alternative, Conservative candidate. "I agreed to be nominated only after I was satisfied that there are a large number of Conservative electors of all classes who would not vote for Sir William Davison on any consideration whatever. I now make this offer to Sir William: If he will withdraw, so will I. A candidate can then be nominated who will unite all Conservative opinion."

"A piece of impudence!" thundered Sir William, when asked to comment. "Why should I stand down? It would make political organizations in this country impossible if a properly selected candidate should stand down because he does not happen to please a small section of the local organization. If I retire, it would smash Conservatism into pieces in South Kensington and allow the Liberals to walk in."

The unhappy election campaign snarled to its close. Sir William Davison, with 28 049 votes, notched a 20 479 majority over Sir Hugh Seely, the Liberal, and Rayner Goddard, K.C., Independent Conservative, came bottom of the poll with 6 365 votes.

Long afterwards, his intimates have summed up this unfortunate incursion. Christopher Clarke, a retired partner in Slaughter & May and an old friend of Rayner's, says: "There was quite a lot of talk about whether it was sensible for him to stand. Quite a few people thought it was a frightfully unhappy incident from Rayner's point of view. He couldn't succeed—and Rayner must have known that he would not succeed. I think it was an error of judgment. I bet Bill Mortimer [Clarke's senior partner and Rayner's closest friend] would have called him a silly old chump. I think we all felt it was not at all sensible." This is also the view of Rayner's daughters. Lord Dilhorne, a Conservative M.P. for twenty years before he became Lord Chancellor, says, "His entry into politics was a mistake which I think he regretted." And Rayner himself once commented wryly on his political experience to the jury he was directing in the Laski libel action: "Just because I sit on the Bench I am not going to pretend that I don't know what goes on at political meetings, and I am not going to pretend that I haven't been to political meetings myself, though I think I can say with perfect honesty that I have never attempted to heckle a political speaker in my life, because I thought he would probably get back on me if I did!"

Before the dissolution of Parliament, on 3 May 1929, the Benchers of his Inn had elected Rayner to be one of their number. In the post-election quiet they welcomed him with warmth, untinged by any aspersion. He may have gone some distance towards making a bit of an ass of himself, but at least his heart was in the right place, as the beneficiaries of the Barristers' Benevolent Association—and of his private generosity—had long known. And, after all, he had been doing no more than seeking to defend the virtues of morality and family obligation, as he saw them; and the Bar of England was hardly going to pillory one of their most popular members for trying to do *that*. His honour was rightly due to him.

Soon Rayner was immersed in a civil action that was to take him right up to the House of Lords. It was an entertaining case in which he represented Cyril Tolley, then the British amateur golf champion, in a suit alleging libel against the well-known firm of J. S. Fry & Sons, Ltd, chocolate-manufacturers.

Mr Tolley was complaining that Fry's had laid him open to a false accusation of conduct unbecoming to a gentleman and an amateur golfer. What had they done? In June 1928 they had published in the *Daily Mail,* the *Daily Sketch* and in sixty-two other newspapers over the country an advertisement which showed a caricature of Cyril Tolley driving at golf, with a caddy looking on and holding up packets of Fry's chocolate. A packet also protruded from the golfer's pocket. The caption was a limerick, which ran:

> The caddy to Tolley said: 'Oh, Sir!
> Good shot, Sir, that ball see it go, Sir.
>   My word, how it flies
>   Like a Cartet of Fry's
> They're handy, they're good, and priced low, Sir.'

Mr Tolley complained that the advertisement meant that he had allowed his portrait to be exhibited for the purpose of advertising the defendant's chocolate; that he had done so for gain, and had thus prostituted his reputation as an amateur golfer by appearing to seek notoriety and reward, which would constitute a declaration that he was guilty of conduct unworthy of his status as an amateur golfer.

His case was put in the High Court before Mr Justice Acton and a common jury by Rayner Goddard, K.C., leading H. M. Giveen. For the defendants, Norman Birkett, K.C. (later Lord Birkett of Ulverston) led Mr W. T. Monckton (later Sir Walter Monckton, K.C., and eventually Viscount Monckton).

Rayner's impact on a client at this time merits recording. Major Tolley (he served in both World Wars, and was awarded the Military Cross) reported breezily[1] at the age of eighty: "A member of my [Stock Exchange] firm suggested I employ Mr Barry Cohen, a very enterprising solicitor. He in his turn suggested Rayner Goddard because he was good and not expensive. His fee was, I think, 30 guineas whereas Birkett's was 150 guineas with Monckton as junior.

---

[1] In a letter to the author.

As I remember Goddard—short, thickset, taciturn, he didn't appear to like Cohen, a fine grasp of detail—thought I had some prospect of winning but not too hopeful. Didn't bewilder the jury and did his work quietly and efficiently. I think he was amused when Birkett, very red in the face after the verdict, said he would pay the money into Court against any appeal."

Birkett's fee of five times Goddard's was set in his record financial year—his fee-book showed £33 500 for 1929, and the annual total remained at around £30 000 until he accepted a judgeship in 1941. Goddard was less a spectacular high-flier, although he did take 5 000 guineas for one untypical day's work[2]—5 000 shillings more than a judge's annual salary in those times. The *Tolley* v. *Fry* session in the King's Bench Division was more run-of-the-mill, even though it did eventually entail appearance in two higher courts.

It was not an occasion for eloquence. To Mr Justice Acton and the jury Rayner cut the cackle and got down to the facts. The defendants had admitted publication, but denied the innuendo, and said that the words in the advertisement were incapable of constituting a libel. Within six days of the first publication, on receiving Tolley's complaint, they had replied "deeply regretting" that the advertisement should have given him offence, but denying liability.

"This is entire humbug," said Rayner forcefully. He produced a file of correspondence between the chocolate firm and its advertising agents. The main subjects dealt with were, first, the "good taste" of acquiring publicity by caricaturing a man unrelated to the enterprise, and without his permission; and secondly, the possible legal liability involved in doing so. One letter from the agents ran:

"On the subject of good taste we feel that the actual caricatures produced by us for you strike a cheerful note in the main. They are not bitter nor scurrilous in their attitude. . . . If you have any doubts (once the legal aspect of the matter is settled to your satisfaction) you might consider sending a proof of each advertisement for the scrutiny of the individual concerned before its appearance in the Press. . . . If, before its appearance, you received an actual protest, it might then be wise to withhold the caricature. . . . We shall however be considerably surprised if any effect other than interest, amusement, and increased sales comes from this service."

This suggestion was rejected by the chocolate firm on the somewhat amazing ground that "we feel that this is rather bad form

---

[2] When giving evidence as an English K.C. on English Commercial Law in a New York court.

and are not agreeable to this procedure".

The agents persisted in trying to get themselves covered in advance. They said that caricatures which they had drawn, and which had already been published in this series of advertisements, included ex-King Constantine of Greece, Michael Arlen, Gerald du Maurier, Mr Asquith, Woodrow Wilson and Sir Alfred Mond—a truly impressive stable of celebrities. They continued:

"Up to date no action, legal or otherwise, or any other than complimentary comment have been forthcoming. This does not, of course, mean that no action for annoyance or nuisance might not [sic] lie."

Among the subjects scheduled for caricature in the series with Tolley and the Caddy were Fender [P. G. H.] with the Fireman, Joynson-Hicks and a Taximan, Austen [Chamberlain] and the Bolshevik, and the Countess and the Chorus Girl. Cartoons of Philip Snowden and Jimmy Maxton, the Socialist celebrities, had been rejected (because they were "not sufficiently well known").

But Rayner revealed that, at a later stage, counsel advising J. S. Fry & Sons had actually turned down eight caricatures which included Inman, the billiards player, Austen Chamberlain, Admiral of the Fleet Earl Beatty and even the Countess and the Chorus Girl. In what seems justifiable alarm the agents wrote to their clients, "We must receive from you a definite guarantee that we shall not be liable to any action by reproducing Suzanne [Lenglen] and Tolley."

It could not be said that the defendants had been unaware that some kind of legal trouble might result from their campaign. But, Rayner put as the final point in his opening, Tolley had been rejected by Fry's when he had offered to halt his action if the firm would announce with equal publicity that they had used his name and likeness without his knowledge or approval and without payment.

Rayner called Cyril Tolley to elicit the simple facts: no financial gain, no consultation, no apology. In cross-examination, Norman Birkett asked the golfer:

"You don't complain of the drawing, do you?"

"It is not a particularly good swing," said Tolley, "and I don't think it's a very good limerick. The presence of a packet of chocolate in my pocket insinuates that I chew chocolate when I play golf!"

"That is hardly libellous," countered Birkett.

Rayner then called an eminent amateur golfer, who said that if he lent himself to a scheme for advertising a great many people would think he was not maintaining his amateur status and it would damage his reputation as an amateur golfer. A secretary to two well-known golf clubs also said, "If an amateur lent himself as a golfer to the advertisement of people's goods, I think he would be called on to resign the membership of any reputable club."

Norman Birkett then submitted that the plaintiff had not made out a case that the advertisement was capable of a defamatory meaning. Mr Justice Acton ruled against him. Birkett called no witnesses—possibly a mistake, since the judgments in the House of Lords later observed that no evidence had been brought to contradict the club secretary's statement that an amateur golfer associated with advertising other people's goods would be asked to resign from his club. Birkett had, however, elicited from Tolley that he had won the British Amateur Gold Championship (for the second time) *after* the appearance of the Fry's advertisement.

The King's Bench jury found for the plaintiff and awarded him £1 000 damages. Upon an appeal the Court of Appeal held that the judge ought to have withdrawn the case from the jury, the damages were excessive, and they entered judgment for the defendants. Rayner Goddard took the case to the House of Lords, appealing on the first point only—the question of whether the advertisement was capable of a defamatory meaning. His client accepted that £1 000 was too much: he was only concerned to vindicate his reputation.

It was Rayner's argument that established the modern law. "The substantial question," he said, "is whether the trial judge was right in holding that the publication complained of was capable of holding a defamatory meaning. The majority of the Court of Appeal held that, in the absence of evidence of special facts known to those to whom the advertisement was published causing them to attach to it the meaning alleged in the innuendo—namely, that the plaintiff had consented to being represented as assisting to advertise Fry's chocolate—the publication was incapable of bearing any defamatory meaning. "The fact", he emphasized, "that the caricature was published by a firm of such eminence as the respondents has an important bearing on this question, because no one would suppose that any respectable firm would have made use of the plaintiff's name to advertise their goods without his permission. The question is not whether the publication is susceptible of an innocent interpretation, but whether no libellous interpretation can reasonably be put on it."

Norman Birkett contended that the document complained of was admittedly not libellous, and it was not capable of a defamatory meaning in the absence of evidence of extrinsic facts known to persons to whom the document was published, causing those persons to attach to it the meaning alleged in the innuendo. He claimed that the appellant was asking the King's Bench jury to infer that words innocent in themselves bore some sinister meaning without giving any evidence of extrinsic facts from which that inference could reasonably be drawn.

But what were those "extrinsic facts"? Rayner had called no evidence to show that anyone seeing the advertisement, and knowing of Cyril Tolley, would assume he must have been paid for his co-operation, and thus have betrayed his amateur status. According to Rayner, he did not need to do so: that was self-evident.

Birkett did not agree. He dealt in somewhat tiresome detail with the evidence of the distinguished golfers and the correspondence with the advertising agency. But Goddard short-cut the meandering argument back on to its original course, and at the same time justified himself for not having called "evidence of extrinsic facts" specifically to prove that the public, seeing a picture of a sportsman sponsoring a product, could reasonably infer that he had been paid for the plug. He spoke bluntly and briefly. "The important point in this appeal is: How far a judge is entitled to rely on his own knowledge. A judge must have regard to ordinary matters of common knowledge."

That was typical of the healthy reality of Rayner's approach to judicial attitudes. He never assumed or supported an ivory-tower ignorance of common life on the part of the Bench. His no-nonsense approach as a K.C. was echoed much later when he himself was a Lord Justice of Appeal. In the nineteen-thirties and forties the magazine *Lilliput,* under its Editor, Stefan Lorant, ran a highly popular series of full-page contrasting pictures. One of these pairs of pictures had on one side a portrait of a famous man-milliner to the Queen tending a hat with flowers on it while there was a flower-study of a pansy upon the other. A libel suit followed, and a subsequent appeal was heard in 1943 in the Court of Appeal by Lords Justices Scott, MacKinnon and Goddard. Referring to the *double entendre* of the word pansy, Scott said, "I personally was not alive to the slang meaning of the word, nor, I think, was my brother MacKinnon, but my brother Goddard fortunately was quite alive to it, having had judicial experience as a result of which he had come to know about it." Doubtless Rayner smiled to himself at the cautious justification of "judicial experience" in the last phrase.

After the Lords hearing of *Tolley* v. *Fry* it was held (by Viscount

Hailsham, Viscount Dunedin, Lord Buckmaster and Lord Tomlin, Lord Blaneburgh dissenting) that in all the circumstances in which the publication took place, as explained by the evidence, the caricature *was* capable of bearing the meaning alleged in the innuendo: Cyril Tolley had been defamed, and there would have to be a new trial limited to the assessment of damages.

Lord Hailsham defined the precise point of importance in the case: "The case is unusual in that the defamatory innuendo does not depend on the words used of the plaintiff but solely upon the circumstances in which the publication takes place. The question here does not depend upon a state of facts known only to some special class of the community, but upon the inference which would be drawn by the ordinary man or woman from the facts of the publication. It is always difficult to determine with precision the amount of judicial knowledge which is permissible to a judge or jury; but I am not satisfied that it would not be open to a jury, acting on their knowledge as ordinary citizens, to assume that no reputable firm would have the effrontery and bad taste to take the name and reputation of a well-known man for an advertisement commending their goods without first obtaining his consent, and without later apologizing or contradicting the imputation."

As the early Thirties dawned, with his own key to the Benchers' private quarters of Inner Temple Hall in his pocket, and his solitary excursion into politics well behind him, Rayner could now have only one remaining ambition to accomplish. Mollie Goddard, full of pride in her husband, had often told their daughters, "Your father will be Lord Chief Justice one of these days!" But he himself had no such pretensions: as the Lord Parker of Waddington, his eventual successor as Lord Chief, has told me, "Rayner would never have thought of the possibility of his being Lord Chief Justice in those days. The position was then purely a political appointment, and it would never have entered into his reckoning."

According to Lord Parker, "Rayner did not aspire to anything more than a county court judgeship". But Sidney Newland does not agree, "As the nineteen-thirties began, he did say to me more than once that he would like to be a judge; but I cannot help thinking that if he only got a county court judgeship I would have been astounded, and I would have hoped he would have refused."

In fact, quite clearly the Legal Establishment had other ideas for Rayner. In the summer of 1931 Mr Justice MacKinnon fell ill, and it was necessary to appoint a Commissioner of Assize to go out on Circuit in his place. That was the traditional method of 'trying out' potential High Court Judge material from the ranks of the senior silks available—and Rayner was selected. For the first time he sat, albeit only temporarily and with the status of a deputy, as a High Court Judge at the Leeds Assizes for July 1931.

Eight months later Prue Goddard, Rayner's 'baby' daughter, received an excited telephone call at the solicitor's office where she was then working as a secretary. It was her father on the line. "I thought I'd like to let you know that I've been sent for by the Chancellor," he said. "I knew what that meant," she comments today. There could be only one reason why Lord Sankey, Lord Chancellor in Ramsay MacDonald's National Coalition Government, was sending for her father: the High Court was about to have a new adornment.

"It was a tremendous day! I told my sisters and his mother. The old lady nearly burst with pride. Poor Father then realized the need for secrecy. He rang her himself and said please don't tell anyone. She said she'd only told one man—the plumber: 'But he's a most reliable man!' So the only people who knew about my father's impending appointment to the High Court Bench were my sisters, myself, my grandmother—and the plumber!"

After Rayner had rung off his mother penned him a letter that he always thereafter kept among his most personal papers: "My dear Rayner," she wrote. "I never can say on the telephone all that I want to say, or even the half of it. But it is just this, that I do feel very proud and thrilled that this honour has come to you, for you have worked hard for it and also your father and dear Mollie would have been so gratified. There is no going back from this, for your father often spoke of it to me and said he had never had one moment's anxiety about you, and he felt sure you would go straight ahead, right on to the end: so it has all come true. From your affectionate Mother, Janet G. Goddard."

But there were those in the profession outside the immediate family circle who knew of the forthcoming appointment before the official announcement appeared in *The Times* on 31 March 1932. Arthur Smith, who had been the 14-year-old junior clerk starting life in the Temple in Rayner's first set of chambers at Mitre Court Buildings back in 1903, was now a judge's clerk, assigned to Lord Finlay, a judge of the King's Bench Division, the division of the High Court which Rayner was now shortly to join. One day Lord Finlay came into his private room and told Mr Smith, "I've got some important news to give you, Smith, but it is highly confidential and I don't want you to tell anybody." Mr Smith swore himself to secrecy, and the judge said, "I've reason to believe that Mr Rayner Goddard is soon to be promoted to the Bench, and when that happens he has asked me to release you so that you can join him." Lord Finlay gave his blessing, and soon arrived a cryptic postcard for Arthur Smith: "Meet me at Mitre Court Buildings at 10 o'clock on Saturday, R.G.". Rayner could not take his beloved Sidney Newland with him on to the Bench, Mr Newland was still only twenty-nine and with a lifetime ahead of him in the Temple; but at least he could have beside him that other young clerk he had befriended some thirty years earlier.

Once the news was made public the letters of congratulations came pouring in. "My dear Judge," wrote Lord Hewart, the Lord Chief Justice, from his home at Totteridge in South Herts, "Warmest congratulations on your appointment, at which I rejoice. May you have long life, health and happiness. But alas! I shall have no more of your persuasive arguments from the Bar." "I should like to send you a line of congratulation on your appointment," wrote Lord Hailsham, a past Lord Chancellor and the present Lord Hailsham's father.

Even the icy Sir John Simon unthawed his fingers to write from the Foreign Office, where he was then Foreign Secretary, "My dear Goddard, Salutations to the new Judge—'and a good Judge too'. You have been marked out for this for some time and if the appointment gives as much pleasure to you as it does to your friends—Inner Temple, Western Circuit, old Uncle Tom Cobley and all—you should be pleased. Good luck."

On 6 April 1932, at the start of the new Legal Term after the Easter Vacation, Mr Justice Goddard, resplendent in his new robes of office, was sworn in before Lord Hewart, in the Lord Chief Justice's spacious, high-vaulted courtroom. An unusually large number of judges were present: not only Mr Justice Avory and Mr Justice Hawke sitting on either side of Lord Hewart for the ordinary business of the court, but six other King's Bench Division judges stood behind their seated brethren to welcome the newcomer (shortly to receive the customary knighthood) to their midst.

The courtroom was filled with barristers and public spectators, and—typically—the new judge's family contingent was so numerous that they had to be divided. Rayner's aged mother and his brother Ernest sat in the well of the court, while his three daughters were placed at the back.

In a clear, strong voice, Rayner, standing beside the Lord Chief

Justice, took the oath of allegiance to the King and the judicial oath binding him to carry out justice and do right "to all manner of men, without favour or affection, fear or ill-will".

As a barrister, he had been sound, competent and able. As a judge, he was to prove of surpassing quality. Now at last, at the age of fifty-seven, no longer a young man, with his wife dead and the shade of his loving father looking down upon him, he had come into his own.

7 The New Judge

Mr Justice Goddard went straight from his swearing-in ceremony to hear his first case. As the new boy, he was assigned to possibly the least impressive courtroom in that vast stone rabbit-warren, the Royal Courts of Justice: Court "B", not even in the main building itself, but virtually a shed, a prefabricated construction erected 'temporarily' in 1915 during the First World War and, alas, at the time of writing, over sixty years later, still in use. The law has always come low in the priorities of spending public money.

A young barrister named David Scott Cairns (now Lord Justice Cairns) had a junior brief in that first case. "It was an action for damages for fraud on the sale of a car," he says. "It was tried by jury, and the jury disagreed. A few months later I met at a friend's house a man who introduced himself to me as a member of that jury. He said, 'It was that stupid woman in the corner seat who would not agree to a verdict in your favour.' About twenty years after, I was sitting next to Rayner at dinner and said, 'Do you remember the first case you heard as a King's Bench Judge? 'Yes,' he said. 'It was a jury case—fraudulent sale of a car—the jury disagreed—the only member of the jury who really understood my summing up was a woman sitting in one corner of the jury box.' "

The new judge's second week was spent as Judge in Chambers, always a testing ordeal for the capacities of a new man. He does not sit robed in open court with generally only one case or, at the most, two to occupy his mind during a working day. He sits unrobed in a small room off the Bear Garden, a large hall in the middle of the Law Courts that owes its name to the babel of noise from the milling hordes of waiting barristers, solicitors and their clerks, and hears, in private, upward of fifteen to twenty summons a day. Nothing is straightforward: it is not just one long case, as with Lord Justice Cairns's action for damages; the new judge has to switch his mind from one branch of the law and then back again to another, within a matter of minutes. Often with a host of tricky little procedural points confusing the issue as well.

Many a new judge dislikes intensely, possibly even fears, his first stint in Chambers. It will soon reveal to his freshly left colleagues at the Bar any chinks in his knowledge of the law. Not so with Rayner: he relished his first tour of duty in that little room off the Bear Garden—and early showed exactly what sort of judge he was going to be.

It was the custom in those days for an attendant to call out the name of each case three times, so that if a barrister or his clerk missed the first call they could always get in later in the day. On Rayner's first morning he sat at 10.30 sharp, and by 11 o'clock he had dealt with all those who had answered the first call, and was sitting in his room with nothing to do. The remaining applicants trickled in throughout the morning, but even so his list was finished before the luncheon adjournment.

"We can't have this hanging about doing nothing and wasting time," Rayner said to Arthur Smith, as his clerk accompanied him back to his private room along the judges' corridor. "Tomorrow, if the parties are not ready to come on when they are called, I shall strike them out."

Such a course was unprecedented: no previous judge had taken such a strong aversion to doing nothing. His clerk, who had, after all, many years' experience himself as a barrister's clerk, tried to point out to Rayner that it had always been the custom for the barrister's and solicitor's clerks to arrange between themselves the order in which they should come on.

"I've no objection to that," said Rayner, "but I've got the strongest possible objection to sitting idle twiddling my thumbs!"

Next morning Mr Smith took care to pass the word round among the assembled clerks in the Bear Garden that they must get their barrister in front of his Lordship's door in time to go in when called, otherwise they would be struck out. Even so, within half an hour of sitting Rayner was waiting for someone to turn up. The cases were called but no answer was forthcoming—so he carried out his threat and struck them all out on the spot. That meant another summons would have to be taken out, another fee paid, and unnecessary delay incurred—all of which would have to be explained to the client.

Mr Smith comments, "The outcome was that during the remainder of the time we were in Chambers summonses were heard more quickly than ever before, a foreshadow of things to come."

As is usual again with new judges, Rayner spent much of his first years on the Bench on Circuit. Some recruits to the judiciary find it irksome to be so withdrawn from the pleasures of their club or the comforts of their home or their delights in the capital; Rayner was not in that category. For him going on Circuit—even if not to his beloved Western Circuit—was, in a very real sense, going home: it was going back to the cradle of his earliest, perhaps happiest, years at the Bar.

Judges, both then and now, did not have completely free choice in the selection of their itineraries. The practice then was for the Lord Chief Justice three times a year, at the beginning of the Michaelmas, Hilary and Easter Terms, to hold a meeting of his King's Bench judges at which, among other things, it was decided which judges would go on Circuit and where, and which would stay in London. In those days, by tradition the most senior judge was allowed to choose his own Circuit, the next senior chose from those remaining and so on down the hierarchy. Today a rota system has been adopted, which is really much fairer to everyone.

Rayner's first outing on Circuit was to the South-Eastern, or "Home", Circuit as it used to be called. Usually no new judge would be selected for it: it was far too much in demand, because of its nearness to London, by the more senior, and more elderly, judges. But in the summer of 1932 the South-Eastern became available at the last moment, and so the new boy was sent out, as a last-minute replacement, to bear the King's justice to the citizens of the Home Counties and neighbouring shires.

Rayner began at Huntingdon, then went on to Hertford, Cambridge, Bury St Edmunds, Norwich, Chelmsford, Kingston, Maidstone and finally to Lewes. Writing in 1959, Arthur Smith was to comment, "Looking back on the events of that Assize and upon the pronouncements which he made, after more than a quarter of a century has elapsed, I am struck forcibly by the extraordinary consistency of the Chief's attitude towards current problems. The directions he gave the East Anglian juries that summer do not vary in emphasis or tone from the summings-up he delivered in his last session at the Old Bailey." "I would say he did not change at all in his attitudes in all his years on the Bench," says Sir Joseph Molony,

Q.C. "He had a strong sense of realities, of what is right and what is wrong. He consistently voiced the commonly held public view that when society has been affronted by some appalling crime, society is entitled to have the crime expiated."

In that first Assize he early showed his forceful command of the English language when imposing sentence. At Hertford he tried the case of five young men who had conspired to steal the Dowager Lady Portman's jewels. One of them had somehow got a job as her chauffeur: the rest had hired a car and lain in ambush. As Lady Portman and her maid were being driven along a lonely stretch of road in Hertfordshire on their way to a country-house week-end their car was stopped, two young men wrenched open the door, seized the jewel-case from under the seat and made off. The chauffeur did nothing to stop them. He did not even try to give chase. Only the maid ran after the thieves, decamping in their hired car, shouting at them furiously—and forlornly—in French to come back.

Rayner was outraged by the story. "This is a plain case of highway robbery," he said. "The law has always taken a very serious view of this crime and it will not tolerate the activities of young highwaymen like yourselves. . . . Besides being of considerable pecuniary value, some of the jewels you stole were, no doubt, of great sentimental value to Lady Portman." He sentenced them to terms of penal servitude ranging from five to three years.

Mark those sentences: for the offence committed, they were by no means excessive—certainly not in the early nineteen-thirties, when stern judges of the old school were handing down, in the days of the Depression and several million hungry unemployed, swingeing sentences for even comparatively minor crimes of theft as a deterrent against violations of the sacred right to property. In later life Rayner Goddard was to be branded a sadist, a paranoiac, a megalomaniac; he was even likened to Judge Jeffreys. But his handling of those five young villains in that 1932 Summer Assize at Hertford was exactly typical of his *real* way of dispensing justice, not that falsely attributed to him: harsh words that lash almost physically the men standing in the dock before him, followed by a surprisingly soft or lenient sentence such as will not grind the culprits down beyond redemption and imperil the possibilities for reform.

"I think this strong language was very often used by him", says Lord Dilhorne, ex-Attorney-General and Law Lord, "to help him pass a lesser sentence than would otherwise have been regarded as right." "He was not a cruel man as so many would appear to believe," says his ex-pupil, the late Lord Tucker. "I don't believe he ever gave a gaol sentence of as much as fifteen years in all his years on the Bench. In principle, he did not favour long sentences: if there was any chance of recovery in the man, he thought it would defeat its object."

And so Mr Justice Goddard and his retinue of clerk, specially hired cook, butler and marshal's man progressed around the English countryside hearing the usual charges of rape, buggery, murder, theft, incest and various other variations on the theme of man's inhumanity to man.

But it was not all grim or serious. An elderly Kent solicitor remembers one of his cases due to be heard at Maidstone Assizes that summer: "The plaintiff and I, with counsel and witnesses, waited all day on Thursday for the case to be called, but it wasn't, and we spent all Friday morning waiting in vain as well. During the lunch interval I suggested to our client and to his counsel that if this case went on much longer the expenses would more than equal any successful claim for damages and the matter ought to be settled.

"The two counsel got together and, after lunch, between witnesses in the case mentioned, they rose and told his Lordship that the case had been settled. His Lordship peered at counsel and said, 'Do I understand that I am being deprived of the pleasure of sitting here tomorrow (Saturday) morning?' We all promptly disappeared!"

Back in London, Mr Justice Goddard—again as the new boy— was assigned to sit as the "Vacation Judge", while his more senior colleagues doffed scarlet and ermine for two pleasant months of summer vacation. Comments Arthur Smith, "He dealt with the matters which came before him with the speed which was to become legendary in later years, and lists which had been expected to occupy three full days' hearing were disposed of on the first morning before the luncheon adjournment."

Lord Hodson, now a retired Law Lord, remembers that as a young man he appeared before Goddard at about that time. "He was Vacation Judge, and the earlier Vacation Judge had adjourned the case so that my client could be represented. Rayner began by telling my opponent that he had read the papers and what order did he want? At once I jumped up and told him that I was on the other side. He soon calmed down then and let me present my client's case. He was minded to be hasty, even at that early stage in his judicial career; you cannot deny that. But if you stood up to him, he could be persuaded to the contrary view—isn't that what every barrister should be, capable of standing up for himself?"

Rayner quickly found his natural level in civil cases. It was in this sphere that his successor as Lord Chief Justice, the late Lord Parker of Waddington, remembered him best. "My clearest recollection of him as a Judge of the First Instance was when he sat in control of the Commercial Court before which I appeared on many occasions. He was, I think, the ideal Commercial judge, in the sense that he had a nose for delaying tactics, and would insist on early trials. I remember one case in which the Midland Bank were suing the defendant on Bills of Exchange. When we came before the Court for directions he sensed at once that there was no real defence. He said, 'This is a case which ought to be tried at once and I am fixing today fortnight'. When the date of trial arrived the defendant acknowledged by his counsel that there was no defence and submitted to judgment."

It was to take over a full year from the date of his appointment before at last Rayner could take the train at Waterloo Station bound for his mother Circuit, the Western. But it was Circuit life as a style for living that was close to his heart, not just his own Circuit, however dear to him. Others who have not shared its joys may regard a Circuit existence—or, at least, the Circuit existence which flourished in the days before the Beeching Report of the late Sixties and the bland, anonymous Crown Courts structure of today—as a way of life for overgrown children, never out of the 'pillow fights in the dorm' stage of their public school. So be it. They may well be right. But that was not Rayner Goddard's view.

Sir Fred Pritchard, formerly a distinguished member of the Northern Circuit and later a High Court Judge, writes:

"After his appointment to the King's Bench Division in 1932, Mr Justice Goddard was a frequent visitor as Assize Judge to the Northern Circuit. This may have been due to the fact that more recently appointed Judges had the last choice of Circuits and the Northern Circuit, being further from London and lasting more than two months, presented the longest and therefore the least popular of the Assizes which were chosen by the Judges in order of their seniority; but the members of the Northern Circuit liked to think, as time went on and he gained more seniority, that Mr Justice Goddard was wont to come the Northern Circuit because he liked it as they liked him.

"In court and out of court, he was second to none in the popularity and affection in which he was held. He was a frequent and popular guest in the Circuit Bar Mess and after dinner it was his wont to say, 'Now Boys! What about a boat race?' Whereupon, seventeen members of the Circuit would arrange themselves sitting with him on the floor in the formation of two eights, each with a cox, in which positions to the great detriment of the seats of sixteen pairs of trousers (including the judicial trousers whose wearer always occupied the position of Stroke of one of the 'boats'), the competing eights shuffled backwards across the floor until one of them crossed as victors the imaginary finishing line.

"In 1946, after his appointment as Lord Chief Justice, I wrote him a letter of congratulation in the course of which I said that I hoped he would find it possible to celebrate his return to the King's Bench Division by making an early visit to the Northern Circuit. At this point I stopped, wondering whether I ought to add, 'and we hope you will once again stroke the boat.' I decided that perhaps I ought to omit this pious hope, having regard to the fact that I was addressing not a mere puisne judge but the Lord Chief Justice himself.

"I could not have been more wrong. The reply came, direct, kindly and to the point—'Thank you for your letter. I am glad to be back in the K.B.D. There wasn't enough work for me in the Lords. I shall certainly come to the Northern Circuit when I get a chance. Do you think I shall be allowed to stroke the boat?' "

In many respects, Rayner was a reformer, but in many others he was a reactionary of such committed views it would be idle to seek to defend them today. One such hobby-horse of his was the to him totally unjustified and even disgraceful way in which public money was spent—wasted, he would no doubt say—on paying for the representation of a person without financial means *who was pleading guilty*. In 1930, two years before his appointment, the Poor Prisoners' Defence Act, an early precursor of modern criminal legal aid, had revolutionized the law and allowed legal representation, paid for out of local funds to "poor prisoners" who were pleading guilty and merely needed someone to make a speech in mitigation on their behalf. The modern view is that, even with a plea of guilty, the skilled presentation of facts to the court is necessary to ensure that all that can be said on the defendant's behalf *is* said; but that was not Rayner's view. He did not begrudge spending public money when the man was pleading not guilty and making a fight of it—that was his right. But a barrister to speak for him, when he was pleading guilty? That was rubbish!

And so in his first Winter Assize, on the North-Eastern Circuit at Leeds shortly before Christmas 1932, Rayner took the chance to fulminate against the Poor Prisoners' Act and criticize the "prodigal use" to which he considered it was being put. "A prisoner's best friend is very often his judge," he said.

Nearly thirty years later, when addressing a meeting of magistrates as Lord Chief Justice, he was still playing the same tune: "You know, Poor Prisoners' Defence certificates now are handed out in the most extravagant way. . . . What is the object of that? The result of it is that someone gets one guinea or two guineas for it and the public have got to pay. All that counsel can say at the trial is, 'My client pleads guilty. My client is a married man with two children and a third on the way.' There is always a third on the way! There is very often nothing else to say.

"If there is any mitigation it comes so much better from the prisoner himself. You may say that the man is shy. Well, my experience is that if you are patient and speak sympathetically and very quietly to the prisoner you will very often get him to talk, and if he has got anything, and very often there *are* points in mitigation, it comes so much better from him and sounds so much more genuine, I think, than if some young counsel gets up and says something for him about matters relevant to his family."

And Rayner went on to tell the magistrates about a case of his at Worcester Assizes, "when there were three boys before me for garage-breaking. There was one boy whom you would have thought was quite the worst. They were not defended, but after a time I got these boys to talk and found that, in the case of the boy who appeared to be the ringleader, it turned out that there was a great deal to be said for him. He was, apparently, a boy born in New Zealand who had lost his parents. It was a very pathetic story which I got out of him gradually. I got the probation officer to check up on it and I found out that the story was all perfectly true, and it enabled me to take a course with him that I should not have been able to take if counsel had got up and said a few words about the boy's family"—i.e. he put him on probation instead of sending him to Borstal or prison.

It could be said that what Rayner Goddard left out of account was that, if his idea of the judge being the poor prisoner's best friend were to be valid, every criminal judge would have to be as humane and understanding as Rayner himself—and that, unfortunately, was not then and is still not the case.

At the same early Leeds Winter Assize Rayner showed already that he could intersperse firmness with humour. One of the most successful junior barristers on the North-Eastern Circuit at that time was a young man, now himself a member of the Court of Appeal.

On the first day of the Leeds Assize this junior met Rayner's marshal by chance in the barristers' robing-room. "You've got a tough judge, haven't you?" grumbled the young barrister. "I've appeared before him five times round the Circuit and have been given thirty-five years all told. Average, seven years per appearance!" The marshal grinned, and later reported the conversation to Rayner.

Next day a prisoner was brought into court on a charge of rape. It is a strict rule of practice in such cases that, if there is no corroboration of the complainant's evidence, the judge must warn the jury in the strongest terms of the danger of convicting: generally speaking, it is considered unsafe to convict a man of rape on the woman's evidence alone. So when this accused asked for legal aid and the Clerk of Assize turned to the judge to tell him the names of counsel in court who were available to take Poor Prisoners' Defences Rayner interrupted him before he had said a word.

He called on the young barrister from the robing-room incident of the morning before, who was sitting in court. "Yes, my Lord?" said the youngster, rising to his feet. "Will you take this case?" said Rayner. "Certainly, my Lord," said the young man—and, as he approached the Clerk of Assize's desk to collect the papers, Rayner said in a loud stage whisper audible to everyone in the courtroom, "This should bring your average down. There's no corroboration."

"As a judge, he was supremely in command from the beginning", says Sir Joseph Molony, Q.C. "He was a very good lawyer, of course—that is why he was a good commercial lawyer. If a man is a good lawyer he can take any specialist line offered to him—that is why it did not matter that Rayner had not done very much criminal work at the Bar for many years. He was a man on top of his job from the start."

In general terms, that may well have been so. But when Rayner did at last for the first time visit the Western Circuit as a judge, in the early summer of 1933, in one case at Bristol his touch was not so sure as it might have been.

Relates Mrs Irving Gradwell, that pioneering local woman solicitor, "An unemployed leader, W. Fairman, had been charged with sedition for a speech he had made at an open-air meeting. He decided to defend himself. Two police witnesses gave evidence that Fairman had said that unemployed men should join the Army and then 'take Lenin's advice, turn their guns the other way and shoot down their officers' rather than be used to suppress unemployed workers' demonstrations.

"Fairman cross-examined these two policemen and asked them to submit to a memory test, reading a passage of equal length to his alleged statement from a book by a Marxist philosopher.

"The first witness broke down after several attempts, and then complained that the atmosphere was very different and he felt self-conscious with everyone looking at him. Fairman suggested that he should turn his back on the court and try again. He made an equally poor hand at it, nor did prosecuting counsel handle the situation competently in re-examination.

"When the second police witness was called and exactly the same process began, Goddard got restive—and was clearly longing to conduct the examination in his own brilliant fashion. He remarked testily, for example, 'Come, come! I can remember it. Surely, you can. It begins . . .' From the Bench he seemed quite unaware of the effect his intervention was having on the jury.

"Finally, when Fairman addressed the jury, he began to make the speech which he claimed he had made, which did not include the passage about Lenin's advice—without which, of course, the speech was not seditious. Goddard stopped him and explained that it was not relevant to deal with other matters; only with the evidence which constituted the charge. Fairman looked puzzled, scratched his head, and started again. After a sentence or two Goddard again stopped him; explained it all again, kindly but firmly. Fairman exchanged puzzled glances with the jury and tried again, each time beginning his speech with a different opening sentence. Goddard got more and more impatient at the man's 'stupidity': and after he had interrupted seven or eight times he had worked the jury into a state of extreme curiosity as to what the speaker *had* said, rather than what he had denied saying! They found him 'not guilty', to the obvious astonishment of Goddard, who never seemed to realize the contribution he had made to the defence."

But in a murder case—*Rex* v. *Morse*—heard at Wells Assizes later on the same Circuit that summer, his first murder trial of note as a judge, Rayner's touch was more assured. It was a country crime of singular unpleasantness: Frederick Morse, a Somerset farm-labourer, was accused of drowning a twelve-year old girl who was not only his incestuous child, the product of a union between himself and his sister, but was also pregnant by him.

In fact, it was the ever-increasing obviousness of her condition that led to the child's death. On some pretext Morse took her out for a walk into the countryside, plied her with rum—then toppled her into a stream. When the child did not return home his first explanation to the police was that a storm had broken, she had sheltered in a shed while he went down into a field to check his rabbit traps—and, when he returned to find her missing, he assumed she had carried out an earlier threat to kill herself. He claimed that he searched for her everywhere along the swollen stream, wading into the water, almost being swept away, before finally he turned for home.

Next day he went out with the police in an organized search party. Late in the afternoon the child's body was found in the water, the stream swirling past her as she was held by the branches of an overhanging tree.

Tried for murder, Morse was, in his own defence counsel's (J. D. Casswell) words,[1] "an appalling witness. Sullen in manner and uncouth in appearance, he repeated stolidly in examination-in-chief the story he had already given to the Somerset police. There was no truth in any talk . . . of his wanting to do the girl harm; she had simply not been in the shed when he had returned from checking his rabbit traps, and all his efforts to find her had been fruitless. In cross-examination he attempted to stick rigidly to this story—indeed, it was his only possible course—but in the course of an exchange with J. G. Trapnell, K.C. (leading prosecuting counsel), he suddenly came out, 'Oh, yes, I'd found the girl's body in the first afternoon before I went back to the village.' "

In other words, all the time he had been talking to the Somerset police and 'looking' for her with them he had in fact known perfectly well she was dead and the exact spot where she lay!

Rayner interposed with one vital, sharp question. "Why", he asked, "haven't you told anyone this before?"

There was utter silence in court. Casswell later recalled, "Morse did not answer. I looked at him and at the jury. By the expressions on their faces I saw that the case was over."

And so it virtually was. After what Casswell himself called a "forlorn" final speech for the defence, Rayner summed up and the jury brought in their inevitable verdict of guilty.

The muttering of an approaching thunderstorm had been heard during their retirement, and as the foreman stood to pronounce the verdict the courtroom suddenly blazed blue with sheet lightning and a massive thunderclap sounded at close hand. Rayner's youngest daughter, Prue (now Mrs Ruth Clayton), was in the courtroom. She

---

[1] In his memoirs, *A Lance for Liberty,* published in 1961 by Harrap, and written in collaboration with the author.

was then not quite twenty-one years of age. She had sat beside her father on the Bench all through the trial. Rayner waited while Morse was asked if he had anything to say. After a silence he addressed the prisoner:

"I do not think that anyone in this court would for one moment doubt the righteousness of that verdict. That little girl was in your care, and by every law of God and man it was your duty to protect her. Instead you outraged her and then you murdered her. For that offence there is only one sentence to pronounce."

This was one of the first times that Rayner Goddard pronounced sentence of death, but, says Mrs Clayton, "he took it all very much in his stride". It was a part, but no more than a specially exacting part, of his job. "He would never throughout his career go out to dinner while a murder trial was in progress," she says. "He simply felt that he must keep his concentration going."

Morse was hanged: on 25 July 1933, at Taunton Gaol, after an abortive appeal. And there is no reason to believe that Rayner lost ten minutes' sleep over the event.

But in the following year he had a far more harrowing experience, when he was compelled to pass on a woman sentence of death which he knew himself could not possibly be exacted. It was a memory that was to remain with him for over twenty years. It was a mercy killing case, and everyone in the law knew that one of the few things on which you could rely in the sometimes haphazard administration of the reprieve system was that genuine mercy killers, though sentenced to death, were always reprieved.

In the early nineteen-fifties, Rayner, when Lord Chief Justice of England, told the Gower Commission that with such people it was his firm view that "it would have been better if they had not been sentenced to death".

This case was the trial at Leeds Assizes in December 1934 of a 62-year-old mother accused of the murder of her idiot son, aged thirty, by first drugging him with an overdose of aspirins and then asphyxiating him from a tube connected to the gas-supply. Her reason was that she was due to enter hospital for a major operation, and throughout that crisis—or perhaps for ever afterwards in his lifetime—her son would have no one to look after him. Her words to the police who arrested her were: "I did not do it feloniously or maliciously. I mercifully put my boy to sleep."

In his summing up to the jury Rayner remarked that no doubt they would return a recommendation to mercy, but with regard to the verdict their duty was clear: "There are no circumstances which amount to justification for the killing of this woman's son. The time may come when it may be the law of this country that an imbecile or idiot may be put mercifully to death. That is not the law at present, and neither you nor I have any right to make law. We have to take the law as it is found. . . . No person has a right to kill another human being because he thinks it would be better for that human being if he should die. Therefore there is no justification for this unhappy act."

A verdict of guilty was therefore returned, with "the strongest possible recommendation to mercy". Nevertheless, Rayner had to pass sentence of death. It has been mentioned that he had a voice which could excoriate a prisoner in the dock. It is also the fact that he had a mildness of tone (it is not too much to call it an intimacy) which he frequently used—to child witnesses, to simple people genuinely unnerved by the panoply of the law, and very frequently in his exceedingly unstuffy address to a jury. But it was against his nature either to rattle off the death sentence in a meaningless monotone or to pronounce it conversationally as if tea and crumpets had just been ordered. It is a very difficult thing to declare, in an offhand manner, "The sentence of the Court upon you is, that you be taken from this place to a lawful prison and thence to a place of execution and that you be hanged by the neck until you be dead; and that your body be afterwards buried within the precincts of the prison in which you shall have been confined before your execution. And may the Lord have mercy on your soul."

Rayner uttered that sentence as lightly as the words allowed, and promptly supported the jury's recommendation to mercy. Within only two days the recommendation was heeded and the woman reprieved. After a very short spell in prison she was released to return to her husband.

It was a death sentence two years later on a woman that brought Rayner his greatest notoriety during his six years' service as a puisne judge. The trial of "Nurse Waddingham" at Nottingham, where she was found guilty of murder and duly sentenced, ended in a riot outside the Shire Hall, where hundreds of angry women, barred from the court, tussled with the police and screamed abuse at the judge who had pronounced the condemnation.

"Nurse Waddingham" was the professional name of a woman of thirty-five, born Dorothea Waddingham, who picked up a smattering of medical knowledge during service as a ward-maid at Burton-on-Trent Infirmary, married an old man called Leech,

moved to Nottingham and kept her husband and children by running an old folks' home, and after her husband's death started
another old folks' home with her lover Ronald Sullivan, six years
her senior, and with the children he begot on her.

No one who personally remembers Nurse Waddingham—and for
the purposes of a newspaper article some years ago, I have discussed
her with a number of people who did—has given her credit for great
intelligence. It is unlikely that Rayner or anyone else saw her as the
equal of a Borgia. His eldest daughter, Mrs Pamela Maurice, then
recently married, was in court throughout the hearing of the case
and describes the prisoner as "a poor, cringing little creature; she
looked a bit mental, frankly". Nevertheless, Nurse Waddingham
and Ronald Sullivan found themselves on trial for a profitable
murder in February 1936.

They had taken in at their nursing-home—where Sullivan had no
post more specialized than that of porter and handyman—a sick old
lady of eighty-seven, Mrs Louisa Baguley, and her spinster daughter
of fifty, Ada Baguley, who was grossly overweight and a hopeless
cripple. Once the Baguleys were installed, at a total cost of £3 a
week, they felt at home and liked the place: owing to the death of
the last inmate, they were soon the only residents. Once the old
ladies were happy, Waddingham and Sullivan gazumped the weekly
fees for their upkeep, giving the alternative that otherwise they
would have to go to the workhouse. The Baguleys did not want to
leave. They had a reserve of some £1 600 between them. Waddingham and Sullivan said that that fortune was a reasonable pledge
for their future. And four months after they had been installed Ada
signed a properly executed will which left all her property to be
shared equally by Waddingham and Sullivan "in consideration that
they have undertaken to look after me and my mother for and
during our joint lives".

Within five days of the signing of the will on 7 May 1935 Mrs
Louisa Baguley was dead. Dr George Manfield, the nursing-home's
regular doctor, had not been present at the end, but he complacent-
ly signed a death certificate naming cardiac muscular degeneration
as the cause of death.

Ada was taken into tight control by Waddingham and Sullivan,
and all her letters were censored. A friend visited her in the afternoon of 10 September 1935 and found her bright and well. But
within twelve hours she was dead. Again Dr Manfield was not present. "I tried to leave a message but you were out on your rounds,"
Nurse Waddingham told him. She described Ada's last hours: "She

wasn't so well yesterday. She had a heavy midday meal which seemed to upset her. About two o'clock this morning she was breathing very loudly and slowly. She was very flushed, and unconscious. Later the colour changed. I thought she was dying and I telephoned you. She was in a coma for about four hours."

The doctor made an external examination and then wrote on the death certificate "Cerebral haemorrhage due to cardial vascular degeneration." His diagnosis of a fatal stroke was consistent with Ada's previous history and her obesity, his examination of the body, and Nurse Waddingham's description of the patient's last hours.

"There is one thing," said Nurse Waddingham. "She wanted to be cremated. Would you sign the form?"

"She never told me that she wanted to be cremated," said Dr Manfield.

"No? But she left a letter for you. Here it is."

Nurse Waddingham produced a letter, dated a fortnight previously, addressed to the doctor and signed by Ada Baguley. The letter ran:

"I desire to be cremated at my death for health's sake and it is my wish to remain with the nurse, and my last wish is my relatives shall not know of my death." The signature was witnessed by R. J. Sullivan.

"Would you sign the proper form for the cremation?" said Nurse Waddingham when the doctor had read the letter.

"You need two doctors to sign a cremation form," said Dr Manfield.

"Oh. Perhaps you would get another doctor to sign it as well."

"All right."

Sullivan collected the dually signed cremation form and took it to Nottingham Crematorium. But the medical referee there did not immediately accept it. He noticed, apart from the strange wording of the letter, that it was all, save the signature, in the same handwriting as that of the witness, R. J. Sullivan. The doctor passed on his doubt to the Nottingham coroner, who ordered an immediate post-mortem. Over five grains of morphia were found in the body, and the post-mortem finding was "Death by morphia poisoning." An inquest was ordered. Nurse Waddingham did not attend, because she was in the last month of her pregnancy with her fifth child—Sullivan's. The inquest was adjourned, but an order was granted to exhume Mrs Baguley. Morphia was found in her body too. Nurse Waddingham was visited by a detective inspector, and police searched the house. They found no morphia. "I know there is no morphia in Mrs Baguley," declared Nurse Waddingham. "I reckon this is a put-up job."

She attended the resumed inquest on Ada Baguley. After four days she went impetuously into the witness box, although the coroner told her that she need not give evidence. She faced interrogation for four hours, and then virtually skipped to put her head in the noose.

The coroner asked her how she thought the morphia got into Ada Baguley's body.

"I gave it to her," she said blithely. "I gave it to her in five separate doses of two tablets each." The coroner asked why she had done it, and where the drug had come from. "Dr Manfield told me to do it. He left me six tablets when he called in August and four more in early September. He told me to give them to her when her pain was bad. I gave her the last two at eight o'clock on the night before she died." Why had she said nothing to the police or the court about Ada's morphia tablets? "Because Dr Manfield told me not to."

The ruinously destructive stupidity of these statements was appalling. She had had a legal representative in the coroner's court, and during his cross-examination of Dr Manfield counsel had made no mention of these tablets, or any prohibition on disclosing their existence, clearly because he knew nothing about them and had no idea that Nurse Waddingham intended to mention them—if, indeed, she did have such an intention when she first went into the box. Nurse Waddingham need have said nothing, and then no one could ever have proved that she either had or had not administered the morphia. She had already told the police, "I have never given Miss Baguley any morphia." And Dr Manfield had already sworn in evidence that he had never prescribed morphia for Ada.

Nurse Waddingham stepped down from the witness-box and Sullivan was called. But when the coroner, alert to the law on self-incrimination, advised him too that he need not give evidence he replied, "I don't think it is necessary." And promptly stepped out of the box.

However, the verdict of the coroner's court was that Ada Baguley had been murdered by Ronald Joseph Sullivan and Dorothea Nancy Waddingham. The couple were arrested immediately and brought to trial with astonishing speed, a separate indictment having been prepared against Nurse Waddingham only for the murder of Mrs Louisa Baguley. The trial began eight days later before Mr Justice Goddard.

After most of the prosecution witnesses had given their evidence Rayner asked Dr Frank Jacob, Ada's old doctor and family friend, to come back into the witness-box. "Tell me, doctor," said the judge, "was the deceased at any time when you saw her in such a condition or complaining of any pain such as a doctor would think it right to administer morphia to her?" Dr Jacob answered, "She never complained to me at all of any such pain." Rayner had elicited from an independent medical witness that there would have been no reason for any doctor to have prescribed this dangerous drug.

However, the judge had certain other qualms. When Norman Birkett, K.C., closed the case for the prosecution Rayner at once said, "What evidence do you say there is against the male prisoner? There is no direct evidence against him of possession of morphia. There is no direct evidence against him of administration of morphia." When Birkett attempted to counter this he was adamant. "No, Mr Birkett," he said. "It seems to me that it amounts to no more than that the prisoner Sullivan *may* have been connected with the matter. Not that he *must* have been."

He ordered Sullivan to be released immediately because of this "hiatus in the Crown's evidence". Justice was seen to be done—by a judge as staunch for the defence as for the prosecution.

The trial against Nurse Waddingham went on, and she was predictably found guilty. "I am innocent," she said dully. But when the news of the verdict was conveyed to the crowd of women outside the Shire Hall a more positive response ensued: there was a great outcry against the judge! The Court was aware of the tumult as the formalities of sentencing began.

It was clear that Mr Justice Goddard was affected.

"I see no reason", he told the Royal Commission on Capital Punishment nineteen years later, "why a woman convicted of murder should not hang equally with the men." Yet when he pronounced sentence on Nurse Waddingham he did not look into her face, but sat with bowed head, making the black cap even more stark against his white wig, and he spoke in choking tones, as once, now twenty-seven years ago, he had movingly ended the peroration that saved the life of Mrs Flora Haskell. The jury had recommended mercy, and the judge's tones became more controlled, and very gentle, as he told Nurse Waddingham that this recommendation would be carefully considered. No doubt it was considered by Sir John Simon, then the Home Secretary, along with the fact that the woman's youngest child was four months old. But it was rejected, and Dorothea Waddingham was hanged.

"I see no reason why a woman convicted of murder should not hang . . ." Whatever *reason* told Rayner Goddard, *feeling* said another thing. But Rayner had covered that point too in the finality of his phrase: ". . . *equally* with the men". He was as concerned with sentencing a man to death as at sentencing a woman; but his traditional appreciation of women—*fin de siècle,* stiff, shy; it may be denigrated ad infinitum—made his conduct towards the woman more of an ordeal. His daughter Pamela, who attended the trial with him, was with him before and after the proceedings, and in their intervals, has this to say about the sentencing of Nurse Waddingham:

"The fact that she was a woman affected him very much. In only one sense it made no difference to him that he was pronouncing sentence of death on a woman instead of on a man, because, whatever people may say, I know he hated pronouncing the death sentence anyway. I remember the atmosphere in the house: a kind of pall. Even we kept quiet."

8 High Court Judge to Law Lord

In his personal life, the mid-1930s were years of mixed joy and sadness for Rayner Goddard. His two elder daughters, Pamela and Peggy, had married within months of each other in 1934, and Prue, the youngest, had taken over, with the assistance of the invaluable "Nicky", the efficient running of his household. In May 1935 his first grandchild had been born, and at last there was a boy in the family—Peggy's son, Richard, with whom Rayner was always to be particularly close, perhaps in some way making of the grandson the son he had never had. Life was of special contentment in that decade of the Thirties, the last great period of the middle class in Britain before Hitler's War and its social aftermath destroyed for ever a way of life just as assuredly as Kaiser Wilhelm's War had destroyed the way of life of the upper classes before 1914. To many looking back now on those years, even if they were then only (as I was) children, it seems as if the middle classes of this nation were all waltzing in the ballroom as the *Titanic* steamed ever closer to the iceberg floating silently down to meet them across the chill waters.

In June 1934 Rayner's mother had died in her eighty-first year. She had already been too ill to attend Peggy's wedding some weeks before. The end came peacefully in the house where she had lived in happiness for so long with her husband and where Rayner had lived right up to his marriage. Now the two women with most influence on his earlier life were dead: his wife and his mother. He stood alone as sole guide to his children, and the children they would in time bear. "He was fond of his mother," says Lady Sachs, "and she was very proud and fond of him. But Uncle Ernest—the youngest of her five children—was her pet. He was a weakly child, and the apple of her eye. She was slightly in awe of Rayner."

In February 1937 Prue, Rayner's youngest daughter, donned bridal white and left her father's home. At St Mary's Roman Catholic Church, Cadogan Street, London, she married Archibald Sands Clayton, a young stock broker, and Lord Hewart, the Lord Chief Justice, and his wife attended the reception afterwards in Inner Temple Hall. Rayner was left alone with "Nicky" as his housekeeper and the normal mid-1930s complement of domestic staff to attend to his creature comforts. Some months after the wedding he moved out of the mansion flat in Oakwood Court, Kensington, where Prue had lived with him, and moved into a pleasant, double-fronted house at 46 Chelsea Square. His friend and judicial colleague, Mr Justice (Sir Charles) Hodson, and his wife lived at No. 48, and later Peggy and her barrister husband Eric Sachs (subsequently Sir Eric and a Lord Justice of Appeal) were to come and live almost opposite on the other side of the Square. It was a contented, almost cosseted, life for a widower in his early sixties, surrounded by family and friends and with work that he found thoroughly congenial.

But soon the nature of his work was to change. In early 1938 Parliament passed the Administration of Justice (Miscellaneous Provisions) Act, enlarging the Court of Appeal by a third: from five to eight regular members. Who were those three new Lords Justices to be? Rayner had by then been a High Court judge for six years, and it was common gossip in the Temple that he would probably be one of those 'to go up'. It could not, therefore, have come as much of a surprise to him when, in the Long Vacation of the summer of that year, he received a private, handwritten letter from Lord Maugham, the Lord Chancellor in Neville Chamberlain's Conservative Government, "My dear Goddard, may I suggest your name to the P.M. as a suitable person to be appointed to the Court of Appeal? It would be a great pleasure to me to do so."

The date of that letter was 28 September 1938. It can be doubted whether the Prime Minister was at that time over-concerned about the question of filling a vacancy in the Court of Appeal. He had other, more urgent, problems claiming his attention. For Britain lived then under the imminent threat of war. He had already twice visited Adolf Hitler in desperate, if not grovelling, attempts to stave off the conflict that the whole country was, with mixed trepidation and courage, fearing; and it was on the very afternoon of 28 September, as an ashen Neville Chamberlain was reporting to a

grim House of Commons the failure of his second peace mission to
Hitler at Godesberg, that a note was passed along the Treasury
Bench and handed to Chamberlain, who read it and with hardly a
pause announced to the almost hysterically relieved M.P.s that the
German Chancellor had invited him to a conference at Munich on
the following day, together with Mussolini, the Italian leader, and
Daladier, the French Premier.

On the evening of 30 September, to cheers from the waiting
crowd, Chamberlain returned to London with the promise of
"peace in our time" and the assurance, equally inaccurate, that he
had accomplished "peace with honour". Seven days later, on 6
October, on the same day as the House of Commons by 366 votes to
144, declared confidence in his Government, Chamberlain's private
secretary wrote to Rayner: "The Prime Minister has asked me to say
that it would give me [surely a mistyping for 'him'?] great pleasure
to submit your name to the King for appointment as one of the
three new Lords Justices of Appeal, but before doing so he would be
glad to know that this course would be agreeable to you." That was
only a formality: Rayner had already replied to Lord Maugham's
earlier note indicating that he would be prepared to accept the
honour. And so, on 14 October 1938, Rayner Goddard, resplendent
in buckled knee-breeches and robes of black flowered damask
trimmed with gold, was driven to the House of Lords to be sworn in
as a Lord Justice of Appeal.

He was formally welcomed to the Bench in the Court of Appeal
just in time to take part in the ceremonial calling "within the inner
bar" of his son-in-law, Eric Sachs, Peggy's husband, whose appointment as a K.C. had been announced on the last day of the last Legal
Year at the end of July. Both of them were, at differing stages of their
careers, new boys.

"With the elevation of Mr Justice Goddard to the Court of
Appeal", an article in the *Daily Telegraph* commented, "the King's
Bench Division loses its most robust personality. I know no judge
who faces life with such zest. There will be no beating about the
bush in the Court of Appeal when he is sitting!" "I hope you like
the work", Sir Travers Humphreys, who he was leaving behind as a
King's Bench judge, wrote to him, "though I shall not be surprised
if your quick brain gets a little bored at having to slow down to the
pace of some others. You will need all your patience." That was, as it
proved, a quality in which Rayner was not over-endowed. For six
years he had been his own master, sole authority in his own court.
Now he had to learn new judicial tricks, to be one of a team of

three—for the Appeal Court normally sat in divisions of three; and to concentrate on legal argument in a court where witnesses were seldom, if ever, heard and the decisions were based on questions of law, on the written record of the proceedings in the court below and on the advocacy of counsel. "When sitting as an appeal judge, he would sometimes say to one of his colleagues 'Balls' in a voice I am pretty sure others in court would have heard," recalls Lord Hodson. "I remember him once, years later when I was a Lord Justice and he was sitting with me in the Court of Appeal to help out as Lord Chief Justice, him turning to me and saying, 'I cannot stand any more of this appeal. You give the first judgment!' He never acquired the ability to suffer fools gladly."

Rayner was a Lord Justice of Appeal for six years. It is something of a paradox that he always thereafter claimed himself that they were his happiest years on the Bench. One would have thought that he would have jibbed at the restraints of being one in three—and, in the earlier days, not even the senior one of those three—and of having to perform his judicial tasks in the rarified atmosphere of the Court of Appeal far, with its air of scholastic quiet, from the rough and tumble of Assizes and Circuit. But it was not so. "He told me", said Lord Denning, in his official tribute as Master of the Rolls in open court upon Rayner's death, "that of all the courts in which he sat, he had enjoyed his term in the Court of Appeal most of all. It was the variety of the problems, the range of the work and the high standard of argument that he found so stimulating."

"If—and it is a very big 'if'—I have been able to contribute anything to English law, it would be found in civil cases of little interest to other than lawyers, and in decisions when I sat in the Court of Appeal," Rayner himself once commented to a friend.[1] In particular, he formed a high regard and affection for Lord Greene, the Master of the Rolls (and President of the Court) throughout his six years as a Lord Justice. The two men worked well and harmoniously together, although Greene, a Chancery lawyer with a whimsical wit and a great love of the classics, came from a totally different legal stable from the rumbustious, solidly Common Law background of Rayner: "I have seldom had so much pleasure from a letter as I had from yours," Lord Greene was to write to Rayner when eventually the time came for Rayner to draft his letter of farewell on his promotion to the House of Lords. "To me too our association has

---

[1] Quoted at page 167 of *Lord Goddard, His Career and Cases* by Eric Grimshaw and Glyn Jones (Allan Wingate, 1958).

brought nothing but pleasure and happy memories . . . I have relied on you more than you can have guessed, and I shall miss your help and support more than I can say. All good things must come to an end, and I must put up with it."

Perhaps the secret of Rayner's success in the Court of Appeal lay in the fact that he never became, as others have done both before and since, a shade too much of an academic, removed from everyday life. "Not much Bar gossip these days," wrote Rayner in one of his war-time letters to prisoner of war Lieutenant Clifford Cohen. "Your latest North Eastern Circuit judge, Hallett, is proving rather long-winded. We had an appeal from him the other day when he took 15 pages of type to decide a simple running-down case.

"MacKinnon [a fellow Lord Justice] made some rather snarkey remarks which *The Times* reported without mentioning the name of the Judge, and the joke was that when Hallett read it he said to his Clerk, 'Hello, Croom-Johnson' [another King's Bench judge] 'has been getting it in the neck!'"

The Second World War had finally broken out on 3 September 1939, but the Law Courts had never ceased to function. Arthur Smith was still Rayner's clerk: "Even during the worst of the Blitz", he tells us, "the Court of Appeal never missed a day. A system of electric bells was installed: at the approach of enemy aircraft, they rang and the Court continued its hearing in the cellar, to emerge when the 'All Clear' sounded."

At the height of the bombing Rayner closed up his Chelsea Square home and went to live, as a paying guest, with the Hodsons, who had moved out to a house in the country at Rotherfield Greys in Oxfordshire. For the first time in his life he became a commuter. His bowler-hatted form was regularly seen boarding the Paddington train at Henley each morning, and stayed unseen in the blue gloom of the blacked-out carriages returning at night. He was still, in his mid-sixties, a robust man enjoying phenomenal good health, although, like so many, he was reluctant to admit to himself the passing years: "I remember him once in our garden during the War," says Lord Hodson, "getting down on tiptoe to show my wife how to start a sprint. He ran like a cloud for a few yards and then tore a muscle in his arm."

When the phoney war ended with the British evacuation at Dunkirk, and the invasion of Britain became an odds-on probability, Rayner had been appointed President of the Midland War Zone Court District, in which capacity he would have been virtual Lord Chancellor of that autonomous area in the event of invasion. It never came to that; but the War came tragically home to him when the Hodsons heard that their elder son had been killed in North Africa. He himself had no son to send to fight, but his sons-in-law were in uniform. As he wrote to Clifford Cohen, "respect is and ought to be paid for men like yourself who went at the instant".

He still indulged in the occasional diversion of a Western Circuit dinner. At one memorable reunion, the congratulatory dinner to Lord Caldecote on his appointment as Lord Chief Justice—at the Royal Hotel, Winchester, on 24 February 1942—which he attended with John Simon, then Lord Chancellor, it was pointed out that the Lord Chancellor, the Lord Chief Justice, the Attorney-General and the Solicitor-General were all from the Western Circuit. The official record of the occasion notes that Lord Justice Goddard's contribution to the post-prandial entertainment was, "in response to popular demand", his classic recitation of his much-loved monologue "The Return of Albert".

In 1943, for the first time, Rayner's name became known to the general public on a wider basis than merely being one of His Majesty's judges. He was appointed by Herbert Morrison, the Labour Home Secretary in Winston Churchill's wartime Coalition Government, to conduct a public inquiry into a disturbing, albeit minor, scandal in the administration of criminal justice. The incident had been blown up by party political heat and the understandable opportunism of penal reformers. In the result, Rayner deflated the issue to reasonable proportions—but at the same time enunciated with the clarity of a bell principles of responsible magistracy and open justice.

The matter arose over what Lord Caldecote—not normally given to strong language—called "a complete neglect of the rules of justice and of the administration of the Criminal Law". In January 1943 the police at Hereford had brought charges of breaking and entry, theft and malicious damage against three boys, aged ten, eleven and thirteen, before the local juvenile court. The youngest lad was dismissed from the case on the ground of his age and lack of capacity for criminal responsibility. The other two boys, having admitted the charges, were each sentenced to four strokes of the birch for the malicious damage, which the prosecuting police inspector had suggested to the court when presenting the case, and had been committed into the care of the local authority for the larceny—the charges of breaking and entry having been withdrawn. The boys were immediately taken away from the juvenile court to the police station for the birching. The parents of the boys had been told that they could be present at the execution of this sentence, but this appeared to have been indistinctly heard. However, they did quickly announce that they would appeal against it. But by that time the boys had been birched. Eventually, nine months after the sentence, the parents' appeal to the Divisional Court for an order of certiorari to quash the conviction was heard by the Lord Chief Justice with Mr Justice Charles and Mr Justice Hallett. All the evidence was by affidavit, and on the basis of this evidence the appeal was allowed, the convictions quashed, and Lord Caldecote declared:

"From the start of these proceedings [in the juvenile court] there seems to have been an assumption that these boys were guilty of the offence without the necessity of proving it against them. It is surprising to find an inspector of police apparently so ignorant of criminal law as to ask the magistrates to take into consideration other offences before even they have heard the case on the charge under investigation."

Among other apparent instances of "gross misconduct", it seemed that probation reports as to the boys' homes had been admitted before the finding of guilt, and the order for birching had been carried out without giving the parents the opportunity to be present.

When a Lord Chief Justice mentions "gross misconduct" the Press leader-writers and Parliamentary back-benches have carte blanche to declare a scandal. The public outcry, besides having the congenial targets of police and magistrates, was emotionally heightened by the aspect of the birching sentence on these two young lads. Herbert Morrison, always a wily politician but in this instance using no more than the conventional weapon in his hand, stilled the clamour by appointing a Tribunal of Inquiry. Lord Justice Goddard was entrusted with its conduct as the sole member of the Tribunal, and he took intensive evidence in Hereford from the boys, their parents, the magistrates and the police, with counsel present. He worked with the greatest application for almost a week, and then came home and wrote an 11 000-word report over the weekend. Eventually it was published as a White Paper.

It was a tour-de-force, and done in record-quick time. It was now five years since Rayner had last sat as a trial judge hearing witnesses give evidence before him, but obviously he had lost none of his dominance in court. The excuse given as to why the birching had taken place before the parents had even had a proper chance to decide whether they wanted to appeal was that the Clerk to the juvenile court had himself raised the possibility of an appeal after the lads had peremptorily been taken off to the police station for the sentence to be forthwith carried out. A messenger was dispatched to the station to stop the birching, but by the time he arrived it had already been carried out.

Rayner asked the Clerk of the Court how long it took to get from the juvenile court to the police station. "About ten minutes, sir," he replied. Rayner was suspicious of the answer. He adjourned the inquiry and set out to see for himself. "I walked it myself and found that, walking at an ordinary pace, it took me just under three minutes," he later stated in his report.

His verdict was right down the line—strong, independent, giving no one complete absolution, and apportioning blame where it properly lay. The nub of his findings was that, contrary to the allegations in Press and Parliament (and, it must be said, in the Divisional Court), there had been no scandalous abuse of procedure by either the Hereford magistrates or the local police. The Lord Chief Justice and his two brother judges had been deceived by the method of preparation of the case before them, for which the magistrates were in part to blame, the solicitor acting for the parents in part, and the police not at all: for the police had not been notified, as they ought to have been, that the certiorari application was going forward, and had therefore not even filed an affidavit putting their case. The first they heard of the affair was when they read the Divisional Court judgment in the newspaper. In fact, the boys *had* pleaded guilty to the charges, but an inexperienced Deputy Clerk had entered their pleas wrongly, and when the time came for the Divisional Court hearing the magistrates, more loyal to the immaculacy of their register and to their Deputy Clerk than to the demands of justice, let that entry stand: which entirely deceived the Divisional Court of the King's Bench and, of course, heightened the false accusation against themselves.

It was an amazing story. Rayner reported:

"There was no wrongful conviction. . . . There was a want of care by the magistrates and the clerk in regard to the Court register. . . . I can find no irregularity on the part of the police, but I think it desirable that police officers, when prosecuting, should refrain from suggesting or referring to possible sentences unless invited by the Court to do so. . . . With regard to the proceedings in the Divisional Court, after hearing the evidence I have come to the conclusion that both the affidavit filed on behalf of the applicant and that of the Justices were such as to give the Divisional Court not only an incomplete but a wholly wrong picture of what took place, so far as the most serious of all the matters was concerned—namely whether there was an admission of guilt as to all or only one of the charges. The magistrates have no ground for complaining, in these circumstances, that the Court passed severe strictures upon them."

Rayner conceded that he saw a genuine difficulty in the wording of the relevant Statute which, when a birching was ordered, said that it should be carried out as soon as "practicable"—which conflicted with the defendant's right to appeal within a fortnight. The only sensible way out of the dilemma was "in future, if corporal punishment is awarded by the Court, a direct question should be put to the parents, if present, whether they desire to witness the birching or not".

The "Hereford Birching Inquiry", as it was popularly known, raised for the first time the name of Rayner Goddard in the context of corporal punishment. As he was later controversially to prove when he was Lord Chief Justice, he was a confirmed believer in the efficacy of birching, although his own private views were not involved in this particular matter. Even so, *The Times* took the opportunity editorially to thunder:

"Although the real gravamen of the criticisms made against the Hereford justices related to alleged irregularities in the trial, popular interest concentrated itself largely upon the sentence of birching. The unanimous finding of a strong departmental committee some years ago was adverse to the continuance of this mode of punishment; and its arguments have been repeatedly supported in these columns. Nevertheless Parliament has not yet seen fit to abolish the power of corporal punishment possessed by the Juvenile Courts; and, so long as the power remains, benches which use it, although they may be considered reactionary by the weight of authoritative opinion, have an unchallengeable right to act according to their own beliefs."

It was, of course, the whistle of the birch in the case that had aroused the most passionate reaction, and in the House of Commons penal reformers like Sydney Silverman sought to make the publication of the report as a White Paper an occasion for a full-dress debate. But Geoffrey Mander, a barrister himself, put his finger on the "curious" outcome of the inquiry. He first, as a Parliamentary Under-Secretary, asked the formal lead-in question which enabled the Home Secretary to say:

"I am obliged to my honourable friend for giving me an opportunity to express in this House my appreciation of the public service which Lord Justice Goddard has rendered by investigating this matter so thoroughly and so quickly, and by writing so admirably clear a report. It is a matter for general satisfaction—and not least to the Hereford justices concerned—that the report has completely dissipated the misapprehension that fundamental principles of justice had been ignored by the Hereford Juvenile Court."

But Mr Mander was holding his supplementary at the ready. "Is it not the case", he asked, "that Lord Justice Goddard has, in effect, unofficially reversed the decision of the King's Bench, and is this not a very curious position?"

Herbert Morrison, quick as ever at the side-step, declared, "As far as I know this is not the case, but in any case my honourable friend is drawing me on the threshold of dangerous and explosive matters, and I think I had better not express an opinion."

Lord Caldecote fortunately did not feel so embarrassed as Mr Mander's assessment might have suggested. He had naturally seen Goddard's report before it was published, having been sent a copy by Lord Simon, Lord Chancellor, as soon as Goddard submitted it. Lord Simon reported within a day:

> *House of Lords, S.W.1.*
> *18th November 1943.*

MY DEAR RAYNER,

Thank you for for sending me a copy of your Hereford Report. I have read it with great interest and with real admiration for its completeness and its tone of moderation. If ever we revive in this country the ancient Roman office of Censor Morum, I shall propose your name for the post, confident that you would do it both thoroughly and with human understanding . . .

At the Western Circuit dinner last night in honour of Walter Lloyd (which was a very pleasant function and gave our friend extreme gratification), I had a word with the Chief, to whom I had sent on my copy of your Report, and it seemed to me that he took the whole thing in an excellent spirit. He made two comments on matters of fact and this morning has written a letter, of which I enclose a copy, about them . . .

Let me thank you again for undertaking this none too pleasant piece of work. I shall wait till the Report is published and then I shall write to the three Magistrates letters of comfort, for they have been most villainously pilloried by the sensational press, and will be greatly relieved by the partial vindication which your Report contains.

> Yrs ever
>
> JOHN SIMON

Some eight months later, on 4 July 1944, within a year of the collapse of Nazi Germany and the formal surrender at Reims,

Rayner received another letter from 10 Downing Street. Lord Atkin, a senior Law Lord and arguably the outstanding civil judge of this century, had just died. So Winston Churchill wrote, "Dear Sir Rayner Goddard, It would give me much pleasure to submit your name to the King for appointment as a Lord of Appeal in Ordinary to fill the vacancy created by the death of Lord Atkin." What seemed the ultimate pinnacle of Rayner Goddard's career had been scaled.

A few days later, his appointment was officially announced —together with the news that George VI, in accordance with established practice, had made him a Life Peer. He took as the territorial designation of his title the small Wiltshire village of Aldbourne, in whose parish church he liked to believe his ancestors lay buried.

It is one of those many eccentricities of the English legal process that, the higher one goes up the judicial hierarchy, the less are the outward trappings of one's office. A King's Bench or Queen's Bench judge has robes of rich red trimmed with ermine and an usher who meets him outside his room and marches before him to the court. As soon as he arrives in the Court of Appeal a Lord Justice wears a sombre workaday gown of black silk, shares an usher with a colleague and is not even escorted to and from his room; the usher waits outside the court for his Lords Justices to arrive. Finally, when he is promoted to the House of Lords the Law Lord loses, except for ceremonial occasions, all his robes completely, has no usher whatsoever—and, for the first time in his judicial career, has no clerk either. One consequence of Rayner's going up to the Lords was that he had to say farewell to Arthur Smith—although neither realized that in two brief years' time they would be back again together in harness. "Dear Sir," wrote Arthur Smith to his departing employer, "I do appreciate to the full the kind letter and gift you have sent me and again take the opportunity of thanking you for the generous offer of help until I get fixed up again. I hope it will not be for long that I shall have to avail myself of your kindness. It is a great relief to Mrs Smith and myself to know that we shall not be without an income and the wife asks me to send her thanks and the hope that you will be happy in your new position.

"It is a wrench parting from you, I have been so happy serving you and enjoyed every minute. . . . If at any time I can be of service to you I shall be delighted to do what I can as a small token in return, not only for the kind regard you have shown towards me as a Judge's clerk, but also for the sympathy you displayed so many years ago to a small shy boy from Bethnal Green. Those days I never have and never shall forget. All my affection and good wishes go with you, Sir."

It was a nice letter to receive, and so was the letter that his other ex-clerk, Sidney Newland, wrote:

"I have found great difficulty in waiting for the official announcement before offering you my congratulations upon the latest and greatest honour you have attained. I do so with great sincerity knowing perhaps as well as anybody how well you deserve the appointment, and with a feeling of pride at my association with you.

"All today I have found myself going over in my mind those countless little incidents in your career, which seem so fresh and which undoubtedly pointed, at the time, to the greatness which has now earned its reward. Without exception, everyone is saying it is a splendid appointment.

"Mrs Newland joins me in wishing you long life to enjoy the distinction and Margaret [Rayner's goddaughter] is tremendously proud."

The new Lord of Appeal in Ordinary received many letters of congratulation from Bench, Bar and friends; but perhaps the most touching came from Sir Edward Acton, the King's Bench judge, now retired, who fifteen years earlier had presided over the court hearing in which Rayner Goddard, K.C., had appeared as counsel for Cyril Tolley in his libel action against Fry's chocolate firm. "In my extreme old age and amid all the horrors and abomination of this mixture of Hell and Bedlam, I felt a delightful sensation of pleasurable excitement when I saw the announcement in *The Times*," wrote Sir Edward. "It was indeed so strong I cannot refrain from letting you know how sincerely it was felt: for though the elevation was expected because it had been so brilliantly earned, expectations are not always fulfilled and the highest merit is not always adequately recognised. With sustained sincerity, I beg of you not to reply to or even acknowledge this expression of felicitations which would never have seen the light if it was to add to your burdens."

The war in Europe was over. Rayner was back at 46 Chelsea Square, cared for once again by the attentive "Nicky" (although she was to retire two years later). He had climbed to the top of his professional tree—but he was restless and not a little bored. He longed for something more to do; for something more to occupy his days than the placid, dignified but unhurried and unexciting passage through their Lordships' House of the occasional lawsuit that actually got as far as the ultimate court of appeal. As it happened, he had to wait for over a year until came the opportunity once again to marshal his abundant energy to a specific and pressing task worthy of the challenge: once again, the Government of the day asked him to conduct a one-man inquiry into an alleged miscarriage of justice in a magistrates' court—this time it was the affair of the secret court at Stoke-on-Trent.

In May 1945 a Roman Catholic priest aged forty-eight was arrested at the swimming baths at Stoke-on-Trent and charged with indecent assault on a young boy. The city of Stoke had two magistrates' courts: one, presided over by the stipendiary, at Tunstall; and the lay magistrates' court at Longton. The case of indecency was of a gravity to require that it should be dealt with, according to long-established practice in Stoke, by the stipendiary. But in fact the defendant was bailed to appear at Longton. The police superintendent in charge of the Longton Division, who was a Roman Catholic, queried this, and the Chief Constable said the case must come before the stipendiary at Tunstall. This change of arrangements was made, but in the intermediate confusion the clerk to the lay magistrates at Longton—a dominating man, Mr George Hawley, a Roman Catholic who had had thirty-five years' experience as magistrates' clerk—having been visited by Father Walsh, the rector of Longton Roman Catholic Church, took the rector for a conference with the police superintendent, and later persuaded the latter to allow him to borrow the papers in the case relating to the charge against the priest, which as a supposedly impartial clerk to the justices he had no right to see before the case.

Finally, it was known to all concerned that the case was to be heard at Tunstall. The defendant's solicitor specifically asked the stipendiary not to begin the hearing before 12.30 because he was engaged in another case. On the morning fixed for the hearing the stipendiary's clerk was telephoned by Mr Hawley, the clerk to the lay magistrates at Longton, who asked for the case to be taken off the list because it had already been dealt with.

Mr Hawley had in fact called a special court at Longton at nine in the morning, an hour before the regular opening of the court. He had informed two junior magistrates who each had about three years' service, and one of whom was a Roman Catholic, that there was a case of a distressing nature to be heard, and that no one else was available—although there were magistrates due by rota to serve that day at ten o'clock, and they had thirty-five years' experience between them. The Press were not present, nor were the public, and nor were the police, who knew nothing about the hearing. The 'prosecution' was apparently conducted by Mr Hawley in the presence only of two junior magistrates, the prisoner and his solicitor, a doctor who had made a report on him and the Abbot of Oulton Abbey, into whose care he was ultimately committed.

The stipendiary magistrate, who had waited in vain for the case to come to him after 12.30, learned something of the circumstances and complained to the Chief Constable. By this means knowledge of what had happened came to the Home Secretary and the Lord Chancellor—then, in Mr Churchill's caretaker Government before the general election, Sir Donald Somervell and Viscount Simon. Lord Goddard was asked to conduct an inquiry.

The report was held up by the delayed announcement of the results of the general election, and was published on the following day under a new and unexpected régime: the Labour Government of Clement Attlee with Lord Jowitt as Lord Chancellor, and Chuter Ede as Home Secretary.

Rayner's report followed the same sturdy, independent line as his earlier inquiry into the Hereford birching case. He began by discounting any suggestion that justice had not been done. The priest had been bound over for twelve months. His character had previously been good, though this was not known to the two magistrates since they had no evidence from the police: "Had I been dealing with the case," said Rayner, "I should have made exactly the same order". But justice had not been seen to have been done, and Rayner launched into a scathing attack on what he considered to be grievously wrongful behaviour. *The Times*, praising him for having "very promptly rendered a lucid and decisive report", subsequently thundered, "It is obvious that there was a deliberate and scandalous contrivance to defeat the fundamental rules of publicity for the proceedings of all courts".

Rayner rejected Mr Hawley's defence of his conduct, given both to the Lord Chancellor and to himself, that he acted "solely with the desire to protect the accused from illegal arrest and with a desire to uphold the dignity of the Longton Bench from police interference". He said, "I entirely disbelieve this. What I do think in part actuated him was a desire to get the better of the Chief Constable and to show him that it was he, Mr Hawley, with whom the police had to reckon.

"I wish I could find that a desire 'to score off' the police was the only motive," he continued. "But the facts appear too strong to permit of that conclusion. They point inexorably to a determination on Mr Hawley's part that so far as possible this case should be heard without any publicity. Two magistrates of comparatively recent appointment and who were not on the rota are approached; a court is fixed at an hour earlier than anyone can remember for a sitting for the court; the magistrates on the rota with their usual chairman were due to sit in fifty minutes, and none of them was asked to attend; notice was given to the accused and his solicitor but none to the prosecution, so that no police officer was in court; no notice was given to any witness for the prosecution, and no information to the magistrates on the rota when they arrived as to what had happened. I asked his counsel if he could suggest anything more that Mr Hawley could have done to render the trial secret, and he agreed that he could not."

Of the two magistrates involved in "this sorry business, this regrettable affair", Rayner commented:

"I acquit them of having consciously taken part in an irregular proceeding; I acquit them of deliberately closing their eyes to the obvious. The lamentable fact remains that they did not recognize what must have been plain to any man of ordinary intelligence.

"I do not under-rate the difficulties which often confront lay justices; they are entitled to rely on their clerk for assistance on questions of law, and for taking care that cases are properly conducted in accordance with the law. But they are not to subordinate their judgment to his dictation, and where, as here, they realized that there was something unusual in the proceedings, it is impossible to have confidence in their capacity to act as justices, seeing that they did not recognize plain irregularities and had not the resolution to demand full and proper explanation from their clerk."

On the religious aspect, Rayner said:

"That Mr Hawley, Mr T— [a magistrate], Superintendent E— and the Rev. Mr W— [the rector of the Longton church] all profess the Roman Catholic faith must inevitably give rise to the impression that there was here a conspiracy to prevent publicity regarding a charge of indecency against a priest of that Church. A conspiracy requires the agreement of two or more persons. I have already said that I acquit Superintendent E— of any religious bias, and as he was deliberately kept in ignorance of the secret hearing he could not have prevented it. Nor do I think the religious aspect affected Mr T—; whatever the nature of the case or the religion of the accused, he would have done anything that Mr Hawley told him to do.

"Mr Hawley's resolve to get the case disposed of in secret can only be attributable to the fact that the accused was a priest of his Church. I think Mr W— [the rector] must have discussed with Mr Hawley the publicity the case was sure to receive, and it was then but a very short step to asking if that could not in some way be avoided.

There is nothing however to suggest that he took any part in arranging for a secret hearing. So if an impression has got abroad that there was a conspiracy to hush up this case, it is Mr Hawley who must take the blame for it. He certainly did all in his power to create it."

Policemen in general recognized that although Rayner emphasized in his report "a breach of a strict construction of police regulations", in that the police superintendent had given Mr Hawley a prior look at the reports in the case, his criticism was well-founded, and he had pointed out that the papers had been shown to "the last person who might be expected to make improper use of them". Semi-official police opinion conceded this; and merely took the opportunity in the next *Police Journal* to pontificate about officials and advocates who attempted to "score off" police officers. It recommended restraint in meeting criticism: "In the subsequent publicity the sympathy and support of magistrates and the great majority of the public generally lie with the policeman", it said with confidence grounded more perhaps on hope than experience.

The outcome of the Stoke-on-Trent report was, unavoidably, that the man at the centre of it, Mr Hawley, resigned. But what of the man who wrote it? Rayner had given proof once again to the world at large of his forthrightness, his speed, his ability to get at once to the heart of a matter—and his astute common sense in summing up character and the mainsprings of human behaviour. But he went back to being 'merely' a Law Lord again, gathering dust on the highest rung of the judicial ladder. Were such bustling talents to remain indefinitely under-used?

It would seem that round about this time he may even have thought of retiring. He had, after all, already served as a judge for twenty-two years: seven more than was required to earn his full pension. In June 1944 his old friend and kinsman, Lord Schuster, had retired after twenty-nine years as permanent secretary to the Lord Chancellor, and in his reply thanking Rayner for his letter of good wishes appear the words "Don't retire or think of retiring. There is plenty more milk in the coconut".

With hindsight, those words seem edged with prophetic irony. For at that time, on any objective view, it could not be imagined that the future held more for Rayner than a few more years of prestigious, but unstimulating, distinction, followed by the inevitable physical decline of surrender of office and faltering progress towards the black valley of death. Yet within less than six months of him submitting his Stoke-on-Trent report a whole new realm of experience was—almost unbelievably—opening up before him.

9 Lord Chief Justice– the Office

The office of Lord Chief Justice of England is one of ultimate legal splendour. To the popular eye, he embodies the law: he is what the title says, the lord chief justice—the highest-ranking judge. In fact, technically speaking, he is not the head of the judiciary. The Lord Chancellor takes precedence as the senior of all judges.

But the Lord Chancellor is a member of the Government; even though he is not always a politician—as in the recent example of Lord Simonds for the Tories in 1951 and Lord Gardiner (ex Gerald Gardiner, Q.C.) for the Socialists in 1964—his tenure of office is as uncertain as the progress of a falling leaf floating through a gale. His robes are splendid, his room in the House of Lords overlooking the Thames magnificent, he chairs their Lordships' debates resplendent upon the Woolsack, he has the right to preside over the Law Lords when sitting as the ultimate court of appeal, he has supreme patronage over the law, appointing all High Court and Circuit judges, Recorders, Q.C.s and magistrates and is consulted by the Prime Minister on all senior judicial appointments above the rank of High Court judge. He is the nearest we have in this country to a Minister for Justice—but he may lose all this glory at the bat of a Prime Minister's eyelid. On the 'night of the long knives' in July 1962 Harold Macmillan gave Lord Kilmuir, Lord Chancellor for eight years, just seven hours' notice of his dismissal from office.

Not so with the Lord Chief Justice of England: he is the senior permanent judge. He cannot be dismissed by a politician rejigging his Cabinet. He stands pre-eminent, and movable only by the rigours of time. He is President of the Queen's Bench Division of the High Court, and as such he may try civil cases in the ordinary way like any other Queen's Bench judge. He also goes on Circuit, attends the Old Bailey and presides over the Court of Appeal (Criminal Division), the Courts Martial Appeal Court and the Queen's Bench Divisional Court. He has the right to sit in the Court of Appeal (Civil Division), in the House of Lords and on the Judicial Committee of the Privy Council. Some of his ceremonial duties, such as swearing in new Queen's Bench judges, are judicial; others, such as receiving the new Lord Mayor of London upon his election in November, are to be found in the ancient traditions of the City of London. He is also a Church Commissioner, a Trustee of Chequers Trust and of *The Times*. As between himself and his fellow Queen's Bench judges, he is *primus inter pares:* they call him quite simply "Chief"—and that about sums up his position, he is 'the boss'. Have a strong Lord Chief Justice and you have a strong judiciary, have a weak Lord Chief Justice and you have a collection of in-dividuals—some weak, some strong, but generally bland. The Chief puts his stamp upon the judges of his era: their colour comes from him.

Pre-eminently is this true of the Criminal Law. It is through presiding over the two superior courts hearing appeals in criminal matters, the Court of Appeal (Criminal Division)—in Rayner God-dard's day it was still called the Court of Criminal Appeal—and the Queen's Bench Divisional Court, that the Lord Chief Justice can most influence and oversee the development of English criminal law and sentencing policy. His presidency of the Queen's Bench Divisional Court, on appeal from magistrates' courts and various tribunals, also makes him the most important judicial influence over administrative law, which deals with the relationship between the in-dividual on the one hand and Ministers, Government departments, local authorities and other bodies that made decisions affecting the citizen's life on the other. The Divisional Court is the channel through which the ordinary man can challenge the decision of authority. It exercises judicial control of administrative acts through the 'prerogative writs' of mandamus, certiorari and prohibition, and through the writ of habeas corpus it ensures the Englishman's basic freedom from unlawful detention. It was the first Lord Chief Justice of England, Sir Edward Coke, who in the early years of the seventeenth century declared proudly, "A man's home is his castle", and defied the wrath of James I to proclaim the independence of the judges.

But a fundamental characteristic of the English way of life is its scant respect for logic. The majority of legal historians agree that Sir Edward Coke was indeed the first to style himself Lord Chief Justice of England, but he was never a 'lord', and his very assumption of the title was that which eventually led to his downfall. In fact, his only official title was Lord Chief Justice of the Court of King's Bench—one of the three old Common Law courts, all sitting together side by side under the vast, vaulted timber roof of Westminster Hall—and when he was dismissed in 1616 the Lord High Treasurer, the Earl of Suffolk, told him, "Amongst other things, the King is not well pleased with the title of the book [Coke's famous *Commentaries on the Laws of England*] wherein you entitled yourself 'Lord Justice of England'. Whereas by law you can challenge no more than Lord Chief Justice of the King's Bench."

For centuries there were two other 'Chiefs', one for each of the two other old Common Law courts, the Common Pleas Court and the Court of Exchequer. Only when all three courts were merged into the one High Court of Justice by the Judicature Act of 1873 did Parliament officially create the post of Lord Chief Justice *of England,* and even then we had to wait until 1880 for the first "true" Lord Chief Justice of England to be appointed—when Lord Coleridge, then Chief Justice of the Common Pleas Division of the High Court, assumed the office upon the death of old Sir Alexander Cockburn, the last Lord Chief Justice of the King's Bench. Only since 1880 has the Lord Chief Justice of England always been, in fact, a lord; always appointed to the peerage on taking office, if not already ennobled.

But if the history of the office affords a prime example of the English taste for a certain charming eccentricity, the nature of the first seven appointments to the full post displayed a quality somewhat less endearing: some might term it hypocrisy. For the first seven holders of this highest permanent judicial office in the State—traditionally, according to all the books, the leader of the judges in their steadfast independence of politics and the Executive—were all to a man political appointments! With one exception, they all gained the office as a reward for political services, and that one exception was a complaisant elderly judge keeping the seat warm for a political nominee. It is not one of the most noble weaves in the many-stranded texture of English law.

As far back in time as 1612 the devious Francis Bacon, then Solicitor-General and plotting his own steady advancement up the hierarchy of power towards his eventual Lord Chancellorship, fawningly addressed James I upon the death of Sir Edward Coke's predecessor as Lord Chief Justice of the King's Bench, "Having un-

derstood of the death of the Lord Chief Justice, I do ground in all
humbleness as an assured hope, that your Majesty will not think of
any other but your poor servant, your Attorney and your Solicitor,
one of them for that place. Else we shall be like Noah's dove, not
knowing where to rest our feet. For the places of rest after the
extreme painful places wherein we serve have used to be either the
Lord Chancellor's place, or the Mastership of the Rolls or the places
of Chief Justices." So when Coke, previously Attorney-General,
moved over in smooth progression from the Chief Justiceship of the
Common Pleas to that of the King's Bench the Attorney-General,
Sir Henry Hobart, moved up to the Common Pleas Chief
Justiceship—and Bacon oozed his way forward into the Attorney-
General's place, thereby confirming his own view of the Law
Officers' "expectations and successions to great places".

Over the succeeding centuries the Attorney-General's 'right' to
succeed to the Lord Chancellorship was never completely established. Such elevation frequently occurred, and still does even
today; but that is simply because "tall oaks from little acorns grow"
and, as lawyer-politicians serving one political party mature and
develop with experience it is a natural progression from being
merely a Law Officer advising a Government to being, at a later
stage in one's life, a Lord Chancellor actually a member of that same
party's Government. This flows from the natural progress of a predominantly politically based career: it does not overtly reek of undesirable patronage, nor is it offensive to the nostrils.

But it proved differently with the Attorney-General's avowed
'right' to the Lord Chief Justiceship of England. That was a claim
most decidedly honoured in the performance. Of all the Lord Chief
Justices of the King's Bench appointed from 1725 to the time of the
Judicature Act in 1873, all but two had previously held the office of
Attorney-General. The translation to the King's Bench was an
accepted perquisite of the lesser post, should a vacancy fall due
during the holder's period of office; and the convention continued
in full vigour after the passing of the Act.

When in 1920 Lord Reading (himself an ex Attorney-General),
then Lord Chief Justice and as ever casting around for new fields
wherein he might bedazzle with his brilliance, wished to become
Viceroy of India, there was only one objection to the Prime
Minister's mind: Sir Gordon Hewart, K.C., the Attorney-General,
would claim his 'right' to succeed Reading—and, with his Government's steadily weakening position in the post-War House of Commons, Lloyd George did not want to run the risk of losing so

stalwart a Parliamentary colleague.

So the Prime Minister, ever wily, suggested this plan to Hewart, which the Attorney-General duly recorded in a private memorandum:

"That Rufus [Reading] should go to India, that the office of Lord Chief Justice should then be offered to me, that I should for the moment decline it, and that then it should be offered to and accepted by one of the more elderly judges, who had earned or almost earned his pension, upon the terms that he should give it up at any time when requested by the Prime Minister, which request might be made in a few months' time and certainly would be made before he [Lloyd George] ceased to be head of this Administration or before the next General Election, whichever event should first happen, and that thereupon I should be appointed Lord Chief Justice. . . ."

Hewart protested, not at the shoddiness of the plot or at its squalid Tammany Hall-like mentality, but not least because of the impression which he felt the public would have that he had been passed over. He told the Prime Minister, "Neither personally nor as trustee of the rights of the great office of Attorney-General can I assent to that suspicion". Later, under pressure, he relented and agreed to fall in with the arrangement, provided that, when Reading resigned and the vacancy occurred, he should be given a real opportunity of declining the post, and that the fact should be officially announced—safe in the knowledge that the stopgap Lord Chief Justice would duly hand over when the time was right.

As it transpired, Lloyd George welshed on the deal. Reading resigned without any public declaration of Hewart's having declined to succeed him. Instead it was merely announced, in April 1921, that the seventy-seven-year-old Mr Justice A. T. Lawrence, who had already served as a conscientious but remarkably dull High Court judge for seventeen years (two more than was needed to qualify for his pension), was to be the new Chief, and had been raised to the peerage as Lord Trevethin.

He did not enjoy his totally unjustified honour for long. Within eleven months Lloyd George's Government was in its death-throes, Parliament was dissolved—and Lord Trevethin read of his resignation from the Lord Chief Justiceship of England in *The Times* newspaper. Not appreciably shaken, he retired to his beautiful home in Breconshire and lived a contented country life for fourteen more years, finally departing this world when fishing in the Wye above Builth Wells at the grand old age of ninety-two.

Hewart's accession to office was totally lacking in dignity, and so, perhaps appropriately, was his leaving it eighteeen years later. By October 1940, when Rayner Goddard had already been two years on the Appeal Court Bench, Hewart's health was failing badly: he was so weak he could hardly hold a pen, he was falling asleep in court. But he held on grimly to office, merely promising Winston Churchill, then Prime Minister, that he would resign "in the near future". Eventually his mind was made up for him by Britain's wartime leader in characteristic fashion: he was called from his sickroom to answer a telephone call from the Prime Minister's office and told curtly that his resignation was to be announced for convenience, along with other Cabinet changes, in the newspapers of the following morning.

His successor, Lord Caldecote, who as young Tom Inskip had been elected to the Western Circuit at Bristol on the same day as Rayner Goddard, was a purely political appointment. He did not want the job. He was aware of his own lack of brilliance, and knew full well of his limitations as a lawyer. Even his biographer Bernard Fergusson could only write of him later in the *Dictionary of National Biography*, "Inskip was a man who attained to the highest offices, not by brilliance, influence or luck, but by character and sound judgement. Apart from his aptitude for hard work he was chiefly characterized by his integrity and his deep religious convictions." He took the job because his political master, Winston Churchill, asked him to: it was as simple as that.

Caldecote, a former Attorney-General, had served the Tory Party well, if stolidly, in several Cabinet posts over the years: Minister for the Co-ordination of Defence under Stanley Baldwin, then Dominions Secretary under Neville Chamberlain, later transferring to the Woolsack on the outbreak of the Second World War (allegedly to keep the seat warm for John Simon!), then after eight months (when John Simon went to the Woolsack) back to the Dominions Office under Churchill, then after five months cynically moved over by Churchill, who had other more important things on his mind, to take over from Hewart as Lord Chief Justice. It is not a record of outstanding singleness of purpose, although it does perhaps reveal a somewhat plodding sense of duty.

As Lord Chief Justice, Caldecote was a pleasant, amiable nonentity who has left no impression on legal history whatsoever—content, through failing health and frank acceptance of his lack of surpassing talent, to lean heavily on the skilled assistance of the ageing Mr Justice Humphreys, that experienced veteran of the Criminal Bench who regularly sat with him in the Court of Criminal Appeal and King's Bench Divisional Court, and frequently deputized for him during his increasingly long periods of absence from the Bench through illness. "Humphreys was almost the acting Lord Chief Justice during Caldecote's latter years", says a retired Q.C. who often appeared before him during that time.

Even Arthur Smith, whose wording is always guarded, speaks about "the feeling of flatness and inertia, of growing disorganization, which was prevalent in the Royal Courts of Justice, due partly to the war and partly to the illness of the Lord Chief Justice, Lord Caldecote, who was not able to give the dynamic leadership needed at such a time".

By contrast, Rayner Goddard was champing at the bit with frustration: his unbounding enthusiasm for work totally unsatisfied by the comparatively few demands put upon it by his prestigious but not overburdening labours as a Law Lord. The Stoke-on-Trent inquiry had only whetted his appetite for more active and inspiring duties.

There he was, in the autumn of 1945, the War over, back living in Chelsea Square with the faithful Nicky returned to look after him. His three daughters all married, five of his six grandchildren already born. Aged sixty-eight, in robust health (he had only missed one day through illness since his appointment to the High Court Bench thirteen years earlier), rich in achievement, proud of his friends and their affection—*yet restless*. He was, to put it simply, bored. He met Arthur Smith by chance in a corridor of the House of Lords and Smith asked him how he was getting on. "Well, Arthur", he replied, "I like the work but feel so strange. I have no room of my own, no one to look after me and I cannot even find anybody who will buy me a 2d. stamp."

It was shortly after this conversation that an event occurred that was to alter Rayner Goddard's life, and bring about a fundamental change in the administration of law in this country. In December 1945 Lord Caldecote had a stroke. He had earlier that year been off duty for six months, his longest period of absence yet, returning only to the courts in October. Now it was clear that he could not much longer continue in office. "Man proposes, God disposes."

The last thing that the new Labour Administration under Clement Attlee wanted was a problem about who should be the new Lord Chief Justice. Returned to power by the General Election of July 1945, the first Labour Government with an effective majority in the history of Britain was poised on the brink of what many believed to be a social revolution. Churchill and the Tories had been con-

signed to the political wilderness. The future for Mr Attlee and his
colleagues was bright, promising and full of excitement.

But whom could they appoint to succeed the fast-failing Lord
Chief Justice? The Attorney-General was Sir Hartley Shawcross,
K.C., a brilliant courtroom lawyer of outstanding ability. He would
undoubtedly make a first-class judge. But he was only forty-five
years of age. All previous Attorney-Generals claiming their 'right' to
succeed to the Lord Chief Justiceship had been of rather more
mature years—and none had been a Socialist! Was Britain, now
adjusting for the first time to 'Red' rule in Parliament, also to have a
'Red' judge presiding over the criminal law? Old ladies in
Cheltenham were already fearing they would be slaughtered in their
beds; the political views of the new Attorney-General were known to
be somewhat militant in flavour—would not the sight of him,
resplendent in scarlet and ermine as Lord Chief Justice, drive them
to the point of distraction?

In the result Sir Hartley did not succeed Caldecote. Rayner Goddard got the job—and the tradition of the Lord Chief Justiceship
being a political appointment was killed, finally and for ever. "Lord
Goddard was the first non-political Lord Chief Justice of recent
times", the late Lord Parker, his successor, has told me. "So was I,
and so was my successor. He will go down in history as bringing
to an end the convention of political appointments to that high
office."

Professor J. Ll. J. Edwards, in his work *The Law Officers of the
Crown*, written in 1964, merely speaks of the custom "being ignored" in Lord Goddard's and Lord Parker's appointments. But
there was much more to it than that. The custom was not ignored in
selecting Rayner Goddard for the post. It was deliberately
abolished. Sir Hartley (now Lord) Shawcross tells for the first time
the full story:

"I *was* offered the post by the Prime Minister, Mr Attlee, and the
Lord Chancellor, Lord Jowitt—although the Prime Minister put it
to me in his typically laconic way, 'I don't suppose you'll want it,
will you?'

"In fact, I didn't want it! It would be stupid to say I would never
want it at any time. It was about the only judicial appointment I
would ever have been likely to accept. But I did not want it then, and
for these reasons: I had often said as a junior at the Bar, as a silk and
as Attorney-General that the whole idea of the Attorney having the
'right' of succession to the Lord Chief Justiceship was wrong. How
could I now go back on that? It would have been a public scandal,

to my mind!

"Besides, I was really more thinking of politics at that time. Even if I had been offered the post four or five years later, and nothing to do with the fact that I had been Attorney-General, I would still have refused it. My interest was in politics. Later, Hugh Gaitskell asked me if I would be Lord Chancellor, if the Labour Party under his leadership, got back into power and I said, 'No, I would much rather be Foreign Secretary.'"

So Sir Hartley Shawcross, from a mixture of personal conviction and personal preference, told Mr Attlee that he did not want the job. "I said, 'No'—but I also said that I thought Goddard was the man, although I did not think my selection was all that important."

Why did he recommend Goddard? Was he a personal friend? "No, I hardly knew him personally at that time at all, although afterwards, yes, we did become close friends. I thought he had the right image. I had appeared before him as a judge once or twice—and found him forthright, succinct and a good judge. He was a strong personality. I felt the judges wanted the leadership of a strong personality and he would give it to them.

"I did not regard him as a hanging, cruel judge at all. I always took the view that if I was an innocent man I would have been quite happy to appear in front of him, but if I was guilty I would have preferred someone else.

"I took the view that, if the appointment was not to be a political one—and I was convinced that it should not be—the job should go to the best man; and that best man, to my mind, was Goddard."

Attlee did not act upon Lord Shawcross's recommendation alone. The Labour Party had no outstanding candidate of their own. The Party was remarkably thin on the ground in supporters among the ranks of the judiciary in the mid nineteen-forties. There could be no 'jobs for the boys' so far as this appointment was concerned for the good reason that, if it had been desired to make that the method of selection, there were no 'boys' available. Even the Government's Lord Chancellor was Lord Jowitt, that veteran turner of many political coats who had been Liberal, Labour, Liberal and now Labour again along his path to high office.

Says the late Lord Parker, "The Government had to go, and rightly went, to the judges themselves for their choice." "I don't believe he did it in any formal way," says Lord Shawcross, "but I believe that Jowitt did, in fact, speak to the judges informally about it. He canvassed their views. I don't think it would have been proper to do it formally, but informal consultations—yes, they did take place. Very likely, Jowitt would have said something like, 'What do you think of Rayner?' "

The result was like asking ballet-lovers what they thought of Rudolf Nureyev. Rayner was one of the most popular judges of the time among his own brethren: they both loved the man and respected his ability. On 16 January 1946, Attlee wrote Rayner this confidential letter from 10 Downing Street:

DEAR LORD GODDARD,
The Lord Chief Justice has written asking to be allowed to resign on the grounds of ill-health, and it would give me much pleasure to submit your name to the King for appointment in his stead. Before taking any steps in the matter, however, I should be glad to know whether this would be agreeable to you. The matter should of course be regarded as confidential.

"He rang me up", says Mrs Prue Clayton, Rayner's youngest daughter whom he had telephoned so excitedly fourteen years earlier on receiving the first intimation of his High Court judgeship," and told me the news. He said it was a complete and utter surprise. He said of course he was going to say yes. He said he was absolutely thrilled because he always liked to run his own show."

Rayner wrote by return accepting the Prime Minister's offer. On that same day Attlee wrote back, "I am much obliged to you for your letter of 17 January informing me that you agree to the submission of your name to the King for appointment as Lord Chief Justice. I am making a submission accordingly and I will ensure that you are duly informed before any public announcement is made."

On the following day, 18 January 1946, came the official confirmation from the Prime Minister's Private Office: "My Lord, I have the honour to inform you that The King has been pleased to approve that you be appointed Lord Chief Justice of England. It is proposed to issue a press notice to this effect to appear in the papers on Monday morning."

Only then did Rayner write to the ailing Lord Caldecote, and received this fond reply dated 20 January 1946, written in the outgoing Chief's fading hand. It enclosed the key to his desk:

MY DEAR RAYNER,
There is a lot I should like to say—but I am not sure that I shall try. I couldn't have wished for anyone more than for you to succeed me. You have said so much in your letter that I can't believe it can be true, but it is

kind and good of you to say it. Good luck to you in your job!

Here is the key. It unlocks all the drawers of my table.

I am greatly relieved at you taking Peter Stephenson [Caldecote's private secretary since 1935]. I will ask him to come down on Tuesday.

I shall look forward to seeing you soon.

Yours ever affectionately,

TOM

There was one other thing to be done that weekend before the announcement in the Press. The new Lord Chief Justice would need a clerk. Rayner wrote to Arthur Smith asking him to come and see him at Chelsea Square. "When I arrived there was an air of suppressed excitement about him which I could not miss", says Mr Smith. "I knew that something tremendous must have happened."

Rayner showed him the Prime Minister's letter asking if he could submit his name to the King as Chief. "I looked up. There was no doubt what his answer had been. 'Well, Arthur,' he said, 'so we're back in harness again. I have a thousand things in mind which I want to do, and I shall need your help."

It was traditional for a new Lord Chief Justice to be offered a hereditary peerage. Rayner's barony was, of course, only a life peerage as a Law Lord. Attlee offered him a hereditary title—but he refused. "I saw no point in it", he was later to be quoted as telling a friend. "I have no son!" Mrs Pamela Maurice, his eldest daughter, confirms this depressingly male chauvinistic view: "He did not take a hereditary title because he had no son. It was very unlikely they would allow the succession to a daughter. They generally only did that for Scots lords or the daughters of distinguished generals. He might have got it, if he had tried—but he didn't!"

On Monday 21 January 1946 appeared the official announcement: "The King has accepted the resignation of Lord Caldecote from the office of Lord Chief Justice of England and approved the appointment of Lord Goddard in his place."

At an age when most men are already in retirement, spending their days on the golf-course or tending the garden, Rayner Goddard was taking on the most exacting task of his already long life. "I'm only a stopgap", he told his daughter Lady Sachs. "I shan't stay a day longer than three years", he told Arthur Smith. "I don't suppose I shall be here all that many years", he told Peter Stephenson, his new secretary inherited from Lord Caldecote.

But he was to reign for twelve long, eventful years into his early eighties. As Pope John XXIII, the 'stopgap' Pope appointed in his old age as a temporary measure, lived on to take the Roman Catholic Church in his strong, gnarled hands and leave his imprint on it for ever, so Lord Goddard, the 'stopgap' Lord Chief Justice, was to prove the most powerful and dynamic man ever to have sat below the embossed Royal coat of arms in the Lord Chief's vast courtroom. The greatest Lord Chief Justice of this century was about to fulfil his own, and the law's, destiny.

10 Lord Chief Justice—
the Man

On Wednesday, 23 January 1946, in the presence of the Lord Chancellor, the Master of the Rolls, the President of the Probate, Divorce and Admiralty Division, the Lords Justices of Appeal and the High Court Judges then in London, Lord Goddard was sworn in as Lord Chief Justice in his own splendid courtroom. His daughters and their families were there, and his brother Ernest "with black cotton gloves and top hat, looking like a High Church church verger", to quote Judge Ifor Lloyd, Q.C.

Lord Jowitt uttered in his most dignified fashion mellifluent words of welcome, recalling that the new Lord Chief Justice in his Oxford days had been a distinguished sprinter, and had "certainly displayed some of his old agility in mounting the judicial ladder". Sir Frank Soskice, K.C., the Solicitor-General, made a speech on behalf of the Bar. But perhaps the most interesting salutation came in a private letter from the one man who more than any other had brought about his selection for the post: Sir Hartley Shawcross, the Attorney-General, confined to his bed by a severe attack of influenza. "Dear Lord Goddard," he wrote that day. "May I send you my best congratulations and good wishes on your appointment. We are very fortunate in having been able to have such a distinguished occupant for this most important position and I hope that you will like the job as much as I know the job will like you."

In fact, from the very outset there was no doubt how well Rayner Goddard and 'the job' took to each other. "Now we shall really get a move on", a leading K.C. told Arthur Smith on that first day; and so it soon proved.

As he explained to his clerk, Lord Goddard took to himself two main objectives. One was to re-galvanize the lethargic and disorganized administration of the courts and the other, to which he accorded even greater priority, was to set the courts firmly against the appalling upsurge of crime which in those early post-War months was already appearing. "If the criminal law of this country is to be respected, it must be in accordance with public opinion and public opinion must support it", he was to say two years later in his maiden speech in the House of Lords; and from his earliest utterances on the Lord Chief Justice's Bench he made it vigorously clear that public opinion, in his view, demanded sternness and authority.

The sentencing policy of our criminal courts is largely set by the standards imposed by the Court of Appeal (Criminal Division), then known as the Court of Criminal Appeal, presided over by the Lord Chief Justice. The Court of Criminal Appeal had enjoyed, ever since it was set up in 1907, the power to increase a sentence on appeal as well as to reduce it or merely leave it alone, but under Lord Caldecote's unsteady hand that power had been little exercised in recent years. Furthermore, the practice had always been on a soft, game-of-cricket basis in that where a prisoner appealed against a sentence which in the opinion of the Court was too light, if the Court gave leave to appeal they always issued a warning that they had power to increase the sentence—as if to say, "Don't go on any further." In Lord Goddard's own words in a 1952 lecture printed in the *Journal of the Society of Public Teachers in Law,* "When I became Chief Justice I thought this practice of giving a warning should be abolished. The statute requires that, if leave to appeal is given, the Court shall impose such sentence, whether greater or less, that they thought proper. It seemed to me, therefore, it was our clear duty if we thought a sentence was inadequate to give leave and act as the statute directed."

On 18 February 1946, within a month of his appointment, the new Chief had the opportunity to announce the changed policy of the Court. A man named Harry John McBain was appealing against a sentence of three years' penal servitude imposed on him by the Recorder of London. He had been convicted of housebreaking. He had got into some flats in Earl's Court and stolen £600 worth of goods. As he was leaving some police officers saw him. They called to him to stop. He produced a revolver from his pocket—which one officer heard click. There was no shot, but the officers were momentarily disconcerted, and McBain got away. Later he was arrested and, after several days' trial, convicted. He applied for leave to appeal against his conviction, which was refused, and against his sentence—which was granted.

The Lord Chief Justice explained why: "The Court gave him leave to appeal for one reason only—in order to consider whether or not they should not substantially increase the sentence. Hitherto, this Court, when considering an application for leave to appeal against sentence has, if in its opinion the sentence was not severe enough, generally warned the applicant that, if he persisted in his appeal, the Court might increase his sentence. This Court is no longer going to take that course. . . .

"The time has certainly come in the state of crime in this country now, when sentences must be severe. This Court will not shrink from increasing sentences where the prisoner appeals if it thinks it right to do so."

A new voice was speaking in the land. But, as Sir Frank Soskice (now Lord Stow Hill) has told me, "Rayner had an impulsive sense of what was fair." The Court did *not* increase the sentence in this first case where the existing practice was changed and a warning for the future given. Rayner 'dressed it up', of course. "One thing, and one thing only, has saved the Appellant from having it increased to a considerably longer term," growled the formidable figure on the Bench. "If he had gone to the flat armed with a revolver, so that he was committing armed house-breaking at the time, the Court would have thought a sentence of three years' penal servitude wholly inadequate and would have doubled it. It appeared, however, that he did not go armed but stole the revolver when he was at the flat. It is not clear whether the revolver was loaded or not. It is a very serious offence and the Court has considered long and earnestly whether it ought not to increase the sentence.

"Taking into account, however, the fact that the Appellant did not go armed, and that he has not been previously convicted, it has come to the conclusion that the sentence must stand; but in its opinion it was a very lenient sentence for a very gross and grave crime. The appeal is dismissed."

Rayner was up to his old trick of stern words masking a not over-stern sentence. It was pure judicial window-dressing, for he surely must have known that so strong a judge as Sir Gerald Dodson, the Recorder of London, would certainly never, even in a rare moment of sublime tenderness, have imposed a sentence of only three years if the man had gone to the flat deliberately armed with a revolver. As someone who appeared on several occasions before him, I can testify that Dodson would not have gone *that* far astray. However, the message to would-be appellants was clear: "Watch out! Ponder well before you appeal in a borderline case; without any chance to turn back, you may well get your sentence increased." And the message to the criminal courts was also clear: "Don't be timid about imposing stern sentences for serious crime. If you don't, and we get the chance, we will!"

Rayner proved as good as his word. A number of prisoners, appealing for a reduction in their sentences, had them substantially increased or even doubled. Gradually the courts, hearing that the Appeal Court considered that a sentence of so many years was the appropriate one for a certain type of case in certain circumstances, fell into line with the superior court's wishes. Sentences all over the country tended to become more severe—or "more adequate", as Rayner himself described them in his 1952 lecture.

Every Monday morning when the courts were sitting, Lord Goddard presided over the Court of Criminal Appeal, and for two to three weeks at a time he would for the rest of the week preside over the King's Bench Divisional Court. He gave high priority to the Criminal Law. He was determined to put backbone into the attitude of the courts towards criminals and their efforts. "My sentiments are more in favour of the victims than for the murderers." "I have never yet understood how you can make the criminal law a deterrent unless it is also punitive. The two things seem to me to follow one on the other." "The age-old causes of crime are still there. They are the desire for easy money, greed, passion, lust and cruelty." "If our criminal law is to be respected, the public conscience has to be satisfied, and it will not be satisfied if gross violence, and sometimes bestial crime, is not punished in a way that will satisfy the public. There are old people who go trembling to their doors at night." All these are typical utterances during his twelve years in office. Is it any wonder that for a large section of the population, I firmly believe for the overwhelming majority of the population, Rayner Goddard as Lord Chief Justice came to represent their most sturdy bulwark against crime and violence?

When this biography was announced in the Press a Mr H.N. Kent of Worthing wrote to me. His words need to be known: "I had not on any occasion the honour of Lord Goddard's acquaintance; I can however vouch for the impression he made while L.C.J. on the British public and on me . . . that Goddard stood for what the public wanted: and that was that human life was to be protected, if necessary, by vigour; that the growing tide of brutal criminality for which the war and certain weak political theories were partly responsible was to be vigorously withstood. He did this always; and I remember the keen apprehension I felt on his announced retirement; my fear was more than justified; since he left the active scene we have had an enormous increase in all kinds of crime, and worst of all, a growing feeling of helplessness among the people, who feel that those who now govern them will on no account give them the stern protection that severe administration of justice used to give. The public has lost confidence in the judgment, wisdom and competence of government and magistrates to a large extent; and anybody with a memory looks back to Lord Goddard's time as to relative paradise."

Reactionary views? I do not think so. I believe that many people reading those words will mutter to themselves, "Hear, hear!" Rayner Goddard was most definitely *not* a do-gooder in the modern, pejorative sense of the word. He would not have agreed with current ideas whereby bail is even granted in pending murder trials, men and women walk free from court having killed a fellow human being because a sympathetic judge sees fit to impose merely a suspended prison sentence for what the law now calls manslaughter, and what would in Rayner's time almost certainly still have been murder; he would have reacted with horror at the current notion that it is legally permissible to include a count for murder—the 'ultimate crime'—in the same indictment as other lesser offences; he would have been appalled by the current flight from authority by members of the judiciary on all fronts of the battle against crime and anti-social forces.

Yet he was for all that not a harsh judge and, according to the standards of his time (that now, alas, already seems so remote), compassionate in his sentences. "What has worried me", the late Lord Parker of Waddington has told me, "is the build-up he got as being a tough judge: the Judge Jeffreys of his day. That is a most misleading view of him. Of course, he was tough when toughness was called for in a time of rising crime. But no one could be more humane.

"I can remember a case where I went in with George Lynskey [Mr Justice Lynskey] to him when I was a Queen's Bench judge before going into the Court of Criminal Appeal, and there was Rayner walking up and down the room: 'What can we do for this young man of eighteen? It's wrong he should go to prison.' I can remember George Lynskey saying, 'You're getting soft!' But Rayner prevailed: he got probation.

"As bad luck would have it, that same young man thereafter came up again in front of Rayner—and then he *was* tough!"

On innumerable occasions the Appeal Court presided over by him set aside sentences of imprisonment and substituted probation orders, especially where young offenders were concerned, where there seemed to be a chance that they would respond to lenient treatment. "I agree with all my heart", he said in his maiden speech in the House of Lords, "that when you are dealing with the sort of cases which come before magistrates daily, and perhaps to a lesser extent before Quarter Sessions—that is, when you are dealing with the young criminal, the boy who is drifting into crime, the man who has made a slip from which he can be rescued, or even the old lag in whom there is still some good that, given a fair chance, he will be able to develop—reformation is the main thing for a court to bear in mind." It is still not generally known, even among lawyers, that it was he who brought about an almost revolutionary change in sentencing procedure—on the side of leniency—by ruling that it was not improper for a probation officer to recommend how the court should deal with a prisoner.

Mr Tom Ashworth, a retired shorthand writer at the High Court and Assizes, recounts an instructive example of Rayner Goddard in action in the early 1950s at Reading Assizes: "He was faced with about a dozen young people, from sixteen or seventeen to about twenty-two, each of whom pleaded guilty to being concerned, in greater or lesser degree, in a considerable number of burglaries, shop-breakings and so on; some asked for other offences to be taken into consideration and some had previous convictions for similar crimes.

"When he came to passing sentence he began at the lower, or higher, end of the scale and sentenced each one individually. The first two or three he discharged conditionally, the next group he put on probation, and the third group he sent to Borstal training. As he passed sentence of Borstal training on one youth in particular, a strident voice called out, 'You're a hard man. My son is no worse than so-and-so and you only put him on probation!' There was a little commotion as the outraged mother was ejected from the court, and then his Lordship continued and concluded with sentences of imprisonment on the last two or three.

"As the last man went down below, Lord Goddard leaned over his desk and spoke to the Clerk of Assize, saying, 'You know, I think that woman was right. I was too severe with her son.'

"Thereupon he had the youth returned to the dock and the

mother brought into court. Truculently, even rudely, she acknowledged she was the boy's mother and in a surly manner answered questions from the judge, and then he said, 'Madam, you were quite right, and I was wrong. Your son was no worse than those I put on probation so I will withdraw the sentence of Borstal training and put him on probation.'

"And that is what he did, and it was in open court."

But crime was not the only major problem with which Rayner found himself faced as Lord Chief Justice: there was also the appalling dilemma of congestion in the courts and long delays in obtaining justice. As a practical innovator and administrator—a side of his activities little seen by the general public—he proved to be of outstanding ability: it was largely due to his efforts that the delays in the civil cause lists, of depressing length when he took office, were reduced to manageable proportions. At his instigation the successful scheme of fixing dates for civil trials was launched. The establishment of the early, prototype Crown Courts in Manchester and Liverpool, that did so much to reduce the congestion of criminal business in those vast conurbations, owed a great deal to his advocacy. He pioneered a complete revision of the time-honoured (and time-wasting) method of taking depositions before magistrates in criminal cases. He even took his passion for saving the court's time to the extent of suggesting, in his speech of welcome to the new Lord Mayor of London in November 1954, that his beloved Common Law should be amended so as to follow the Scottish example and permit majority verdicts—a 'reform' that eventually came into the law years after he left office and, at least in the author's view, has sacrificed principle on the altar of expediency.

Yet his greatest single contribution to shortening "the law's delays" was the potent force of his own example. In his first appearance presiding over the King's Bench Divisional Court he got through seventeen cases in a week that were expected to last a full fortnight. During the first three weeks of his tenure of office the officials of his Division found that in his hands the lists melted away just about twice as fast as they could be replenished. A case that had been expected to last for five hours disappeared in forty minutes, a two-day case was disposed of in an hour: "To appear before him is at the same time a test and an exhilaration, astringent and salutary as a cold shower," said a barrister in a broadcast in the BBC's General Overseas Service in June 1953. "It is not an experience for the soft or the vague or the muddle-headed or the half-prepared. The Chief seizes the point, fastens on to it, and brushes aside all irrelevancies with ruthless brevity and abrupt vigour."

"He wondered why there was a delay in the courts", says Mr William ("Tiny") Fell, who sat with him for many years as Court Associate and was later appointed by him to be Clerk of the Lists, "because he could deal with so many cases in such a short time. I have sat with him with one or two or three cases in his list, with which he dealt quite summarily—and then been anxious to get more work, and taken one or two more cases from other courts. It wasn't very easy for the barristers appearing in front of him—but he did not worry too much about that. As far as I could see, he dealt with those cases quite satisfactorily: he used to cut out the preliminaries and used to like to get on with it—'Get on with it, Mr So-and-so', he would always be saying.

"He was insatiable for work. On one occasion in the Divisional Court we had thirteen cases in the day's list, about double the usual number, and he got through them all. It was murder for me: as Associate, I had to draw up all the orders. It beat all records!"

Rayner went out on Circuit—'to encourage the troops'— probably far more than any other Lord Chief Justice before or since. In 1955, at the age of seventy-eight, he set off and covered in one session two separate Circuits, something it is said no other occupant of his office has even attempted. A month after his seventy-ninth birthday, in 1956, he conducted Assizes in seven towns so as to speed up the trial of a large number of cases pending in the lists. "Uppermost in his mind was the need to do the work on Circuit", says Peter Stephenson, the private secretary whom he inherited from Lord Caldecote. "He went to every Circuit there was and almost every Assize town, but he was never away from London for more than three weeks consecutively—he wanted to be back for the Court of Criminal Appeal and the Divisional Court.

"I know he loved going on Circuit—he always told me he did—for personal reasons as well as because he considered it his duty as Chief. But it was not done 'as of right'. That was not his way of doing things. He always asked the other judges if they minded his going. At the Judges' Meeting on 1 October, when the Circuits were chosen, he would always start by saying, 'I would like to do X, Y and Z—would you please bear that in mind."

With Rayner Goddard, swiftness in court was as much a natural reflection of his instinctive way of doing things as a conscious desire to speed the processes of justice. An anonymous profiler, writing in the *Observer* newspaper in July 1952, gave a vivid picture of the Lord Chief Justice in full throttle: "He is short, powerfully built, and the impression that he gives as he comes in—of a man in a towering hurry—is confirmed by the day's proceedings. He stands no nonsense. To one barrister he says, 'This appeal is of an impudent nature.' To another, 'What I might call—the usual defence.' To a third, 'This is quite an idle application.' To a fourth, 'I don't know whether you are trying to wring my withers', a task that one gathers might be difficult."

After Mr Justice Humphreys's retirement, Rayner's old friend Mr Justice Cassels used frequently to sit as his senior colleague on his right-hand side in the Court of Criminal Appeal. He often used to say, "I'd better hurry otherwise Rayner will have given judgment in the first case before I get into court!"

Rayner was adored by his judges: there can be no doubt of that. "It was the most 'direct running of the Division you could get," says Peter Stephenson. "If an emergency occurred on Circuit, he would say to his clerk or the Clerk of the Lists: 'Who can we afford to release from London?' He himself would approach a judge and say, 'Do you mind?' There was no half-hearted approach, he was always most direct—and thoughtful.

"For instance, it had always been the custom for all judges to meet on the first day of each Term except for the Whitsun Term. Before, no one told absent judges what had happened. From the day he took office, he caused minutes to be circulated so that everyone was kept in the picture.

"He was always available to his judges and a great many members of the Bar as well, even on personal matters. I know that, in my own case, when my father died some four years after he took office, he virtually took the place of my father with his advice and his concern over my welfare. On one occasion, he was written to by a lady member of the Bar: her letter said she would like to go out on Circuit as a judge's marshal. It was unheard of, and there was no chance in those days of it being possible; and certainly Lord Goddard, with his views on such matters, would never have approved. But he saw her—very fatherly, kind and gentle but definite: 'No, it wouldn't do, my dear!'"

This extreme approachability is confirmed by Sir Fred Pritchard, a retired High Court judge: "To have been a judge of the King's Bench division during the time when Lord Goddard was Lord Chief is perhaps the greatest privilege which any member of the legal profession can have enjoyed.

"He insisted always that his relations to the members of his team was that of *primus inter pares,* and he lived up to this principle in every way. For instance, if he wanted to talk to you on any topic he never sent a message requesting your presence in his room. Instead he would drop in quite casually into your room, and after the preliminary inquiry 'Have you got a minute?' tell you what it was he wanted to say."

But although a quick judge and a strong judge, Rayner did not impose his views on his brethren. "Anyone sitting with him noticed how quick he was," says the late Lord Parker. "But he was always willing to eat his words. That was an essential characteristic of Rayner. I remember once I was sitting with him as the junior judge of the three, on his left-hand side. He had early on formed a very definite view of the case, and counsel was battling on to try and make his arguments prevail. I quite frankly talked too much, and by my interventions endeavoured to assist counsel in his task.

"After lunch, I promised Rayner to stop it and not talk too much. 'Hubert, I think I'm beginning to see the point,' he replied. 'Speak a bit more.'

"Later, during the course of the afternoon, he turned to me and said, 'I'm quite convinced now. You give the judgment!'"

Independence was a quality he allowed others as well as himself. Sir Fred Pritchard relates, "It was the custom for one member of the Court in the first instance to consider applications for leave to appeal before the full Court sat which had been constituted to deal with the current list. When I did this work I used to act on the principle that I would refuse leave to appeal against sentence except when I formed the view that the sentence was excessive and ought to be reduced. In the determined drive which he made to conquer the crime wave after the War, the Lord Chief Justice took a different view of the way in which the Court should discharge its functions, and he was known on occasions to advocate the granting of an application for leave to appeal when he considered that the sentence under review was not sufficiently severe in order that the full Court might consider increasing it.

"On one occasion in my room I was dealing as the single judge with a number of applications which included an application for leave against sentence by a man whom I shall call 'X'. It was a bad case, and I formed the view that 'X' had been lucky to receive only the sentence which had been imposed; and accordingly I marked the application 'Leave refused' and initialled this 'decision'.

"I was proceeding to deal with further applications when a knock on my door announced that I had a visitor in the person of Lord Goddard. After a short talk during which he ascertained the nature of the work on which I was engaged, he said, 'Have you dealt with the case of 'X' yet?' I said I had, and added that I thought he had been lucky and that his application ought to be refused. The Lord Chief Justice said that he took the view that it was such a bad case he would have been minded to give leave to appeal and then revised the sentence in order to make a closer fit between the punishment and the crime.

"I told him that this was not in accordance with the principle on which I normally worked, and was adding in deference to his greater experience and responsibility, 'but if you think so I will look at it again'—but he interrupted rather abruptly, saying 'No. You have already dealt with this case and your decision must stand.'"

It was not only his fellow-judges whose independent views and personal ability Lord Goddard respected. The same trait was reflected in his attitude to the barristers who appeared in front of him. "He never resented people standing up to him," says Sir Joseph Molony, Q.C. "'Oh, did I, did I?' he would say if you presented some previous judgment of his in which he was saying the opposite of what he was saying now. 'Oh, I was wrong then!' But he was always prepared to say he made a howler in the past or was making one now."

Lord Justice Cairns relates one case of his own as counsel in the Divisional Court arguing before Lord Goddard, Mr Justice Byrne and Mr Justice (now Lord) Devlin: "Faced with an earlier decision of a Divisional Court, including two of them, and realizing they had been wrong, he turned to Byrne and said, 'You were as much to blame for that hash—you'd better give the first judgment here.' But, of course, he gave the first judgment himself and freely admitted that they had been wrong in the earlier case."

"I appeared before him on many occasions as a junior counsel, as a silk and later as Attorney-General," says Lord Dilhorne. "He was a very good judge. He would take a view and leave you in no doubt as to his view. But if you argued with him and you were persistent, there was always a chance you could persuade him to change his mind—but never more than once!

"I don't think Rayner changed very much in all the years I knew him on the Bench. He always seemed the same to me. He did not suffer fools particularly gladly—but then why should one? He was always kind to a young man who he thought was doing his best, but he could be pretty tough with an older man who he thought was wasting time and could do better."

The late Lord Parker confirms this picture: "I appeared frequent-

ly before him in the Divisional Court when I was Treasury 'devil'.
You had to know his idiosyncracies and understand him. He did not
suffer fools gladly. He would listen carefully to what you had to
say—provided it was not verbose."

Rayner could not abide long-windedness—as was, indeed,
manifest in his conduct of the Laski libel case and his attitude to
Professor Laski in the witness-box (see Chapter Twelve). And he
generally did not mind how he showed his abhorrence: Sir Anthony
Highmore King, retired Crown Office Master and Registrar of the
Court of Criminal Appeal, recounts one incident. "I went to see him
one Friday about something, and when he had finished he pointed
to a pile of Criminal Appeal papers, and said, 'Look at that lot
you've sent me for the weekend. Is there anything in them?' I said I
didn't think there was, and he picked up a particularly fat bundle
and asked, 'What about that one?' I replied, 'Never heard such balls
in my life.' He cocked an eye at me, and I said, 'Oh! I've judicial
authority for that phrase.' 'No! Whose?' 'Yours.' 'Never!' 'Yes, indeed.' One day X.Y. [there is no point in giving the name of this
elderly, loquacious and now long since dead barrister] had been
going on the whole morning, and when you rose at one you said to
your junior as you passed him, 'I never heard such balls in my life!'
'Did I?' said the old man with a look of horror. He never seemed to
realize that his *sotto voce* remarks could rattle round the Court."

But did he really not realize it? Mr Fell, his Associate, remembers
an occasion when Rayner found himself saddled in the Divisional
Court with a comparatively new judge sitting as his junior on his
left-hand side. He soon proved remarkably wordy. "Instead of
being content with saying simply, 'I agree' when the Chief had given
the leading judgment as the No. 2 judge was, this junior would go
on and on. Finally, the Chief, realizing that he was stuck with this
fellow for about a fortnight, got a bit tired of it and leaned over and
said in a stage-whisper that I, and am sure many people in court
could hear, 'You know, you don't have to say something *every*
time!'"

Says the late Lord Parker: "He has been criticized as being too
quick, making up his mind at an early stage, not listening to what
counsel had to say. He *was* very quick. But by contrast he was
patient, courteous and helpful to the young. I used jokingly to say to
him, 'If I have a poor case, I'll send over the youngest man in my
chambers. I know he'll get a patient hearing whereas I might be out
in the corridor in five minutes.'"

I can myself bear witness to this: in 1955, aged twenty-six, with only four years' experience at the Bar, I was appearing for a woman estate agent in an appeal to the Divisional Court brought by a police superintendent against the Bow Street magistrate's dismissal of a summons alleging she had knowingly let premises in Mayfair for use as a brothel. The upper part of a house in Curzon Street was divided into two separate flats, each let—and there was no dispute about this—to a prostitute who plied her trade there. But the two flats were not self-contained: the one shared a kitchen with the other, and it was well-established law from Victorian times that "premises cannot be regarded as a brothel if they are only used by one woman". So the question was: What were the "premises" let by the estate agent—the whole upper part or the two individual flats? The Bow Street magistrate decided, after inspecting the building, that the "premises" were the individual flats: only one prostitute was using those premises, so the charge must fail. The police superintendent appealed.

Counsel for the appellant, a highly experienced practitioner and now a distinguished Lord Justice of Appeal, argued with considerable force and authority. As counsel for the woman estate agent, inexperienced and nervous, arguing my first major case before the Lord Chief Justice, I did my best to contend with both my opponent and the Court. At one point, somewhat fazed by a quite proper intervention from my opponent, I lost my place in a Law Report: "Page 608", said Lord Goddard with a gruff smile. In the end of the Court veered from allowing the appeal to dismissing it: "There was no evidence as to the nature of the joint user of the kitchen?" the Chief asked counsel for the appellant—pinning the vital point that ruined his case.

Sir Peter Rawlinson, Q.C., M.P., former Chairman of the Bar and a former Attorney-General, has a somewhat similar tale to tell: 'I loved the old man! I am partial, of course, and mainly I suppose due to the fact that once, as a young man, he was knocking me about on a legal aid appeal in the CCA and I got rather cross and told him the Single Judge had certified there was a point of law which should be argued and I intended to argue it. At the end he leant down to the Registrar and said audibly, 'Double this young man's fee!' So, of course, I loved him!"

"He was a very kind man, very anxious to give a young man at the Bar a chance," says Mr Fell. "One young man was doing very well in front of him, but was being harassed by a very experienced counsel, who was 'playing rank' rather and doing everthing he could to unnerve the youngster. But he stuck to his guns and got the decision.

After pronouncing judgment in his favour, Lord Goddard handed down to me a note which I read and handed to the usher to pass on to the young man. I saw him open it. It read, 'Congratulations. You did very well!' The young man blushed to his roots and started to rise to his feet. I knew he wanted to say how grateful he was, but I motioned him down with my hand: I knew that was the last thing Lord Goddard would have wanted."

Mr Eric Crowther, a Metropolitan stipendiary magistrate, tells of his first appearance before Rayner over twenty years ago, not long after he was called to the Bar: "I was briefed to appear at the City of London Quarter Sessions to defend a lad of seventeen who had pleaded guilty before the Alderman at the Mansion House to being in possession of an offensive weapon, a sock filled with sand. The defendant had one previous conviction, for stealing a glove by finding when he was nine, and the Alderman, in view of his "character and antecedents" had committed him in custody to the Quarter Sessions for sentence, with a view to Borstal Training.

"The boy lived with and supported his widowed mother, was in work and his employer spoke well of him. He lived in a big block of council flats in the East End, and the caretaker of the whole estate and several neighbours were prepared to come to court to say what a kind and helpful boy he was, especially in running errands for old people, lighting their fires, etc.

"Unfortunately, in those early days at the Bar I did not know where the City of London Quarter Sessions were held, and my then Clerk, who was more used to civil work, assured me that the solicitors had made a mistake and really intended the *County* of London Sessions, which in those post-War days were held in what had formerly been Marylebone Swimming Baths, to which I repaired. The case was not listed in any of the four courts sitting there, and I returned, worried and puzzled, to Chambers, only to learn that the City of London Quarter Sessions in fact sat four times a year at the Old Bailey, that my client had appeared there that morning, had said nothing and had not called any of the witnesses who were there to speak on his behalf (he having expected me to rise from among the serried ranks of bewigged before him to conduct his defence) and had been sent to Borstal by the Recorder of London, Sir Gerald Dodson.

"By the time this news reached me the Court had risen, and I regarded the Recorder as *functus officio,* so I set off for Wormwood Scrubs Prison where I found my client, very forlorn and depressed in the wing set aside for boys awaiting allocation to Borstal institutions. I told him what had happened, advised that his only possible remedy now lay in appeal to the Court of Criminal Appeal, obtained the requisite forms from the prison staff and set about helping him to draft the notice of appeal.

"Under 'Grounds of Appeal', I wrote: 'My counsel went to the wrong court and in consequence no mitigation was advanced on my behalf and none of the character witnesses who attended court to speak for me was called', and I got him to sign it.

"Weeks passed before the case was listed to come on before a court presided over by the Lord Chief Justice, with Hilbery, J. and Hallett, J. as the other members. My friends at the Bar advised me that this was not the ideal tribunal for my purpose." (As any practitioner who remembers those two other quite frightening 'Old School' judges will readily agree.) "I saw two convicted murderers' appeals disposed of somewhat, as it seemed to me, summarily, and the dejected appellants led away towards their deaths. I wondered what was going to happen to me. In my mind's eye I could already see the evening paper's banner headline: 'Barrister went to wrong court. Disgraceful, says L.C.J.' and, next morning: 'Barrister Disbarred.'

"At about ten past four my case, the thirty-seventh in a list of forty, was called on, and I rose weakly to my feet for the first time in that enormous courtroom, 'May it please your Lordships, I appear—.' 'Wait a minute,' said Goddard gruffly, 'we haven't read your notice of appeal yet. You want us to read that, I suppose?'

"'I'm not sure,' I murmured.

"He studied it, and so did the other two, and he conferred briefly with his brethren, talking with his hand in front of his mouth.

"'Mr Crowther,' he said eventually.

"'My Lord,' I replied, waiting for the worst.

"'You don't want to say too much about this case, I should imagine.'

"'Not if it can be helped, my Lord.'

"'I didn't think you would. This young man's been punished far too much already. He'll be put on probation for two years.'"

My Crowther comments today, "This is my answer to those who say that Lord Goddard was unkind to young barristers. He had a wonderful opportunity so to be if he had wished, but instead he did everything he could to save me from embarrassment for my mistake. Moreover, the offence was one of a kind that he was supposed to detest—potential violence by a youngster. Yet he could set all that aside because he felt that this particular young man had been unjustly treated."

This then is the Lord Chief Justice of England whom we are going to see in action in closer detail in the further chapters of this book.

11 Two Important Murders

Rayner Goddard came to the office of Lord Chief Justice in a post-War situation when much of the idealism of the struggle had gone, but there remained many of the wartime restrictions on personal freedom and on freedom of acquisition. These are circumstances when at least two of his "age-old causes of crime"—greed and the desire for easy money—had full play in the corruption of the black market, and these often gave release to the passion, lust and cruelty which always wait in attendance on man's baser motives. It was a black-market setting that dominated the crime which was the occasion for Rayner's first important judgment as Lord Chief Justice, and it is still regarded as the classic statement of the law on the subject of separate trials for co-accused. The case became known as the "Russian Robert Murder".

Russian Robert was a black marketeer whose dead body was found on the morning of 1 November 1945 shot through the head in his car in Chepstow Place, North Kensington. Two Poles—recent Army deserters who had previously had distinguished war records—were charged with the murder. One of them, 32-year-old Marian Grondkowski, had in his possession all the personal property and most of the money that Russian Robert had been carrying when he died—he was due to meet and pay for a consignment of stolen Scotch whisky. Furthermore, Grondkowski's clothes bore traces of blood, his trousers had a specially made pocket for the murder weapon, a .32 revolver, and his fingerprints matched bloody prints found on the steering-wheel of the murdered man's car.

But Grondkowski denied the murder, saying, 'I tell you

everything . . . I no shoot Robert. Malinowski shoot him. He always carry a gun.'' The person so charmingly betrayed was Grondkowski's 'friend' and associate, Henryk Malinowski, a good-looking 24-year-old. Grondkowski was only too happy to tell the police the address where they could find his ex-wartime comrade. He was duly arrested—and, perhaps not unexpectedly, said, "I was there, but I do not shoot. Grondkowski kill him." The spectacle of thieves falling out is almost as ancient as crime itself.

Both men individually described the night of the murder. They had met Russian Robert at Edgware Road tube station at 11.10 p.m. The Poles were both hard up, and the Russian had stood them several large Scotches each at a club near Marble Arch. Later they had called at Grondkowski's former flat and he had gone upstairs. When he came down Robert tried to start his car but the battery was flat. The two Poles got out to push while Robert stayed at the wheel. They got the car going and jumped in while it was moving—one in the front passenger seat and the other at the rear. After they had gone some distance the man in the back seat shot Russian Robert through the head from behind, and as the driver collapsed on to the steering wheel the killer leaned over him to grab the wheel, and yelled to his companion to pull on the handbrake. The car juddered and stalled in silent Chepstow Place. The killer pulled Russian Robert out of the driving seat and bundled him into the back, rifling his body and pockets of jewellery and cash, including a wallet containing £150. He then sat in the driving seat, took the wheel with bloodstained hands and—the battery still not working—told the other man to get out and push. Between them they could not start the car, and they abandoned it with Russian Robert's body sprawled on the back seat.

This was an entirely credible story, and it was repeated under separate interrogation in almost exact detail by both men. But when Grondkowski told the tale he said he had been the man in the front seat and Malinowski was the killer. When Malinowski made his statement he reversed the roles and said he had been the man sitting in front with Grondkowski, sitting in the back, as the killer.

As the police pursued their inquiries it seemed rather more likely that Malinowski, the younger of the two, was perhaps the one telling the truth. It was quite clear that he had known 'Russian Robert' considerably better than the older man: he had been his associate in various previous shady deals. So would it not be more probable that he would sit in front? Admittedly, the murder weapon was found in his suitcase, but he explained that by saying that, after the killing, he had prevailed upon Grondkowski to hand it over to him as a token of their mutual good faith. "I said to him, 'Do you trust me?' and he said, 'Yes', and I then said, 'Then give me the pistol', and he shook hands with me and say, 'We are friends', and he give me the pistol."

The case between the two men was very finely balanced, the jury could well believe either as to the actual facts of the shooting itself—but one thing was undisputed; whoever fired the fatal shot, both had shared in the booty. Cash that could only have come from the dead man was found in *both* the accused men's possession.

Malinowski was defended upon his trial at the Old Bailey by the late J. D. Casswell, K.C., and Victor Durand (later also a silk), with Grondkowski represented by Melford Stevenson, K.C. (later Mr Justice Melford Stevenson), and Lewis Langdon. Wrote Casswell later in his Memoirs[1]: "Undoubtedly if the two men were to be tried side by side this feeling of 'two rogues together' would be so strong that the prejudice against both would almost certainly condemn both to the gallows. Malinowski's only hope, slender as it was, of an acquittal hinged largely upon whether I could persuade the trial judge to order separate trials."

The trial judge turned out to be Mr Justice Croom-Johnson. "At 10.30 on the morning of Monday, February 11, 1946, Marian Grondkowski and Henryk Malinowski entered the dock in No. 1 Court at the Old Bailey . . . Before they were asked to plead to the charge I rose to my feet and told the judge that I was applying for them to be tried separately. The terse reply of Croom-Johnson was far from encouraging: 'I remember my powers', he snapped." Undeterred, Casswell went on to point out that an essential part of each prisoner's defence amounted to an attack on his co-prisoner, and in those circumstances there was, in his submission, abundant authority to say that the interest of justice required separate trials. The defence of each would be greatly embarrassed if they were tried together.

Melford Stevenson, understandably, supported Casswell's application for separate trials—but Anthony Hawke (later knighted and Recorder of London), who appeared with Henry Elam (later a Circuit Judge at Inner London Crown Court), for the prosecution, equally understandably, rigorously opposed it. In the result Mr Justice Croom-Johnson dismissed the application. "I have no doubt the situation between these two men will plainly develop itself," he

---

[1] *A Lance for Liberty,* by J. D. Casswell, Q.C. (Harrap, 1961).

said tersely, "and I have no doubt that if I fail to make it plain to the jury I shall be corrected elsewhere."

'Elsewhere' meant, of course, the Court of Criminal Appeal, and it was to there, on 18 March 1946, that the case was brought after the almost inevitable conviction of the two accused. The principal ground of appeal was Croom-Johnson's failure to grant separate trials. "The joint trial in this case constituted a miscarriage of justice," Casswell uncompromisingly told a Court consisting of the new Lord Chief Justice, Mr Justice Hilbery and Mr Justice Sellers. "Separate trials should have been ordered, as it was plain from the outset that an essential part of the defence of the appellant Malinowski constituted an attack on his co-prisoner."

For once, Rayner did not rush through the proceedings. The argument by all three leading counsel took the better part of a day. Then the three judges conferred in *sotto voce* discussion on the Bench, and eventually Rayner announced, "The appeals by both men will be dismissed, but as important issues have been raised the Court will give their reasons in writing at a later date." At that early stage in his career as Chief, he was taking no chances.

A week later everyone—including the two Poles sitting uncomprehendingly in the green-curtained dock—repaired again to the Lord Chief Justice's Court to hear Rayner read one of his few written judgments in the Court of Criminal Appeal. It is still cited today in criminal courts up and down the land, and is the standard authority on the subject.[2] There could be no doubt about the new Chief's legal erudition: he refers to several old cases in the course of the judgment that counsel had not even mentioned during the argument—a somewhat unusual circumstance.

Rayner began by stating the law in terms that in some respects were a prophetic forerunner of his later pronouncements in the case of Craig and Bentley (see Chapter 17). "Each prisoner sought to put the blame for the actual shooting on the other, and each denied that he intended to offer violence or even to rob. There was ample evidence from which the jury could infer a common intention to rob and to use such violence or other means as was necessary to effect that purpose. Which of the two actually fired the fatal shot was therefore immaterial. . . ."

As to the issue of separate trials, Rayner laid down the law as follows: "*Prime facie* it appears to the Court that, where the essence

---

[2] The judgement in *Rex.* v. *Grondkowski and Malinowski* is reported in Criminal Appeal Reports (Vol. 31) at page 116.

of the case is that the prisoners were engaged on a common enterprise, it is obviously right and proper that they should be jointly indicted and jointly tried, and in some cases it would be as much in
the interest of the accused persons as of the prosecution that they
should be. . . .

"But it is said that there is now a rule of law that, where it appears
that the essential part, or an essential part, of one prisoner's defence
is or amounts to an attack upon another prisoner, a separate trial
should take place." That had been argued by Casswell as being the
effect of a decision by Lord Hewart in a 1940 case, but Rayner would
have none of it—"In our opinion, that case is not to be read as
laying it down that, wherever it appears that one prisoner is going to
lay the blame on the other, or another, there must be separate trials.
The law is, and always has been, that this is a matter of discretion for
the judge at the trial. . . .

"The discretion, no doubt, must be exercised judicially, that is,
not capriciously. The judge must consider the interests of justice as
well as the interests of the prisoners. It is too often nowadays
thought, or seems to be thought, that 'the interests of justice' means
only the 'interests of the prisoners'. If once it were taken as settled
that every time it appears that one prisoner as part of his defence
means to attack another, a separate trial must be ordered, it is obvious there is no room for discretion and a rule of law is substituted
for it. There is no case in which this has ever been laid down, and in
the opinion of the Court it would be most unfortunate and contrary
to the true interests of justice if it were."

These were grim and forceful words, and Rayner ended, "The real
test, after all, which must be applied by a Court of Criminal Appeal
on a matter which is essentially one of discretion is, has the exercise
of the discretion resulted in a miscarriage of justice. . . . In this case
we are satisfied that there has been no miscarriage, and this ground
of appeal therefore fails." The two Poles, in law equally guilty of the
murder of their erstwhile black-market associate, were led off back
to their condemned cells to await the scaffold. Eight days later, on 2
April 1946, at Wandsworth Prison, they were hanged.

"I had no doubt that the prisoner was insane. . . ." said Lord
Chief Justice Goddard to the Royal Commission on Capital
Punishment.

"You would not have thought it proper that he should hang?"
asked Dr Eliot Slater, a member of the Commission.

"I should have thought it very proper that he should have been hanged," affirmed the Lord Chief Justice.

"Even though he was insane, and presumably, from the ecclesiastical point of view, not in a fit state to make his peace with God?"

"He could make his peace with God, I think, quite well. I do not know what his religion was, but the only reason he committed the murder was because he mistakenly believed that the man had committed adultery with his mistress. . . ."

"I think the medical point of view", said Dr Slater, "would be that the disease had altered his personality so as to make such wickedness possible."

"If that is the medical point of view", said Rayner with Johnsonian finality, "I am afraid, frankly, that it does not appeal to me at all. If that is the case I think it is one of the reasons why he should have been put out of the way."

These stark words sharpened the die which stamped the reputation of Lord Chief Justice Goddard as a hard judge. Immediately he came into office he had stressed that his answer to the violence of post-War crime lay in heavy sentences. Within three weeks he had announced, in the case of Harry John McBain, the man who pulled the trigger on two policemen chasing him after his raid on an Earl's Court flat, "The time has certainly come in the state of crime in this country now when sentences must be severe."

Having established that standpoint, Rayner Goddard went on to pursue the campaigns buttressing capital punishment and corporal punishment which are separately considered in this work. And in the midst of these long battles he made plain an attitude to certain types of insane criminals which was widely regarded as more primitively Mosaic even than the not markedly liberal approach of the ancient English law-makers; for the Royal Commission cited weighty authority from Coke to Blackstone when declaring "it is contrary to the Common Law to execute an insane criminal". This was one respect in which Rayner failed to see eye to eye with his beloved Common Law of England.

The case which the Lord Chief Justice was referring to as justification to put a paranoiac 'out of the way' was the trial of Thomas John Ley for what was known as the Chalk-Pit Murder. It was held at the Central Criminal Court before him in March 1947. There was a second defendant, Lawrence John Smith, whose fate was decided by the decision on the principal prisoner, Ley.

The motive of the murder is timeless, a tale of jealousy as deep as

Othello's. Yet it is curiously crystallized by its period setting of London immediately after the War: the Brompton Road, where even by walking to Harrods you could never be sure to get a taxi in those days of shortage; Beaufort Gardens, where the murder was committed—a square of tall houses all being feverishly and shoddily converted into flats after wartime dereliction; the Crown and Sceptre pub almost opposite, where over pints of beer a half-baked plot was agreed by a jobbing carpenter and an ex-pugilist running a car-hire firm; and an apartment house in Wimbledon, where the First Murderer wrongly suspected his ex-mistress of having what he called "high jinks" with an innocent barman from the Dog and Fox on the corner.

The tale of detection began with that fresh-faced barman, Jack Mudie, being found dead, trussed and strangled, in an inexpertly dug hollow in a chalk pit at Woldingham, between Biggin Hill and Caterham. Jack Mudie in life had been a pleasant, quiet man. His landlady, who had mothered him a little, remembered him for his blue eyes and the resemblance she saw in him to Bing Crosby. Jack Mudie in death was wearing his chalk-stripe demob suit with the waistcoat heaved up to the top of his chest. His overcoat, inside out, was tied round his head. His clothes were streaked and streaming with the chalky clay of a two-day rainstorm, but the soles of his shoes, which projected into the air out of the hollow, were clean of any sludge. He had not walked to that grave.

Inside his jacket Mudie's clumsy murderers had left a visiting card bearing his full name. His address was soon traced—he had recently begun a new job as barman at the Reigate Hill Hotel. In his room at the hotel the police found letters from Thomas Ley giving the address of 5 Beaufort Gardens, Brompton Road. A pickaxe by the body, evidently abandoned after a swift attempt to deepen the grave, was traced to 5 Beaufort Gardens, where Ley was having his house converted into flats. A brown-stained green rag which gagged Mudie's mouth was matched with more green rag at 5 Beaufort Gardens, where it had been used for french-polishing. Two Surrey landscape gardeners, as soon as they heard of the murder, reported to the police that three days previously—that is, on the day before the murder, as the pathologists deduced from the state of the body—they had seen a car inside the chalk-pit entrance, and a man prospecting the pit. The man seemed to panic when he saw them, ran to the car, had great difficulty in starting it, but finally drove away in the dusk. Both gardeners remembered the figures of the registration number as 101, though they could not recall the letters.

Lawrence Smith, a joiner employed as foreman builder in the conversion of 5 Beaufort Gardens, was found to have hired a Ford car, index FGP 101, from a firm in Beauchamp Place, one street west of Beaufort Gardens. And in a later identity parade one of the gardeners picked out Smith as the driver. In the meantime John William Buckingham, the 'third man' who had conspired with Smith at the Crown and Sceptre, voluntarily reported to the police on hearing of the murder, because he had not known that that was what he had been mixed up in. The police took statements from Ley, Smith and Buckingham, and eventually charged them with the murder of John McNair Mudie. Buckingham turned King's Evidence, and Ley and Smith were taken into the dock at the Old Bailey on 19 March 1947 for trial before the Lord Chief Justice and a jury.

Counsel for the Crown were Anthony Hawke (later Sir Anthony, Recorder of London) and Henry Elam. For Ley, Sir Walter Monckton, K.C., led Phineas Quass (later himself a Q.C.) and Gerald (later Mr Justice) Howard. For Smith, Derek Curtis-Bennett, K.C., led Malcolm Morris (later also a silk).

The task of the defence counsel was near-hopeless. The best they could do was to suggest that it was a case of manslaughter or suicide, or even an accidental nudge by an extraneous house-breaker who, not entirely fortuitously, turned up in the witness-box. The story of the murder was intensely bizarre. Its execution was madly incompetent. Its detection was certain. The only faint doubt centred on whether the First Murderer could bluff or buy his way out.

The Hon. Thomas Ley was sixty-six years old, reasonably rich, and he bore the half-title because he had been Minister of Justice in New South Wales for half a dozen years in the 1920s. He had emigrated from England to Australia at the age of eight, and began his prosperous career by selling newspapers on the streets. He graduated as partner in a firm of Sydney solicitors and then entered politics and share-pushing. He was a Minister by the age of forty-two, but after scandals and disappointments he left Australia for England in 1929. One year later he brought over Mrs Maggie Brook, who had been his mistress ever since he entered Government in Sydney. For the next sixteen years until the murder of John Mudie he lived mainly with her, supporting his wife successively in English hotels and in Australia. Ley developed into an abnormally obese man. Mrs Brook was exactly his age, sixty-six at the time of the trial, and both she and Ley averred that they had had no sexual relations for the last dozen years. But Ley had certainly maintained a sexual *relationship*. It was his crazed sexual jealousy regarding Mrs Brook that alone prompted the murder.

In June 1946 Mrs Brook went temporarily to an apartment house at 3 Homefield Road, Wimbledon, to look after the flat belonging to her daughter and son-in-law, Mr and Mrs Arthur Barron, while her daughter was in hospital. Two other men with flats, or serviced bed-sitters, in this house were Mr Arthur Romer and Mr John Mudie. A few days after Mrs Brook had taken up residence in the flat, Ley called at the house. But he did not ring at Mrs Brook's bell. He went upstairs and listened outside the door. He said in evidence at the Old Bailey that he heard the voices of Mrs Brook and of a man she was calling "Arthur", and Ley said that he deduced that the two people were having sexual intercourse. He repeated in detail the intimacies which he claimed he had overheard.

He immediately suspected that the man was Arthur Romer, the resident in another flat. Later he contrived a meeting with Arthur Romer, was doubtful about the identification, and decided that Mrs Brook was having intercourse with her son-in-law Arthur Barron. He tried to inveigle Arthur Barron to his house in Beaufort Gardens, but Barron would not come. Ley said in court, "I tried to get him along under conditions when he would listen to me, talk and give information." "You may possibly think that it was lucky for Arthur Barron that he was not induced to go along to Beaufort Gardens," Rayner later commented to the jury in his summing up. When Ley could not confront Barron, although he did not entirely rid his mind of suspicions regarding Arthur Romer and Barron, he switched to a strong belief that Jack Mudie—who was some thirty years old—was having an affair with Mrs Brook. He coarsely voiced this suspicion as he quizzed the resident landlady of the Wimbledon flats. "Oh, they had high jinks at the flat upstairs," he said, "and of course she couldn't keep the pace." It must be emphasized that Mrs Brook, who physically conceded all of her sixty-six years, unhesitatingly denied any liaison with anyone. Indeed, she did not know Arthur Romer at all, and had met Jack Mudie only once, being introduced on the staircase by their landlady.

Ley learned from the landlady that Mudie had changed his job, his ambition promoting him from the Dog and Fox to the Reigate Hill Hotel, with the object of getting enough experience to take over his own licensed house. Ley suspected that Mrs Brook was not only having an affair with Mudie, but was about to subsidize him in setting up his own business. Ley instructed his solicitor to initiate a fiendishly intricate manoeuvre—sending irrelevant cheques to

Mudie, who did not know him, to pass on to Mrs Brook for signature as a co-director of one of his businesses. Ley's object was, if Mudie did pass over the cheques, to convince himself that Mudie and Mrs Brook had some sort of understanding or intimacy. Mudie, however, had no idea what to do with the cheques, and they were returned to the solicitor. Ley then went down to Reigate to interview Mudie on a fabricated excuse: this was the first time he met him. From that date onward, 7 August 1946, Ley was determined to murder Mudie. The operation took nearly four months.

Ley asked a hotel porter in Bloomsbury if he knew "a man with a car who could look after himself and keep his mouth shut". He said that such a man "could earn a year's salary in a matter of weeks". The porter introduced Buckingham, whose hire-car company was used by the hotel, and he was 'dropped' £10 for the introduction. Meanwhile Ley began with some frequency to take out to dinner at the Normandy Grill, Knightsbridge, the joiner Lawrence Smith, who was working at 5 Beaufort Gardens in charge of the flat conversions. Smith was eventually found guilty of the complete conspiracy and act of murder, so the extent of his prior knowledge may be deduced. Buckingham may have known less. He told the police that he understood that Ley, as a solicitor, was anxious to confront a blackmailer who was extorting money from two woman clients—a girl whom the blackmailer had seduced and the mother of the girl. The blackmailer was named as Mudie, and the problem was how to get him to 5 Beaufort Gardens.

Buckingham's fee was to be £200. He first suggested that he should go to the Reigate Hill Hotel with his son, that he should pretend to be drunk, that the son should ask Mudie's help in getting his father back into the car, and that once outside the two Buckinghams should overpower Mudie and drive off with him. Buckingham and Smith blithely set off to do this, but as they emerged from the Crown and Sceptre in Brompton Road, where they had been planning their coup, they found that Buckingham's car had been stolen. Next day they mentioned the failure to Ley. Ley, whatever fantasy world he was inhabiting, still had sufficient criminal realism to veto a dangerously crude kidnapping, if not to vet more thoroughly the final murder. He rejected this plan. Eventually it was arranged that a woman friend of Buckingham's should scrape an acquaintance with Mudie, and should then invite him to use his one night off in the week to make some extra money by running the cocktail bar at a private party she was giving. This was done. The woman said she would come with a chauffeur to pick him up and take him to Lon-

don. Mudie agreed, and the date was fixed: Thursday, 28
November. The murder had been arranged.

On 27 November Smith prospected the chalk pit at Woldingham
as a place in which to dump the body. On the next evening Smith
and Buckingham drove to Reigate in the 8 h.p. Ford FGP 101 which
Smith, using Ley's money, had hired for the week. Buckingham's
son, in chauffeur's uniform, and Buckingham's woman friend drove
down in another car, picked up Mudie and returned to London,
shadowed by Smith and Buckingham until the last few miles, when
the Ford went ahead.

Smith and Buckingham went into 5 Beaufort Gardens. They
alerted Ley, who had been waiting in his own flat there, and the
three men moved down to the basement which Ley used as offices.
But Ley then moved away, up a few stairs. The second car arrived.
Mudie had the back door opened for him, then the woman and
Buckingham junior made an excuse, slammed the door with Mudie
inside, and went across to the Crown and Sceptre for a drink. As
Mudie passed an angle in the corridor Smith caught hold of him
and pinned his arms. Buckingham threw a carpet over Mudie's
head. Mudie, caught entirely unawares, struggled violently and
yelled, "You are stifling me!" Buckingham said, "You are breathing
your last."

Smith tied Mudie tightly, as he was held in the dark of the basement, from the ankles to the trunk with rope he had previously
bought. Smith and Buckingham 'jumped' Mudie—propelling him
in a series of hops which ended when Buckingham fell heavily on
Mudie—into an office of Ley's, and they sat him in a swivel chair
opposite a desk. Between them Smith and Buckingham found cloth
for a gag from rags that had been used for french-polishing, and
stuffed Mudie's mouth, tying the rag at the back of the neck. Ley
dismissed Buckingham, giving him a package containing £200,
and Buckingham joined his son and the woman in the Crown and
Sceptre, after which they went on a long pub crawl. Smith and Ley
were left in the house with Mudie.

At some time within the next hour John Mudie was killed through
being asphyxiated by the constriction of a rope being tightened
round his neck, and sustained upward pressure being exerted. That
is, he was strangled while his trunk was in a hanging position, a
form of death demanding some minutes to complete, rather than
the instantaneous severance of the spinal column effected in a
judicial hanging. No innocent man ever died more cruelly than this
bewildered, bright young barman in the demob suit he had put on

to start a new career in private catering. The body was taken to the chalk pit that night. Smith went home with a packet of two hundred £1 notes. Six days later, Ley paid him a cheque for £300, but Smith returned it ten days before Scotland Yard invited him to make a full statement. Buckingham had gone to the police as soon as he heard that he had taken part in a murder, and not a blackmail confrontation. Smith and Ley were not charged until 28 December, exactly one month after the murder, although they had been interviewed, and remained under supervision, for a fortnight beforehand.

Dr (later Professor) Keith Simpson, the pathologist, was called by Sir Walter Monckton to give evidence for the prisoner Ley, in a somewhat bizarre attempt to persuade the jury that Mudie had committed suicide. He said that he deduced from his examination of Mudie's body that death was due to asphyxia by suspension, but there was nothing to indicate whether it was accidental, suicidal or wilful strangulation.

Rayner was astonished. "But this body was lying in a trench in a chalk pit?" he interjected.

"Yes, my Lord," said Keith Simpson. "I am describing the conclusions I draw from this mark [on the neck]. One could *imagine* a great deal, but there was nothing to show. [The body] had been lifted in some way at the side of the neck, but *how* there was nothing to show."

The Lord Chief Justice pressed the witness strongly to get an opinion on whether Mudie had been unconscious before his death, and whether he had suffered any appreciable physical violence before death—a matter on which Dr Simpson differed from the Crown's pathologist, who had conducted the autopsy while he had a watching brief. The importance of this point was that, if violence or unconsciousness before death could be proved, the possibility of Mudie's having committed suicide was virtually extinguished. Hawke cross-examined Dr Keith Simpson lengthily on this matter. Both pathologists agreed that there was a bruise on Mudie's head. Dr Simpson said it was trivial; the Crown pathologist said it was an important injury which would seriously have affected Mudie. Hawke put it to Dr Simpson that, if Mudie had been hit while he still had a carpet over his head the bruise might be trivial but the injury it denoted might be important. He asked, "Have you heard the evidence in this case, as well as Dr Gardner's?" [Dr Eric Gardner, the Crown's expert witness, was consulting pathologist at the Weybridge Hospital.] "No," said Dr Simpson, "I have heard only Dr Gardner's evidence."

145

"We have been told by a man called Buckingham", continued Hawke, "that before this man was tied up a rug or blanket was thrown over his head. You will take that from me, I have no doubt?"

"I don't accept the evidence, but if you are going to base a question on it I shall answer it."

"I am going to base a question on it."

"What I mean is I don't necessarily accept the evidence."

Rayner, who had started at the penultimate answer, reinforced the roar he had been preparing when he heard the last. "You are not asked if you accept the evidence, Dr Keith Simpson," he said. "You are being put what has been said in this case, and what you know quite well has been put in this case."

"I accept that, my Lord," said Dr Keith Simpson, without noticeable humility. "I have not heard it."

The cross-examination continued, and the frequency of Lord Goddard's interruptions intensified. Facing fire from two flanks, Dr Simpson only became more precise. "Whatever else you and Dr Gardner may disagree about," Hawke said soothingly, "you agree about this: that this man died of asphyxia?"

"Yes."

"He died of asphyxia as a result of having, I would say *mainly* as a result of having, a rope tied tightly round his neck?"

"Drawn and lifted."

"You can trust me not to leave anything out."

"I am not trying to give the impression that you are trying to trap me; I am merely anxious for accuracy."

"You and I know each other too well for that. The rope had been tied tightly?"

"And lifted."

"You want to add lifted?"

"Yes. That was the significant thing in this point."

"Why?"

"Because in other cases it wouldn't necessarily cause death; it was the lifting that did it."

"If it was a sustained death, is it consistent with a sustained death by somebody pulling up the rope, like *that*?"

"Not necessarily somebody."

"Not necessarily somebody?"

"No, I don't think we have any evidence to show . . ."

"Not necessarily somebody?" Hawke repeated with renewed emphasis.

"No. I don't think there is any evidence."

"Is it your theory this man was hanged?"

"I am not anxious to propound a theory; I am anxious if possible to draw proper conclusions from what I saw, and not to enlarge upon them."

"Did you find this man had been found with a rope round his neck which had been pulled tight and lifted?"

"Yes."

"And that had killed him?"

"Yes."

"Leaving out, for the moment, if you will, anything that may or may not have happened to him before, that would be consistent with a man possibly having hanged himself?"

"Yes."

"Knowing the facts as you know them now, you do not think this man hanged himself, do you?"

"I think it is possible."

"What? After he had been gagged and tied up with a rope?"

"I have nothing from my examination to show that he had been."

"We have got evidence."

"I am trying to interpret my findings."

The Lord Chief Justice broke in:

"Yes, but you know, doctor, you are being asked, as a man of common sense, having heard the facts in this case, do you think they point to suicide?"

Dr Keith Simpson was firm: "I saw nothing in the condition of the rope-marks round the neck . . ."

"We are not asking you about that," Rayner interjected. "We are asking you to take the whole facts of this case into account. Was there any trace of his having been hanged from a tree near where he was found?"

"There need be no traces left."

"Were there trees there?"

"There were trees all around."

"Was there any suggestion of that?"

"I made no search; a search was made. I am not suggesting there was. I am not suggesting he was hanged. I do wish to give my evidence so far as it is proper, not to give it further—not to have it drawn further."

Simpson was making a remarkable stand for scientific integrity, committing himself solely within the confines of his own specific knowledge. Rayner yielded slightly from the attitude of confrontation, and eased his inquiry into neutral:

"What you are asked is, from what this man showed on his death, was it consistent with his having been hanged from a tree?"

"From being suspended in some way" was Simpson's amendment. "We have no evidence."

"Having heard the evidence, do you think it is not inconsistent?"

"I say the disposition after death naturally aroused suspicion."

"Well," said the Lord Chief Justice, with perhaps an over-elaboration of tolerant good humour. "Well, at any rate, we have got as far as that."

But Dr Keith Simpson still had a comment upon the comment.

"I might make the additional statement", he observed, "that suspicion has often arisen where the death has been natural." Rayner did not win every courtroom joust—even as Lord Chief Justice.

As for the evidence of Ley, the principal defendant, his manner in the witness-box was indicative of the condition of his mind, in which he only accepted as real that which he wished to believe—and shut his consciousness to all other reality. His attitude was arrogant stonewall: he knew nothing about the murder, he had had nothing to do with the unfortunate Mudie's death. He met every piece of evidence against him with a blank denial: "No, it didn't happen", to the Bloomsbury hotel porter's account of his asking him if he knew "a man with a car who could look after himself and keep his mouth shut". "No" to the detailed incriminations of Buckingham and Smith's confessions to the police. "No" to virtually everything.

Where was he when the murder was being committed? He claimed an alibi—that he was with, of all people, Mrs Brook for part of the time. Described by many observers in court as looking like a frightened woman, she did indeed testify that she had been playing gin rummy with him from 7.45 p.m. to 11.0 p.m. on the fatal evening—but the first time she ever hinted at this partial support of Ley's alibi was in her cross-examination at the Old Bailey.

Rayner shrewdly intervened: "Did you not tell anybody, when you knew this man you had been living with was accused of murder, that you could account for his movements?"—"Oh, I didn't," said the nervous Mrs Brook.

In his summing-up, Rayner was not slow to emphasize to the jury the implications of the blanket denials that formed the core of Ley's testimony and defence:

"Now it must have struck you as remarkable, although it is not impossible, that in this case this curious body of evidence that has been led here has been met by Ley with simple, positive, flat denials.

There is no question of his saying: 'Yes, so far that is true. I engaged Buckingham for some purpose and he misunderstood the purpose', or whatever it was. He has simply given a flat denial of this and says there is not one word of truth in it from beginning to end. Of course to that you will give such weight as you think fit. You see, one of the things which he has most positively sworn to is that he never knew Mudie was brought to that house at all. Members of the jury, do you remember one piece of evidence that Ley gave while he was in the witness box? You will remember there were three people of whom he had suspicions with regard to their conduct with Mrs Brook—Romer, young Barron, and Mudie—and he said in the course of his evidence, and I took it down, 'I wanted Arthur Barron to come along somewhere where I could get information, to Beaufort Gardens'. Is not that exactly what Smith and Buckingham say he wanted with regard to Mudie? You may possibly think, members of the jury, that it was lucky for Arthur Barron that he was not induced to go along to Beaufort Gardens. But if he was wanting, as he has told you in the witness-box, that Arthur Barron should go to Beaufort Gardens to get a statement from him, does it not strike you as altogether remarkable that he should have procured Mudie to be brought to Beaufort Gardens?"

And Rayner followed these observations with his only reference to insanity in connection with Ley *made at the trial*:

"If the motive of this man, you know, was jealousy, and jealousy is one of the most powerful emotions and leads very often to the most incalculable and unhappy results—if you think what he said to young Barron shows that he was suffering from this, shall I call it insane—that only means unreasoning, it does not mean he was mad, no one suggests he is mad, but unreasonable—jealousy in this case—this, you may think, throws a flood of light upon the whole of this story."

Rayner was telling the jury that no one suggested Ley was mad. But later he told the Royal Commission on Capital Punishment that—presumably, based on prior prison medical reports—he knew Ley was mad.

Ley and Smith were fairly speedily found guilty by the jury, and were sentenced to death. Four weeks later, their appeals—based mainly on insufficient direction to the jury on the possibilities of manslaughter, accident or suicide as the cause of Mudie's death—were dismissed. Eleven days after that their application for fiat to appeal to the House of Lords was refused, and they could look forward to but a few more days to live. Three days before the date set for execution the Home Office announced—the Home Secretary was Chuter Ede, with whom Rayner was to have bitter brushes later—that Ley had been pronounced insane by doctors, and he was to be sent to Broadmoor. At the same time the sentence on Smith was commuted to one of penal servitude for life. (If the reasoning behind Smith's reprieve was that the secondary conspirator should not die if the First Murderer was respited, this logic was abandoned by Sir David Maxwell Fyfe in the case of Craig and Bentley.) Ten weeks after Ley had been pronounced insane he died from a stroke in Broadmoor.

"I have no doubt that the prisoner was insane," Rayner told the Royal Commission on Capital Punishment, recapitulating the case of Ley three years later:

"His whole conduct, including his demeanour and evidence at the trial, showed a typical case of paranoia. But he refused to allow his counsel to raise the defence of insanity, and would have been horrified at any such suggestion. This is all part of the disease. His case was this: he believed that not only the youth he murdered, but others, were committing adultery with his former mistress. It became an obsession. He therefore conceived a hatred against this young man and set to work to have him murdered, deliberately murdered, meaning that he should be murdered. He did it by hiring some bravoes to kidnap the boy and bring him to his house and tie him up there. He then bribed another man with five hundred pounds to murder him, or help to murder him.

"What excuse was found for that? Merely that the man had got the delusion this boy had been committing adultery with his woman friend. Supposing he had been told by people he thought he could trust, that the boy and the woman had been committing adultery? He might have honestly believed it, but that could not have excused what he did, having this boy kidnapped, brought to his house, strangled, and then the body taken away to be buried, whereby he hoped to avoid detection. I say that seems to me to show the wisdom of applying the M'Naghten rules, which put the test of responsibility not on the ground of whether or not you can say that the man has got some unsoundness of mind—after all, who is there to say that anyone has not got unsoundness of mind in some form or another?—but on the question whether he knows what he is doing and whether he knows that he is doing wrong.

"This man knew that he was murdering that boy. I had no doubt that Ley was what you may call a pathological case by the way he gave his evidence, in which he simply denied everything flatly. You see, he had gone to work in the most deliberate and cunning way, first in finding out the people who could be trusted to kidnap the boy, providing them with the money, promising sums and paying them, and then having the other man ready to commit the murder at his house. The whole thing was planned in the most elaborate way, and he was a very wicked man."

It was here that Dr Eliot Slater interposed the question already cited: "You would not have thought it proper that he should hang?"

"I should have thought it very proper that he should have been hanged."

That, for the historical record, was the judgment of Lord Goddard: undiluted, unequivocal, unrecanted.

12 The Laski Libel Action

As Lord Chief Justice, Rayner Goddard roundly faced his responsibilities and his critics on all the general issues of principle in which his position involved him. Yet one case, a solitary case not establishing a general point of law or a restatement of a clouded verity, never ceased to trouble him. Eighteen years afterwards he said, "I have never worried about a case I have tried so much as this. . . . I can say that it has been on my conscience."

The case in question was the Laski Libel Case: an action brought by Mr Harold Laski, Professor of Political Science at the London School of Economics, against the Newark Advertiser Company Limited, publishers of the *Newark Advertiser,* and against Mr C. E. Parlby, editor of that newspaper, claiming damages for libel alleged to have been uttered in a report of a political meeting at Newark published on 20 June 1945. Libel actions for similar reports were instituted against the *Nottingham Guardian* and Mr H. C. C. Carlton, who had written a letter published in that newspaper, and against the *Daily Express* and *Evening Standard* of London, which reproduced this letter. Because it was likely that the result of the first action would be accepted by both sides as the probable result of the other actions, the various defendants agreed to combine in resisting the first action, and the *Daily Express* took over the conduct of the case against the *Newark Advertiser.* The defendants applied for, and obtained, an order that the cause should be tried before a special jury, seven people presumed to be in a more prosperous and better-educated station of life than 'common' jurors.[1] The action was tried

---

[1] Special juries were abolished three years later, in 1949. They were considered to be unrepresentative of the modern kind of juror.

before the Lord Chief Justice in the King's Bench Division of the High Court on 26, 27, 28 and 29 November and 2 December 1946, seventeen months after the publication of the alleged libels.

The Laski case was a microcosm of the social conflicts that had led to the Labour Party's triumph in the 1945 general election and ironically, as we have seen, to Rayner's own elevation to the Lord Chief Justiceship. It was a courtroom struggle against a background of politics.

Harold Laski was born in Manchester in 1893, the son of Nathan Laski, J.P., cotton-shipper, philanthropist, a leading figure in the local Jewish community and a constant friend of Winston Churchill.

Harold left Manchester Grammar School and married, at the age of eighteen, Frida Kerry, a vigorous Scots lecturer in eugenics, birth control and women's suffrage. For this offence he was virtually kidnapped and beggared by his family, and was forced to pass his three years' stint at New College, Oxford, almost incommunicado from his wife. It was she who, nine years later, effected a family reconciliation by formally entering the Jewish community. In June 1914 Laski took first-class honours in history at Oxford. In August he tried to enlist, but was rejected on medical grounds. In September he took a post in McGill University, Montreal, which enabled his predecessor there to return home and enlist—but the man was seconded to the Civil Service! In January 1916 Laski took a tutor's post at Harvard, lecturing on history and political theory and becoming book editor of the *Harvard Law Review*. In 1920 he began his lifetime career as a lecturer, later a professor, at the London School of Economics. Laski was a Marxist, but not a Communist. When he lectured in Moscow he was fiercely attacked there. He was the intellectual leader of the Labour left wing—but, incidentally, was on cordial first-name terms with Franklin D. Roosevelt, and was never averse to giving the President his advice. When Clement Attlee joined the British wartime Coalition Government as Deputy Premier Laski was for long his personal aide. Laski fully supported the wartime leadership of his father's friend, Winston Churchill, but he maintained, as a Marxist student of revolution, that the radical changes towards State capitalism which Churchill and Attlee made within wartime Britain had paved the way for even more radical changes towards State socialism which would present themselves after the War: "With such changes we could hope for a peaceful transition to a Socialist Britain over a period of years." Laski was enunciating his own theory of *revolution by consent* as a natural development of Marxism, the controversial tenet—as alive today as it was in 1945—which was the real issue of the historic Laski libel case.

Two weeks after the surrender of Nazi Germany in May 1945 Winston Churchill had tendered to George VI the resignation of his wartime Coalition Government, and formed a Tory Administration as caretaker during a general election campaign which began on 15 June, and was decided on 26 July. The Japanese were still very much in the War, and the Potsdam Conference between Stalin, Truman and Churchill was planned to begin on 17 July. Churchill asked Clement Attlee, his former Deputy Premier, now Leader of the Opposition as head of the Parliamentary Labour Party, to accompany him to Potsdam. "There will be an opportunity", he told Attlee, "for it to be shown that, though Governments may change and parties quarrel, on some of the main essentials of foreign policy we stand together."

Professor Laski immediately burst into the ring and, as current Chairman (for one year) of the Labour Party National Executive, declared, "It is essential that if Mr Attlee attends the gathering he should do so in the role of observer only." Attlee retorted publicly, "There has never been any suggestion that I should attend 'as a mere observer'. There seems to me great public advantage in preserving and presenting to the world at this time the unity in foreign policy which we maintained throughout the last five years." Laski was called for a private dressing-down by the deceptively mild Labour leader, and afterwards announced, "Everything has now been satisfactorily cleared up."

But in a speech at Scunthorpe delivered that very same day, Laski repeated that Attlee's visit must not bind him to Churchill's foreign policy: "When we win this election we want to be free in Socialist terms to make our own policy for our own Socialist purposes."

And during that same weekend, on the night of 16 June 1945, Laski made the speech at Newark in Nottinghamshire, at the meeting which led to the critical libel action being brought.

In a sense, he only had himself to blame. He had virtually typecast himself as the Labour Party's 'bogey-man' for that vital post-War election: a positive gift to the mainly Tory-controlled popular press, a sort of Anthony Wedgwood Benn of thirty years ago—with vague undertones of only half-expressed anti-Semitism to add murk to the scene.

In the Conservative Party's *Notes for Speakers and Writers,* issued for the use of Party hecklers and speakers, he appeared with two heckle-worthy extracts from past speeches against his name. At Bournemouth on 13 December 1941, he was quoted as having said—and he agreed with the accuracy of the newspaper report—"The Labour Party is not fighting to preserve traditional England, and if Mr Churchill thinks we share with him any other end than the end of Hitler he is mistaken. The Party is concerned, not merely with victory, but the purposes for which victory is won. The process upon which we are now engaged is a process the fulfilment of which must begin before the War is over; we have a choice of revolution by consent now or revolution by violence after the War."

At Bishop's Stortford on 22 November 1941 Laski was quoted as having said—but he disagreed with the accuracy of the newspaper report—"The Labour Party must not wait till after the War to reconstruct. They must do it now as part of the war-effort. If they did they would not get the same disillusionments and disappointments that followed the last War. Unless they demand great things now the vista of unemployment and all the other problems would open up again. Their choice was very simple: to begin social transformation by general consent now or do it by violence after the War."

Those quotations had been used at a political meeting on the night before Laski came to Newark by Colonel Sidney Shephard, the local Conservative candidate. They were also in the hands of the gentleman who was acting as publicity adviser to Colonel Shephard, Mr James Wentworth Day. Wentworth Day, then aged forty-six, six years younger than Laski, was and still is, an author, journalist and publicist. He had been publicity manager of the *Daily Express*, editor of the *Saturday Review*, the *Illustrated Sporting and Dramatic News* and *The Field,* a war correspondent at the beginning of the Second World War, and had, as he expressed it, "conducted a High Tory campaign in nine by-elections". He went to the Newark meeting addressed by Laski, quite rightly and properly, for the purpose of heckling him.

"Frankly I disliked Laski intensely for two reasons," he has written to me,[2] "(a) he represented that type of glib foreigner who comes here for political freedom and then abuses the hospitality of this country by attacking its institutions; and (b) he had all the insufferable conceit of the pseudo-intellectual, a type I dislike as much as a dog dislikes a cat. These two phases of dislike can, I think, fairly be classed as 'political'." Readers remembering that Laski was born in Manchester, the son of a Justice of the Peace, may perhaps think

---

[2] In a letter dated 5 February 1976.

of another word to describe the nature of Mr Wentworth Day's dislike.

In any event, in the Newark Market Place, before an audience of 1 500 people, Laski addressed the meeting for three-quarters of an hour. The Labour candidate, Air Vice-Marshal Hugh Champion de Crespigny, spoke for a further quarter of an hour. And then, as the meeting was beginning to break up, without any questions having been asked, Wentworth Day shouted, according to his later evidence in court, "In November 1941, when most of us were fighting and I personally was on a minesweeper, you said at Bishop's Stortford and Bournemouth: the Labour Party must not wait until after the War to reconstruct; that it is very simple to begin now or do it by violence after the War. What does the bloodthirsty Professor mean by 'violence'; and why did you spend the whole of the last War in America? Why did you openly advocate revolution when most of us were fighting, or other men were being bombed at home?"

In some heat Professor Laski dealt with the question about his 1914–18 war service, quoting an apology which had been made to him in the House of Commons after previous allegations reflecting on his behaviour at that time. He then turned to the matter of his advocacy of revolution. It was a long answer. Even the summary of it which he gave later in court was extended:

"I said it was quite untrue to allege that I preached revolution; I was saying a very different thing, that in an epoch where people are engaged in a war and in making immense changes, that is the period for great experiment and that if great experiments can be made by consent, so much the better. I pointed out that in my speech I had referred to hard conditions in this country in the inter-war years—housing, nutrition, unemployment, and similar matters—and I said that it was often the case that during the Great War men expected the redress of grievances, that where that redress was achieved by consent and the great revolution was accomplished by social transformation by agreement, that was admirable; the danger always was of a drift away from the temper that permitted great experiment to a temper where men had forgotten the great experience to which they had been subjected, and that where that drift away was concerned, the abyss between those who ruled and those who were making these demands was such that there might be a slow evolution to a revolution, and that that would be a terrible disaster that we ought to evade and that we should evade it by making great social changes now, 'now' being the time at which the meeting was held. I then quoted Edmund Burke, who had said,

"The people have no interest in disorder. Where they do wrong, it is their error and not their crime." And I referred to the saying of Henry IV's minister, Sully, whom Edmund Burke himself quoted on that occasion, "All popular violence arises from popular suffering," and I urged the desirability of preventing popular violence by assuaging popular suffering."

Wentworth Day did not allow this answer to be given without interruption. He challenged repeatedly on the subjects of Professor Laski's unmilitary career and revolutionary zeal, and at the height of the angry interlude was told by Laski, in words which both sides later confirmed, "Judging by the temper you display, you would naturally be one of the objects of violence when it does come." The meeting ended on what all present agreed was "a lively note".

The *Newark Advertiser* had a very experienced shorthand reporter present by the platform, and when the weekly edition of the newspaper was published on Wednesday, 20 June 1945, it carried not only a full report of the main speeches, but a separate item on another page which ran as follows. This publication was the substance of the libel action against the *Newark Advertiser*:

REVOLUTION BY VIOLENCE

Professor Laski Questioned

"There were some lively exchanges between Mr Wentworth Day and Professor Laski following the latter's speech in Newark Market Place on Saturday night.

"Mr Day asked the Professor why he had openly advocated 'revolution by violence' in speaking at Bishop's Stortford and Bournemouth during the war, 'whilst most Englishmen were either fighting or being bombed at home', and why he (Professor Laski) had spent the whole of the last war lecturing in America. If he were unfit, why did he not join the Red Cross?

Rejected

"Prof. Laski replied that he was twice rejected in this country during the 1914–18 war and had medical certificates to prove it. He also attempted to enlist in Canada, and then he went to Harvard University, and he had a certificate from the Medical Officer of the British Army in New York of his inability to be accepted on medical grounds. He also said concerning the other part of the question: 'That was said about me in the House of Commons ... and if you

Lord Goddard

look at Hansard for 29 November, 1944,[3] you will see an ample and generous apology made to me for being as insolent as you are in suggesting it now.'

Reference to Violence

"As for violence, he continued, if Labour could not obtain what it needed by general consent, 'We shall have to use violence even if it means revolution.' When people felt it was the moment for great experiment, for innovation, because when war is over people so easily forget—especially those who had the power in their hands—that was the time for experiment. Great changes were so urgent in this country, and if they were not made by consent they would be made by violence, and judging by the temper his questioner had displayed he would be perfectly naturally one of the objects of violence when it came.

"Mr Day submitted to the Professor that when general consent was against him he substituted revolution.

"Prof. Laski said it did not lie in the mouth of any member of the Tory Party, who helped to organise mutiny in the British Army over Home Rule in 1914, to discuss the question of violence. When a situation in any society became intolerable—and when 25 per cent of the people had inadequate nutrition it did become intolerable—it did not become possible to prevent what was not given by generosity being taken by the organised will of the people.

Not an Asset

"Mr Day: 'You are precisely the sort of bloodthirsty little man, full of words, who has never smelt a bullet, but is always the first to stir up violence in peace.

" 'We expect serious constructive thought from the Chairman of the Labour Party, but since you have consistently attacked everyone and everything from Mr Churchill to the leaders of your own party and the constitution of this country, and have been disowned by Mr Attlee only this morning, how can anyone take you seriously? I suggest that you are not an asset to the Labour Party but a liability.' "

This account had been written up by the *Newark Advertiser* reporter, James Opie, from his own shorthand notes and from another document. The second document was a report of the "lively

---

[3] Mr Laski later agreed that the date he had given was mistaken, and the apology was given in the Commons on 14 December 1943.

exchanges" at the end of the meeting written by Wentworth Day himself, and handed to Cyril Parlby, the editor of the *Newark Advertiser*, at the request of Mr Parlby. This report began:

"At a meeting in the Market Place on Saturday night Mr Wentworth Day asked Professor Laski why he had openly advocated 'revolution by violence' in speaking at Bishop's Stortford and Bournemouth during the War, 'whilst most Englishmen were either fighting or being bombed at home', and why he, Professor Laski, had spent the whole of the last War lecturing in America. If he were unfit, why did he not join the Red Cross? Professor Laski replied that he had volunteered for service in the 1914/18 War, but had been rejected, and that as for violence, if Labour could not obtain what it needed by general consent 'we shall have to use violence even if it means revolution'."

When James Opie, the shorthand reporter, had been told to collate the two accounts for the final published story he pointed out to Cyril Parlby that Wentworth Day's first paragraph—with the reference "*openly advocated revolution by violence*"—was not substantiated by his, Opie's shorthand report. He later agreed that the other published reference to violence—"*As for violence, he continued, if Labour could not obtain what it needed by general consent, 'We shall have to use violence even if it means revolution'*"—was also taken from Wentworth Day's account and not from his own shorthand note, which contained merely the phrase, "Great changes are so urgent in this country that if they are not made by consent they will be made by violence".

Cyril Parlby, the Editor of the *Newark Advertiser*, later explained in court how the much stronger sentence—"We shall have to use violence even if it means revolution"—got into his newspaper's report: "Mr Opie drew my attention to the fact that that particular sentence was not in his shorthand note. I pointed out to him that I had been to the meeting, and that from the fragments I had heard I was of opinion that that sentence should be in—and also on the Monday morning I had seen the letter in the *Nottingham Guardian* from Mr Carlton and that further reinforced my view that those words had been used, knowing the *Nottingham Guardian* to be a most careful paper and that anything that appeared in the Nottingham Guardian would be most carefully edited."

That "letter from Mr Carlton" was the substance of the libel actions against the three other newspapers involved, the *Nottingham Guardian,* the *Daily Express* and the *Evening Standard*. Who then was "Mr Carlton"?

A Nottinghamshire county councillor, Mr Henry Carlton, had been present at part of the Newark meeting, and had heard part of the interchange between Laski and Wentworth Day, knowing that the latter had intended to heckle the speaker. According to his evidence given later in court, he was so deeply shocked by what he had heard that he wanted to get a letter published in a newspaper to say so. It was Saturday night, and the *Nottingham Guardian* was to be published on the following Monday. Mr Carlton telephoned a reporter of that paper early on Sunday morning, telling him of the incident and asking him to get the account in the paper. The reporter said he would draft a 'Letter to the Editor' and pass it back for Mr Carlton's approval. This was done and, after the Editor had questioned Mr Carlton by telephone to check the authenticity of the letter, it was published in the *Nottingham Guardian* next day, Monday 18 June. This letter began:

SIR,
Attending a meeting in the Newark Market Place on Saturday night I was horrified to hear Prof. Harold J. Laski, Chairman of the Socialist Party, when enumerating reforms he wanted to see, declare: 'If we cannot have them by fair means we shall use violence to obtain them.'
A member of the audience immediately challenged him and said: 'You are inviting revolution from the platform.'
Prof. Laski replied: 'If we cannot get reforms we desire we shall not hesitate to use violence, even if it means revolution.'
I think the widest publicity should be given to this statement, for I feel that electors all over the country should know what is really behind the Socialist mind. . . .

H. C. C. CARLTON

An hour before midnight on Tuesday 19 June Professor Laski, aware that the *Daily Express* would carry in the morning a front-page splash on the Carlton Letter, denied to the Press Association news agency that he had made the statement attributed to him, gave his version of what he had said at Newark, and announced that he would take out a writ for libel "against the man who wrote it and against anybody else who reproduces the letter". The letter was already set up in type and print for publication in a number of newspapers, not only in London, on Wednesday 20 June. The *Daily Express* published its front page according to plan—the headlines read: "Laski Unleashes Another General Election Broadside: Socialism Even If It Means Violence"—and included Mr Laski's denial in later editions. The Editor of the *Evening Standard* decided to publish the letter that afternoon along with the denial. The *Newark Advertiser*, with its independent story, appeared as scheduled on the Wednesday. Professor Laski issued writs against the *Nottingham Guardian* and the *Daily Express* on the Wednesday and against the *Evening Standard* and the *Newark Advertiser* on the Friday. The matter was in *sub judice* limbo. Lord Simon, the Lord Chancellor, possibly over-heated—for once—by election fever, suggested publicly during an election speech at Carshalton that Laski had issued the writs only "to stop people's mouths" and made the public wager that "as soon as this election is over you won't hear anything more about these writs". It was an impermissible remark by a head of the judiciary, and Simon later apologized.

As sheaves of interrogatories were put and affidavits sworn, Laski was already appalled by the costs he risked when the case came for trial before the Lord Chief Justice and a special jury at the end of November 1946. For the plaintiff, G. O. Slade, K.C. (later Mr Justice Slade), led, supported by Sir Valentine Holmes, K.C., and Peter Bristow (later Mr Justice Bristow). For the defendants, Sir Patrick Hastings, K.C., led Holroyd Pearce, K.C. (later Lord Pearce), Arthian Davies (later Lord Justice Davies) and Anthony Gordon.

Gerald Slade, in his opening, ran through the sequences by which the *Newark Advertiser* report had been compiled from the parallel sources of the notes of the official reporter and the account of Mr Wentworth Day, noting that the nub of the libel was not in the shorthand report. He drew attention to the reliance of Cyril Parlby, Editor of the *Newark Advertiser,* on the letter signed by Mr Carlton which had already been printed in the *Nottingham Guardian,* and observed that, since the Wentworth Day version was not to Parlby's hand when he read it, this was the first suggestion that Laski had mentioned violence in pursuit of socialist reforms *before* there had been any provocation by a questioner. Slade promised that any such suggestion would be denied in court by the Air Vice-Marshal who had been present as the Labour candidate.

Although he was an accomplished libel expert, his opening speech was long, rambling and woolly. By contrast, Sir Patrick Hastings, as soon as he rose to cross-examine Harold Laski in the witness-box, showed that it was going to be a contest of silver-tipped rapier against blunderbuss.

"Mr Laski, do you believe that the use of violence to achieve your political ends is practically inevitable?" Hastings asked.

Laski hesitated: "No", he said. "In a country where there is a long constitutional tradition of mature and literate people, I think that consent . . ."

"Is the answer 'No'?" Hastings interrupted.

"The answer is 'No'."

"As far as possible, would you keep your answers short? Have you ever believed that which I have put to you?"

"No."

"Do you agree with me that anyone who for years had preached such a doctrine would be a public danger?"

"No, not necessarily."

"Have you preached it for years and years?"

"No."

"You do not think such a person would necessarily be a public danger?"

"I do not understand quite what you mean by that."

"Could you answer that 'Yes' or 'No'? Supposing a person for years were preaching this doctrine to a dissatisfied proletariat, 'The use of violence to achieve your political aims is practically inevitable', don't you think such a person would be a public danger?"

"That would depend", said Laski, "upon the degree of his power to persuade those to whom he spoke."

"You mean to say he might be useless, and therefore not a danger or powerful and then a danger?"

"Yes."

"Would you consider yourself, with the innumerable qualifications which Sir Valentine read out to us, a person sufficiently powerful to be a public danger?"

"I should have said not."

"In this court you would say not. On public platforms you take rather a different view, do you not?"

"I have never said on any public platform anything that could be construed into a belief that I am a significant public figure in the national life."

"I am quite content with the two answers you have given me," said Hastings. "I want to add one more. Do you believe that if achievement of political aims cannot be arrived at without the use of violence, then violence is justifiable?"

"Not in all circumstances," said Laski. "In circumstances where a burden is intolerable, violence may be inevitable because the burden is intolerable, but not otherwise."

"In the circumstances which existed on the 16 June, 1945, the date you made this speech, did you then believe that if the aims of the proletariat could not be achieved without the use of violence, then

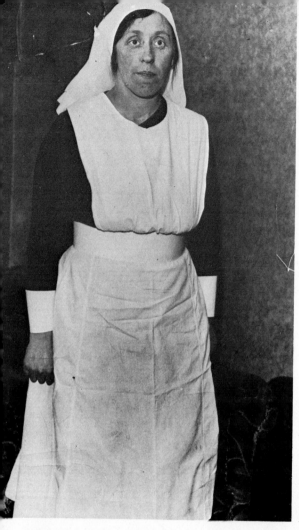

Nurse Dorothea Waddingham, sentenced to
death by Mr Justice Goddard in 1936
Photo Mirrorpic

The cordon of police somewhat
unnecessarily strung across the road leading
to Winson Green Prison, Birmingham, on
the morning of Nurse Waddingham's
execution
Photo Radio Times Hulton Picture Library

Two famous cases in Rayner's first year as 'Chief'

Thomas John Ley, the ex
Justice Minister who plotted
the Chalk-Pit Murder
Photo Keystone Press

Professor Harold Laski,
whose libel action before
Lord Goddard failed
Photo Keystone Press

Rayner Goddard as his family and friends knew him: the Lord Chief Justice of England relaxing in the garden of a friend's house

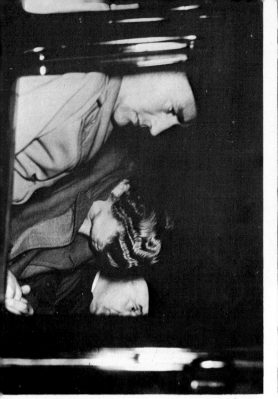

The Craig-Bentley Case

The two young defendants leaving Croydon Magistrates' Court after being charged with the murder of P.C. Sidney Miles. *Top left* Craig, *bottom left* Bentley

Photos Keystone Press (Craig) and Syndication International (Bentley)

Right
The knuckleduster which Craig handed to Bentley before the murder, and on which Lord Goddard commented strongly at the trial

Photo Syndication International

violence was justifiable?"

"No."

"Do you agree that anyone who preached that doctrine would be a public danger?"

"Yes."

"*And have you preached it for twenty years?*"

"No."

"We shall have to see. If you have preached it for twenty years, you agree you would be a public danger?"

"If I had preached to the proletariat the inevitability of violence for twenty years, I should certainly be a public danger."

"And you would not complain of what was said about you in this action?"

"I should have complained of the untruth of the words attributed to me on the occasion, but not the general description that you are seeking to give my personality."

"We shall have to see whether you have been preaching," said Sir Patrick Hastings.

"If you please," said Professor Laski.

Whereupon Hastings virtually put the witness on trial for his political beliefs, culled from his many books and articles. But Laski presented no grotesquely pitiable figure. If he talked too much it seemed often because of his donnish enthusiasm to cover every possible contingency, rather than to put up a smoke-screen to disguise his views. In particular, he persistently resisted the repeated tactic of cross-examining counsel to show that when, in his writings, he analysed revolution he was really inciting it—that 'diagnosis was exhortation'.

"You are asking me, Sir Patrick," he said at one point, "to say that passages in the book which you choose to read out show how difficult it is to maintain a happy relationship between capitalism and democracy, and how on occasions—as for instance in Austria or Spain or Italy or Germany—those are to be taken as the general expression of my view. That is untrue. I take the view that the maintenance of social peace and the avoidance of violence is one of the most vital things at which our society can aim. That is why I am a member of the Labour Party and not a member of the Communist Party. This is at no point (nor is any of the material you have so far quoted) exhortation. Every part of the material that you have quoted is careful, and I hope accurate, diagnosis; and I think that you put me in an unfair and an unjustifiable position by asking me to accept diagnosis as exhortation."

Hastings was reduced to temporary silence by this direct speech, and almost immediately he was struck a blow which pierced the armour of even this steely advocate. Laski, as quoted by Hastings, had been dealing with the gap between the privileged and the unprivileged. Hastings wanted to shift those terms to mean the capitalists and the socialists. "Are there any privileged in the Socialist Party?" he asked.

"Why, indeed, Sir Patrick," said Laski. "When you were a member—"

"No, Mr Laski," the Lord Chief Justice swiftly interrupted.

Sir Patrick Hastings, as a member of the Labour Party, had been Attorney-General in 1924 and had handled the Campbell Case (the 'Zinoviev Letter' scandal in which a letter advocating rebellion and now presumed to be forged was used to bring down the first Labour Government). The private or political lives of counsel may not be referred to in court, and Rayner was quick to smother this attempt by Laski to allude to Hastings's political past; although curiously he did not silence Gerald Slade when, in his closing speech to the jury, he commented on the incident and said, "I think at least I should have said, *'Touché!'*, if that answer had been given to me."

What Hastings did say, with some petulance, was: "Do not be rude."

"It is the last thing I want in the world," said Laski.

"It may be difficult for you to be courteous, but do not be rude," persisted Hastings.

"Not in the least."

"You are rude to everybody, are you not?"

"I don't think so."

And so the cross-examination continued, with the tension and the prickles obvious even from the bare, flat written record of the evidence. The trial transcript shows, as far as words can show without reference to mood, that Laski was fighting back spiritedly. Yet the *impression* which many of those present in the courtroom have recorded, and which presumably the jury absorbed, is that, in the words of one commentator,[4] "Hastings, at his most subtle and incisive, made Laski look helpless and shifty." And the Professor also had to face the perhaps less subtle, but certainly no less incisive, questioning of the Lord Chief Justice.

When Laski said that violence would not be justified "if there were a large majority of the community opposed to the demands of the working class" Rayner interrupted.

---

[4] Louis Blom-Cooper, Q.C., at page 120 of *The Law as Literature* (The Bodley Head, 1961).

"I do not quite understand," he said. "The working class. There might be a large proportion of the working class opposed to it."

"Yes," said Laski, "I am assuming that."

"You have to remember that not so very long ago a very large Conservative majority was returned?"

"I agree."

"I was wondering whether you would tell us whether in your view, if there is a very large majority of Conservatives returned, the same principles would apply as set forth in your books, that the Labour Party ought then to give an undertaking that they will not reverse the legislation which the Conservatives bring in?"

"May I answer that in this way, that Conservative legislation does not alter the fundamental framework of the State."

"It may; I don't know why it shouldn't. But are the same conditions to apply when the Labour Party are in opposition as are to apply when they are in Government?"

"I think certainly," said Laski. "That is the nature of constitutional government."

"Then what becomes of Parliamentary opposition?" persisted Rayner "Then you can never get a reform?"

"Yes," said Professor Laski. "I am arguing that an Opposition—" But Rayner interrupted, "Please do not think I am putting this against you or for you, but I only want to follow what was in your mind in some passages that have been read, and which you are perfectly entitled to explain by reading others. But still, perhaps I had better not go into it any further."

In one of his longer answers—few of which were short—Laski stated, "I am saying that you must carefully divide (and I should have thought, Sir Patrick, that you would have known that you must carefully divide) the supporters of socialism into those who believe that socialism ought to be achieved by constitutional methods within the framework of a constitutional democracy and those who do not believe that that is the case. The first are in the Labour Party to which I have the honour to belong. The second are outside the Labour Party."

"I do wish", said Hastings, again visibly nettled, "that you would not make speeches, Mr Laski."

"May I suggest", said the Lord Chief Justice, "you have got the words, Sir Patrick, and you have made your point. Now cannot you pass on?"

At the end of Laski's evidence, Rayner commented, "Professor Laski, let me say, I think has given his answers and explanations extremely clearly. . . . Your thesis has been throughout, Professor, as I understand: 'I am in favour of a revolution in the sense of a complete change of social circumstances. I have never advocated revolution by violent means. I have always suggested the ballot-box rather than the lamp-post'?

"Yes," said Laski. "And, if I may add, I have always pointed out the immense danger to society."

"I was just going to add that," said the Lord Chief Justice. "That is your view. The jury will take that into account. The jury must form their own opinion, and nobody else, as to what the ordinary meaning of the words used is."

It surely cannot fairly be said that Professor Laski, in court, was intimidated by the law, or displayed any of the passivity of a corpse in a dissecting-room, as in defeat he talked himself into believing.

Counsel for the plaintiff then called ten witnesses, all of whom said that they had been present at the meeting in Newark Market-place, and all of whom denied that Professor Laski had used the words "As for violence, if Labour could not obtain what it wanted by general consent, we shall have to use violence, even if it means revolution." The best that Sir Patrick Hastings could do against them was to quote other controversial remarks which Laski conceded he had made during the heckling—and confirm that the witnesses did not admit to having heard these either. When Air Vice-Marshal Hugh Champion de Crespigny, the Labour candidate for whom Laski had been speaking at Newark, was twitted with not having heard a significant passage he claimed, "There was nothing vital that I would not have heard", to which Hastings scored a hit with his swift riposte: "If you did not hear it, how do you know whether it was vital or not?"

Early on the third day of the trial the defence called its witnesses after a half-hour opening by Sir Patrick, who ended his speech:

"'If we could not obtain what is needed by general consent the people will have to use violence even if it means Socialist revolution.' He said it over and over and over again. What is he complaining about? Do you not think the explanation of this case is that when this speech was made the Labour Party, who were fighting for their lives at the last election, may have said to themselves, 'Heaven and earth, Laski again! He's got to stop this', and so Mr Laski issues writs to say he never said it. . . ."

And there was much else in similar vein from the learned counsel who could so easily get upset when the witness was "rude" to him, and complain about his "offensive" behaviour.

The principal witness called by Sir Patrick for the defence was James Wentworth Day. He recounted how, having gone to the Newark meeting as the Conservative candidate's publicity adviser for the purpose of heckling Professor Laski, he had written down a report of the encounter which he had handed by request to the editor of the *Newark Advertiser*. Cross-examined by Gerald Slade, he said, "I was so astonished by Mr Laski's remark to me: "We shall have to use violence, even if it means revolution" that the moment I got home I copied that out on a writing pad." He said he intended his question regarding Laski's war service to be "very personal and very challenging", preferring the word "challenging" to "offensive". He agreed that the coupling of the reference to war service with the points from the speeches at Bishop's Stortford and Bournemouth was designed to provoke Professor Laski.

He agreed with Slade that when at the meeting he had asked Laski why he had openly advocated "revolution by violence" in previous speeches, and when Mr Day repeated that phraseology in his report to the newspaper "there is no doubt that what you intended to convey by those words was that Professor Laski had openly incited the population to revolution by violence". Later in the cross-examination, however, he withdrew this and said he had not been intending to convey anything: "I asked Mr Laski a question. I wanted his answers to that." The words of the second reference to violence—"If Labour could not obtain what it needed by general consent, we shall have to use violence even if it means revolution"—had been spoken directly at him and quite loudly, and he understood those words to be a direct incitement to revolution by violence.

On the morning of the fourth day Gerald Slade took the step—which in retrospect he may have regretted—of cross-examining Mr Wentworth Day about a book of his, not yet published but in proof, which referred to the Newark incident. His object was to assess that Mr Wentworth Day had personal animosity against Laski, and this was denied. The practical effect of the venture was to read into the ears of the jury, who no doubt welcomed a little light relief at this stage, a witty—but, Mr Wentworth Day maintained, not disparaging—description of Laski, which Mr Day was delighted to justify from the witness-box:

" 'I determined to have a look at him'," Slade read from the book. 'I did not know Professor Laski, but his writings had depressed me. He seemed to find so much solace in the revolutionary standards of less happy countries and so little comfort in the Britain which his ancestors had adopted as a place of profitable residence, and he wrote and talked so much about it all—evidently a man with a disturbed mind. . . . Professor Laski appeared on a sort of French Revolution cart fitted with a microphone instead of a guillotine, dressed in a tight-fitting hip-slinky overcoat of the sort that dance-band leaders wear.'

"Was that intended to be offensive?" asked Slade.

"That was not intended to be offensive," said Mr Wentworth Day. "It was intended to draw a striking parallel between his attire in a country town and the general people surrounding him. I thought it was entirely out of place in a rural market-place."

"'An overcoat that dance-band leaders wear.' That is intended to be a disparaging remark, is it not?"

"Not at all—a pictorial description."

"'He addressed the crowd with an air of quite remarkable superiority'?"

"That is perfectly true."

"'For the better part of an hour he sprayed us with an oleaginous stream of rhetorical oratory'?"

"That is my description of it, sir, and I stick to it."

"Oily, you mean?"

"Yes, oily, and very condescending, I thought."

"'Full of sly half-truths'?"

"That I also stick to."

"Meaning that a half-truth is worse than a lie?"

"Meaning that it was a half-truth."

"Do you regard a half-truth as being worse than a lie?"

"I regard a half-truth, Mr Slade, as being half a truth. . . ."

"'His gibes at Mr Churchill and 'that imp' Beaverbrook, his cocksureness, his irritating air of condescension, his Manchester accent which married so ill with the affectation of Oxford donnishness.'"

"I think that is a legitimate observation."

And there was much more in similar vein, while the unfortunate Harold Laski had to sit by, perhaps pretending not to hear the perfectly fair answers to his counsel's none too wise questions.

The cross-examination of James Wentworth Day galloped home to a rousing finish in which Slade asked him in seven separate questions whether he had been setting a trap for Mr Laski. Mr Day said the words "we would have to use violence even if it means revolution" were spoken to him "In quite a clear voice but not a shout. He was looking at me. He was in a white heat of anger and he added that when that violence or revolution came I should quite naturally be one of the objects of it. This was said to me in a most menacing fashion with his arm up like that."

"Was there a lamp-post anywhere near?" asked Rayner.

"My Lord," said Wentworth Day, "I had a vision of myself being dragged off to one."

"Were you trying to lay a trap for Mr Laski?" asked Slade.

"I think Mr Laski is far too experienced a public speaker to fall into any trap," replied Mr Day.

"I did not ask you whether your trap succeeded. Will you listen to my question. Were you trying to lay a trap for Mr Laski?"

"No. I was asking him to clarify his previous statement and state his object clearly and plainly."

The next witness was Major Richard Breene, British Consul at Trebizond, who had been present at the Newark meeting seventeen months earlier. His evidence had been taken on Commission at the British Consulate at Istanbul and was read to the court. "Of the interruptions I have mentioned," Major Breene deposed, "Mr Laski, in reply to the second one, said, 'If the Labour Party does not obtain the reforms desired, it may be necessary to use violence' and he added 'if that means revolution', or words to that effect. . . . When he made the last statement I turned round to my wife, who was with me, and said, 'My God, Laski has slipped there. That's a pretty serious statement.' "

In cross-examination at Istanbul, Peter Bristow, junior counsel for Professor Laski, could not get Major Breene to support Laski's statement that although it had been Wentworth Day, not Laski, who had first phrased the alleged threat to achieve revolution by violence, Laski himself had never afterwards used it. "It is not my recollection of it, and the reason I am fairly confident about it is that that evening, after I went back to the hotel, I made a note of what had happened actually and it bears it out."

"Major Breene," Bristow had asked him, "if your recollection of what you heard was right your view was, I take it, that Laski had been trapped into saying something silly by a deliberate and careful bit of heckling?"

"Yes," was Major Breene's not unimportant answer.

The next witness for the defence was Councillor Henry Carlton, who said he had missed much of the heckling exchange but his memory of what Laski had said from the platform was, "If we could not get it by fair means we should have to get it by revolution even if it meant violence." In cross-examination he said he had previously met Wentworth Day, who had told him he was going to the meeting to heckle Laski. Mr Carlton explained how the letter to the *Nottingham Guardian* had been compiled over the telephone. During re-examination, when the Lord Chief Justice asked him why he had thought it was his duty to write this letter he replied, "Because I thought it was a dangerous speech to be making at such a time." "That is all I wanted," said Sir Patrick Hastings.

Hastings made his closing speech in a jocular mood. "After long experience I have never yet known a case in which anything that I have said has had any effect on the jury one way or the other, and therefore I have come to the conclusion that the shorter the time I take in saying it the better for everyone. You know, members of the jury," he said with colloquial confidence, "this is not very far away from being a storm in a tea-cup, this case. If there had not been an imminent election, it would have passed, Mr Laski would have gone home and his supporters no doubt would have said, 'Good old Laski, he's at it again'; but because there is an election don't you think somebody said, 'Laski, you have got to stop this at once'? And once you start issuing writs, you know, you have to go on. . . .

"I told you I was only going to be a few minutes. I have been fifteen, and I am afraid that is too long. I wish you good luck in the hope that Mr Slade will not be four times as long. Whether you will get that good luck or not, I don't know. I doubt it."

His words proved prophetic. Gerald Slade, in his closing speech, spoke for the rest of that Friday afternoon and for a considerable part of the following Monday morning when the case was resumed. He took a very long time to put, in effect, Professor Laski's basic contention that he had never said the offending words alleged to have been uttered at the Newark meeting—and that if he had he had "succumbed to a careful trap" provoked by "a blatantly offensive question by a blatantly offensive questioner"; and that the newspaper report was not fair and accurate because it made no reference, on the same page, to the long and peaceful political meeting which had taken place before the heckling started.

When it came to Rayner's turn he summed up for twenty minutes before lunch on the final day and for only an hour afterwards: refreshingly, and characteristically, brief after a case which had droned on for five days. "The case with which we are concerned", he told the jury, "is essentially what may be called a political case, a case with a strong political flavour and it would be a most undesirable thing (indeed almost impossible) that a judge, whose duty it is to keep himself clear of politics and to express no political views one way or the other, should try an action of this sort; and it is essentially one in which both parties would desire, I think, to have the verdict of a jury."

He outlined the law in England regarding the right of discussion: "A citizen of this country is entitled to hold what opinions he pleases and he is freely entitled to express and to write those opinions. He can do it in books and he can do it in newspapers, and other newspapers and writers in books can take the opposite view and can express what opinions they like. There is no special privilege attaching to newspapers or to writers or authors of books. When we talk about freedom of the Press, whether we are talking about the Press as newspapers or the Press as books, you have to remember that exactly the same privileges and disabilities attach to writers in the public Press and writers of books that they put out for sale and distribution among the public as to any other person, and that there is no special privilege which attaches to any of them."

He quoted Dicey: "'A man may in this country publish anything which twelve common people, that is to say, twelve jurymen'—now it is seven, but that does not matter and I will say 'seven'—'selected at random from a panel of jurymen think it is expedient should be published; he may not write or publish anything which seven of his countrymen think ought not to be published'."

"But," the judge continued, "newspapers have one privilege and, as far as I know, one privilege only, and it is this: Parliament . . . has said that if a fair and accurate report of a public meeting on a matter of public concern and which it is to the public benefit should be known is published in a newspaper, the newspaper is protected. . . . The first and most essential thing before the newspaper can claim that protection is that the report should be fair and accurate; it must be both. . . . To be fair it must not take words out of their context, and above all, of course, it must not attribute to a speaker what he did not say."

The case they were trying, Rayner said, arose from an election meeting when "tempers run high; repartees are made and questions are asked very often which a speaker resents and may rightly resent. No one ought to be too thin-skinned at election time if they choose to come down and make speeches and submit themselves to the electorate as supporting either this or that. But because a man ought not to be too thin-skinned he is not to have matters fastened on to him and attributed to him which he did not utter. On the other hand, if the report of his speech that is published, though it may be in condensed style, does accurately represent what he said, so that those who read the newspaper are fairly and truthfully informed of what the speaker said, then he cannot complain. . . .

"Members of the jury," Rayner commented, "I dare say you will have noticed that no two witnesses, as far as I know, are in agreement as to what was said." The newspaper reporter, Mr Opie, had not taken down in shorthand all that was said. Mr Wentworth Day's report of his own remarks was not textually accurate. But Mr Wentworth Day's evidence was that he asked Laski why he had openly advocated revolution by violence, and Laski agreed that that was the question.

"Now . . . I should imagine you would think that with the possible exception of Mr Day no one is in a better position to know what he was asked than Mr Laski, and if that is so, you will have to ask yourselves, in considering if it is likely that the words were used, having been asked that question is it likely that he would answer it, and does the sentence which is complained of appear to be an answer to that question? . . . If he did use the words it is nothing to the point to say, well, he was trapped into using them. The whole object of hecklers going to meetings and putting questions is to trip up a speaker if they can. What else do they go for? They generally say they go there, of course, to elucidate matters; but they generally go to these meetings in order to upset speakers, if they can, so as to put a different political complexion on the case.

". . . A man may always express his opinions provided that he avoids defamation, blasphemy, obscenity and does not fall, on the other side, into what I may call the pit of sedition. . . . You may say as a matter of your political creed that you hate this and you hate that; you may say that I believe in a political theory, and my political theory is that if you do not take this or that course, certain results may follow; but you must not use language which can fairly be taken as an incitement to violence and to lead to revolution. . . . You may, of course, indoctrinate people to such an extent that your words do amount to incitement. . . .

". . . Now, Sir Patrick on behalf of the defendants has really said to you, as I understand it, this: If you take the Professor's books and his speeches, it may be that he pays lip-service to the fact that he is only warning in a pessimistic or regretful tone people that if this does not happen, or if this reform is not granted, or this programme is not accepted, there must be violence; but if you say that often enough and in the way that he did say it, why, that is in effect inducing people to say: 'Well, we are told and we are urged to have violence.' . . .

"I do say one thing. There was one point that Mr Laski made when giving his evidence. It was one which, speaking only for myself, I was a little surprised to hear. On reflection, I think he may be entitled to say in the passages which have been read out that he does in some passages say: 'Well, the people who will attack are the capitalists who will fight in defence of their capital and their institutions'. But, on the other hand, I think it is fair to say that a good many people would read his warning as meaning: 'If the capitalists do not give way, it is the proletariat or working classes or labourers, or whatever you like to call it, who will use violence for the purpose of getting their way.' If a man stops me in the street and says, 'Give me your wallet'; well, of course, if I consent to that and hand over my wallet, there is no need to use violence; but if I do not hand it over at once, then violence may be used. And then Charles I and the French Revolution are referred to. It is true that in the French Revolution the French aristocracy fought for their privileges. It is equally true, I suppose, that the first violence came from the proletariat who rose and attacked them first by taking the Bastille, which was the beginning or the symptom of the revolution, and afterwards by the attack which they made."

The jury took only forty minutes to make up their minds. That the report in the *Newark Advertiser* was a fair and accurate report of a public meeting, and that it dealt with a matter of public concern which it was beneficial for the public to know. Rayner Goddard gave judgment for the defendants with costs.

Harold Laski was physically and morally shattered. He immediately tendered his resignation from the Labour Party National Executive, on the ground that his continued association might harm the party; but this was not accepted. The greatest blow to his ego was the shame of being branded as, in Rayner's words to the jury, a "sedition-monger", when he had always considered himself "an honourable servant of a great movement". For a time Laski believed he was financially shattered, too. The costs, which he had been told were £20 000, were finally taxed at £13 000, but the sum was raised—with a £2 000 surplus—in small contributions from the Labour Party rank and file and a $6 000 testimonial from a hundred of Laski's American friends. That affectionate reaction did little to soothe his emotional defeat. Six months after the verdict he wrote to his lifelong friend Mr Justice Felix Frankfurter of the United States Supreme Court, apologizing for his "unforgiveable" silence: "The simple truth is that, ever since my grim defeat in that libel action, all the strength and energy I have had has gone into keeping my head up, and convincing myself that I was not really a disastrous failure who injured those I love and all the principles for which I care. . . . Morally, I believe, I think honestly, that men not in the least of my way of thinking thought the result unjust. And, of course, my own philosophy ought to have taught me not to expect any other outcome."

Laski would have experienced the greatest surprise if he had known the truth that one of the most unsuspected "men not in the least of my way of thinking"—Rayner Goddard—thought the result unjust. But, in his ignorance—and, it must be said, in his amazing political naivety— Harold Laski had the most scurrilous opinion of the Lord Chief Justice. His wife has written:

"My husband had great confidence in the English legal system & therefore the result of the case gravely undermined his confidence in the English judiciary—this so much hurt him that he was more up- set when told by one of the Judge's relations or friends (I don't know which) that Lord Goddard was an owner of property & feared that the Socialists might deprive him of some of it, therefore he felt he was right in finding against a Socialist who was then Chairman of the Labour Party. I think this libel action shortened my husband's life as he died within 2 years; never having forgotten the case."[5]

Rayner Goddard's thoughts on the Laski libel action will be con- sidered shortly. Of more than passing interest is Laski's reaction to Goddard himself—not the childish acceptance of hearsay recorded by his wife, but the detailed and immediate evaluation set down after days of living in the shadow of Goddard's presidency.

Harold Laski's reflections were left in his desk drawer, un- published, in a manuscript written very shortly after his defeat. They are a testament of hypersensitivity. His reaction to Sir Patrick Hastings was extreme:

"He performs his war dance about you like a dervish intoxicated with the sheer ecstasy of his skill in his own performance. . . . He moves between the lines of sarcasm and insult. It is an effort to tear off, piece by piece, the skin which he declares no more than a mask behind which any man of understanding could have grasped the foulness of your purpose. He treats you, not as a human being, but as a surgeon might treat some specimen he is demonstrating to students in a dissecting room."

---

[5] Letter from Mrs Frida Laski to the author, 10 January 1972. Professor Harold J. Laski's death from a burst abscess on the lung occurred on 24 March 1950, $3\frac{1}{4}$ years after the libel verdict.

Laski goes on in this strain for much longer, on a note of consistent nausea. But his response to Lord Goddard was more organically subtle:

"And all the time, there sits above you the brooding and impassive judge, to whom this operation is no more than another day in an endless routine of similar days ... [*At the beginning of the summing-up*] The judge seems a kindly old man, with a winning smile that lights up his eyes. He speaks with unemphatic quietness, so that, sometimes, you have even to bend forward to catch what he says to the jury in an easy, almost conversational tone. When he tells them of some point the defence has made, or, with a half-amused smile, describes to them the nature of a political campaign, or urges them to realize the passionate care the Bench has taken to safeguard discussion, you almost feel that you are back in some pleasant lecture room of an Oxford college where an elderly don is retailing the details of some ancient trial decided long ago.

"Then, suddenly, his transition to another part of the evidence makes you wonder when he is going to stress that point in the first part which told so strongly in your favour; how he is going to comment on the curious methods of this witness, the subtle way in which your opponent's counsel tore endless passages from their context to paint his picture of your ugly purposes. He will not, surely, forget your counsel's comment on this suggestive point; he cannot have failed to notice that vital combination of circumstances so carefully omitted from the speech in which your opponent's counsel sought to prevent the jury from seeing the gap it revealed in his case. You cannot believe that he will studiously refrain from noting that the charges made against all you have ever said or written these twenty years not only have never been made before, but, were they true, ought obviously to have resulted in your appearance in the dock at Old Bailey. At some time, you are confident, he will bid the jury take notice of the massive testimony your own witnesses have given without an effort at serious contradiction. At least, so you think in growing uneasiness, he will remember that in your five-hour duel with opposing counsel you stood your ground, answered with straightforward clarity, did not fall into the traps he laid that you might grow angry or confused or irritated, and so be led into the situation where he is notoriously able to have a witness at his mercy.

"And then, with a sudden gasp, you realize that he is not going to put your case at all. He makes his point; he is careful always to emphasize to the attentive jury that it is for them, and them only, to choose whether they will accept the points he makes. But they are always your opponent's points, and you note, almost within the first half-hour of his summing-up, that he is conveying, not without some subtlety, what Mr Justice Holmes meant when he said that judicial decisions depend upon the 'inarticulate major premises' of the man on the Bench. And you understand at that stage that the case is lost.

"The judge not only hates the opinions you hold, but will explain to the jury that they are dangerous opinions. And since, at your opponent's instance, the jury is a 'special' jury, you know how unlikely it is that will have an atom of concern for anyone with dangerous opinions. What, you swiftly see, is the real issue at stake is not what was said at some place on a definite occasion, but the fact that you hold unpopular opinions which both judge and jury are convinced it is bad to hold and worse by far to express."[6]

Harold Laski never commented on James Wentworth Day, the principal witness against him. Mr Wentworth Day has, however, at my invitation, kindly given his own reflections on Rayner Goddard:

"My impression of Lord Goddard concerning Laski was that he regarded the man with some irritation, particularly when Laski subjected the Court to his usual flow of arrogant omniscience. The LCJ looked as though deep within he intensely disliked being lectured.

"I think he regarded me with amused understanding and tolerance. This was particularly evident when he asked me 'Was there a lamp post near?' and I replied: 'My Lord, I had a vision of myself being dragged off to one.'

"His question to me regarding my dislike of Laski—'You are distinguishing personal from political?'—was, I thought at the time, designed to be helpful to me . . .

"Some years after the trial was over, Lord Goddard was staying in this County [Essex] for the weekend and dined with friends of mine. His hostess said: 'You know a friend of ours, Jim Wentworth Day.' Goddard replied: 'I had plenty of opportunities to study Mr Wentworth Day during the Laski trial—he was a very able witness in a grave miscarriage of justice.' This was said with a broad smile, a chuckle and almost a wink. He certainly did not convey the impression that he really thought the verdict had been a grave miscarriage of justice. Nonetheless, I have been known in certain quarters of this County ever since as 'the Great Miscarriage' . . .

"Incidentally, the *New Statesman* declared after Laski's death that I had killed him. I certainly did not send a wreath. . . ."

---

[6] Harold J. Laski, posthumously published *Atlantic Monthly* Nov. 1952.

Fifteen years after the death of Harold Laski, his brother Neville Laski, Q.C., then aged sixty-five and recently retired as Judge of the Crown Court at Liverpool, had a conversation of remarkable tenderness with Lord Goddard, then aged eighty-eight. At the suggestion of a friend in whom he had confided, Neville Laski wrote a record of this conversation, and it is to this friend of the late Neville Laski—Mr H. Phillip Levy—that I am greatly indebted for a copy of the original document. This is the first time the full version has been published.[7] In addition to the account of Neville Laski's striking personal experience on the night of the verdict, it puts on record perhaps the most poignant self-disclosure ever made by Rayner Goddard.

Neville Laski wrote:

13.6.65

On Thursday last, June 10th, at 3 pm I was alone in the Smoking Room of the Benchers' suite in the Inner Temple. Lord Goddard entered and having sat down at once asked me 'Was your brother very grieved and angry with me for my conduct of his libel action?' I replied 'The first I knew of the case was when I read the account of the first day's hearing in the "Evening Standard". Whenever I sought to speak to him about the case he always brushed me off and in effect refused to discuss it.

'I know he was very deeply hurt and this is confirmed by what my cousin Norman Laski has told me. Norman said he went to court and insisted on taking Harold home so collapsed was his condition.'

Lord Goddard then said 'The reason I am speaking of this is very important to me personally. I have never worried about a case I have tried so much as this. Lately there has has been a revival of the case on the wireless and I have received numerous letters mostly critical—some of which I have answered.

'I did not agree with the finding of the Jury. I thought [*A. B., a Defence witness*] was lying throughout and I did not like any of the evidence for the Defence. I gravely considered whether there was anything I could do, but as a Jury was involved I was helpless. I have been unhappy about this case always and often think about it. I can say that it has been on my conscience. I do want to add that your brother was not a good witness. He could not answer simply 'yes' or 'no' and made long speeches. Slade was no match for Pat Hastings.'

I said that I was very grateful to Lord Goddard for his frankness. I reminded him that on the night of the verdict he and I, as a then Junior Bencher, were dining at the Inn. We were at opposite ends of the room. A

---

[7] A partial version of Neville Laski's account was quoted by Mr Levy in his letter to *The Times,* published on 12 June 1971.

fellow Bencher sensing that perhaps we both felt awkward took me across to Lord Goddard who of himself put out his hand shaking mine and said 'I hope no hard feelings.' I replied 'Of course not.' I ended by saying that I had always been appreciative of the way he had treated me personally in Court and as a fellow member of the Bench.

NEVILLE LASKI

That is a mellow note on which to leave this disturbing case, in which—whatever the rights or wrongs of the matters in issue—the pride and self-respect of a brilliant man were blasted.

13 Capital Punishment

By April 1948 Rayner was already well established within his own profession as a forceful and out-of-the-rut Lord Chief Justice: the undisputed master of his realm. His conduct of the Laski libel case and the chalk-pit murder trial, extensively covered in the newspapers, had also enabled him to make a considerable mark on the general public; but the first full blast of his quite extraordinary explosion upon the national scene was now at hand. No longer was he to be merely a lawyer's lawyer or even just the judges' own choice as their leader: now, at the age of seventy-one, he was to become truly a national—and highly controversial—figure, which he was to remain for the rest of his active working life. Even in the late nineteen-seventies, several years after his death, he still remains for many people the only judge they know of by name.

The starting-point for all this was a worthy but, in its original form (apart from one provision), quite unexceptionable piece of legislation—the Criminal Justice Bill of 1948. The legal framework for the administration of the Criminal Law had virtually not been brought up to date since the Criminal Justice Act of 1925. The task was long overdue, as all those concerned in the legal profession from the Lord Chief Justice downward readily conceded. The Bill dealt with five main topics: young offenders, probation, habitual criminals, various necessary reforms in the administration of the penal system—and the proposed abolition of corporal punishment, which was to be retained only for serious breaches of prison discipline. This last topic was the only part of the original draft of the Bill which Lord Goddard—and others—found (decidedly) not to their liking. As Rayner later told the House of Lords, "There are in this Bill many provisions which I welcome wholeheartedly, matters which relate to what I may call the everyday working of the courts."

But what prompted Lord Goddard's tenacious opposition to the Bill, on a scale unprecedented for a Lord Chief Justice in modern times, was not only the proposed abolition of flogging in the original draft, but also the proposed suspension of capital punishment contained in an amendment to the Bill introduced in the House of Commons by the late Mr Sydney Silverman, M.P., one of the most dedicated pioneers in the anti-hanging lobby. When originally introducing the Bill to the House back in November 1947, the late Mr Chuter Ede (later Lord Chuter-Ede), the Home Secretary, had pointed out that crimes of violence had increased so greatly since the end of the Second World War that the Attlee Government did not feel it right for them to propose abolishing capital punishment in their own Bill—but Mr Ede added, with the cowardice normal to Governments of all political persuasions in these 'delicate' areas, that if an amendment were introduced on the floor of the House at a later stage the question could be decided by a free vote and without the intervention of the Party Whips. Mr Silverman and his like-minded colleagues in both major political parties (although more on the Labour side than on the Conservative) gladly took the hint; and on 14 April 1948 the Commons approved by 245 to 222 votes (a majority of 23) an amendment to the Bill suspending capital punishment for an experimental period of five years.

Mr Chuter Ede had himself voted against the Silverman Amendment, but two days later—and it would seem without much prior thought of the full constitutional implications—he hurriedly announced that he would automatically reprieve all prisoners sentenced to death in the courts until the future of the Amendment was finally resolved: it would, of course, have to go to the House of Lords, together with the rest of the Bill, and receive their Lordships' assent before it could become law.

Twelve days later, on 28 April 1948, Lord Goddard went down to the House of Lords, and on the peers' Second Reading of the Bill made his maiden speech as a member of that august House. He had been a member for nearly four years ever since becoming a Lord of Appeal in Ordinary in July 1944, but he had never yet taken part in a debate. Now at 3.48 p.m. he rose from his place on the cross bench—symbolizing his non-involvement with any political party—and, in a conversational voice, just as if he was starting a summing-up to one of his juries, said, "My Lords, I have not had the privilege or honour of addressing your Lordships' House before, but it occurred to me that you would expect the holder of my office—because I suppose I am the head of the Criminal Judiciary—to say a few words today upon the practical working of this Bill, as I see it."

He doffed a hat to the constitutional niceties. He did not propose "to address your Lordships on the policy of much of the Bill. Of course, we all welcome and greatly look forward to the working of the probation provisions. But upon questions of policy I do not propose to embark, because I profoundly believe that the less judges have to do with policy, the better. Any Act which Parliament sees fit to pass we carry out to the best of our ability."

He went on to welcome some of the detailed "everyday" provisions of the Bill, dotting the 'i's and crossing the 't's of many of the clauses. The peers sat back; all seemed in order. Then at last the trumpets sounded: "Much of the debate which has so far taken place on this Bill has related to the question of capital punishment"—and he launched into a powerful statement of his own personal point of view, "I should like to look at the matter from another angle."

He said he could not "help feeling that this is really part of a much wider subject—the true functions of criminal law in regard to crime and punishment. Reading the debates in another place and leading articles that have appeared in responsible and weighty journals ... it has seemed to me that there is a great tendency nowadays to consider that punishment should never be punitive, only reformative. I agree with all my heart that when you are dealing with the sort of cases which come before magistrates daily, and perhaps to a lesser extent before Quarter Sessions—that is, when you are dealing with the young criminal, the boy who is drifting into crime, the man who has made a slip from which he can be rescued, or even the old lag in whom there is still some good that, given a fair chance, he will be able to develop—reformation is the main thing for a court to bear in mind.

"But that class is not the only class of criminal with which the law deals; and when you get to the Court of Assize an entirely different picture is presented. There you get cases in which there is definitely no question of reformation as it is ordinarily understood. . . ."

He went on to illustrate the examples of the ordinary motor-car manslaughter case where a perfectly respectable man kills through criminal carelessness, the persistent bigamist, the professional abortionist, the homosexual who corrupts small boys, the professional receiver, the normal, law-abiding citizen who slips into crime "perhaps because of some unlucky speculation or some unfortunate incident" and then "goes through hell". "They will never do it again. But can the judge overlook it? Can he pass it over?. . . . Yet one is not sentencing them for reformative purposes. They are sentenced because it is society's method of showing that if that conduct or those acts are persisted in certain consequences which must be unpleasant and must be punitive will result. I have never yet understood how you can have the criminal law a deterrent unless it is also punitive. The two things seem to me to follow one on the other."

He was now well into his stride, and the whole House listened with rapt attention to the rare sight of a great criminal judge expounding his own personal—and highly pragmatic—philosophy of the relationship between crime and punishment: "There is one other consideration which I believe should never be overlooked. If the criminal law of this country is to be respected, it must be in accordance with public opinion, and public opinion must support it. That goes very nearly to the root of this question of capital punishment. I cannot believe that the public opinion (or I would rather call it the public conscience) of this country will tolerate that persons who deliberately condemn others to painful and, it may be, lingering deaths should be allowed to live. . . .

"I know that in uttering this sentiment I shall not have the sympathies of everyone but, in my humble opinion, I believe that there are many, many cases where the murderer should be destroyed." To at least one trained observer, the representative of the *Daily Telegraph* newspaper, those words, spoken in unemotional tone, "had the finality of a judgment". To millions more, not then present in the House or even yet born, but contemplating today the grim world of the nineteen-seventies with its IRA terrorists and its so-called 'urban guerrillas', they will seem like a classic statement of truth.

A Departmental Committee under Sir Edward Cadogan, a former Conservative M.P. of impeccable distinction and appointed to the task by Sir John Simon when Home Secretary, had reported unanimously as far back as 1938 that corporal punishment should be abolished for all offences except as the ultimate sanction for grave disciplinary offences inside prison. It was a barbarism that should not remain part of the normal canons of the Criminal Law.

But Rayner would have none of that; and in his thunderings against the proposed abolition that now followed he did not even deign to mention the Committee's unanimous finding. It is perhaps the sole part of his criminal ethic with which his present biographer is totally at variance. But Rayner was adamant—"When I hear that there should never be corporal punishment in the case of an adult, I am sometimes inclined to say, 'If that be so, I wish you would tell me what I am to do with certain cases.' I may be wrong. I shall be the first to admit it if it can be shown that I am wrong, but I believe that in many cases involving youngish men—men up to twenty-five or thirty years of age and so forth—it might be far more beneficial to give them a very short sentence of imprisonment and something in the way of a whipping for the crime that they have committed, rather than send them to a long sentence."

He was not in favour of retaining the 'cat'. He said that every judge on the Bench would welcome its removal from the law's armoury: it was "a weapon or an instrument which ought not to be used".

"But are we so certain about the birch?" And he told the story of one of his cases at the Cambridge Assizes last summer where "a young man of twenty, a big, fine, hefty fellow", a farm-worker with an excellent character reference from his employer, went into a jeweller's shop in Ely and asked to see a watch. He chose a watch and said he would have a few other trinkets as well. The shop-keeper, a man of sixty-eight, offered to wrap them up, and while he was doing so the young farm-worker whipped a two-inch spanner out of his pocket and struck him on the head, knocking him to the floor. Then, just to make certain he would cause no trouble, he gave him two more crashing blows as he lay on the floor.

"I do not believe that that boy will ever do a thing like that again," said Rayner. "But was he to get away with it? Was he not to be punished for so cowardly and brutal attack upon an old man?"

The assembled peers, among whom the grey hairs far exceeded the dark, waited for the answer: "I gave him two months' imprisonment and twelve strokes of the birch rod, and I was not then depriving the country of the services of a good agricultural labourer over the harvest. I cannot help thinking that that was a better punishment than a sentence (which otherwise I would have had to impose) of at least two years' or possibly three years' penal servitude."

And there, for the moment, the matter rested. The House did not divide on the Bill's Second Reading, but the Government were made to realize that they had a new and unexpected adversary on their hands—the nation's senior criminal judge whom they had themselves appointed. As for the general public, Lord Goddard's name was all over the newspapers in banner headlines the next morning and for the first time the ordinary man in the street began to feel the full force of his personality.

Some four weeks later, on 28 April 1948, *The Times* newspaper carried the rare announcement that the Lord Chief Justice had tabled four amendments to a major Government Bill. Three were of only minor significance, but the fourth would have limited the abolition of corporal punishment to the cat o' nine tails: whipping with a birch rod would remain. Battle was now really joined: the floggers on one side, with the Lord Chief Justice at their head, and the Government—plus most informed sections in the community—on the other. It was not an ideal array of forces.

But Rayner's next personal outburst on to the scene was reverting to the question of capital punishment. At 4.08 p.m. on 2 June 1948, on the Committee Stage of the Criminal Justice Bill, he rose in the Lords to speak again about hanging. Earlier in the debate Lord Schuster, ex Permanent Secretary to ten successive Lords Chancellor and perhaps Rayner's oldest family friend and kinsman, had told the peers, at Rayner's request, that the unanimous view of the twenty King's Bench judges was opposed to the abolition of capital punishment.[1] "I am bound to say that I thought and think that they do represent a fair cross-section of the community," said Rayner, not without a certain air of self-satisfaction.

But he had another, more potent, stick of dynamite to throw in the Bill's path. For some six weeks now Mr Chuter Ede, the Home Secretary, had been doing exactly what he had announced he would do: he had automatically reprieved every prisoner sentenced to death for murder since 16 April. Four men had thus arbitrarily had their lives spared, and in at least three of the cases there could be little doubt that, in the ordinary way, a reprieve would not have been granted, and they would have been executed. "I speak merely as a lawyer," said Lord Goddard, "but judges are, after all, concerned with the constitutional law of this realm. I venture to submit to your

---

[1] A month later, on 30 June 1948, Rayner was to apologize to his fellow-peers for an unwitting error on his part. The judges were *not* unanimous. "I knew that they were not unanimous on the question of corporal punishment," he told the Lords, "But I thought they were unanimous on the subject of capital punishment. Two of the judges informed me afterwards that I was mistaken. I apologize to your Lordships and I am sure they will acquit me of having in any way intentionally misled them. Two of the judges told me (it shows what tricks memory can play) that they would support a proposal for an experimental period of five years."

Lordships, I hope without risk of being accused of exaggeration, that that is exercising a dispensing power which has been repudiated by Parliament ever since the days of James II. Such a situation is enshrined, in fact, in the Bill of Rights. Action of this sort is declared to be illegal. And if this is not altering the law by administrative action, I do not know what is . . . It is not too much to say—and I say this with the due sense of its importance—that this raises a most important constitutional issue."

Those were strong words from a Lord Chief Justice to describe the conduct of a Home Secretary: "illegal", "altering the law by administrative action", a charge of unconstitutional behaviour. Rayner went on, in an impressively forthright speech, to spell out yet again the arguments, as he saw them, against the abolition of hanging. He was, as ever, powerful and effective. But in a sense, perhaps, he really need not have bothered: the lordly backwoodsmen were out in force that day—quite a few of them even more extreme in their views than the Lord Chief Justice—and the Silverman Amendment was rejected by the overwhelming majority of 181 to 28.

That was not an end to the Government's worries. On the following afternoon, in the House of Commons, the Conservative Opposition were quick to avail themselves of this surprise weapon with which to belabour and embarrass the Government Front Bench. With that air of passionate concern worn by all politicians when seeking to make party capital out of an issue that really has nothing to do with party politics, Mr Anthony Eden (later Lord Avon), then the Deputy Leader of the Opposition, called for a Government statement in view of the charge that had been made of unconstitutional behaviour. That wily parliamentarian Herbert Morrison (later Lord Morrison of Lambeth), the Leader of the House, countered adroitly by saying there could be no such statement until the Bill formally returned to the floor of the House of Commons—and besides, if the point was so important, why had Her Majesty's Opposition not raised it themselves when the Home Secretary had made his announcement over six weeks earlier? Point, counterpoint: the politicians of Britain were at their usual game.

But the debate continued with increasing heat outside Parliament. Leader-writers thundered in the newspapers, angry letters—on both sides—were written to *The Times*, articles sprouted in magazines and journals: the nation was divided. The Government realized that its whole Criminal Justice Bill was in dire jeopardy over this one stumbling-block of a five-year suspension of capital punishment.

(The Lords had accepted Lord Goddard's amendment on retaining flogging, although restricted to the birch. But when the clause came back to the peers, restored to its original version by an unrepentant House of Commons, Lord Goddard did not press the matter to a division. He wanted to concentrate all his efforts on the capital punishment issue.)

The result was inevitable: the Government tried a compromise. On 15 July 1948, Mr Chuter Ede moved a Government amendment in the Commons in place of the Silverman Amendment. For the first time in English law, the notion of two categories of murder was put forward in a Government Bill. For a five-year experimental period, it was proposed that hanging should be retained only for certain specified kinds of "capital murder" committed with intent to kill or endanger life with life-imprisonment as the penalty for all other kinds of lesser "non-capital murder". The amendment ran to over hundred lines of somewhat turgid print, but in essence there were to be five categories of "capital murder":

(1) Murder committed in the course of robbery, burglary, housebreaking, wounding or inflicting grievous bodily harm by three people or more in concert, murders by explosives or other destructive substances, rape and indecent assaults on females, sodomy and indecent assault on males;

(2) Murder in the course of resisting or preventing arrest or escaping from custody or obstructing a police officer or anyone assisting him;

(3) Murder committed by the systematic administration of poison;

(4) Murder of prison officers by prisoners;

(5) Murder where the accused has already been convicted of a previous murder.

Complicated the new proposal may have been, but it was at least an attempt to try and placate both sides of the argument. Would it get the Government off the hook and their much-needed Bill on to the Statute Book? The House of Commons abolitionists were content with half a loaf as better than no loaf at all. The amendment was carried by 307 to 209, a majority of 98 as against the Silverman Amendment's earlier majority of only 23.

The abolitionists may well have been confident at that stage. With such an impressively strengthened majority in the elected House, surely the non-representational Upper Chamber must now give way? But such optimism, if it existed, would have been ill-founded. For it would not have taken into account two things: one, the Commons vote had nothing to do with the elective basis of its membership, it had been a free vote with each M.P. voting according to his own personal conscience and not according to any mandate from his electors; and two, Rayner Goddard was waiting for the Amendment in the House of Lords, ready to speak out as something the M.P.s were not on this fundamental issue: the Voice of the People.

On 20 July 1948, with the Parliamentary Session drawing to a close and with the Government having only a bare two weeks in hand to get their coveted Bill through Parliament or else have it go over into the next session, Rayner rose to address the assembled Lords: "This matter, as we are all agreed, transcends all Party considerations," he began. "A few weeks ago your Lordships rejected by an emphatic vote the clause which had been sent up from another place abolishing capital punishment. It is agreed on all hands—it has been conceded in another place and certainly in the public Press—that the action of your Lordships was in accord with the opinion of the vast majority of people in the country. If that is so, I ask: what is there to compromise about? With whom are we compromising? Why should there be a compromise? If your Lordships' vote on the last occasion has received the unqualified approval of the people of the country, I venture to submit to your Lordships that for us to depart from it and to compromise in some way on a matter of this substance, by bringing in some milk and water amendment, would not be doing the duty which the Constitution places upon us."

He then, item by item, took the Lords through the proposed Government amendment as if they were a jury and he was summing up to them in a complicated trial of major importance. Indeed, he virtually put the Government's new clause on trial—and had little difficulty in exposing, as with so many rushed compromises, its grim stupidities and contradictions. "I believe", he said, "that in the Criminal Law there are three very desirable principles that we should all strive to attain. The first is simplicity, the second is certainty, and the third is that, in its application so far as possible, it should be neither fortuitous nor capricious." The clause offended against all three principles.

For example: "I yield to none in my desire to support and protect the police, but I believe, and I am sure that every police officer would think, that the lives of the humblest of His Majesty's subjects are as valuable as the lives of police officers. It seems to me not right that a man who, in the height of passion or temper, kills a policeman—perhaps not deliberately in the sense that he pointed a revolver at him—but in the struggle to avoid arrest ... should be told that he is guilty of a capital crime; whereas a man who has taken an axe or hammer, perhaps to a sick or ailing wife, and had battered her brains out should be told that he has committed non-capital murder."

Then there was systematic poisoning. "Are we really to be told at this time that it is to be a capital offence if you administer more than one dose of poison to a person, though if you have taken the precaution to give them a fatal dose in the first instance then it is not a capital offence? I submit that if that law is put on the Statute Book it reduces the law of murder in this country to a laughing-stock."

His peroration was masterly: "There is only one last observation I wish to make. I suggest that public opinion was opposed, and resolutely opposed, to the original clause, I see no indication that public opinion has been stirred in favour of this compromise clause—perhaps because few people except lawyers can understand it. However that may be, I have seen and heard no demand in the outside world for a compromise on this question. It is said that the clause will effect a reform in the law. Gibe as much as you will at judges, who, it is always said, are opposed to alterations in the law. That is not true. I believe that if you go through the many reforms in the Common Law which have taken place in the last century and in the present century you will find that nearly all, if not all, have had their inception in judgments which have been given from the Bench indicating where changes in the law are necessary. I have said already that I would welcome some reform of this law of construc-tive murder;[2] but let us remember that Criminal Law is part of the Common Law of this country, and the Common Law of this country is a very precious heritage. It is to the Common Law and not to the judges—for they only adminster the law—that we look for the protection of our property, our liberties and of our lives. Surely we ought to hesitate before we alter the law, and ought not to alter it unless we are convinced that those who live under it demand and will approve of the alteration."

The majority by which their Lordships rejected the clause was staggering: 99 votes to a bare 19. There had been Lord Chief Justices before who had thundered in the House on behalf of the

---

[2] A highly artificial concept of the existing law which allowed juries to convict of murder in certain cases where there was no express or factual 'malice' (i.e. intent to kill or maim) in the act of killing but merely 'constructive malice' implied from the circumstances.

law, and what they considered to be its special position in society and the need to preserve its integrity (Lord Hewart is an obvious example of this type of Chief); but there had never been before—or since—a Lord Chief Justice who had claimed to speak as the champion of the public conscience. And above all in a dispute with the public's elected representatives! In many ways, the rejection of the Attlee Government's somewhat pathetic attempt at a compromise solution to the problem of capital punishment was one of Rayner Goddard's most signal achievements.

For, of course, the Government, faced with their renewed defeat in the Lords, had to give way. Two days later Mr Chuter Ede told the House of Commons that if it insisted on the clause the entire Bill would be lost; it could not possibly pass into law that session. Under the Parliament Act of 1911, the Lords could stymie the Bill's passage for two years. He urged the House to accept the view that they would not be acting in the public interest if they lost this important and much-needed measure simply to give further expression to their disagreement with the Lords. He threw out one consolation: the Government proposed to explore "without delay" what practicable means there were of limiting the death penalty to certain crimes of murder in a manner which would not be open to the objections raised against their amendment.

The M.P.s knew when they were beaten. They gave way. The Criminal Justice Bill passed into law without the Government amendment. The question of abolition was put on the shelf, to gather dust while a Royal Commission announced by the Government four months later—that classic escape-route for Governments in difficulty—amassed evidence, heard its witnesses, held its meetings, deliberated long and hard, and took four years to bring out a report. Ironically, by the time the Royal Commission on Capital Punishment, under its chairman, Sir Ernest Gowers, finally issued its report in September 1953 the ground-swell in favour of abolition had returned with even greater force and was running at gale-strength—not the least because of an Old Bailey trial in December 1952 which was perhaps Rayner's most famous case, the trial of Craig and Bentley, and which we will meet in Chapter 17.

14 The 'Strong' Chief Develops

Believing that all power corrupts, and absolute power corrupts absolutely, there were influential people within Great Britain as the half-century chimed in 1950 who feared for the corruption of Rayner Goddard. Their panic was unfounded. He had now emerged as an unmistakably strong Lord Chief Justice—that adjective was the most frequent description of him in all the formal valedictory tributes when he retired after twelve years as Chief. The term 'strong' Lord Chief Justice can, of course, have two implications: either that he makes his brother justices seem weak, in which case he is well on course for absolutism; or that by his own strength he tempers the quality of his brothers, so that, as Sir Hartley Shawcross eventually wrote of Rayner upon his retirement:[1]

"Perhaps his greatest claim on the gratitude of his country is that under his distinguished leadership we probably have the strongest Bench of Judges England has ever had. No longer, it may be, are there the 'characters' whose personal foibles used to attract attention. But we have also lost that excessive judicial detachment from the realities of life, that tiresome judicial pomposity, and those occasional political or social prejudices which sometimes seemed to detract from the objectivity and fairness of judicial administration. The influence of Rayner Goddard has brought tremendous strength and cohesion to the Bench. I have no doubt that he will always rank among the greatest of English Chief Justices."

Rayner Goddard never underestimated public opinion and public

---

[1] In a Leader-page article in the *Daily Telegraph* on 21 August 1958.

support. The blistering homilies he addressed to prisoners after a finding of guilty—before sentencing them, occasionally with breathtaking severity, sometimes with heartstopping mild-ness—were directed, in a sense, almost as strongly towards the Press box as to the dock: not through any personal vanity or seeking after publicity for its own sake—he was the last man to do that—but because what is the effect of an official curse if the public cannot observe the bell, book and candle? And Rayner *needed* public opinion—and mainly retained it even when he could not command Parliamentary opinion, during his abrasive 'strong' campaigns. "If the criminal law of this country is to be respected", he had said in his first House of Lords debate in April 1948, "it must be in ac-cordance with public opinion, and public opinion must support it."

Public opinion is represented by more artillery than *Times* leaders. Rayner Goddard did not habitually denigrate the 'sensational' Press, because in many ways he was himself a 'sensational' operator: not always in good taste; often deliberately introducing a tinge of the shocking; didactic but never dull. Witness the stories he used to tell at public functions. Some combined morality with outrage, and mixed them with laughter. Some were straight show-offs, perhaps as meretricious as an executioner's boasting. An example of the latter: his often-repeated anecdote of the occasion when he left Winchester Assizes, having just sentenced three prisoners simultaneously to be hanged; and a barrel organ in the street was playing the *Eton Boating Song*, 'we'll all swing together'. Mr George Greenfield, a diner-out who heard it too often, commented years later:[2] "How the relatives of the condemned men—and of the victim—would have relished his keen sense of humour". An example of the former style: his story against psychiatrists, which he said he had as gospel truth from Mr Justice Lewis. A man was arrested in the act of rape. A girl was screaming with agony, the man was wearing strong spectacles. The prisoner had no defence, so he spent money on a psychiatrist, "which is sometimes better than a defence". The psychiatrist, giving evidence, told the judge that the prisoner's conduct was due to his short sight, which had given him an inferiority complex. "What he needs, my Lord, is not punishment but a new pair of spectacles."

Pointed, funny, sometimes perhaps insensitive, always human, sensational. The recipe is the same for Goddard as for the *Daily Mirror*. In fact, unknown to any of his colleagues on the Bench or to

---

[2] In his letter to *The Times* that appeared on 12 June 1971 in the post Levin spate of correspondence, see Aftermath.

any of his profession at the Bar, five years later Rayner virtually wrote an article in that very newspaper. Lord Cudlipp, then its Editor, relates the incident in his book *At Your Peril*:

"The *Mirror*, in its series of erudite 'Spotlight' pamphlets on Defence, Education, Anglo-American Partnership, Britain's Voice Abroad, Honours & Awards, Trade Unions, The Future of Television, The New Africa, and The Common Market produced one on Justice which so impressed the Lord Chief that he wrote a six-page foolscap commentary on what our writers recommended. 'In commenting upon certain aspects I do so in the confident belief that no publicity will be given to my remarks, at least as coming from me,' he wrote. The opportunity to publish his views was too important an occasion to miss, and after further correspondence he wrote:

> Royal Courts of Justice,
> London, W.C.2.
> 9 December 1954.

DEAR SIR,

I have no objection to your publishing the gist of my letter to you and if you like to put in somewhere some such words as 'The Lord Chief Justice has pointed out' or 'We have ascertained that the Lord Chief Justice is taking such and such a course' I should have no objection. All that I desire is that it should not appear that I am taking part in a newspaper discussion, though as I have told you I take no exception to the tone of your pamphlet or to much that it contained. There were only a few points which I could supplement and perhaps correct.

> Yours faithfully,
> GODDARD

"So the *Daily Mirror* became the first newspaper to publish the views of a Lord Chief Justice on his administration of the courts during his term of office: the headline was 'How Lord Goddard is trying to speed up Justice', the signature was Paul Cave's, but the thoughts were those of the Lord Chief Justice."

This is all the more remarkable when it is remembered that one of the three 'keystone' cases of 1949–51, with which this chapter is mainly concerned, was, as we will see shortly, one involving the *Daily Mirror* and ending in its then Editor, Mr Silvester Bolam, going to gaol!

All three of these 'keystone' cases attracted and consolidated further prodigious publicity for Rayner Goddard, who was developing as the first legal figure for many a decade—apart from professional oddities like Lord Darling—to be a popularly recognized, caricaturable 'character', and certainly the first—and so far only—Lord Chief Justice in history to capture something of the affection as well as the awe of ordinary people, in a Churchillian manner. Indeed, the two men got on very well;[3] not for nothing, as related in the very first chapter, did Sir Winston dub him "Lord God-damn".

It was this Churchillian quality that manifested itself to the full in Rayner's judgment in the case of *Willcock* v. *Muckle* in July 1951. Most of the people who, during his lifetime and even after his death, were happy to berate Rayner for his 'reactionary' views and so-called championing of the dark forces of ignorance and repression almost certainly do not realize that, in large measure, they owe it to him that we no longer have to carry around with us wherever we go State 'identity cards', individually numbered like the brands on cattle in a cattle pen.

These grubby statutory National Registration documents, as they were officially called, had come into existence during the Second World War. Perhaps then they had some value or at least some justification, but they had been scandalously perpetuated by an opportunist bureaucracy, so that the British had been forced by arbitrary regulation to carry their rotting remnants for twelve years after the Hitler panic had caused them to be issued in 1939 and for as many years of peace—six—as for years of war.

In the early nineteen-fifties Mr Clarence Henry Willcock, an enthusiastic member of the Liberal Party, decided that enough was enough.

In somewhat the same manner as the current 'drink-drive' legislation lays any motorist open to a breathalyser test once he has come technically within the observation of a uniformed policeman, any pedestrian citizen could at that time be asked for his identity card if

---

[3] Sir Clement Penruddock, who was Secretary to the Chequers Trust from 1941 to 1972, has told me of one occasion when Churchill was Premier and Rayner Goddard, as Lord Chief Justice and therefore Senior Trustee of Chequers, had gone down to the Premier's country home for some special matter of business. "After dinner, came the time when the entourage were told to leave. The two old boys were left in the dining-room. Time went by, and an assistant was pacing anxiously up and down in the hall. What had happened to them? He put his head round the door—and there were the two old boys, with arms round each other's shoulders, singing 'A bicycle made for two'!"

he had come into official contact in any way with the police—picking up lost property (so why report it?), witnessing suspicious loitering (so why stick your neck out?), or, of course, getting sufficiently involved with summary justice to be taken to the nick anyway. The additional penalty for not producing an identity card, either on the spot or within the next two days at a police station, was a fine of about the same weight as a modern parking fine.

Once Mr Clarence Willcock had decided to challenge the identity card regulations, he was unconscionably delayed—with the usual reformer's luck—in finding any opportunity to demonstrate his stand: no police officer would ask him for his card. Eventually the law deigned to notice Willcock's new habit of driving home at five miles over the speed limit—nothing dangerous, just a tidy statutory offence. The police courteously stopped him and inspected the three motoring documents which Willcock was not objecting to carrying. With the driving licence in his hand, a constable asked for Willcock's identity card. Willcock said how glad he was to be able to say that he would not show his identity card, he would not produce it later at a police station, and he would welcome the legal action against him that he foresaw.

Eventually he was summoned to appear before the Hornsey magistrates. His solicitor, Mr Lucien Fior, another active member of the Liberal Party, developed a keen argument to convince the court that the War was over. It was, after all, nearly six years since VE Day. He reminded the Bench that the Courts (Emergency Powers) Act, which had introduced many short-cuts and temporary time-saving legal procedures as wartime measures, had recently been terminated by Order in Council, for the specific reason, as stated in the preamble, that the Emergency had come to an end. The National Registration Act which instituted identity cards, and the Defence Regulation which gave the police extraordinary powers to demand their production, was renewed every year by a formal Emergency Laws (Transitional Provisions) Act. But if the Emergency was over—*vide* the authority of the Order in Council cited—then the National Registration Act 1939 and the Defence Regulation bolstering it were void, since their duration had been expressly stated as *the period of the present Emergency*.

The magistrates did not capitulate to Mr Fior's argument. They convicted Willcock, but gave him an absolute discharge and agreed to state a case for an appeal to the Divisional Court. In the King's Bench Division three judges adjourned the case for argument by the Attorney-General, then Sir Frank Soskice, K.C., before a court of seven judges. By now Willcock's enterprise as the village Hampden representing the country's 'little men' had started an avalanche of disruption. For if Willcock's contention was right, and the observation that the War was over which had justified the cessation of the Courts (Emergency Powers) Act extended to other Emergency Acts, then some thirty surviving wartime statutes would go crashing into the gulf along with the National Registration Act. And the effect of such a disorderly abrogation of State power would greatly upset the methods by which much administration in the country was effected, and even much business carried out. Establishment and good order would be more neatly served if the decision went against Willcock. This would mean in effect that although the War was over from the point of view of the framers of the Courts (Emergency Powers) Act, it was still on for the National Registration Act and some thirty others; and the phrase 'period of the present Emergency' had an Alice-in-Wonderland elasticity which meant a different thing, and a different length of time, to every Minister who was profiting by the continuance of an Emergency Act—the "Emergency" was different for the purpose of each Act.

That, in fact, was the legal position, ruled on 26 June 1951 a King's Bench Divisional Court of seven judges presided over by Lord Goddard. It was a decision of five to two—with Sir Raymond Evershed, the Master of the Rolls, and Mr Justice Devlin 'doubting', though not formally dissenting from the majority view. Logic, if not liberty, was on the side of the State: "It was argued", said Rayner, "that there can be different aspects of the same emergency, and that, if the Crown considered that a particular aspect no longer existed, so that the emergency which occasioned that particular Act to be passed was ended, it would follow that all the Acts dealing with other aspects of the same emergency were terminated. In my opinion, and that of the judges who agree with me on this point, (that) argument is correct, and on the true construction of this formula, used in so many of the Acts passed at the outbreak of the War, it is contemplated that to bring any of those Acts to an end there must be an Order in Council dealing with that particular Act.

". . . as there is no Order in Council terminating the National Registration Act, 1939 we cannot say that the Act has been terminated."

But the Lord Chief Justice of England was not prepared to leave the matter there. "This Court" he said—and he carried all six of his fellow-judges with him in these words—"wishes to express its emphatic approval of the way in which the magistrates dealt with this case by granting the defendant an absolute discharge. Because the police have powers, it does not follow that they ought to exercise them on all occasions or as a matter of routine. From what we have been told it is obvious that the police now, as a matter of routine, demand the production of National Registration Cards whenever they stop or interrogate a motorist for whatever cause. . . . This Act was passed for security purposes: it was never intended for the purposes for which it is now being used . . . I hope that, if a similar case comes before any other Bench of justices, they will deal with the case as did the Hornsey Bench and grant an absolute discharge."[4]

Almost immediately the Home Secretary drew the attention of all Chief Constables to the remarks of the Lord Chief Justice, and instructed them: "In future, the police will demand the production of identity cards only when it is absolutely necessary; for example, in cases where there is reason to· suspect serious crime, or when the person concerned is suspected of being a deserter or absentee without leave from H.M. Forces."

Two champions of the common man had triumphed: Clarence Willcock[5] and Rayner Goddard. But Rayner, for all that his critics may in ignorance say, was always independent, always refusing to toe any official line, whether drawn by the Government of the day, the police or anyone else. Some four years earlier, in a case where a policeman had gone into a public house to take a bet off a street runner so that the man could then be prosecuted for an offence against the 1906 Street Betting Act, he had exploded:

"The Court observes with concern and disapproval the fact that the police authority at Derby thought it right to send a police officer into a public house to commit an offence. It cannot be too strongly emphasized that, unless an Act of Parliament provides for such a course of conduct—and I do not think any Act of Parliament does so provide—it is wholly wrong for a police officer or any other person to be sent to commit an offence in order that an offence by another person may be detected. It is not right that police authorities should instruct, allow or permit detective officers or plain-clothes constables to commit an offence, so that they can prove that another person has committed an offence".[6]

---

[4] The judgment is reported in (1951) 2 All England Reports at page 367.
[5] Mr Willcock died two years later, at the age of fifty-eight, when addressing a Liberal Party meeting. "Mr Chairman, I don't think I can go on," he suddenly said, and sat down and died.
[6] *Brannan* v. *Peek*, reported in (1947) 2 All England Reports at page 572.

Snoopers who travelled on road coaches to see if they were properly licensed, Ministry of Agriculture officials who made dispossession orders which were bad in law, Inland Revenue officials who with "cruel delay" did not bring an income tax case for two years, an officious immigration officer who was assaulted, magistrates who abused their powers and automatically asked their clerk to retire with them when considering the *facts*—as distinct from the law—of a case or imposed excessive costs upon a defendant as a punishment: all were castigated from the Bench by this stalwart Lord Chief Justice. He had an instinct for fairness.

And it was that instinct, more than anything else, that was affronted by the conduct of the *Daily Mirror* in the celebrated Haigh-Bolam contempt of court case in March 1949. It has long been an essential principle of English (and, indeed, Scottish) law that an accused person should not unfairly be put in peril by premature disclosure of what is already known about him. It may be chauvinistic liberalism to claim that this is an outstanding British concept. Trial by newspaper is tolerated in many other countries in the world, not least in some of our fellow-members of the European Economic Community and in the United States of America. It is worthy of record that Rayner Goddard, the 'strong' Lord Chief Justice, tenaciously fought *for the rights of the accused* in many of his public stances. His long-fought campaign for the reform of the Court of Criminal Appeal, for instance, so that it should be able to order a new trial, offered, as we shall see in the next chapter, and as he himself said, a second chance of acquittal to a convicted man—never another attempt to convict an acquitted man.

And so he was particularly angry about the conduct of the *Daily Mirror* in virtually condemning a man—John George Haigh —before ever he had stood his trial for murder; or even been brought before a court.

On 27 February 1949 the nation's newspapers reported the disappearance from a London hotel of a wealthy widow named Mrs Olive Durand-Deacon. On the morning of 28 February most of them published interviews with John George Haigh, who said he was 'tired of being questioned by the police'. At the same time they commented on the previous disappearance of five other persons. From that evening, and for forty-eight hours afterwards, Haigh— however "tired" he was—was further questioned at Chelsea Police Station, and on 2 March he was charged at Horsham with the murder of Mrs Durand-Deacon, of whom a few pathetic remnants had been found in a sludge emptied from a drum of acid at nearby Crawley.

In the course of his interrogation, Haigh made a number of admissions about the five other persons who had been named as missing, and on 3 March the police held a Press conference, "off the record", which divulged much of what he said, even to his very phraseology.

The decision to make these revelations was taken by the police, and can probably be viewed as a token of their camaraderie with the Fleet Street Press and of appreciation of their forbearance during many frustrating episodes in the past when crime reporters, who sometimes knew more than the police, had obligingly helped with information on the one hand and stayed publicly silent on the other. "Lads," the mood seemed to be, "you have been wonderfully cooperative with us in the past. Now we can do something for you by letting you in on the hottest story we have had for donkey's years—but it is up to you to get it past your editorial lawyers!" Every newspaper has, of course, its own team of resident lawyers available for almost immediate consultation.

The decision to make the revelations having been taken by the police, the further decision to divulge them was taken by the editorial executives of the *Daily Mirror* with Sylvester Bolam, their Editor, at their head—and the man who, in accordance with established practice, would take ultimate liability. It was decided to publish the facts without specific reference to the murder charge against Haigh in connection with Mrs Durand-Deacon—but virtually alongside the report of his appearance in court on the charge relating to her. How it was thought that subterfuge would keep the matter within the law, it is difficult to imagine. "The truth is that the '*Mirror*' perpetrated a blunder", says Lord Cudlipp in his book *Publish and be Damned.*

For on 4 March, 1949, the day after the police Press conference, this was the lead story in the first edition of the *Daily Mirror:*

VAMPIRE WILL NEVER STRIKE AGAIN

"The vampire killer will never strike again. He is safely behind bars, powerless ever again to lure his victims to a hideous death.

"This is the assurance which the *Daily Mirror* can give today. It is the considered conclusion of the finest detective brains in the country.

"The full tally of the vampire's crimes is still not known. It will take squads of police many weeks to test the ghastly tale which has come tumbling from his own lips as he sat, wild eyed and drawn, under a powerful guard.

"But as the police have listened, appalled, to his sadistic story of mass murder, mutilation and the drinking of his victims' blood, confirmation has been flashed back of his earlier boasts.

"During interrogation the vampire explained that he was not happy about his first murders.

"'It was a messy business,' he said. 'I found that my technique improved later.'

"It was as if a great artist were looking back on his handiwork. He told his questioners that he had cut the throats of the people he had killed, and sucked their blood through a lemonade straw.

"And, so far, he has named in his catalogue of murder five people only. They are:

"Dr Archibald Henderson, Mrs Rosalie Mercy Henderson, his wife, Mr Donald McSwann, Mrs Amy McSwann, his wife, and Mr Donald John McSwann, their son.

"Dr and Mrs Henderson disappeared a year ago. Mr Donald McSwann, property owner, of Kenilworth Avenue, Wimbledon, vanished three years or more ago.

"Hour after hour, to relays of shorthand writers and detectives crowded into the buff-painted interrogation room of a London police station, the vampire has recalled his orgies.

"Drinking mug after mug of strong police tea—but never forgetting to crook his little finger genteelly away from the coarse china, the maniac has shown himself a man of easy manners.

"He wears a quiet suit of immaculate cut, with a discreet tie. His hair is sleekly brushed, his nails well-kept. From the interrogation room he has gone back to his cell where he is already awaiting trial for another offence."

As soon as the *Daily Mirror*'s first edition had been seen by senior officers at Scotland Yard the police issued to the Press a warning that the matter of the "disappearance" of five people other than Mrs Durand-Deacon was *sub judice,* as of course was the known murder charge. The statement detailing vampire practices "may be offered in evidence, and any stories which refer to that statement and its contents may be held to prejudice the trial of the accused. Publication of any such statement or references to it would be most improper and would doubtless become a matter for consideration of the Court before whom the accused appears."

The *Daily Mirror* made slight amendments of phrase in following editions, and deleted the third to the seventh paragraph of its original story. But on 8 March Gwyn Morris (later a Q.C. and Old Bailey judge), on behalf of Haigh, applied in the Divisional Court for leave to issue a writ of attachment against the Editor of the *Daily Mirror* in respect of material published on 4 March. The application was granted, and was heard on 21 March by Lord Chief Justice Goddard, Mr Justice Humphreys and Mr Justice Birkett. Sir Walter Monckton, K.C., appeared for Haigh and Sir Valentine Holmes, K.C., for the Editor of the *Daily Mirror,* Sylvester Bolam.

Lord Goddard crystallized the essence of the alleged contempt of court by observing that the *Daily Mirror* presentation "accuses the man not only of the murder in respect of which he was remanded, but of other murders".

Sir Valentine Holmes said that Mr Bolam accepted responsibility for the material complained of, and expressed his sincere apologies. He said that Bolam's instructions to his staff had been that, so long as no charge had been preferred in connection with the five missing people, stories of the disappearance of those five should be published but without the identification of any person as responsible for their disappearance. He had believed that in this manner he would not be committing contempt of court, but he now realized he had been wrong. When the Scotland Yard warning came through he ordered the deletion of any reference to a confession. In the haste with which modern newspapers were produced a quick decision had been called for, and in this case a serious error of judgment had occurred.

"No one", growled the Lord Chief Justice, "could say that this was an error of judgment. What has been written are some of the most horrifying things it is possible to read. It is alleged that a man committed murder after murder and the most horrible details were given. This was no error of judgment. This was policy."

He ruled that in a case of such gravity the proprietors of the newspaper should be brought before the court to answer an allegation of contempt, and they were to appear with the Editor at the end of the week. And on 25 March Rayner gave judgment:

"In the long history of this class of case there has, in the opinion of this Court, never been a case approaching such gravity as this, or one of such a scandalous and wicked character. It is of the utmost importance that this Court should vindicate the common principles of justice and, in the public interest, see that condign punishment is meted out to persons guilty of such conduct.

"In the opinion of the Court this has not been done as an error of judgment, but as a matter of policy, pandering to sensationalism for the purpose of increasing the circulation of this paper. Indeed, it having come to the knowledge of the Commissioner of Police that this paper—or some paper—was likely to issue some details concerning this case, in the course of the evening a warning was issued from the office of the Commissioner of Police to this newspaper. But that this had any real effect on the newspaper, in spite of what has been said in the affidavit that has been filed, it is impossible seriously to believe.

"There was some alteration in the last edition, but very little. The last edition itself was a gross contempt, not, perhaps, quite as bad as the other two which had been issued. The fact that a warning had been given by the police does not affect the question one way or the other. It was an offence whether notice had been issued or not. It may aggravate the case that more attention was not paid to the warning. As I have said, in view of the gravity of this case the Court ordered the proprietors of the newspaper also to be brought before it.

"I will add a word of warning. Let the directors beware. They know now the conduct of which their employees are capable. They know now the view this Court takes of the matter. If, for the purpose of increasing the circulation of their newspaper they should again venture to publish such matter as this, the directors themselves may find that the arm of this Court is long enough to reach them and to deal with them.

"The Court has taken the view that there must be severe punishment in this case."

At that point, he paused. I was present in court as a second-year law student at the time, and I can still remember the heightening of the tension as the Lord Chief Justice then said, very deliberately, "Stand up, Sylvester Bolam."

An ashen Bolam got to his feet. He looked as if he had never realized the case would get as far as this. "The writ of attachment will issue against you," said Lord Goddard, "You will be taken in the custody of the Tipstaff and committed to Brixton Prison for three months. The newspaper proprietors—the limited company—will be fined ten thousand pounds and ordered to pay the cost of these proceedings. The money is to be paid to the Master of the Crown Office by twelve o'clock on Monday."

The shaken élite of Fleet Street staggered to the El Vino wine bar, while Sylvester Bolam was led away to prison. The judgment was not questioned, and indeed could not be officially disputed. Under the law as it then was, no appeal was possible from a sentence imposed for a contempt of court. "Bolam took his punishment and did not complain," Lord Cudlipp has told me. "He was gaoled in Brixton where I visited him. He died three years after his sentence while smoking after breakfast. He was forty-seven."

The 'contempt', as it happened, did not cause the prisoner any disadvantage: all Haigh's 'vampire' statements—which had been correctly enough reported in the *Daily Mirror*—and his references to the other five missing people were put in evidence at his trial, buttressing an attempt by the defence to prove him insane, on a 'the more the madder' basis. It failed. He was eventually hanged.

Rayner's judgment caused a shudder of fear to run down Fleet Street—even leading up to board-room level. In fact, "the Street" over-reacted. There grew up, alongside a renewed respect for the law, a virtual terror of Lord Goddard. Individual writers in certain newspapers—notably, Michael Foot in the *Daily Herald*—continued to engage in political criticism of Rayner Goddard on points of legitimate controversy, such as any perceived confusion between his status as legislator and his function as Lord Chief Justice. But for the most part the Press—even those editors and proprietors with a reputation for truculence, which is no bad quality in the journalism that upholds causes—shied off Rayner as a man with an incalculably long arm.

The writer Peter Black contributed to the *Daily Mail* a review of a book concerned with Rayner's career and cases, published some months before the Lord Chief Justice retired. The review contained some mildly expressed criticisms. Mr Black recounted, long afterwards:[7] "The Editor confided to me that what I had said was well said, was worth saying and ought to be published; he was equally confident that to publish it was out of the question. Whether his fear of a massive retaliation by the law was sound or imaginary its effect was as real as the stones of the Old Bailey."

In March 1950 the Lord Chief Justice sent down Klaus Fuchs, the atomic scientist, for fourteen years for treachery. There was never any doubt as to the sentence. It was the maximum—and Fuchs himself, who had pleaded guilty to four counts of having communicated to persons unknown information which might be useful to an enemy, mistakenly expected death.

He had made a full confession. Without it there could have been no prosecution, for the security services could not lay hands on a single witness to the crimes committed. The statement was not only

---

[7] In a letter to *The Times* that appeared on 12 June 1971 in the post-Levin correspondence.

factual, but highly introspective. This introspection, mainly into the intellectual and emotional sequences governing the actions of a Communist, curiously dominated the proceedings. Rayner, presiding over the Old Bailey trial, ostentatiously slapped it down on occasions when it was raised, yet he himself, in finally addressing Fuchs, made use of the same source.

Certainly this approach was used by the Attorney-General, Sir Hartley Shawcross, who opened for the Crown from the core of this theme. "The prisoner is a Communist," he said, "and that is at once the explanation and indeed the tragedy of this case. Quite apart from the great harm the prisoner has done the country that he adopted and which adopted him, it is a tragedy that one of such high intellectual attainments as the prisoner possesses should have allowed his mental processes to have become so warped by his devotion to communism that, as he himself expresses it, he became a kind of controlled schizophrenic, the dominant half of his mind leading him to do things which the other part of his mind recognized quite clearly were wrong. Indeed, my Lord, his statement (and so far as we have been able to check it, we believe his statement to be true) is a very object lesson in the meaning of communism, and before I say a word as to the facts perhaps I might be permitted to add this, because it has an immediate bearing on the case:

"In this country the number of Communists is fortunately very few, and it may be that a great number of those people who support the Communist movement believe, as the prisoner at one time apparently believed, misguidedly if sincerely, that that movement is seeking to build a new world. What they don't realize is that it is to be a world dominated by a single Power and that the supporters of the Communist Party, the true adherents of communism, indoctrinated with the Communist belief, must become traitors to their own country in the interests—or what they are told to be the interests—of the international Communist movement.

"My Lord, it was because of these facts that this man, brilliant scientist as he is, now undoubtedly disillusioned and ashamed, came to place his country and himself in this terrible position."

Fuchs, said the Attorney-General, was a 21-year-old student at Kiel University in 1933 when Hitler came to power. He had joined the Communists to fight the Nazis, and he was immediately beaten up in the initial stages of the great Nazi purge of the universities. His experiences during the first month of the régime only confirmed his conviction that he would have to stay on the extreme Left to oppose Hitler, but he would need to go underground. "In the universities", he declared in his statement, "there was hardly anybody who stood up for those who were dismissed either on racial or political grounds. . . . People whom you normally would have respected because of their decency had no force in themselves to stand up for their own ideals or moral standards." A month after the takeover he was on his way by train to attend a students' congress when he read in a newspaper of the burning of the Reichstag. "I immediately realized the significance and I knew that the underground struggle had started. I took the badge of the hammer and sickle, which I had carried until that moment, out of my lapel."

In Berlin Fuchs was, in fact, instructed to go abroad to finish his education and be ready to return and help build the new Germany after the defeat of Hitler. After a period of privation he reached England in September 1933. He became a research worker in physics at the University of Bristol, and later at Edinburgh. Politically he was inactive. At the time of Dunkirk he was interned as an enemy alien and sent to Canada, being imprisoned mainly with confirmed Nazis. He was eventually returned to England and took a research post in Birmingham. His task was to make abstruse mathematical calculations in one section of the enterprise which was working on the development of the atomic bomb. When Russia was invaded by Germany he sought out a Russian agent and passed over the results of his own work. In 1943 Fuchs went to America as a member of the British team—he was now naturalized—working on the atomic bomb. He continued to pass information. He remained in the United States for almost a year after the dropping of the bombs on Hiroshima and Nagasaki, and came back in July 1946 to take the post of head of the Theoretical Physics division of the British Atomic Energy research establishment at Harwell, Berkshire.

Fuchs detailed his career elaborately in his statement. In 1947, after a considerable period of quiescence, he again sought out the Russians and began to pass information. But his devotion to the Russians gradually weakened as the firm friendships with brother-scientists at Harwell grew. Moreover, Harwell itself, as an intellectual institution, began to claim from him some of the loyalty a man gives to his university. He analysed this breakaway in words which were read in court:

"I began naturally to form bonds of personal friendship and I had to conceal them from my inner thoughts. I used my Marxist philosophy to establish in my mind two separate compartments: one compartment in which I allowed myself to make friendships, to have personal relations, to help people and to be in all personal ways the kind of man I wanted to be, and the kind of man which, in a personal way, I had been before with my friends in or near the Communist Party. I could be free and easy and happy with other people without fear of disclosing myself because I knew that the other compartment would step in if I approached the danger point. I could forget the other compartment and still rely on it. It appeared to me at the time that I had become a 'free man' because I had succeeded in the other department in establishing myself completely independent of the surrounding forces of society. Looking back on it now, the best way of expressing it seems to be to call it a controlled schizophrenia."

Fuchs said that he began to have doubts about actions of the Russian Government and the Communist Party and he diminished his information to the Russians. Finally he stopped passing any—and seven months after that decision Russia exploded her first atomic bomb.

By the autumn of 1949 the Americans had some information that information about the bomb had been passed, probably by someone in the British camp, and inquiries were begun at Harwell. Rightly or wrongly, Fuchs believed that if he made no confession, but retired from Harwell, the matter would be solved. With increasing introspection, he analysed this decision and its consequences:

"I denied the allegation and decided that I would have to leave Harwell. However, it became clear to me that in leaving Harwell in these circumstances I would do two things. I would deal a grave blow to Harwell, to all the work which I have loved; and furthermore that I would leave suspicions against people whom I had loved, who were my friends, and who believed that I was their friend.

"I had to face the fact that it had been possible for me in one half of my mind to be friends with people, to be close friends, and at the same time to deceive them and to endanger them. I had to realize that the control mechanism had warned me of danger to myself, but that it had also prevented me from realizing what I was doing to people close to me.

"I then realized that the combination of the three ideas which had made me what I was was wrong: in fact every single one of them was wrong: that there are certain standards of moral behaviour which are in you and that you cannot disregard. That in your actions you must be clear in your own mind whether they are right or wrong. That you must be able, before accepting somebody else's authority, to state your doubts and try and resolve them. And I found that at least I myself was made by circumstances."

And so, Fuchs recounted, in the statement from which the Attorney-General was largely reading in the Old Bailey Court, he came to the decision to make a confession in full. He ended with one generalization:

"Before I joined the [Harwell] project most of the English people with whom I made personal contacts were left-wing, and affected in some degree or other by the same kind of philosophy. Since coming to Harwell I have met English people of all kinds, and I have come to see in many of them a deep-rooted firmness which enables them to lead a decent way of life. I do not know where this springs from and I don't think they do, but it is there."

Sir Hartley Shawcross stressed the unchallenged instances of Fuchs's guilt from the precise details given in the statement, and ended his address. Derek Curtis-Bennett, K.C., for Fuchs, rose to make some plea for mitigation. He based this almost entirely on the pressures which had shunted Fuchs into the Communist Party in Germany, and the superior allegiance that eventually was claimed from all Communists. He said that in England Fuchs never pretended to be anything but a Communist.

The Lord Chief Justice queried, "I don't know whether you are suggesting that was known to the authorities?"

"He made no secret of the fact," said Curtis-Bennett.

"I don't suppose he proclaimed himself as a Communist when naturalized or when taken into Harwell or when he went to the USA," persisted Lord Goddard.

"If I am wrong", said Fuchs's counsel, 'Mr Attorney will correct me. It was on his records in this country at the Home Office that he was a member of the German Communist Party."

Sir Hartley Shawcross conceded this, but said there was no record of any association with the British Communist Party.

"Anybody who has read anything of Marxist theory", continued Curtis-Bennett, "must know that any man who is a Communist, whether in Germany or Timbuctoo, will react in exactly the same way when he comes into possession of information which would advance the ideas of communism. He will almost automatically, unhappily, put his allegiance to the Communist ideology first. The prisoner has said in his statement—and, my Lord, I do in part rely upon this statement as an explanation, although not an excuse, of the course of conduct pursued by the prisoner over the last seven years. ...."

And counsel read the long passage already quoted analysing Fuchs's 'compartmentalization' of his friendships and ending: "The best way of expressing it seems to be to call it a controlled schizophrenia."

Rayner intervened: "I have read this statement with very great care more than once. I really cannot understand all this metaphysical talk, Mr Curtis-Bennett, and I don't know that I should. I am not concerned with it. What I am concerned with is that this man gave away secrets of vital importance to this country. He stands before me as a sane man, and not one relying on the disease of schizophrenia or anything else."

It was notable that the Lord Chief Justice had let go by the earlier allusion by the Attorney-General to Fuchs's 'controlled schizophrenia', although he bridled at its repetition by Mr Curtis-Bennett. Fuchs's counsel disclaimed any undue emphasis on schizophrenia.

"I am not relying on any such thing with a long medical name," he said. "But I would submit to your Lordship that a man's state of mind at the time of the commission of the offence is a relevant factor."

"His state of mind", pronounced Rayner grimly, "merely goes to show that he is one of the most dangerous men this country could have within its shores. Go on."

"I have to endeavour to put before your Lordship", said Curtis-Bennett, "this man as he is, knowing that your Lordship is not going to visit him savagely, but justly, both in the interests of the State and the interests of this man. . . . I am not going to confuse this case with long medical terms. He is not mad. He is sane. But he is a human being, and that is what I am trying to explain."

Curtis-Bennett, a mercurial counsel, was not at his best that day. Soon the time would come for the expressionless man in the dock to speak for himself. "Prisoner at the Bar," said the Clerk of the Court, in the time-worn phrase, "you stand convicted on your own confession of felony. Have you anything to say why sentence of the court should not be imposed upon you according to law?"

Fuchs, a spare man of thirty-eight with a high forehead and round gold-rimmed glasses, spoke firmly with a slight German accent:

"My Lord, I have committed certain crimes for which I am charged, and I expect sentence. I have also committed some other crimes which are not crimes in the eyes of the law—crimes against my friends—and when I asked my counsel to put certain facts before you I did not do it because I wanted to lighten my sentence. I did it in order to atone for those other crimes."

He remained standing in the high dock almost level with the gaze of the Lord Chief Justice. An American reporter said the judge's eyes were 'like icicles'.[8]

"Emil Julius Klaus Fuchs," said Lord Goddard, "in 1933, fleeing from political persecution in Germany, you took advantage of the right of asylum, or the privilege of asylum, which it has always been the boast of this country to extend to people persecuted in their own country for their political opinions. You betrayed the hospitality and protection given to you with the grossest treachery.

"In 1942, in return for your offer to put at the service of this country the great gifts Providence has bestowed upon you in scientific matters, you were granted British nationality. From that moment, regardless of your oath, you started to betray secrets of vital importance for the purpose of furthering a political creed held in abhorrence by the vast majority in this country, your object being to strengthen that creed which was then known to be inimical to all freedom-loving countries.

"There are four matters which seem to me the gravest aspects of your crime. In the first, by your conduct you have imperilled the right of asylum which this country has hitherto extended. Dare we now give shelter to political refugees who may be followers of this pernicious creed and may well disguise themselves treacherously to bite the hand that feeds them?

"Secondly, you have betrayed not only the projects and inventions of your own brain for which this country was paying you and enabling you to live in comfort in return for your promises of secrecy. You have also betrayed the secrets of other workers in this field of science, not only in this country but in the United States, and therefore you might have caused the gravest suspicion to fall on those you falsely treated as friends and who were misled into trusting you.

"Thirdly, you might have imperilled the good relations between this country and the great American republic with which His Majesty is allied.

"And fourthly, you have done irreparable and incalculable harm both to this land and to the United States, and you did it, as your statement shows, merely for the purpose of furthering your political creed, for I am willing to assume you have not done it for gain.

"Your statement which has been read shows to me the depth of self-deception into which people like you can fall. Your crime to me

---

[8] Quoted in Arthur Smith's *Lord Goddard* at page 6.

is only thinly differentiated from high treason. In this country we observe rigidly the rule of law, and as technically it is not high treason [aid to a belligerent enemy], so you are not tried for that offence.

"I have now to assess the penalty which it is right I should impose. It is not so much for punishment that I impose it, for punishment can mean nothing to a man of your mentality.

"My duty is to safeguard this country, and how can I be sure that a man whose mentality is shown in that statement you have made may not, at any other minute, allow some curious working of your mind to lead you further to betray secrets of the greatest possible value and importance to this land?

"The maximum sentence which Parliament has ordained for this crime is fourteen years' imprisonment, and that is the sentence I pass upon you."

Note the words used by Rayner Goddard in that stern imposition of sentence. They manifest his ability to lash a prisoner with a discerning awareness of his most vulnerable inner part. For in his statement read to the court Fuchs had spoken of his fear of leaving "suspicions against people whom I had loved, who were my friends, and who believed that I was their friend. I had to face the fact that it had been possible for me in one half of my mind to be friends with people, to be close friends, and at the same time to deceive them and to endanger them."

Rayner, who had closely studied the statement, used almost the same words when he referred to a betrayal of hospitality and protection, the doubts about offering political asylum in the future and the danger that "you might have caused the gravest suspicion to fall on those you falsely treated as friends and who were misled into trusting you". The judge's perception of the sensitivity of the man standing before him in the dock enabled him to wound him with more than just the severity of the maximum sentence for his crime.

Yet many months later, he was to tell Arthur Smith, his clerk, that, "although he abhorred the offence to which Fuchs had pleaded guilty, he was filled with pity for the man who possessed, so he believed, a certain warped integrity". A judge's public and private face so seldom are one. Few if any present in court that day could have believed, listening to Rayner's growled sonority, that compassion was in his heart for the prisoner he was condemning.

15 Middle Years as Chief

The Labour Government survived for another eighteen months. Then in October 1951, Mr Attlee, the Prime Minister, called a general election, and the Conservatives under Winston Churchill were returned to power. The Government's position had been shaky for some while, and their defeat was not unexpected: certainly not by that wily lawyer-politician, Viscount Jowitt, the Labour Lord Chancellor who had started his career in politics twenty-nine years earlier as a Liberal M.P. and had changed and rechanged his political coat several times since then. No word of this unfortunate suggestion leaked into the Temple at the time, but, aged sixty-six, and with the distasteful smell of imminent loss of office in his nostrils, he had the temerity to ask Rayner Goddard, seven years his senior and the one-time stop-gap Lord Chief Justice, to stand down so that he could succeed him.

"The old man forthrightly and correctly refused," says Sir Eric Sachs, Rayner's son-in-law. For a Prime Minister to move around the members of his Government like cards in a pack is undoubtedly one of the prerogatives of political life. But for the holder of the highest legal/political office in the land to resort to this kind of manoeuvre is quite another matter.

Lord Caldecote, Rayner's predecessor, had, after a five-months' interim appointment as Dominions Secretary, himself gone from being Lord Chancellor to Lord Chief Justice. The precedent was most certainly there; and in the immediate past. But it was hardly a happy one, and for Rayner now to have followed it would have undone all the constitutional good done by his own original—non-political—appointment. Besides, he did not want to give up being "Chief". He still had a lot of work to do.

Rayner steamed indomitably on. "Admiration for him comes easily to me," says Sir Eric Sachs, "but I was horrified at the magnitude of Lord Goddard's task as Lord Chief Justice. Apart from his onerous court duties, there was, of course, all the administrative side. Everyone came to him—for example, it was a question of new Judges' Lodgings on Circuit? Right, off he would go to see for himself what the situation was. If there was any complaint about Lodgings, it always seemed to come to him! He was responsible for the Circuits' work in the sense that all reports came to him: 'We are in arrears, can we have a Commissioner?' They had to telephone him personally. Furthermore, he was technically responsible for the administration of the Queen's Bench Division in the Royal Courts of Justice themselves—there was no Clerk of the Lists to help him in his early years as Chief.

"He was completely responsible for the criminal side of things: all the work of criminal appeals with its avalanche of paper that used to descend upon him! And a high proportion of law-reform projects came up to him for consideration and comment; and he did, of course, preside over one law-reform committee himself—in 1953—inquiring into the law of animals.

"The Chief decided when the sittings of the courts on Circuit should start, when they should end and how long they should last at each place.

"It was a prodigious work-load, but Lord Goddard seemed to thrive on it."

As Rayner himself wrote to his old friend, Sir Arthur Bryant, after his retirement; "Without undue vanity I think I can fairly say that in one respect I did a good job. I pulled the QB Division together.... I made a good many changes in the Circuit system so far as was possible without legislation, and a certain number in the practice of the Division which speeded up trials and business generally.

"But then I had an advantage such as no other Chief had. I had been a judge and a Lord Justice, so I really knew the ropes; I had not been promoted straight from the Bar, and if I had made a mess of it I could not have pleaded lack of experience. I think I can fairly claim to have left the Division in a far better state than I found it, but that gives no title to being a great CJ."[1]

At the exact half-way mark of his tenure of office, in May 1952,

---

[1] Quoted by Sir Arthur Bryant in an article in the *Illustrated London News* after Lord Goddard's death in June 1971.

Lord Chief Justice Goddard reintroduced in the House of Lords a proposal for the reform of the Court of Criminal Appeal of whose need he had long been convinced. Indeed, he had previously proposed it during the parliamentary debates that preceded the Criminal Justice Act of 1948 when, although his amendment had been accepted by the Lords, it was rejected by the Commons, and he withdrew it in order to save the Bill. What led him now to revive the issue was a particularly sad and unnecessary murder in Liverpool, and its surprising sequel.

Mrs Beatrice Rimmer, a 52-year-old widow living in Wavertree, a working-class suburb of the city, came back to her home at about ten o'clock on the evening of Sunday, 19 August 1951, after spending the day with her younger married son, an ex-policeman. Local gossip had it that she had quite a bit of money stowed away about the house, and that story—only partially true—led to her death. Holding some flowers her son had given her, she unlocked her front door and walked alone into her entrance hall—where at 7.15 p.m. the next evening her son found her, lying dead. She still had her outdoor clothes on, the flowers had fallen from her hand and lay scattered beside her and she was covered with blood.

She must have been struck down as soon as she closed her front door. She had fifteen wounds in her head, made by two separate instruments, but, despite the appalling violence, the poor woman had not died immediately, but lingered for hours lying alone in her own hall as life ebbed slowly away.

Robbery could be the only possible motive, but nothing was missing from the house. It looked as if Mrs Rimmer's two assailants—the different instruments indicated two men—must have got in through a broken rear window. Then, it was assumed, they waited for her return, intending to make her tell them where she kept her money hidden. But they must have hit her too hard, panicked, gone on hitting her as she lay defenceless on the ground, then fled.

For a long time the police inquiries led them nowhere. But after more than a month they received a tip-off that a prisoner in Walton Gaol knew the identity of the murderers.

Since all the surviving participants in this wretched enterprise are still in their forties, and they may have reformed after a universally appalling criminal youth, they will be referred to by pseudonyms in this account.

The police visited the prisoner in Walton, who will be known as Mackie. He was a professional burglar, and, in Rayner Goddard's estimation as offered in his later narrative to the House of Lords, he gave the police his information because "he was shocked at the murder that had been committed. . . . The professional burglar seldom uses violence; he does not think it in accordance with the best traditions in his trade." Mackie said that a fortnight before the murder two men had approached him in an all-night café and suggested his co-operation in a well-planned burglary at the house of the murdered woman. He agreed, and the date was fixed, but on the Friday before that Sunday he was arrested as an Army deserter and was in gaol at the time of the robbery.

Mackie named the men concerned as Alf Burns and Ted Devlin of Manchester. The police concentrated inquiries on these suspects. They traced two girls who were, in the police phrase, associated with them, and in everybody else's language including Rayner Goddard's, sleeping with them—intermittently, at least. They were a 17-year-old habituée of Liverpool's all-night cafés whom I shall call Molly Mills and a 21-year-old girl from Manchester with similar tastes whom I shall call Julie Oldham. Julie said that Burns and Devlin had invited them to assist with "a job with an old woman in Liverpool". They were to engage the victim in conversation at the front door while the men broke in at the back. Julie said—and Molly confirmed it—that she had refused to have anything to do with it. Molly said that she had agreed to help them and that she had met them at Wavertree at nine o'clock on the Sunday night, but for some reason Burns and Devlin had changed their plan and they told her that they no longer needed her, but that she was to meet them afterwards.

Molly Mills did meet them in a café later that night, and they were both "very nervous". She recounted that Devlin had asked, "Will the woman live?" Burns had said, "To hell with the woman. We'll be out of Liverpool before long."

Having accumulated this and other evidence, the police decided to bring in Burns and Devlin, young men in their twenties who already had many convictions for house-breaking. Edward Francis Devlin was arrested in Manchester, and immediately denied his guilt. "I was not in Liverpool at the time of the murder and I did not hear of a murder while I was there or since," he said. His alibi was the somewhat unusual one that he could not have been committing a murder in Liverpool because he was doing various break-ins elsewhere at the time: "Round about the time of the murder I was doing screwing jobs at Manchester and other places. I was screwing on 10 August to the end of the month, and I was probably screwing a gaff on 19 August [the night of the murder]." Alfred Burns was picked up in residence at Strangeways Gaol. He said, "I didn't do the murder. All the time from the day we first met the girls and for the next two or three weeks I was with Devlin. I can't say exactly where I was, but my mother will be able to give me an idea."

The mother, though she may have had few objections to filling in Alf's engagement diary, declined to confuse the rôles of social secretary and alibi-supporter, and was no help. The police had little evidence apart from the identifications by Mackie, Mills and Oldham. In the intervening eight weeks the clothes of Burns and Devlin had been cleaned, and the forensic scientists could find nothing very definite. No murder weapon had been found. There were no incriminating bloodstains or fingerprints. After preliminary hearings Burns and Devlin were committed for trial at Liverpool Assizes. "I was present at the magistrates' court during the committal proceedings," Mr Richard Whittington-Egan, then a leading crime reporter in Liverpool, has told me.[2] "Devlin was insolent—whispering and sniggering to his companion in the dock. I never saw two people on a serious charge so unaffected by the circumstances in which they found themselves. I was later to see them at the trial. I expected to see a change in their demeanour after their long weeks in prison. But they were still as cocky as ever. They saw themselves as gangster heroes."

Two unpleasant young men. But were they murderers, and could the Crown prove its case?

The trial opened on 13 December 1951. Burns was defended by Sir Noel Goldie, K.C., and Devlin by Miss Rose Heilbron, K.C. (later Mrs Justice Heilbron) with Basil Nield, K.C. (also later a High Court judge) leading for the Crown. There was no untoward incident until about halfway through the fourth day when Sir Noel Goldie asked a Liverpool detective inspector, "Am I right in saying that on the night of the alleged murder a burglary and breaking-in was committed at the Sun Blinds Ltd., 6 Great Jackson Street, Manchester?" At once Nield rose to object that the question was irrelevant, but Goldie countered, "I don't want it to be said at a later stage that I am taking my learned friend by surprise."

For Devlin's earlier statement to the police "I was probably screwing a gaff on 19th August" had now become crystallized into a definite assertion that it was the premises of Sun Blinds Ltd. at 6 Great Jackson Street that had been the subject of their attentions.

---

[2] Cited in *Scales of Justice* by Fenton Bresler (Weidenfeld and Nicolson 1973).

And when the two young defendants went into the witness-box they both gave sworn evidence to that effect. They did more than that: their counsel called from prison, as a witness for the defence, a man who had been convicted of the crime. He claimed under oath that he had not done it alone, but along with the two men in the dock.

"There was no doubt", Rayner later told the Lords, "that a factory had been broken into at Manchester over the weekend, but when it was broken into was quite another matter. The factory was broken into some time between midday Saturday and early Monday morning, when the crime was discovered." Both defendants had some knowledge of the facts of the break-in, but that could have resulted from direct participation, or from what they had heard about it from criminal contacts.

In his final speech to the jury Basil Nield called the alibi "a manufactured alibi" and asked them to ignore it. Sir Noel Goldie countered, "Far from being manufactured, it is proved absolutely up to the hilt. I submit to you with the utmost confidence that it would be most dangerous to convict in this case on the evidence that has been called before you." It was left to the judge, Mr Justice Finnemore, to point out quietly in his summing-up that both the prosecution's case and the defence claim that the men had been in the Manchester raid could be true. No one had been able to pinpoint the hour of the break-in: Burns and Devlin *could* have got back to Manchester from Liverpool in time to do it on that same Sunday night.

After a ten-day trial the jury took only seventy-five minutes to convict both men of murder, and they were sentenced to death. An appeal was lodged in the Court of Criminal Appeal. At this hearing, presided over by Lord Goddard, Miss Rose Heilbron strongly urged the Lord Chief Justice and his two fellow-judges to allow her to call new evidence. The main testimony would be that Julie Oldham had confessed to 'shopping' her ex boy friend, Devlin, for a 15-year-old girl would say that Julie Oldham had told her that she had not spoken the truth when she said that Devlin and Burns plotted the robbery and asked her to join in. The true murderer, Julie Oldham was alleged to have said, was the father of her child, who was not Devlin.

Lord Chief Justice Goddard told the Lords of the impact of that defence application: "What was urged upon us was that we should hear fresh evidence of a most important character . . . and it went to show that Julie Oldham, the importance of whose evidence I have already emphasized, had committed perjury and had admitted that she had committed perjury, and, secondly, that another man had admitted that he had committed the murder.

"That second man can be briefly disposed of, because he very soon retracted his confession. It is the commonest thing in the world, after any murder has been committed, for various exhibitionists to say that they have committed that murder—why they do it I do not know. But we were seriously asked in the Court of Criminal Appeal to consider evidence which it was suggested went to show that Julie Oldham had committed perjury, and to inquire into the confession of this other man.

"We declined to consider that evidence, and we declined for very good reasons. Matters of this sort have often previously been before the Court of Criminal Appeal, who have always in these circumstances refused to hear such evidence, mainly on the ground that they have no power to order a new trial. Your Lordships probably know that all the Court can do is to quash a conviction or dismiss an appeal. We have no power to try anybody. We have power, under the Act, to admit fresh evidence, and the Court has often done it where it is relevant to some matter that has been raised by the defence. For instance, the sort of case that comes most quickly to my mind in which we have done so is where the defence has been an alibi and some evidence has been discovered at a time subsequent to the trial which would strongly support the alibi and which had not been before the jury. If the evidence we had been asked to receive in this case had been evidence to strengthen the alibi that these men committed the crime at Manchester when they were said to have been murdering the woman at Liverpool, we might, if certain well-known rules had been applied—such as that certain evidence could not have been called at the trial because it was not known, and so forth—have admitted that evidence.

"But how could we, without usurping the functions of a jury, which is something our Court has always refused to do, investigate the case and come to a conclusion as to whether Julie Oldham had committed perjury or not? If we were to quash the conviction of these men on the ground that the girl's evidence was untrue, we could do so only if we came to the definite conclusion that the girl's evidence was untrue—and only a jury could do that.

"One of the things I am contending for in the Motion[3] I am put-

---

[3] "To call attention to the recent case of *R.* v. *Devlin and Burns* for murder; and to consider how far the necessity for extra-judicial inquiries after conviction and dismissal of an appeal would be obviated if the Court of Criminal Appeal had power to order a new trial; and to move for Papers." *Hansard,* Lords, 8 May 1952, cols. 745 *et seq.*

ting forward is to uphold the sanctity of trial by jury. It is only a jury which can decide whether a woman has been committing perjury and only a jury which can decide whether another person has committed a murder. If we had embarked upon it we could not have avoided giving some pronouncement on whether this girl had committed perjury or whether this other man had committed the murder.

"Supposing we had said that we did find that she had committed perjury, how could she then have been tried afterwards by a jury? The prejudice that would be against her, the Court of Appeal having found that she had committed perjury, would be so great that she could not, I should think, expect to get fairly tried. So, as I say, the Court has always refused to go into questions of this sort, as to whether a witness has committed perjury at the trial or whether some other person has committed the crime. It applies for the reasons which I have endeavoured to explain, in cases not only of murder but also of other crimes that may come before the Court.

"But now see how different it would be if the Court had power to order a new trial. Then it would be for a second jury to pronounce upon the matter as to whether witnesses were committing perjury or not, or whether these people had been wrongfully convicted. We, the Court of Criminal Appeal, might no doubt consider the evidence afterwards tendered and see to what issues it went, and if we thought it established a *prima facie* case, whether it be of perjury or of wrongful conviction or of miscarriage of justice, then, instead of dismissing the appeal or quashing the conviction (which would indicate that we were satisfied that someone else had committed the murder) we could say: 'There is a case shown here which ought to be reinvestigated. Let it go down for a new trial. Then these men who have been convicted will have the benefit of this new evidence which they say they have discovered. They will be able to cross-examine witnesses, to ask them if it was not true that they had committed perjury and to put to them matters in respect of which they allege that the witnesses have committed perjury. Then, when there has been a proper trial before a jury, if the jury come to the conclusion that their case is right no doubt they will acquit the man.' And a man, if once acquitted, as I have already said, is acquitted for ever, because the Court of Criminal Appeal has no power whatever to deal with acquittals."

The Court of Criminal Appeal did not, in the case of Burns and Devlin, allow Miss Heilbron to call new evidence, but indicated, in Rayner's words, that she should submit the matter "to those whose duty it is to advise the Crown in these matters. It is not a matter which this Court can go into." Miss Heilbron took the hint, and the result was that the Home Secretary, Sir David Maxwell Fyfe, K.C., appointed a leading barrister on the Northern Circuit, Mr Denis Gerrard, K.C. (afterwards Mr Justice Gerrard), to conduct an immediate inquiry into the reliability of the new evidence, and to "consider any further relevant information laid before him and to report whether, in his opinion, the result of his investigation affords any reasonable grounds for thinking that there has been or may have been a miscarriage of justice".

The execution date had already been fixed, but was postponed by a week. Working in secrecy and against the clock, Mr Gerrard, in the words of the Lord Chief Justice, "in fact, re-tried the case. He had to hear all, or a great many, of the witnesses who had already been before the Court, and he had to make up his mind whether or not there had been a miscarriage of justice."

Four days before the postponed execution, Denis Gerrard produced his report. "He came to the conclusion", Rayner recounted, "that there had been no miscarriage of justice. He found that Julie Oldham had not committed perjury, and the other man, who had said he had committed the murder, he dismissed as a mere drunken exhibitionist." Why, then, had Julie Oldham lied to the 15-year-old girl, and retracted her later statement before Mr Gerrard? Was she this time trying to shop the father of her child? "Her motives for making the untrue statements are a matter of speculation only," reported Mr Gerrard.

The battle to save the lives of Burns and Devlin continued. Their solicitors, with the help of Miss Heilbron and her junior counsel, drafted a memorandum setting out grounds for a reprieve, and rushed it to the Home Secretary. The widowed mothers of the two condemned men gathered signatures for a petition, and wrote pleading for mercy to the Queen. But at nine o'clock on Friday, 25 April 1952, the two men were hanged at Walton Gaol.

Within a fortnight of the execution Rayner rose in the House of Lords to put his motion urging that the Court of Appeal should have power to order a new trial. After his detailed exposition of the facts of the latest case, he reiterated that his amendment to the law would never be a means of enabling the Crown to put a man in fresh peril by ordering a new trial against him if he had been previously acquitted. But to a convicted man it would offer "a second chance of being acquitted". And he ended with a not unmoving reference to his own age and experience—which antedated the Court of

Criminal Appeal—and to his desire to see that Court "still more perfect in the attainment of justice":

"I bring this question again before the House not in the interests of prisoners, and assuredly not in the interests of prosecutors. I do it in the interests of justice. Those of us who have been in the profession as long as, I regret, I have are tempted to look upon the Court of Criminal Appeal as a new Court, and certainly it was not in existence until I had been called to the Bar for nine years. But it has been in existence now for forty-four years, and I believe that no one would deny that it has justified itself and that it has gone far to justify the hopes and intentions of its founders. It is because I want to see it if possible made a still more perfect instrument in the attainment of justice that I beg to move for Papers."

Goddard sat down and Viscount Simon rose to submit—in a speech which curiously combined the prolix with the perfunctory—the opposing argument. Rayner, in opening the debate, had referred to John Simon's opposition, combining the acknowledgment with a graceful compliment: "I hardly like to differ from him, as I have for him all the feeling that a pupil has for a master, for he was my earliest master in the law."[4] But Goddard mentioned that he had an advantage over Simon in his long experience of the work of the Court of Criminal Appeal through his services as a puisne judge and as Chief Justice. Simon blandly accepted the tribute to him, but could find nothing more to praise in his 76-year-old junior beyond the narrative skill with which he had retailed so expertly to the Lords the sordid tale of the crime of Burns and Devlin: "If he did not happen to be Lord Chief Justice of England, he might be another Edgar Wallace, with every conceivable claim to interest the public in shocking crimes of violence." Simon repeated the argument against the proposal to give the Court of Criminal Appeal power to order a new trial: that it denied that tenet of English law that a man cannot be charged a second time with the same offence (though this does happen when juries disagree). And Lord Simon reminded the House of the history of this proposal—rejected after debate in 1907, in 1948 and, he forecast, now in 1952.

The Lord Chancellor, Lord Simonds, showed a warmer spirit. He said that Lord Goddard's proposed reform had not yet gathered such a weight of opinion behind it as would justify Her Majesty's Government in introducing a controversial measure into a crowded

---

[4] Simon had been senior to Rayner as an undergraduate at Oxford over fifty years earlier.

legislative programme. But then he added, not as a Minister but for himself: "My personal view is most emphatically in favour of that which the Lord Chief Justice has pronounced—and so it has been these many years. I beg him to go on 'ploughing the wilderness' in the hope that in time he may overcome the anti-prejudices of his master. He will remember how many years those who advocated anti-slavery measures had to bring their Bills before the other House and in this House at the end of the eighteenth and the beginning of the nineteenth centuries. It often takes a long time for the beneficent reform to find its way into the heart of the public. I beg him to go on with his crusade."

Rayner Goddard, the reformer, did continue 'ploughing the wilderness'. The Home Secretary set up a special committee to investigate the powers of the Court of Criminal Appeal. And eventually—twelve years later—the Criminal Justice Act of 1964 gave the Court power to order a new trial. A power that, as Rayner said, could only be used to offer a convicted man "a second chance of being acquitted".

Rayner Goddard was steeped in the history not only of the law but of English institutions, and his sources ranged from Magna Carta to *Pickwick Papers*. "You should read the case of *Bardell* v. *Pickwick*," he had told a prosecuting counsel at Chester Assizes in 1951. "There's lots of legal history in that." He explained how jurymen could be impressed from the bystanders in the court when by accident there were not enough in the box, cited Dickens as a reliable chronicler of this manoeuvre of "praying a tales"—and what Serjeant Buzfuz had done in the 1830s was repeated on the North-Western Circuit 120 years later.

Among the many ancient duties of the Lord Chief Justice is the reception in the Lord Chief Justice's Court of the new Lord Mayor of London, whose formal presentation and swearing-in before the Queen's Bench Divisional Court owes its origin to a Charter granted to the Barons of the City of London by King John in 1215. Indeed, this ceremony is in fact the only formal reason for the parade of the Lord Mayor's Show, escorting the Chief Citizen from Guildhall to the Law Courts. Rayner, relishing tradition, saw to it that his addresses of welcome contained every year different nuggets of historical information concerning the sometimes delicate relationship over the centuries between the City, the Sovereign's judges and the prickly, privilege-conscious Inns of Court. "He took a great deal of care in preparing his addresses," says Lady Sachs, "and was very proud of them indeed. He wrote them all out in longhand beforehand."[5]

To one Lord Mayor he detailed the origins of the ancient feud between the Guildhall and the Inner Temple which had been formally healed only in the current year when, after almost three centuries, the Lord Mayor dined with the Benchers of the Inner Temple on Grand Night in Trinity term—and tactfully did not insist on bringing a naked sword, point upright, which had caused the last riot in 1669. To another Lord Mayor he explained the reason why the Lord Chief Justice and the Queen's Bench Judges then receiving him in scarlet robes and ermine hoods wore, in addition, their black caps:

"Many of the large and distinguished company that are here assembled are, I expect, regarding our headdress with wonder or amusement or perhaps both. It is the only occasion on which we wear our Black Caps superimposed on full-bottomed wigs. Let me assure you that we wear them neither to intimidate you nor to entertain the company but because they are the official headdress of a judge when wearing his scarlet robes. They are in fact a soft description of the academic cap, generally if irreverently described as a mortar-board. The reason we wear them is that you, my Lord Mayor, on this occasion exercise your undoubted privilege of coming into court wearing your hat before us, so we, not to be outdone, wear our caps before you, but we make no attempt to compete with the magnificence of your hat, which I believe has a mystic significance, and without it no Lord Mayor is complete."

To Sir Rupert de la Bere, Lord Mayor of London in Coronation Year, the Lord Chief Justice recalled the previously unremarked historical snippet that the grand council meeting attended by the Lord Mayor immediately after the death of a sovereign was the only gathering of the old Norman *curia regis,* the successor to the Saxon *witan:*

"You will remember that on the 6 February Her Majesty was proclaimed Queen 'by the Lords Spiritual and Temporal of the Realm assisted with those of His late Majesty's Privy Council, with the representatives of other members of the Commonwealth, with other principal Gentlemen of Quality and with the Lord Mayor, Aldermen and Citizens of London'. This assembly at St James's on the afternoon of the day on which our late well-loved Sovereign

---

[5] The Court of the Lord Mayor and Aldermen of the City of London thought so highly of these Addresses that, upon Lord Goddard's retirement, they ordered to be privately printed two slim bound volumes of his twelve addresses during his period of office.

died was in truth a meeting and the only meeting of the ancient Magnum Concilium or Great Council of the Realm, but on this occasion for the first time in history is recorded the attendance of other members of the Commonwealth. It is not a meeting of the Privy Council, and is attended by many who are not members of that body."

Lord Goddard reminded Sir Noël Bowater in 1953 that in the previous century there were six of H.M. Judges trying jury cases in his Guildhall. "You will remember", he said, possibly more in hope than in anticipation, "that what is perhaps the most famous trial in fiction, *Bardell* v. *Pickwick,* was tried there before Mr Justice Stareleigh, a thin disguise for Mr Justice Gaselee, who was a Judge of the Common Pleas in 1831, the year of that trial."

He went on to give an explanation—fascinating to lawyers if to nobody else, because of the simplicity of the words he used to present a difficult sequence, as if he were summing up for jurymen— of why the term *nisi prius* is used to denote a civil cause. No encyclopaedia has expressed this more simply, or more satisfyingly:

"By a provision of Magna Carta the Court of Common Pleas had always to sit at ... Westminster Hall [and a jury from the county in which the cause of the action arose had, whatever the distance, to travel arduously thither]. ... These journeys were in fact undertaken until that great legislator Edward I by the Statute of Westminster II passed in 1285 introduced for the first time a great and far-reaching reform, so that juries from the provinces should no longer have to come to Westminster. That Statute established what was known as the award of *nisi prius.* The jury process directed to the sheriff of a county other than London or Middlesex ordered him to cause a jury to come before the Court at Westminster on a certain day unless before that day (you observe *nisi prius*) the Justices of Assize have come into his county, in which case the jury were to attend the Assizes. ... From that time forward civil actions were tried in the county to which they belonged. It is for this reason that to this day civil cases set down for trial are always referred to as being in the *nisi prius* list."

But at the next Lord Mayor's presentation in 1954 the Lord Chief Justice told Sir Seymour Howard that he was stumped for a subject. This was a sheer artifice of expediency. Rayner had something immediate to say, and did not wish to meander amid the pageantry of history. Every year, at the Mansion House Banquet given in July specifically for the honour of H.M. Judges, the Lord Chief Justice made a speech of deliberate policy. But now it was November. He held an invitation to the Lord Mayor's Banquet that evening, but on this occasion the limelight and the headlines belonged by tradition to the Prime Minister. Rayner was not a speaker at the Banquet that night, he could not wait until July, and he took the only course open to him, barring the initiation of a full-scale debate in the House of Lords, by making a policy address at this comparatively private gathering in his own court.

However, he first made a modest bob in deference to the protocol he had himself instituted of discussing some aspect of the tradition of the occasion. "My Lord Mayor," he addressed Sir Seymour, "once again it is my pleasant duty to receive the Chief Magistrate of the City of London and together with my brethren admit him to his illustrious office. I have on previous occasions referred to the antiquity of this ceremony held every year since 1215, and like many others in this old country it has continued though the purposes for which it was originally ordained no longer apply. There is I think no doubt that the reason for the appearance of the Mayor of London before the Barons of the Exchequer on his assuming office was because the Corporation of which he was the head was in ancient days accountable to the Crown for the revenues derived from the fermes of London and Middlesex. Now the object is to lay claim to the rights and privileges of the City which will I feel sure long remain undisturbed."

The Lord Chief Justice then changed his theme: "Hitherto when I have had the privilege of presiding at this ceremony I have usually referred to some legal matter connected with the City or your office which I hoped might be of interest, but as this is the ninth occasion on which I have received the Lord Mayor you will perhaps not be surprised if I say that I cannot think of any topic of this nature with which I have not already dealt, so I should like briefly to deal with a matter of more general interest which is not I think inappropriate as you, my Lord Mayor, are *virtute officii* the Senior Commissioner of the Central Criminal Court."

The Lord Chief Justice then went on to reinforce the argument which he had first propounded at the Mansion House Banquet for the judges in the previous July, suggesting that in the interests of speedier justice there should be an alteration in the law so that a majority verdict—he proposed nine to three—might be returned by a jury and be valid in criminal as well as in civil cases.[6]

---

[6] This was another of Lord Goddard's proposed changes in the law that later came into effect—in the Criminal Justice Act of 1967. But the necessary majority was slightly stronger: ten to two.

However, having flown his kite twice, he did not persist in launching it again before the next captive Lord Mayor: in the following November he returned to a traditionalist topic, and gave Sir Cuthbert Ackroyd a somewhat detailed disquisition on all the ancient courts which had once existed within the City.

16 Corporal Punishment—
a Last Try

It was at a Lord Mayor's annual banquet at the Mansion House for the judges that Rayner Goddard launched his most famous campaign for a change in the law. But this was not in aid of reform or forward-looking change; this was to put back the clock. It was, furthermore, a campaign that many felt (and not without reason) would better have fitted a propagandist for causes than a Lord Chief Justice. The date was 3 July 1952. The issue was the highly emotive one of corporal punishment.

"Flog 'em!" had been the stern injunction of King George V to his new High Court judge when Rayner had knelt before him at Windsor Castle to receive the accolade of knighthood upon his appointment to the Bench.[1] It was an exhortation that this late-Victorian hardly needed. He had not returned at any length to the subject since his ill-fated attempt to preserve the birch—as distinct from the cat—during the Parliamentary debates on the Criminal Justice Act of 1948. When in 1950 Lord Lloyd had brought the matter again before the House of Lords Rayner had specifically told his fellow peers that it was too early to impose a penalty removed only two years earlier.

But by the summer of 1952 the much-publicized cosh-boy menace was at its height, paraded before the whole country in banner headlines in the newspapers (rather like the spate of mugging reports that appeared twenty years later in the early nineteen-seventies), and Rayner clearly thought the time had now

---

[1] Private information, Lord Hodson to the author.

come for something like John Foster Dulles's "agonizing reappraisal" of the situation. So what more effective opportunity to hoist the standard of battle than when replying to the Lord Mayor's annual toast to "Her Majesty's Judges"?

He spoke, in measured tones, of "the great and disturbing increase of crime which is disgracing the country at present, and, more especially, the crimes of violence which are so prevalent". He suggested that the abolition of corporal punishment had led thugs to believe that violence was worth while, and that the remedy for gangsterism was to restore corporal punishment—"and to extend it, not limit it".

He propounded one of his favourite, and most justified, themes: "In the administration of the criminal law, I believe that for years past we have thought too much of the criminal and not enough of the victim. It may be that a change of heart may now come over those in authority. If public opinion gets seriously disturbed by the amount of crime that is prevalent—and I have been to Assizes and heard that old people have dreaded to answer a knock on the door because they don't know what thug may be standing there to take their life savings—there will be a strong tendency for the public to take the law into their own hands."

Lord Simonds, the Lord Chancellor, was sitting a few places away, waiting to propose the health of the Lord Mayor, Sir Leslie Boyce, and the Lady Mayoress, but he felt that he could not let the occasion go by without making some kind of response to the Lord Chief Justice's outburst. He uttered the bromide that no subject was under more active consideration than the relation of crime with penalty, and added, "So far as we can tell at present, it is not established that the removal of flogging has resulted in an increase in the number of crimes for which the penalty would-formerly have been imposed."

The Lord Chief Justice had, in the most public fashion, thrown his cap in the ring, and soon the nation was racked with controversy. On the very next day, Lord Templewood, President of the Howard League for Penal Reform, retorted that Rayner had overlooked a vital factor: the chief crime punishable by flogging before the Criminal Justice Act was robbery with violence, and only three weeks previously Lord Simonds had said in the Lords that the number of cases of this crime had dropped from 842 in 1947 to 633 in 1951. Mr George Benson, Labour M.P. and Chairman of the Howard League, followed up two days later with a letter to *The Times* recalling the Cadogan Committee's unanimous report in 1938 condemning corporal punishment as ineffective and not a deterrent.

"Subsequent history fully confirms the committee's conclusion", wrote Mr Benson. "From 1939 to 1948 corporal punishment was used more frequently than ever before but, in spite of this, robberies with violence quadrupled. Since it was abolished, this particular crime has fallen while the number of crimes has increased. That the Lord Chief Justice should advocate the reintroduction of corporal punishment on grounds so glaringly contradicted by facts cannot but create confusion in judicial wisdom and in judicial ability to interpret evidence."

It was then left to another *Times* correspondent, a Mr P. Barr-Taylor, to make the obvious point in reply: "Do we know that this type of crime would not have increased five times during the war-time period if it had not been for corporal punishment? . . . Do we know that it would not have fallen to a greater extent (after 1948) if it had been retained?"

Battle was joined. On the day before George Benson's letter had appeared in *The Times,* it was announced that Earl Howe had tabled in the House of Lords a motion "to call attention to the continuation of crimes of violence towards women and other defenceless persons, and to ask whether the existing punishments which the courts have power to inflict in such cases are adequate to protect the public". That motion would be debated in the autumn session. The build-up for the confrontation really got under way.

Statistics were quoted against statistics. M.P.s waxed eloquent on both contending sides. A Liverpool schoolmistress organized a 1 000-name petition demanding the return of flogging. A clergyman observed that "our Lord Himself used a whip, with some devastating results".[2] The Housewives' League demanded action. Magistrates bemoaned from the Bench that they could not order the birch. Associations of Conservative ladies expressed themselves forcefully on the subject. As the summer months wore on it became a combination of serious national debate and 'silly season' agitation.

Finally, on 22 October 1952, Earl Howe rose to initiate the debate on his motion in the House of Lords. "Flogging was abolished in 1948," he said, "and I should like to know whether anyone can tell us what symptoms of reform it has been possible to detect in gangsters since that date."

---

[2] Cited in *Lord Goddard, His Career and Cases* by Eric Grimshaw and Glyn Jones (Wingate, 1958) at page 118.

Rayner made the second speech in the debate. He assured his listeners of "the public disquiet that exists on this subject. . . . My postbag is sufficient reminder. Hardly a day goes by in which I do not get three or four letters from people all over the country wanting to know, with that charming ignorance so many people have of a judge's powers, what I am going to do about it, when I am going to restore flogging, or what I can do to prevent the reign of terror which exists in some places. . . . Nonetheless, it is true, from the evidence I have in this correspondence that, not only in country districts but in places as near here even as South Kensington many old people are terrified to answer a knock on the door at night."

It was a telling phrase. And the Chief continued, "It is time that it is realized that crime—and serious crime—has increased in this country to an alarming extent, so much so that the amount of criminal work which has to be done at Assizes bids fair to put the whole legal machine out of gear. . . ."

But what had this to do with corporal punishment? "I know that I shall be told in this debate—and I willingly accept it," he said, "that robbery with violence is less now than it was two or three years ago. Unfortunately, the statistics do not distinguish between simple robbery and robbery with violence." And he treated the House to a disquisition on the statistics of the matter which makes remarkably boring and tiresome reading in the columns of *Hansard,* and in the end got not very far. Both sides in this debate—as in so many others—used official figures to help try to prove their point, and both equally failed. Flogging was always a subject beyond rational argument, with both sides dedicated in passion to their diametrically opposed points of view: it was a gut reaction in each—and Rayner's proposed solution went even further than that of some of his supporters. Still holding to his aversion to the cat,[3] he wanted the birch brought back, not merely for pre-1948 Act robbery with violence but to be available, at the discretion of the court, "for all forms of felonious violence . . . for felonious wounding, wounding of police with intent to evade arrest and for attempted murder."

---

[3] His reason for rejecting the cat had, in fact, changed. In 1948 he had described it in the Lords as "having an element of brutality". Now he said that he had been—and still was—opposed to it "not because I thought the cat was a terrible instrument . . . but because the fact remained that if a man was given the cat he was too often looked on among his fellows as a hero or a martyr, and that was a bad thing. . . . [Whereas the birch rod] gave criminals a taste of something very unpleasant and very often led to considerable ridicule when they came out. And nothing kills quicker than ridicule."

That proved rather too much for the mild Lord Simonds, a former Chancery lawyer not used to the more robust attitude of some of the judges who dealt with the Criminal Law. Winding up for the Government at the end of the four-hour debate, the Lord Chancellor said, "It is suggested today that not only should we reverse the legislation of 1948, but we should extend the penalty of corporal punishment to a degree which surpasses anything that has been permissible in the last 130 years. Is not that in the nature of panic legislation?"

Their Lordships may have terminated their deliberations, but the debate went on with increased ferocity in the country at large. The following month the Magistrates' Association sent out ballot papers on the subject to its 9 350 members, and the *Sunday Express* announced its own poll among Members of Parliament. One newspaper poll had already claimed that eight out of ten members of the public favoured a return to corporal punishment for violent crime. So the *Sunday Express* sent every M.P. a telegram asking, "Would you support a Bill, if introduced now, for the return of the birch or the cat?" Only 200 M.P.s answered directly—and it was noticeable that of those who replied in favour nearly all were Conservatives, and of those who were opposed nearly all were Labour.

At this time, having initiated the popular debate and having twice spoken in it—at the Mansion House banquet and from the cross-benches of the House of Lords—it would have well behoven Rayner to leave the subject alone for a while, and certainly not to pronounce further upon it from his seat of judgment in court. But that is what he did, and unfortunately his comments were not entirely based on fact.

On 3 December 1952, two brothers, one aged seventeen and the other fourteen, appeared before him at the Old Bailey. They pleaded guilty to robbing two boys in Epping Forest while armed with an airgun and an air pistol. They were also said to have made other boys, younger than themselves, dance in cold water before lining them up and relieving them of their property. They had both already three times been placed on probation.

It was clearly a very bad case, and Rayner was at his sternest: "Nowadays", he commented, "the cane is never used at school. It would have done them good if they had had a good larruping. What they want is to have someone who would give them a thundering good beating and then perhaps they would not do it again. I suppose they were brought up to be treated like little darlings, and tucked up in beds at night."

"What can I do with these young blackguards?" he asked Philip Panto, their young defence counsel. Mr Panto said he had a letter from the local vicar, according to which the older boy was a steady fellow and a member of the church youth club.

But the angry Lord Chief Justice was not mollified. "It would have been a good thing if the small boys who were robbed had a father who had come along and given these two brothers a thorough good hiding," he said, "but then I suppose he would have been summonsed before the magistrates!"

He turned towards the two youths, now standing before him awaiting their sentence. "You are two detestable young bullies," he said. "Nowadays, courts cannot deal with you boys as you ought to be dealt with. Magistrates can do nothing to you, and this court can do hardly anything to you." He sent the elder brother to Borstal, the younger to an approved school.

The use of the almost extinct nineteenth-century word larruping,[4] and indeed Rayner's whole conduct in the matter, would seem to indicate that this was no deliberate intervention by him from the Bench as an intentional contribution to the controversy raging outside his courtroom. He was merely reacting instinctively, using naturally the language of his childhood and adolescence, to the sickening crime these "two detestable young bullies" had committed. Unfortunately, these two lads came from a broken home, and had for some time been beaten almost every night—exactly the treatment that Rayner said would have prevented them committing the anti-social behaviour that brought them before him; and this eventually became public knowledge.

Twenty-four years later Philip Panto, their counsel, then retired from the Bar, could not remember when I asked him whether or not the written reports in the case would have told Rayner of the home circumstances of the two defendants. "Even so," he comments, "I am of the opinion, having appeared in front of Lord Goddard on several other occasions as well, that he would have made up his mind quickly and sounded off accordingly.

Whether or not Rayner should have known from a more careful perusal of the papers before him the true circumstances of the lads, there can still be no denial that at least on this occasion Mr Michael

---

[4] *"larrup; larrop* and *lirrop.* To beat, thrash: col. and dial.: from ca. 1820."—Eric Partridge, *A Dictionary of Slang and Unconventional English,* Routledge and Kegan Paul (4th Edition), 1956.

Foot had a semblance of right on his side when in the *Daily Herald* some weeks later under the heading "O Wordy Judge!" he wrote:

"When is a judge not a judge? That novel conundrum is posed by some recent utterances of Lord Goddard, Lord Chief Justice of England.

"As a judge, his duty is to administer the law, and the duty of other citizens is to accept his decisions without demur or comment.

"Her Majesty's judges are virtually irremovable. They can be displaced only on a petition of both Houses of Parliament.

"No one complains about that system; indeed, it is one of the bulwarks of British freedom. For if the judges were not completely independent, justice would be certain to suffer.

"But Lord Goddard is not only a judge. He has another profession. He is also a propagandist. He holds strong views on how the law ought to be changed. That he has every right to do. But sometimes he seems to express the same views in a court of law.

"Who then is speaking? Is it Lord Goddard, the judge, or Lord Goddard, the would-be law-maker? Sooner or later the question must be settled. For, if the present situation continues, Her Majesty's judges will soon be debating with one another from their rival Benches. That would not be good for the law or anyone else.

". . . In short, should not Lord Goddard save his opinions on corporal punishment for the House of Lords? There they can be answered."

The Lord Chief Justice's critics sharpened the knives of their abuse. On 14 January 1953, the text of a Private Member's Bill, standing in the name of Tory back-bencher Wing Commander Eric Bullus and supported by eleven other Conservatives, was announced to restore birching for male defendants convicted of crimes of personal violence. On the following evening Lord Chorley, a retired university professor, and a Vice-President of the Howard League for Penal Reform, addressing a public meeting in London, denounced the new Bill and said, "It is difficult for Englishmen not to feel ashamed when the Lord Chief Justice is leading a crusade to bring back this form of punishment. There can be no doubt that the fact that the Lord Chief Justice has been using his position in the way he has is one of the main reasons why this agitation for the restoration of flogging has become so prominent.

"Of course, it is in the tradition of Lord Chief Justices. One hundred and fifty years ago Chief Justice Ellenborough, opposing the reduction in capital punishment, said that nobody would be able to sleep in his bed if a man who stole five shillings' worth of goods out of a shop was not sentenced to death.

"The Bench in this country has a bad record in this sort of thing. It by no means follows that because the Lord Chief Justice wants to reintroduce flogging it would be a good thing to do so."

It was an intemperate speech, and so was that which followed from Mr F. T. Willey, a Labour back-bench M.P. "I would like to know who the Lord Chief Justice thinks he is," said the scandalized Mr Willey. 'We have had an investigation and a full discussion in Parliament, of which Lord Goddard is a member. He failed to persuade Parliament that he was right. His action now is bringing the courts into criticism. He is not saying, "We have discovered new facts which I think ought to go before another committee.' He is saying Parliament was wrong. This is intolerable. This is very wrong."

It was left to a third speaker, equally as dedicated a Socialist as Lord Chorley or Mr Willey, but with rather better manners, to state the opposition to Lord Goddard in more appropriate terms. "It is not only Lord Goddard," said Gerald Gardiner, Q.C. "All the Lord Chief Justices for the last one hundred and fifty years have opposed any relaxation of severe punishment. They were sincere men who believed what they said—and they were always proved wrong."

Three days later Rayner was attacked again, and this time from a totally unexpected quarter. Mr John Parris, one of the two defence counsel in the case of Craig and Bentley (which was treading its path through the law to Derek Bentley's eventual execution at this time—and with which we will deal, at some length, in the next chapter) was, as well as a practising barrister, prospective Labour Party candidate for Bradford North. On the evening of 18 January he rose to speak at a political meeting in his hoped-for constituency, taking as his theme "Crime and Punishment".

"Most of what I said went unrecorded," he later wrote,[5] "and the only notes I had were a few scribbled down that afternoon on the back of an envelope." But he did not dispute that, at the end of his speech, he referred to the "present emotional campaign for the reintroduction of flogging" and said that the unfortunate thing about it was that it was largely—almost entirely—instigated by Lord Goddard.

According to Press reports, he continued, "At the moment Lord Goddard is rather like the cat with two heads which figured in a recent law case. One head is the judge's; the other the politician's. I

---

[5] At page 69 of *Under My Wig*, published by Arthur Barker (1961).

have to stroke the whiskers on one of those heads. The whiskers on the other I am entitled to twist." Nor was that all. He went on, "The public are entitled to think that anyone who holds high judicial office will be a model of courtesy, fairness and impartiality. For that reason alone it is undesirable that anybody holding high judicial office should place himself in a position where he must be criticized for political utterances."

"I then went on to quote parts of various of Lord Goddard's speeches," writes Mr Parris in his book, *Under My Wig*, "and to criticize them at length.

"As to what followed next there was a considerable difference in the newspaper reports. The *Daily Telegraph* . . . reported me as saying that I could not say anything about the manner in which the Lord Chief Justice conducted criminal trials. The *Manchester Guardian* had another slightly different version which was, in substance, the same." The *Yorkshire Post* alone carried a report, quoting John Parris as saying, 'Unfortunately, I am precluded from expressing in public the universal consensus of opinion in the legal profession about the manner in which he conducts criminal trials"—a very different observation for a practising member of the Bar to make on a current Lord Chief Justice, and on a political platform to boot.

All the Press reports were substantially agreed that Mr Parris then went on, in his observations on Lord Goddard, "But I am entitled to say that many of his recent utterances in the House of Lords are sensational and untruthful nonsense. Many of the members of that House now regard them with complete contempt. Another judicial officer, the Lord Chancellor, who incidentally is the only one entitled to engage in politics, is as firmly opposed to the reintroduction of corporal punishment as Lord Goddard is in favour of it. But because the things the Lord Chancellor says are not sensational, are presented with restraint and sanity . . . they are not so well known . . . as the outbursts of Lord Goddard."

Rayner, with his characteristic indifference to criticism, could well have shrugged off this remarkable attack from a junior barrister. But there was the honour and position of his high office to consider, and the Benchers of Mr Parris's Inn—Gray's—took the view that it was conduct unbecoming a barrister to imply in a public speech that "the universal consensus of legal opinion is that the Lord Chief Justice conducts criminal trials improperly". They considered Mr Parris guilty of a considered attack "by a member of the Bar on the Lord Chief Justice in his judicial capacity", and suspended him from practice for four months.

The Benchers' decision was reached in April 1953. By then, ironically, the whole flogging campaign had all but fizzled out, and Rayner Goddard had fired no more thunderbolts on the subject.

What had happened was that on 13 February 1953 the Magistrates' Association announced the result of the ballot among their members. It showed a majority of more than two to one in favour of bringing back corporal punishment: of those who voted (and more than 3 000 abstained), 4 412 were in favour and 1 886 against. But on the following day the House of Commons had voted on the second reading of Wing Commander Bullus's private member's Bill to restore the penalty—and had decisively rejected it by 159 votes to 63, a majority of 96.

"The starting-point for today's debate . . . should be a clear understanding that Parliament is being asked to set aside the deeply considered principles on which the nation's penal system has come to rest," *The Times* had said magisterially that morning; and M.P.s took their cue from that line of reasoning. Sir David Maxwell Fyfe, the Home Secretary, reiterated the Government's standpoint that the case for the return of corporal punishment had not been established, and Mr Chuter Ede, his Socialist predecessor in office, congratulated him on what he said was the most courageous speech he had heard in that Parliament.

Rayner was attacked yet again during the course of the debate (as indeed he had been, although in moderate terms, in *The Times* leader of that morning); but now that it was clear that, under a Conservative or Labour Government, the politicians had closed ranks and the return of corporal punishment really was no longer a viable proposition, he seems to have accepted the situation philosophically, and, metaphorically shrugging his shoulders, turned to other things. In public thereafter he seldom if ever returned to the subject again. Even Rayner Goddard did not go on banging his head against a brick wall indefinitely.

17 Craig and Bentley–the Trial of the Century

The trial of Christopher Craig and Derek Bentley for the murder of P.C. Sidney George Miles that opened at the Old Bailey before the Lord Chief Justice of England on 9 December 1952 still remains a quarter of a century later one of the most controversial examples of our criminal law in operation. A policeman was shot dead, a 19-year-old youth was hanged, and some nineteen years later, in 1971, within months of his own death, rich in years and honour, the judge who presided over that trial was posthumously pilloried for his conduct of the case in an article of some ferocity by the redoubtable Mr Bernard Levin in *The Times*[1] and in a book devoted to the case by a young man named David A. Yallop called *To Encourage The Others*.[2] The book—sub-heading: "Startling New Facts on the Craig/Bentley Murder Case"—was a great success. It was serialized in the *Observer* newspaper, and formed the basis of a television documentary-drama that was screened in 1972 and described at the time by the B.B.C. as the scoop of the year. It was so successful that it was repeated in 1973, and, as the magazine *TV Times* wrote on 20 November 1975, it earned Mr Yallop (described as a relaxed man with a well-drilled mind) "a large and rightful measure of acclaim".

What, indeed, are the true facts—"startling" or otherwise—about the Craig and Bentley Trial? Goddard "acted throughout less like a judge than an extra prosecuting counsel. Re-reading the transcript (I have just done so) is a horrible experience; Goddard not only

---

[1] Appearing on 8 June 1971, ten days after Rayner's death.
[2] Published by W. H. Allen, London, 1971.

behaved with vindictiveness, but injected a crude emotionalism into the case," has written Bernard Levin. To what extent is that judgment totally fair or itself coloured by "vindictiveness" and "a crude emotionalism"?

The story will already be known in general outline to most people reading this book, but it needs to be told again, and told objectively and without bias or favour, so far as everyone connected with the case is concerned. It will be related in some detail, using wherever possible the participants' *words at the time*: not those recollected two decades or more later. Yet, where necessary, subsequent statements by the principal parties *will* be referred to, directly quoted from their own published utterances or, more frequently, from their statements direct to me, recorded in my notebook. The memory of Rayner Goddard calls out for justice. This chapter is an attempt to answer that call.

Christopher Craig was the youngest of the eight children of a bank official living in Norbury. Mr Craig senior had served in the London Scottish in the First World War, became a captain at the age of twenty-two and was mentioned in dispatches. He had been a keen rugger player in his youth, and had also won prizes for amateur boxing. In the Second World War, he had been a company commander in the Home Guard. He was a thoroughly respectable and law-abiding citizen. But the family life of Mr Craig proved a perfect example of the old Swedish proverb: "Children are certain sorrow but only uncertain joy."

His eldest son Niven Craig was a professional criminal of the most dangerous kind. Sentencing him to twelve years' imprisonment for his part in an armed robbery on 30 October 1952—three days before the killing that was to form the basis of his younger brother's trial—Mr Justice Hilbery told him, "I have watched you carefully during the course of this trial and I can say that ... I do not remember in the course of some seventeen years on the Bench trying various crimes of violence a young man of your age [he was twenty-six] who struck me as so determined as you have impressed me as being."

Christopher, who was ten years younger than Niven, idolized his brother. He was his great hero-figure. And the lad *did* have his own problems: he was what we would now call dyslexic. In his father's words at the trial, "He never managed to read or write. He suffered from what, I believe, is known as word blindness." The only thing he could just about take in were comics—because they were just "small words"—and films: he used to go to the pictures about three or four times a week. Generally, to see gangster films.

But he had a compensation for his feeling of inadequacy: an obsession with firearms. He admitted in examination-in-chief that between the ages of eleven and sixteen he had had about forty or fifty guns of his own, starting from an antique weapon over a hundred years old. He swapped them and bought them off boys at school, used to take them to school with him. "Whenever you had a weapon, you took it to school?" his counsel, Mr John Parris, asked him at his trial. "Yes, sir."—"Why did you do that?"—"To show it to the boys."—"Why did you want to show it to the boys?"—"To make myself look big, I suppose, sir; to make myself look big because I had got something they had not, sir."

He claimed at the trial that his interest in firearms was totally innocent: that to be a gunsmith was his ambition in life. But when he left Norbury Manor Secondary School in the summer of 1951 the job he eventually took was as a petrol-pump attendant at a garage in Camberwell. "Now, when you left school did you ever take a gun with you to work?"—"Yes, sir"—"I used to take them nearly every day, sir."

The weapon that, according to the prosecution's evidence, killed P.C. Miles was a .455 Eley Service revolver (commonly, but inaccurately, called a .45 Colt). It was undoubtedly Craig's weapon. It had a sawn-off barrel. "Why was the barrel sawn off?" asked his counsel—"So that I could carry it, sir, take it to work, sir"—"Why did you want to do that?"—"It was smaller, sir. You could put it in your pocket"—"Why did you want to take a gun to work?"—"*It just made me feel big, sir*".

Derek Bentley came from equally respectable parents, albeit rather down the social scale. His father was no chief cashier at a bank but a radio and television engineer who admitted frankly in a book[3] published some four years later under his own name that his family of two sons and a daughter had known hard times and considerable financial want. Derek Bentley was nineteen-and-a-half at the time of the events with which we are concerned. He had gone to the same school as Christopher Craig, but because of the age-differential had left at more or less the same time as Craig joined the school.

Craig claimed at the trial he had only known Bentley properly, as a friend, for the past eight months or so. By that time, it would

---

[3] *My Son's Execution* (W. H. Allen, 1957), by William George Bentley.

seem, Bentley had already been demoted from his council job as dustman to that of road-sweeper—and was soon to lose even that employment. He was none too bright. Like Christopher Craig, he could not read or write, and had been rejected for National Service in February 1952 as "mentally sub-standard" and placed in Grade IV. He had been diagnosed as suffering from petit mal as a child, had been sent to an approved school for a minor piece of theft, was a withdrawn, introspective youth who seems to have been devoted to his parents and a member of a close-knit family. In 1952 he was still liable to an occasional epileptic fit.

Craig, though over three years younger, was much the stronger character. Mr Bentley disapproved of his son's new-found friend. He and his wife tried to persuade Bentley to discontinue the association. And this was not without reason: David Yallop, whose book advances the proposition that both these young men were innocent of the crime of murder, writes nevertheless: "During the summer of 1952 Craig was very 'busy'. With Bentley, he broke into a large number of properties, stealing anything that they took a liking to. Without exception all the crimes that these two teenagers committed together were completely non-violent."

One may wonder about that last remark. But certain it is that when, on 1 November 1952, Craig committed what is so far as is known his first armed robbery—upon an elderly couple called Howes—his 16-year-old accomplice was not Derek Bentley but a much brighter local grammar-school boy whom it is not now necessary to name. Within an hour of committing that crime, Craig was visiting the Bentley home and asking for Derek. He was out —but he proudly showed Mrs Bentley a knuckleduster he had made himself at work. He claimed it was better than the ones you could buy.

In his book Mr Bentley relates how his wife told Craig not to be "a silly boy", and to "throw that thing away before there is any trouble". The previous Sunday an anxious Mr Bentley had visited the local police station and asked a sergeant for his help in keeping Craig away from his son: he regarded him as a dangerous influence. Perhaps understandably, all he got was sympathy: there was not much the police could do—at that stage.

Now just check this time-table: on Thursday 30th October 1952, Niven Craig gets 12 years for armed robbery at the Old Bailey. Christopher is shattered by the news. On Saturday 1 November, together with his accomplice, he commits his first armed robbery on the elderly Howes couple and later visits the Bentley home with his knuckle-duster—*and,* according to Mr Bentley's book, tells Mrs Bentley: "They've just given my brother, Niven, twelve years. Do you think I'm going to let them get away with that? I'm going to get my own back some day—and how!"

The next day—Sunday 2 November 1952—Craig again visited the Bentley home just before lunch. His father gives, in his book, this account of what transpired:

"Derek went to the door accompanied by Denis [his younger brother] who told us what passed between them.

"Craig said, 'Come out. I want to talk to you,' 'No,' said Derek. 'You are on your own?' 'No. Dad and Mum are in the garden.'

"Then Craig saw Denis standing behind his brother. 'Send that kid away. I've got something to say to you.' Denis backed behind the partly closed door and listened. He heard Craig talking in a low voice but couldn't make out what he said. Then Derek broke in:

"'I don't want anything to do with it. Leave me alone.'

"Denis ran into the garden and told me that Craig was at the front door. He repeated Derek's words to Craig. I walked into the house and saw Derek in the hall. The front door was shut. 'Where's Craig?' I demanded. 'He's gone, Dad.' 'What's he want with you?' Derek looked at me dumbly. 'Come on out with it! I want to know all about it.'

"Silence.

"'Look, Derek, something's going on. You've got to tell me. Denis says he heard you say, 'I don't want anything to do with it.' What did you mean by that? What's he after?'

"He was deathly pale. I caught him by the arm and shook him. "Tell me,' I said. 'It's nothing, Dad, it's nothing. The bloke's barmy.' And that is all I was able to get out of him."

Is that imagination—or what? Mr Bentley now is dead, but perhaps we are lucky we do not always know what our children are doing. For David Yallop, who at least has had the benefit of long conversations in recent years with Christopher Craig—he was released from gaol in 1963, having served ten-and-a-half years for his crime—tells us in his book that in Derek Bentley's pocket that Sunday were nestling the keys to a butcher's shop in West Croydon, in Tamworth Road, keys that Bentley had stolen the previous after-noon when the butcher's back was turned. Whatever that remark, "I don't want anything to do with it. Leave me alone", may mean (if, in fact, it was ever said), Yallop maintains that Bentley and Craig had already planned to break into and steal from that butcher's shop that Sunday night.

Indeed, at about 8.30 p.m. Craig called for Bentley. Mrs Bentley beat her son to the front door and told Craig—wrongly—that Bentley was not in. Craig needed Bentley: he needed those keys. A few minutes later a well-spoken youth with another young companion rang the Bentley front-door bell. It was the lad who had gone out on the armed robbery with Craig two nights earlier. But, of course, the Bentleys knew nothing about that. Bentley was allowed to "go for a walk" with this nice, well-spoken boy and his friend.

There are no prizes for guessing what happened next: Bentley and the other lad walked to the end of the road where Craig was waiting for them. Bentley and Craig teamed up. The other two went off on their own. Bentley and Craig boarded a 109 bus to West Croydon.

At this stage Craig was armed with a loaded revolver, a spare clip of ammunition and a knife. Bentley had a sheath knife in his coat pocket, and Craig handed him that vicious knuckleduster with the spike he had specially made in the garage.

Did Bentley know that Craig was carrying a loaded gun? For what purpose did he think Craig was handling him that knuckleduster? Of course, these were to be vital questions at the trial on the question of joint enterprise, and, indeed, the answers would also have a bearing on Craig's later contention that he shot at the police officers only with the intent of frightening them, not of killing them.

In 1970 Craig told Mr Yallop, "The gun didn't come into what we were going to do. If he'd thought that I was likely to get a gun out of my pocket Bentley would never have come out with me that night."

Wouldn't he? One wonders. Compare that view with these passages from the trial:

First, Lord Goddard on the knuckleduster when interrupting the cross-examination of Craig by Christmas Humphreys (later an Old Bailey judge) leading for the Crown:[4]

THE LORD CHIEF JUSTICE: "What is that spike for?"
A "I just put it in it. There was a hole."
Q "What is it for?"
A "I just put it there."
Q "What is the knuckleduster for?"
A "To put it on your hand."
Q "You put it on your hand to hit anybody?"
A "Yes, sir."
Q "What is this dreadful spike on it for?"
A "That was in there, sir."

---

[4] At page 86 of the official transcript.

Q "I know, but you say you made it. I want to know what you put this dreadful spike in it for."

A "I did not, sir. It was there. That was just a block of steel, and I rounded off things and filed it a bit."

Q "So if you have it on your knuckles, then you have got *this* as well?"

A "Yes, sir."

THE LORD CHIEF JUSTICE: "A dreadful weapon."

Second, Lord Goddard on Bentley's knowledge of the gun when summing up to the jury at the end of the case:[5]

"Now, let us see what the evidence is with regard to Bentley. The first thing that you have to consider is: Did Bentley know that Craig was armed? . . . Can you suppose for a moment, especially when you have heard Craig say that why he carried a revolver was for the purpose of boasting and making himself a big man, that he would not have told his pals he was out with that he had got a revolver? Is it not almost inconceivable that Craig would not have told him, and probably shown him the revolver which he had? . . . I should think you would come to the conclusion that the first thing, almost, Craig would tell him, if they were going off on a shopbreaking expedition, was: 'It's all right. I've got a revolver with me.'"

Third, Lord Goddard on the knuckleduster again later in his summing-up:[6]

"Then see what Bentley had on him. Where is that knuckleduster?" (The judge called for the exhibit to be handed up to him and held it in his own hand as he continued addressing the jury.) "Apparently it was given to him by Craig, but Bentley was armed with this knuckleduster. Have you ever seen a more horrible sort of weapon? You know, this is to hit a person in the face who comes at you. You grasp it *here,* your fingers go through—I cannot quite get mine through, I think—and you have got a dreadful heavy steel bar to strike anybody with; and you can kill a person with this, of course. Then did you ever see a more shocking thing than *that*? You have got a spike with which you can jab anybody who comes at you; if the blow with the steel is not enough, you have got this spike at the side to jab. You can have it to see, if you like, when you go to your room. It was a shocking weapon."

On this question of the knuckleduster, Bernard Levin's comment in *The Times* nineteen years later was: "When Craig was being

---

[5] At page 136 of the official transcript.
[6] At page 137 of the official transcript.

questioned about the knuckleduster Bentley had taken on their criminal venture, Goddard began to demand of the defendant what the spike projecting from it was for. The judge, of course, knew perfectly well what it was for; it was to make injuries even more frightful than the knuckleduster would have made without it. (The weapon, incidentally, was not actually used on the raid.) Yet he asked the question again and again, pumping up the emotional atmosphere in the court, and he returned to the point, even more crudely, in his summing-up.''

It is surely a little naive of Mr Levin to comment that the knuckleduster "was not actually used on the raid". It *was* carried by Bentley on the raid, and was in his right-hand coat pocket when he was arrested on the roof moments before P.C. Miles was shot. So was it not a vital factor in the case?

His Honour Christmas Humphreys, Q.C., shortly before his retirement from the Old Bailey Bench, told me in January 1976: "I could see nothing wrong in Lord Goddard's references to the knuckleduster. I have done a similar thing many times myself in my years on the Bench and so, I would have thought, have many other judges. 'Members of the jury,' the defendant says, 'this knife'—or whatever—'is only a penknife or used for getting out stones.' Well, you look at it for yourself and see what you think its real purpose was. Do you think it would need a knife as long and sharp as *that*? That sort of thing is perfectly proper, and done every day of the week. Lord Goddard was doing no more than that, in his own forceful way."

Mrs Pamela Maurice, Rayner's eldest daughter, was present in court during the trial. "Much play was made with the fact that my father showed his horror when the spiked knuckleduster with which Bentley was armed was produced in court," she has told me. "It must be remembered that in 1953 the use and display of such weapons was not nearly so common as it is now, and I think even the judge could be forgiven the gasp of horrified amazement that went round the court when the exhibit was produced. Everybody was horrified, not only my father."

But to return to the events of 2 November 1952:

The two young men duly went to the butcher's shop they were minded to break into and steal from, only to find a light on on the premises which put these two brave young marauders off their stroke. They then reconnoitred an electrical shop to see if they could break in, but found a young couple rather earnestly occupied with each other in the alleyway leading to the back entrance. So—third time lucky—they decided to try to get into the warehouse of Barlow and Parkers, a confectionery wholesalers, also in the same road. The place was plunged in darkness. They decided to climb over the six-foot, spike-topped iron gate at the side of the building. It was 9.15 on a cold November night in a side-road in West Croydon. Two agile young men could surely do that easily and quickly without being seen.

But it was not to be. A 9-year-old girl, being put to bed by her mother at No. 74 Tamworth Road, a house opposite, happened to look out of her bedroom window and saw these two suspicious characters. She called over her mother, and the startled woman saw the two young men jump over the gate. She telephoned at once the near-by Croydon Police Station, and within four minutes—that was her evidence—the police arrived on the scene.

That was indeed remarkably quick. First to appear was D.C. Frederick Fairfax, who had been parking his car in the yard at the police station when the phone message "suspects on premises, Barlow and Parker, Tamworth Road" came in. With P.C. Norman Harrison and two other officers—P.C.s Pain and Bugden (who did not afterwards give evidence)—he jumped into a police van, and hastened to Tamworth Road. He arrived just slightly before police patrol car 7Z, driven by P.C. Sidney Miles accompanied by radio operator P.C. James McDonald, which had been alerted by police radio. The police officers split up: Fairfax and McDonald got over the gate, just as Craig and Bentley had done. Harrison (who seems to have been the only one with a torch) worked his way round to the back of the building and got in eventually into the garden next-door at No. 26. P.C. Miles, who was of course the driver of the patrol car, seems to have gone off to get the key to the premises.

By this time Craig and Bentley had clambered up a drain-pipe beside the 30-foot-high building and got onto the warehouse's central flat roof. A word about that roof. It was 54 ft wide and 90 ft long. Roughly in the middle were four roof-lights like miniature greenhouses rising to a maximum height of 4 ft 6 in. At the far end at the back on the right, before the roof became a series of glass and asbestos roof-tops rising and falling over the rest of the building, was an 11 ft 6 in-high lift-shaft. Halfway along the left-hand side of the roof was a brick hut containing the top of the staircase leading on to the roof from the floor below. Both structures would give shelter to anyone hiding behind them.

The first that Craig and Bentley seem to have known of the presence of the police is Craig spotting P.C. Harrison's torch shining in the next-door garden. At the trial Craig claimed it was then, and only then, that he told Bentley he was carrying a loaded gun. It seems almost incredible, but that was his evidence.[7] Incidentally, in Bentley's evidence[8] he says nothing about Craig then—or at any time—telling him he had a gun: at his trial he denied throughout that he knew Craig was armed *before* Craig started firing.

That was now to start. For this part of the case, I can do no better than quote at some length from D.C. Fairfax's evidence at the trial: he was the first police officer on the flat roof, and for some time he was the *only* police officer facing those two young men—one of them armed with a loaded revolver. This bare account of his actions will suffice to explain why he was subsequently promoted Detective Sergeant and, much more important, awarded the George Cross. It is an extract from his examination-in-chief by Christmas Humphreys:[9]

Q "What did you do when you got on the roof?"

A "I saw two fellows. ... They were standing between the roof lights and the lift stack. ... I walked towards them, and as I walked towards them they backed away and went behind the stack. ... I got to within about six feet of the stack ... and I shouted out to them, 'I am a police officer. Come out from behind that stack.' One of them shouted back—"

Q "Just a moment. Do you now know having heard them speak which that was?"

A "Yes, sir."

Q "Who?"

A "Craig, sir."

Q "What did Craig say?"

A "He shouted back, 'If you want us, fucking well come and get us.' I said, 'All right'. I rushed behind the stack and got hold of the accused Bentley. I pulled him out into the open and then I pushed him round the side of the stack of which Craig had just previously gone out of; I pushed Bentley round with a view to closing in on Craig ... I pushed him round to the left as Craig had previously gone out to the left ..."

Q "So, with one man in your grasp, you pursued the other?"

A "Yes, sir. I pursued the other."

---

[7] At page 87 of the official transcript.
[8] At page 98 of the official transcript.
[9] These vital extracts from Fairfax's evidence start at page 18 of the official transcript.

Q "What happened?"

A "As we got to the corner of the stack, Bentley broke away from me, and as he did so he shouted, 'Let him have it, Chris'. There was then a flash and a loud report and I felt something strike my right shoulder which caused me to spin round and fall to the ground."

Q "At that time how far away were you from Craig?"

A "About six feet, sir."

Q "What happened then?"

A "As I was getting up from the ground I saw one person moving away from me to my left, and one person moving to my right. . . . I made a grab at the fellow on my right and found that I had again got hold of the defendant Bentley. I struck him with my fist and he fell to the ground. As he did so there was a second loud report . . . and I then pulled Bentley up in front of me as a shield. . . . I then pulled Bentley to the side of the roof light. . . . When we were behind there I felt over the defendant's clothing to see if he was carrying a gun. He was not carrying a gun [but Fairfax found in his right-hand coat pocket the knuckleduster and in his right-hand breast pocket a knife]. . . . He said, 'That's all I've got, guv'nor; I haven't got a gun!' "

Q "What did you say to Bentley?"

A "I said to him, 'I'm going to work you round the roof to that escape door over there [the door to the stair-case stack on the other side of the roof] . . . Bentley said, 'He'll shoot you.' "

Q "Did you work him round until he was sheltered with you behind the staircase head?"

A "Yes, sir . . . Craig had followed us round . . . then he retreated along back to the top right-hand corner of the roof."

Q "As you were with Bentley under the cover of the brick wall behind the staircase head did you hear your colleague P.C. McDonald coming up the drain-pipe?"

A "Yes, sir."

Q "Did he want help and did you go and help him?"

A "Yes, sir."

Q "Did he then join you by the staircase head?"

A "Yes, sir."

(Twenty-three years later, on 20 November 1975, answering questions that I put to him, in my chambers in the Temple, Mr Fairfax, then retired from the police force, said, "Bentley was left alone by the brick wall. He was sitting at that stage. He did not try and take advantage of my going to help P.C. McDonald to join Craig or to go anywhere else.'')

Q "You went down with Bentley?"

A "Yes, sir."

Q "Were you given something at the bottom of the stairs?"

A "Yes, sir; I was given a pistol."

Q "Did you hand over Bentley to some other officer and return to the roof?"

A "Yes, sir."

THE LORD CHIEF JUSTICE: "What happened when you got back to the roof?"

A "I shouted to Craig 'Drop your gun; I also have a gun,' and he shouted back, 'Come on then, copper, let's have it out.' I jumped out of the doorway on to the flat roof, and as I did so there was another flash and a loud report; and I rushed at Craig in a semi-circular direction and I fired two shots as I went. Before I reached Craig he vanished over the roof."

(In answer to my questions, Mr Fairfax, in November 1975, made two further points: "From the time that P.C. McDonald appeared on the roof Craig was not on the flat roof itself at all. He was sitting up on top of the first row of asbestos and glass gabled roofs and the end of the flat roof so that he had a commanding view of the flat roof itself and anyone who came on to it. Also, I can assure you that he jumped of his own free will from that position at the end of it all—nobody pushed him! It was his own deliberate act.'')

To P.C. Stewart, who was the first officer to reach him lying on the ground at the back of the building and, although in great pain from a badly injured back, miraculously still conscious, he said, "I wish I was fucking dead. I hope I've killed the fucking lot." And there were other similar expressions used to police officers by his bedside in hospital over the next few days. At his trial Craig claimed that his taunts on the roof-top—including the line "Come on, you brave coppers, think of your wives!"—were mere bluff, that he meant no harm; his shots—so he said—were deliberately fired in the air or wild. As for the things he said in hospital afterwards, he claimed that he did not say them or did not remember them or, if he did say them, he was under the influence of medical drugs.

Such matters need not long delay us. If Craig had been alone that night and over the age of eighteen, he would almost certainly have been hanged for murder and (apart from one specific matter raised for the first time in his book by Mr Yallop) almost no one would have questioned his guilt and few would have criticized his paying what was then the ultimate penalty for the crime he committed.

But of course Craig was not alone. Bentley was his accomplice. Bentley was already under arrest at the time P.C. Miles, that brave officer, was shot dead between the eyes. Was he guilty of murder? Should he have suffered the fate that Craig escaped merely because of the accident of birth?

The absolutely single vital factor in considering the case of Derek Bentley is that five-word sentence: "*Let him have it, Chris.*" Detective Sergeant Fairfax's evidence was not the only one on that score: P.C. McDonald clambering up the drain-pipe to join Fairfax on the roof also swore that he heard it—and so did P.C. Harrison, then standing by the chimney-stack on the roof-top of No. 25 Tamworth Road some thirty to forty feet away.

Were those three police officers lying? Derek Bentley's father claims in his book that "Derek never called Craig 'Chris'; always 'Kid' or 'Kiddo'". But this was never put to any of the police witnesses at the trial by the extremely competent and experienced counsel, Frank Cassels (later a Circuit Judge) acting for Bentley—nor does Mr Yallop mention this alleged fact. John Parris, who represented Craig, maintains in his book *Most of My Murders*[10] that there was a *third* youth on that rooftop or in the immediate vicinity that night and that it could have been *he* who exhorted "Chris" to 'let him have it'. But again this theory stands on its own: it is nowhere else put forward, and would seem to have a lodging place in the extensive mythology of this case.

Rayner Goddard put it in his own characteristic way in his summing up:[11] "Now, of course, the most serious piece of evidence against Bentley is that he called out, if you believe the evidence, to Craig 'Let him have it, Chris!', and then the firing began, and then the very first shot struck Sgt. Fairfax. Gentlemen, those words are sworn to by three police officers, Sgt. Fairfax, Police Constable McDonald and Police Constable Harrison; they all swear that they heard Bentley call that out, and the firing started. There is one thing I am sure I can say with the assent of all you twelve gentlemen, that the police officers that night, and those three officers in particular, showed the highest gallantry and resolution; they were conspicuously brave. Are you going to say that they are conspicuous liars?—because if their evidence is untrue that Bentley called out 'Let him have it, Chris!', those three officers are doing their best to

---

[10] Published by Frederick Miller, Ltd, London, 1960.
[11] At page 137 of the official transcript.

swear away the life of that boy. If it is true it is, of course, the most deadly piece of evidence against him. Do you believe that those three officers have come into the box and sworn what is deliberately untrue—those three officers who on that night showed a devotion to duty for which they are entitled to the thanks of the community?"

Personally, I am not at all sure that one can always equate courage with truthfulness as a witness. Some judges of today, in the nineteen-seventies, might well feel that the issue could have been—nay, should have been—more temperately put to the jury.

Even so, one still feels, as Christmas Humphreys said to me in October 1975, "It seems unfair that Bentley should have died because of those five words while the other chap got away with it because he was too young to be hanged. Yet I have no doubt those words were said!"

Nor were they the only words said by Bentley indicating a knowledge—indeed, a prior knowledge—of the fact that Craig was armed with a loaded gun. There was his interjection on the roof-top when P.C. McDonald asked Fairfax what sort of a gun Craig had, and Bentley butted in, "He's got a .45 Colt and plenty of bloody ammunition too". And, while being driven to the police station from Tamworth Road, he suddenly said—according to two police officers' testimony—"I knew he had a gun, but I didn't think he'd use it. He's done one of your blokes in."

It must be stated that in his signed written statement to the police on the following day—preceded by his telling Detective Chief Inspector John Leslie Smith, "I didn't kill him, guv. Chris did it."—Bentley maintained, "I knew we were going to break into the place. I did not know what we were going to get—just anything that was going. I did not have a gun and I did not know Chris had one until he shot." Incidentally, throughout that fairly lengthy statement Bentley always referred to Craig as "Chris": no mention of "Kid" or "Kiddo".

Indeed, on the question of whether he said "Let him have it, Chris!", Dr David Haler, the pathologist who performed the post-mortem on P.C. Miles, has told me that he still remembers quite clearly the police officers telling him when he arrived on the scene on the Monday morning that Bentley had called out on the roof-top, "let him have it, Chris!" If it *was* an invention, it was invented pretty smartly after the event.

The trial was due to start before the Lord Chief Justice at the Old Bailey on Thursday, 4 December 1952—the day after Rayner's 'larruping' case—but that would have put John Parris in considerable personal difficulties. He tells in his book *Most of My Murders* how his brief arrived two days before the fixed date of trial with a one-sentence set of instructions. He was still engaged in a receiving case at Leeds Assizes, which case could not possibly be over by the Thursday of that week. So he describes in *Most of My Murders* how he came specially down to London on the Wednesday morning and saw Lord Goddard, together with the other counsel, in his private room to explain his predicament, and "after a great deal of argument", the Lord Chief Justice agreed to adjourn the case until the following Tuesday, 9 December 1952. Mr Parris tells us that he had to charter a private plane to get himself back to Leeds in time to take over his receiving case again in the afternoon.

At all events, he was back in London on the following Monday for a joint conference with his co-defender, Frank Cassels—and he tells us that Cassels's first remark to him was: "I think both little beggars ought to swing." Mr Parris continues, "It was a view that was widely shared at the time and the fact that he held it did not, of course, prevent him doing his duty faithfully as counsel for one of them." That reads like a sneer, and if so is unfounded: for it would be a bad day for the independence of the Bar and the quality of our justice if counsel were only to represent causes with which privately they were in sympathy and persons for whom, as individuals, they have feelings of liking or affection.

The trial took four days. It is not necessary in this already overlong chapter to go into it in any more detail, save only for two matters.

First, Bernard Levin, in his article in *The Times,* instanced as "the worst example of Goddard's bias" the fact that allegedly "he even forbade Bentley's counsel to question one of the medical witnesses about the possible angle of one of the bullets (the lawyer was trying to show that the shots were fired at random, not with intent to kill)."

In fact, Dr Nicholas Jazwon, on duty as Casualty Officer on the night of 2 November 1952 when Detective Sergeant Fairfax was brought in, had since moved up north to Manchester. His brief technical evidence about having found that the police officer was suffering from a bullet wound over his right collar-bone was purely formal, and he had been conditionally bound over after giving evidence at the committal proceedings in the magistrates' court. So that, unless the defence specifically requested his attendance at the trial, the signed deposition of his testimony before the magistrates would be read to the jury. His attendance at the Old Bailey was, however, requested, and he had travelled down from Manchester to go into the witness-box.

The reason for this soon became clear as John Parris began his cross-examination. The official transcript enables us to form our own views on whether Bernard Levin's strictures on Rayner's performance are justified:[12]

Q (by John Parris): "That is what I think you describe, doctor, as a searing wound."

A "Yes, sir."

Q "Indicating that the bullet had passed over the surface of the skin and not penetrated it?"

A "Yes, sir."

Q "Am I right in thinking that it shows signs of going upwards and over?"

A "Yes, sir."

Q "It goes up and over the shoulder?"

A "Yes, I suppose you could put it like that."

Q "That would indicate to you, doctor, that the bullet had come from a low level?"

A "Yes, it would appear to be like that."

THE LORD CHIEF JUSTICE: "It is a self-evident proposition, *is it not?*"

A "Yes, my Lord."

THE LORD CHIEF JUSTICE: "I do not know why the doctor has been brought from Manchester to say that."

MR PARRIS: "I thought the jury might like to appreciate it. Now, doctor, I want you to draw some inferences from this. That officer found a bullet somewhere round his back braces. Is what you found in your examination consistent with a bullet ricochetting off the floor, going up, searing the shoulder, and going down behind?"

THE LORD CHIEF JUSTICE: "Well, are you competent to answer such a question?"

A "No, I think not, really."

MR PARRIS: "You prefer not?"

A "I prefer not."

THE LORD CHIEF JUSTICE: "The doctor is here to give medical evidence, not to speculate on the flight of bullets."

MR PARRIS: "I was asking whether what he found is consistent with that theory—the wound."

THE LORD CHIEF JUSTICE: "That is a matter you can address the jury on. It is not a matter for the doctor."

---

[12] It starts at page 50 of the official transcript.

MR PARRIS: "If your Lordship will not allow me to ask the question, that is all."

THE LORD CHIEF JUSTICE: "I very much regret that you have been brought all the way down from Manchester. The procedure of binding over was introduced for the purpose of saving the time of people who have been conditionally bound over. The wound you have given evidence about and the passing across the skin could have been perfectly well read, and I regret that you have been brought. You are now at liberty to go."

"Lord Goddard was always very kind to medical witnesses, and did not like their time being wasted," says Dr David Haler.

Second, Rayner's direction to the jury on the law as to Bentley's involvement in the killing needs to be stated:[13] "Well, now I turn to Bentley. Members of the jury, these two youths are tried together, and they are both tried for the murder of the policeman. It is quite unnecessary, where two or more persons are engaged together in an unlawful criminal act, to show that the hand of both of them committed the act. . . . Where two people are engaged on a felonious enterprise—and warehouse breaking is a felony—and one knows that the other is carrying a weapon, and there is agreement to use such violence as may be necessary to avoid arrest, and this leads to the killing of a person or results in the killing of a person, both are guilty of murder, and it is no answer for one to say, 'I did not think that my companion would go as far as he did'."

That, with all respect to Lord Goddard, was perfectly sound law. It did not matter, *in law,* that at the time Craig actually fired the gun Bentley was already under arrest: that was a matter that went only to the question of a possible reprieve. It was in the realm of mercy, an argument in mitigation of guilt; not an argument for non-guilt. Indeed, before all three counsel started their final speeches to the jury, Rayner had said, in the course of discussion with counsel in open court on the law applying to the case, "[Bentley] must be aware that Craig was armed, and the jury must be satisfied that he intended with Craig to offer violent resistance," and had specifically asked Frank Cassels, his counsel, "I do not think you quarrel with that, do you, Mr Cassels?" and Cassels had replied, "No, I do not, my Lord."[14]

The trial concluded with the conviction of both prisoners of murder. Since he was under eighteen, Christopher Craig could not

---

[13] At page 136 of the official transcript.
[14] At page 110a of the official transcript.

be hanged, and was sentenced to detention at her Majesty's pleasure. Derek Bentley, *in whose case the jury recommended mercy*, was sentenced to death. Even had he not wished to do so, Lord Goddard would still have had to pronounce sentence of death: recommendations for mercy were a matter for the Home Secretary, not the trial judge.

Rayner had interrupted during the course of the hearing no less than 250 times. He had strong views throughout which he expressed trenchantly and with force—as in so many of his cases. But in this trial did he go too far?

One incident cited by David Yallop in his book may help to assess the value of the criticisms made of Lord Goddard's conduct of the trial, and the weight to be attached to them. At the conclusion of the summing-up, the foreman of the jury stood up and asked if the jury could have Sergeant Fairfax's coat and waistcoat with them when they retired to consider their verdict. This is how Mr Yallop describes what then took place:[15]

"Throughout the trial the courtroom was also packed with members of the legal profession. One of them, a young barrister named Anthony Samuelson, described to me what transpired when the foreman of the jury made his request to see Sergeant Fairfax's jacket and waistcoat.

"Lord Goddard completely lost control of himself. He quite literally screamed at the members of the jury. 'You will remember you are not considering the wounding of Sgt. Fairfax. You are considering the murder of a policeman.' When he uttered the words 'murder of a policeman' he smashed the knuckleduster that was on his hand down on the bench. The jury at this point had nearly all gone out; only a few of them heard and saw this frightening display.

"This account comes, not from a person unversed in courtroom procedure, but from a member of Lord Goddard's profession. It should convince any reader still in doubt about the matter of Lord Goddard's determination that his point of view should prevail in this trial."

The official transcript[16] has a somewhat different version:

THE FOREMAN OF THE JURY: "My Lord, I would like to see Sgt. Fairfax's coat and waistcoat."

THE LORD CHIEF JUSTICE: "Yes. You will remember, of course, gentlemen, you are not considering the wounding of Sgt.

---

[15] At page 205 of *To Encourage The Others*.
[16] At page 159.

Fairfax. You are considering the death of Police Constable Miles."

It would have been grievously improper if the presiding judge had referred to "the *murder* of a policeman" before the jury had brought in their verdict. It was for the jury to decide into which legal category to put P.C. Miles's death. Craig's counsel had run—however forlornly—the defence of manslaughter (unintentional killing) or accidental death, and Bentley had similarly denied any complicity in a murder. For Goddard to use the word 'murder' at that moment would have been a disgrace.

But did he say it? I have asked Christmas Humphreys if he can remember any such reckless outburst. Mr Humphreys says that he has prosecuted in 250 murders when at the Bar, and quite honestly does not remember very much about the facts of this particular trial; but he is quite sure that if such an episode had occurred he would have remembered it.

So on 26 September 1975 I wrote to Mr Yallop, care of his publishers, as I could find no other address for him, asking if he would be good enough to give me the address of Anthony Samuelson and to confirm that he was indeed "a young barrister", as I had been unable to find him in the current Law List or in one for some years back, 1969.

I handed in that letter at offices in Mayfair of Mr Yallop's publishers on 26 September 1975; but although a charming receptionist promised me that it would be sent on, I have received no reply or acknowledgment from David Yallop. However, I continued my own researches. The Law List for 1953 shows a Neville Anthony Wylie Samuelson, called to the Bar in 1950 and a member of the South-Eastern Circuit but without any Chambers address given; and the records at the Senate of the Inns of Court and the Bar in April 1976 showed no documentation or evidence of the continued existence of the same Mr Samuelson. Then inspiration belatedly struck, and I looked up 'Samuelson' in the London telephone directory. A letter of inquiry to a Mr N. A. W. Samuelson, listed in the directory, brought this courteous and revealing reply:

"You are right in thinking that I am the Anthony Samuelson referred to in David Yallop's book. The incident was so indelibly imprinted on my mind that, when I heard that Yallop was writing his book, I took the trouble to get into contact with him through his publisher. This is a thing that I have never done either before or since. I am not the type who pushes himself forward into controversial situations.

"At the time I felt very strongly that, whether or not Bentley was guilty in law of murder, he was not seen to be getting a fair trial. I do not think it matters very greatly whether Goddard said 'Death' or 'Murder' and if the official transcript said 'death' then I would not question its accuracy. The thing which stuck in my craw (and has stayed there for two decades) was the unjudicial and partisan manner in which Goddard said what he said; and the fact that he said it, not to the whole jury, but to less than half of them; in fact the stragglers who were bringing up the rear.

"I think I was only 22 or 23 years old at the time. With the perspective that one gets from growing older I am now inclined to think that a strong Lord Chief Justice during those post war years was probably of great and lasting value to the country. I could not see it at the time, but what was at stake may have been the very existence of the Rule of Law as we had known it. Should one, then, accept that there were bound to be one or two casualties? I don't know."

Craig did not appeal: indeed, in law, such a course would have been entirely hopeless. But Frank Cassels, who is supposed to have been so faint-hearted for his client, *did* battle on before the Court of Criminal Appeal. The appeal was heard on 13 January 1953 before a court consisting of Justices Croom-Johnson, Ormerod and Pearson. Within an hour it was dismissed: "This is nothing more than an ordinary appeal in a murder trial," said Mr Justice Croom-Johnson, "an appeal which is, in our judgment, without foundation and which is accordingly dismissed." Rayner Goddard—and many other judges of his time—had given judgment in the Court of Criminal Appeal in like terms. Merely because an appeal involved a conviction for murder did not necessarily mean that it bore any legal substance.

Public concern, however, understandably fanned by the Press, was becoming more pronounced. The date was fixed for Bentley's execution. It is fair to say that most people expected a reprieve: the lad's youth, the fact that the murder was committed when he was already in custody, the jury's recommendation of mercy, the fact that Craig was not to die—all these, and other considerations, seemed to indicate that Bentley would not be hanged. When it was announced that Sir David Maxwell Fyfe, the Home Secretary, had refused a reprieve it undoubtedly came as both a surprise and a shock to very many people, and it evoked a wave of indignation. As level-headed a journalist as the late Kenneth Allsop wrote that the nation was plunged into an emotional upset comparable to only two other recent events—Dunkirk and the death of King George VI.

In a desperate effort to force the Home Secretary's hand and make him disclose in public his reasons for disregarding what R. T. Paget, Q.C., M.P., has called "the assembly in the highest degree of every ground upon which the Prerogative of Mercy has formerly been exercised", Sydney Silverman, M.P., put down on the Order Paper of the House of Commons a motion "respectfully dissenting" from Maxwell Fyfe's decision and urging him to reconsider the matter. The motion was signed by two hundred Members, including ten ex-Ministers, but the Speaker, feeling himself bound by the rulings of previous Speakers in earlier cases, ordered the motion to be removed from the Order Paper.

The following day Mr Silverman forced a debate on the propriety or otherwise of the Speaker's decision. The late Aneurin Bevan cried, "A three-quarter witted boy of nineteen is to be hung for a murder he did not commit and which was committed fifteen minutes after he was arrested. Can we be made to keep silent when a thing as horrible and shocking as that is happening?" Other Members took part in the discussion, but it all turned on the question of whether the Speaker was right in ruling that the Home Secretary's decision in a capital case could not be debated in Parliament until after the sentence had been carried out. A great deal of oratory was thundered, but Maxwell Fyfe was not flushed into making a single public statement as to why he had decided that Bentley must be hanged.

The Speaker maintained his ruling, and it was supported by a majority vote in the House of Commons.

Public protests continued. Various M.P.s went to see Maxwell Fyfe. Crowds congregated outside Wandsworth Prison, where Bentley was in the condemned cell. But on 28 January 1953 he was hanged.

David Yallop describes the final scene in these words: "Bentley was crying silently. He was guided to a chalk-mark on the trap. Taking his last look at the men gathered about him he sobbed, 'I didn't say it. I didn't tell Chris to shoot that policeman.' Pierpoint [sic] placed the white cap over Bentley's head, then put the noose round the youth's neck and adjusted it. His assistant meanwhile had been securing Bentley's legs with a leather strap. Pierpoint gave a sign for everyone to stand well clear of the trap, then he kicked the release bolt from the lever. The heavy oak doors dropped open and life began to leave the body of Derek William Bentley."

It would be interesting to know the source of Mr Yallop's statement that, at that very last moment of his life, Bentley sobbed 'I didn't say it. I didn't tell Chris to shoot that policeman'. Albert Pierrepoint, the hangman, in his autobiography *Executioner Pierrepoint*,[17] confines himself to stating tersely: "At the execution of Derek Bentley I did not shake hands with the prisoner on the afternoon before his death. I did not make any notes about him. The Governor of Wandsworth Prison did not have to urge me to get on with my job. Derek Bentley did not cry on the way to the scaffold. I cannot be provoked into giving the witnessed details which would disprove these tales, but I state unequivocally that they are false."

That tragic last line, "I didn't say it. I didn't tell Chris to shoot that policeman," so movingly re-enacted in the television documentary—was it said or not? Mr Pierrepoint's account seems to rule it out, but the point is not specifically covered. So I asked someone very close to Albert Pierrepoint in the writing of his autobiography, someone who has discussed the execution with him in detail, "Was it spoken?" The reply: "Nonsense! There was nothing like that at all. I can assure you that Pierrepoint was quite adamant that at Bentley's execution there were no 'extras'."

Two final questions remain to be resolved.

(1) Should there have been an execution? Should Maxwell Fyfe have advised the Queen to reprieve Bentley?

I must first trail my own petticoat. In my book *Reprieve: A Study Of A System*, published in 1965,[18] I took the view that, in common humanity, once Craig—the principal in the crime—was not to be hanged, then this mentally slow, illiterate companion—even though he *did* say, "Let him have it, Chris!"—should not also have been executed. For it should not be forgotten: "Let him have it, Chris!" was directed at shooting Fairfax, who was only wounded; *not* some minutes later at Miles, who was shot dead.

But my personal views are unimportant. What *is* important is: Why did Maxwell Fyfe, who took such a "courageous" line on not bringing back flogging (to use Chuter Ede's phrase), take the opposite view? In his Memoirs, *Political Adventure*, published twelve years later,[19] Maxwell Fyfe does not really tell us: "After brooding unhappily over the problem for what seemed an interminable period, I decided that Bentley's case did not warrant the recommendation for mercy. My decision was announced on Monday, 26th

---

[17] *Executioner: Pierrepoint, An Autobiography* (Harrap, 1974).
[18] By Harrap, London.
[19] By Weidenfeld and Nicolson, London, 1964.

January, and brought down on my head a storm of vituperation without parallel in my career"—and that is virtually all we are told. So I decided to try and find out from the one person still living, close to Maxwell Fyfe, who *could* tell us: his widow, now the Dowager Countess de la Warr.

"He discussed it with me a lot," she says. "He always did. He never attempted to involve me in his decision-making, but he did always talk things over with me—as he said, to clear his mind. I know he had many awful nights on this decision. His reasoning, as I remember it, was that, if a young man of Bentley's age got off because he went out on that kind of enterprise with an even younger man who did not hang, it would happen again. It would be an encouragement to similar exploits in the future.

"He felt strongly that you had to protect the police, if you did not want to arm them and he *very* much did not want to arm them! He felt all young men would take out someone slightly younger on a felonious enterprise armed with a gun, it would be a marvellous escape-hole for the guilty.

"He was not in any way someone to feel that everyone else was wrong and he was right. His judgments were based on reason. I don't remember a time when making the decision on a reprieve was as difficult for him as then. We were living in Gray's Inn at the time, and we had to have a double guard. You have to be really brave. There were an awful lot of threats on his life at that time."[20]

But what about Lord Goddard's role in the post-courtroom decision on whether the death sentence should be carried out?

In 1970, David Yallop tells us in his book, he interviewed Rayner, then aged ninety-three and within months of his own death.[21] He quotes him as saying, "Yes, I thought Bentley was going to be reprieved. He certainly should have been. There is no doubt whatsoever in my mind. Bentley should have been reprieved."

In a pre-publication reference to the book in "The Times Diary" feature by "PHS" in the week after Rayner's death, he was quoted as having said he was "very unhappy" about Bentley having been hanged. It was that comment which prompted Bernard Levin to write his article "Judgment on Lord Goddard" in *The Times* from which several quotations have already been made (and see After-math). "If Goddard did indeed claim this, it was a breathtaking

---

[20] Interview at Lady de la Warr's London home on 21 November 1973.

[21] In fact, Mr Yallop does not give the exact date of his interview, but states (at p. 14) that it took place within the sixteen months prior to February 1971.

piece of hypocrisy, in view of his conduct of the case," commented Mr Levin.[22]

Mr Jeffrey Simmons, the managing director of David Yallop's publishers, has told us—in a letter to *The Times* following Mr Levin's article—that "Mr Yallop has a tape of his interview—the only personal interview Lord Goddard is believed to have given," Mr Simmons added.

In fact, Lord Goddard *did* give an earlier "personal interview"—but not at the age of 93 and nearing death. It was as a vigorous 84-year-old and on Friday, 12 January 1962; that he received me in his top-floor flat at Queen Elizabeth Building in the Temple in answer to a request for an interview to help in background research for the book *Reprieve*. At that stage Lord Goddard would not allow himself to be quoted by name, but he did permit grateful acknowledgment of his assistance to be made in the Preface to the book. In the course of the interview he expressed himself forcefully on the case of Derek Bentley; fortunately, over all these years I have kept my notes.

Those notes only serve to confirm my clear recollection that what Lord Goddard was saying in vigorous old age was very different from what he is tape-recorded as having said some eight years later and in the last ebbing stages of his life. "Although Craig's offence was the greater of the two, they were both equally guilty of murder and should equally have hanged," is what Rayner Goddard said in January 1962. "Once Parliament has said that persons can be hanged over the age of eighteen, I don't see why the Home Secretary should be expected to observe a higher age limit." He was not impressed by the argument that, since Craig escaped hanging because he was under the permitted limit, Bentley should also not be hanged because he was over the limit. "Because they couldn't hang the one doesn't mean to say they shouldn't have hung the other," he said, sitting in his high-backed armchair in his front room looking out on the Thames.

Some years later, I recounted those words to the late Lord Parker of Waddington, his successor as Lord Chief Justice, and his reaction was: "That sounds like Rayner Goddard. That is what I would have expected him to say!"

And Lady de la Warr told me, "I would have said that David [Maxwell Fyfe] did discuss it with Rayner. I think he always discussed

---

[22] Old men's memory plays strange tricks. In March 1971 Rayner told Timothy Daniell, a young Bar student (see Chapter 21), that he had not discussed the case with the author of a forthcoming book on it, and that his housekeeper had turned him away.

a capital case with the judge—he had every line thought out. He was first and foremost a lawyer."

Yet there is one more strand to weave. At the time of the Craig and Bentley trial Rayner was being cared for by a superb housekeeper of the old school, Mrs Nellie Walpole. I have visited her, a splendid old lady, in her retirement home in Norfolk. She remembers that she was very concerned about Derek Bentley. She thought it was terribly unfair that he should be hanged while his partner got away with it because of his age. She says that when Lord Goddard returned from the Old Bailey at the end of the trial and she was helping him off with his overcoat, he said, "Well, I had to sentence him to death. But don't worry. He won't be hung!"

How does that square with what he later told me, and, indeed, his failing to indicate publicly in court—as he could have done—that he concurred in the jury's recommendation to mercy? Lady de la Warr's proffered explanation is interesting: "He could have said it to his housekeeper in a derogatory sense. He would have been frightened that David Maxwell Fyfe would have been too weak to stick to his guns."

The final matter that remains to be canvassed about this case only arose in 1971, with the publication of David Yallop's book. It is this: Was the whole case a grim farce anyway? Is the truth that—and this is Mr Yallop's hypothesis—P.C. Miles was not murdered at all, that the bullet that killed him was not fired (deliberately or otherwise) by Craig's gun, but was a stray bullet fired by the police themselves?

It seems a fantastic suggestion to put forward—Mr Yallop admits, "Everyone has assumed that it was Craig who shot at and killed the unfortunate policeman. *He even accepts it himself.*" But Mr Yallop yet considers it possible to advance his alternative theory, and indeed to state positively: "I am convinced that Christopher Craig was innocent of the murder of P.C. Miles."

What are his grounds for such a startling proposition? He starts with the fact that undoubtedly at some stage during the roof-top battle the police were armed with weapons and ordered to load them. We know, for instance, from Fairfax's own evidence that he came back up on to the roof himself with a loaded gun and faced young Craig. Yallop also prays in aid the undoubted fact that no bullet was ever recovered as being the fatal bullet: so how can anyone be certain which bullet—and which gun—killed Sidney Miles? The bullet that killed him went right through his head and out the other side we know not where.

Mr Yallop relies very much upon what he says Dr David Haler, the Crown pathologist, said to him during his research for his book. He quotes first the pathologist's report on the dead policeman: "There were two wounds in his head. One was at the inner side of the left eyebrow and was a typical wound of entry of a large-calibre-bullet. The other, slightly to the right at the back of the head, was the exit wound of the said bullet."

He then continues: "When the pathologist, Dr David Haler, gave evidence during the Old Bailey trial, the information elicited was basically the same as in his report. His appearance in the witness box was brief and, perhaps understandably, neither Defence Counsel cross-examined him. If they had, just two or three questions might well have shattered the Prosecution's case. When I interviewed Dr Haler I asked him if he could define the term 'large calibre bullet' more precisely. He had privately formed the opinion that the wound could have been caused by a bullet of a calibre between .32 and .38. Craig was firing a .455 Eley. If Dr Haler's estimate of calibre is right then either Craig shot P.C. Miles between the eyes, firing a .38 bullet from a .455 gun (which a ballistic expert showed me was impossible) at 39 ft. in the dark, or Craig did not fire the fatal shot."

Dr Haler's recollection is different.[23] David Yallop phoned him up out of the blue, told him he was writing a book on the case, agreed to travel out to Dr Haler's home at Weybridge to see him. "But we only had about half an hour to talk. It is not correct to say that I expressed any such private opinion to him as he states in his book." In fact, Dr Haler has sued Mr Yallop for libel and the case has been settled out of court.

The *Guardian* newspaper printed an item relating to a repeat of the Craig and Bentley documentary on B.B.C. Television, and Dr Haler sued them as well. On 8 April 1974 the case ended with a statement in open court giving him a full apology: counsel on his behalf saying, "In order to correct any misleading impressions which may have been given . . . the plaintiff wishes to emphasize that the calibre of the bullet which killed P.C. Miles was never established because the bullet was never found. The plaintiff had no information which would have enabled him to give any definite evidence at the trial of Craig and Bentley as to the size of the fatal bullet beyond saying that it was apparent from the wound that it was caused by a bullet of large calibre. The precise calibre could not have been determined from the wound."

---

[23] Interview with author, 3 November 1975.

Counsel on behalf of the *Guardian* newspaper then told Mr Justice Mocatta that his clients "regret that their comments should have caused any distress to the plaintiff and they accept that the plaintiff had no information which would have enabled him to give any definite evidence at the time of the trial as to the matter in question. The defendants are happy that this unfortunate dispute can be terminated on this matter being clarified."[24] They agreed to pay damages and Dr Haler's costs, and the record of the action was withdrawn.

Earlier on 21 November 1971, two weeks after publishing the relevant extract as part of their serialization of David Yallop's book, the *Observer* newspaper had printed a letter from John Parris: "The extracts you published . . . convey the impression that as counsel for Craig I neglected my duty to my client by failing to inquire about the calibre of the bullet which killed P.C. Miles. It is suggested that had I so inquired, it would have been discovered that the bullet was a .32 and not the .44 used by Craig. In fact, Dr Haler the pathologist reported at the time that the wounds had been made by a 'large calibre bullet'. If he then believed it to be a .32, I can think of no reason why he should not have said so. Craig admitted killing Miles and in the clearest possible terms: 'That copper. I shot him in the head and he fell down like a ton of bricks. . . . There can . . . have been no reason whatever why the question should have been asked : still less is it probable that it would have brought the answer suggested."

In any event, Mr Yallop's contention does not make sense. The exact wording of Dr Haler's post-mortem report, of which he has supplied me with a copy, refers to "a typical wound of entry of a large calibre bullet" and "a typical wound of exit of the same bullet". I have asked him what he meant by "a large calibre bullet". His reply: "*anything above a .38—.38 of an inch*". Craig's weapon was a .455 Eley firing undersize bullets of *.44* calibre—large calibre, according to Dr Haler's definition. The police issue of guns was .32, *small* calibre. So what is it all about anyway? It just does not make sense!

But we live in an age when it is only too easy to question authority and make a whipping boy of the established forces of the law. None of the considerations of elementary logic set out above prevented the almost inevitable letter being written to *The Times* within a short time of the publication of Mr Yallop's book calling for a full inquiry

---

[24] The specific terms of the Statement in Open Court as drafted by counsel for Guardian Newspapers Ltd, 5 November 1973.

into the case. Over the signatures of William George Bentley (Derek Bentley's father), Louis Blom-Cooper, Q.C., Lord Gardiner, Livia Gollancz, H. Montgomery Hyde, Arthur Koestler, Nancy Silverman and Lord Soper appeared a letter on 10 December 1971 stating: "With regard to the innocence of the two youths, we believe that a prima facie case has been established and we urgently call on the Home Secretary to open a public enquiry or grant a Free Pardon to Craig and Bentley". How easy it is nowadays to bandy about the word 'innocence' when the full machinery of the courts has already sat in judgment and pronounced guilty!

On 25 May 1972 a Labour back-bench M.P. asked Reginald Maudling, then Home Secretary, in the House of Commons whether he had yet had an opportunity of seeing the B.B.C. television documentary on the case and whether, in view of the documented evidence it contained, he was prepared to recommend a public inquiry into the circumstances surrounding the trial and execution of 19-year-old Derek Bentley.

"I have fully reviewed the facts of this case in the light of Mr Yallop's book and television production, and the Commissioner of Police of the Metropolis has at my request made some further inquiries into those matters on which it is suggested that new or different evidence is now available," said Mr Maudling in a written reply.

"In the light of these inquiries and of my study of all the facts, I have found nothing to justify any action on my part in regard to the conviction, or to warrant more extensive inquiries."

One final factor remains to be stated to destroy any lingering doubts in anyone's mind. When the police were called to Barlow and Parker's on that November night in 1952, long before the days of urban guerrillas and I.R.A. terrorists, no one knew that the suspicious characters spotted by the woman opposite going over the gate were armed. The police did not carry weapons. They did not know that Craig was armed with a loaded revolver until that first bullet blazed across the roof-top and struck Frederick Fairfax on the shoulder, spinning him round with its impetus. It must have taken some time before the startled police—especially in those days—could get a message back to Croydon Police Station and have themselves issued with arms. After all, this was Croydon and not Chicago.

On this aspect of the case, the last word should be given to Frederick Fairfax, now a semi-retired private detective: "It was not until some time after arrival at Tamworth Road that it was known that Craig was in fact armed. This was when Bentley was arrested and I was shot, after having climbed to the roof.

"Following this the 'key-holder' was sent for and it was when he had opened the premises that P.C. Miles came to the roof. He stepped out on to the roof, faced Craig and was shot. I would make two points at this stage. Firstly, at this stage, Craig was the only person present with a firearm. Secondly, whether it was an accident or not, I do not know. All I can say is that Craig fired and P.C. Miles fell dead. I do not remember the number of shots he fired; but of the number he fired, he managed to score a hit twice.

"It was later that a number of revolvers were brought to the premises by a police officer in a despatch bag. The bag was handed to Inspector Cook in the Managing Director's office in the presence of the firm's Managing Director. At this point everyone knew that Miles had been killed previously."

This statement is taken from a letter to me dated 11 November 1975, and Mr Fairfax confirmed specifically and by word of mouth in my Chambers on 20 November 1975: "At the time of Miles's death there were no police weapons whatsoever on the scene."

Yet now Christopher Craig, through the accident of his date of birth, is alive and well, and, it is believed, living a decent, honourable life—while Derek Bentley is dead, hanged in ignominy. I have asked Mr Fairfax his thoughts on the case, looking back now after all these years: "The verdicts were true—I'm not so sure the sentences were correct. I suppose at the time my attitude was: 'That's one out of the way and it's a pity we couldn't have them both.'

"But returning to sanity and looking back now, I think it would have been justice to have reprieved Bentley. Why? That's the 64,000 dollar question! I suppose afterwards you are able to look back and appreciate the fact that he was sub-normal, of low intelligence and his age-bracket wasn't all that much different from Craig's—*and that Craig did not hang!*"

According to Mr Yallop's taped interview, towards the end of his long life Rayner Goddard came round to the same view. It is one that, with all respect to Sir David Maxwell Fyfe and the younger Lord Goddard, should have prevailed at the earlier time. Of murder there can be no doubt that, in law, both these young men were guilty—up to the hilt. But once Craig was saved from the scaffold, so should have been Derek

Bentley. The logic of compassion is irrefutable. Yet it is to be regretted that the wish for posthumous justice for Bentley should have caused so much posthumous injustice to the tough, vigorous, old-fashioned, but fundamentally fair judge that heard his case.

18 Capital Punishment–
the End

A unique occasion for Lord Chief Justice Goddard was his appearance with the Earl Marshal, in full state dress and preceded by
officers of arms and the tabarded pursuivants and heralds—Rouge
Dragon and Bluemantle, Richmond, Somerset, York and Lancaster—in the High Court of Chivalry, which had not been con-
vened for 250 years. The Court was recognized as the province of the
Lord High Constable, and after his extinction the Earl Marshal as
head of the College of Arms. The Duke of Norfolk, fighting shy of
the law, appointed as his Surrogate Lord Goddard, D.C.L., not in
his office as Lord Chief Justice of England but as a counsellor
learned in the law.

The only authority remaining to the Court was to adjudicate on
heraldic matters, and this first dispute remitted to it after two centuries tickled Rayner's fancy. On many occasions during Manchester
Assizes in the pre-War years when the music hall was still at a peak
he had sat incognito with his *own marshal* in the stalls of the Palace
Theatre to watch the whirligig of variety and hum the songs—he
sang the words of all the old ones. Now the Corporation of
Manchester was suing the Manchester Palace of Varieties, Limited,
for displaying on the pelmet above the main curtain of the
auditorium in the Palace Theatre, Manchester—and with additional
audacity displaying on the company's common seal—represen-
tations of the arms, crest, motto and supporters granted to
Manchester Corporation by the Kings of Arms in 1842.

On 21 January 1955, as Surrogate, Rayner gave an extremely

lengthy reserved judgment.[1] Evidently he had enjoyed the whole performance. He noted that the defendants had denied the jurisdiction of the Court on the grounds that the case against them was not covered by the appropriate statutes of King Richard the Second. He spent much time justifying the existence of the Court, even if it had not sat for so long, and confirming its jurisdiction over the display of arms. Coming to the present complaint, he said that if it had concerned only the display over the front curtain in the auditorium he would not savagely correct it:

"It is common knowledge that armorial bearings are widely used as a decoration without complaint. Hundreds, if not thousands, of inns and licensed premises throughout the land are known as the So-and-So Arms, and the achievement of a nobleman or landowner is displayed as their sign. The arms of universities, colleges or dioceses displayed on tobacco jars, ashtrays, teapots and other articles of domestic use are to be found in shops all over the country and are dear to the hearts of souvenir-hunters and tourists, American and others, as well as seaside visitors. I suppose that, in strictness, none of these people have any right to use or display articles thus emblazoned. . . ."

But Rayner's tolerance did not extend to the use of the Manchester Corporation arms on the common seal of the Manchester Palace of Varieties, Limited, which could be interpreted as an attempt to identify the company with the Corporation of the City, and therefore he thought the Court might properly inhibit and enjoin the Manchester Palace of Varieties from any display of the Corporation's arms, crest, motto or supporters.

To deliver this judgment Rayner Goddard had but recently returned from his own variety turn at the College of William and Mary in Williamsburg, Virginia, where he had up-staged the Chief Justice of the United States, Earl Warren, who was on the same programme.[2] The occasion had been a ceremony in celebration of the 175th anniversary of the establishment of the first Chair of Law in the United States. Goddard gave an address on Blackstone. The *Washington Post* headline ran 'Scarlet-Robed Briton Steals Show at W & M,' and the story began:

"A gentleman who looked right regal and forbidding in a scarlet

---

[1] Reported in (1955) 1 All England Reports at page 387.
[2] Seventeen years later, upon Lord Goddard's death, Chief Justice Warren's successor, Chief Justice Warren E. Burger, was to send Lady Sachs a rare tribute from the head of a foreign legal system, a telegram stating, "My colleagues join in expressing our deep sympathy on the loss of your father. His distinguished career is one of the great legacies to the Common Law World."

gown turned out to be not that way at all and stole the legal-academic show at the College of William and Mary today.

"For putting a nice light touch on impressively heavy proceedings, all honors were won easily by Rayner Goddard, Baron Goddard of Aldbourne, England's Lord Chief Justice.

"Lord Goddard was speaking in appreciation of the contributions to the study of law of Sir William Blackstone, England's first law professor (he pronounces it Blekstun)...."

Goddard was wearing his robes as Doctor in Civil Law at Oxford. His old college, Trinity, had made him an Honorary Fellow in 1940. He held in addition honorary D.C.L.s from Montreal and New York, and LL.D.s from Cambridge and Sheffield.

Rayner Goddard therefore entered his last year of office luminous with honours and mature in tradition. It would be a conventional garnish to add that he was mellowed with age, but this is an unnecessary hypocrisy. Goddard had had a private reputation for mellowness all his life, and when he reached the stage when honours were showered upon him that reputation was even translated into Latin. The Public Orator at Oxford, introducing Rayner for the honorary degree, discoursed at length in Latin not only about Goddard's speed at the sprint and "the measures he has taken to expedite the course of justice". He then referred to his ripe urbanity [the Latin is translated]:

"I should like to banish any thought that some scowling Rhadamanthus is being presented to you. Listen, then. At that evening hour, when dessert is served, that hour when we who sit in his company have seen 'The nuts passed round, with *wine Oporto ships*', we never feel that we are conversing with some forbidding Monster, but with a companionable and courteous and polished raconteur, who can charm us with his talk until far into the night, as Ulysses once held Alcinous."

The Orator at Cambridge went one better, and must be recorded as a pioneer in mentioning Gilbert and Sullivan with Albert and The Lion in the same congratulatory sentence—and in Latin:

"Multo gratius esset, si rumori credemus, omnibus vobis doctum hunc iudicem de infelici puero Alberto leonisque ferocitate narrantem audire quam oratorem Latinas ineptias garrientem. Nec mirum. Nonne enim (ut Domini Cancellarii verba mutuer) quicquid est excellentiae incorporat Lex, Legemque ipsam incorporat hospes noster?"

("If we are to believe the talk of the town, it would be much more agreeable to all of you to listen spellbound to this learned Judge telling the tale of poor little Albert and the ferocious Lion, rather than lend a casual ear to an orator prattling Latin trivialities. And small wonder. For is not (to borrow the words of the Lord Chancellor) 'the Law the true embodiment of everything that's excellent?' And does not our guest 'embody the Law?'")

As at Oxford, the Cambridge Orator also praised Rayner's geniality:

"Who has not enjoyed his after-dinner speeches? It is an article of faith with him that true authority does not demand the maximum sentence in frowning, and does not desert a man who sees no harm in occasionally 'fooling in season' with his friends."

But geniality was not the keynote of the speech that Rayner delivered to the House of Lords on 10 July 1956. The occasion was sombre, and Rayner's style impressive and grave. He was then in his eightieth year, and it was to prove his last major intervention in a House of Lords debate. The subject was capital punishment and the renewed agitation for its abolition.

The Royal Commission on Capital Punishment promised by the Home Secretary, Chuter Ede, in November 1948 as the Attlee Government's sop to the abolitionists after the House of Lords, with Goddard at their head, had blocked the abolitionist clauses of the Criminal Justice Bill, had taken four years over their work since their formal appointment under the chairmanship of Sir Ernest Gowers in May 1949. Rayner, as Lord Chief Justice, had submitted a memorandum and given oral evidence in public of his views before the Commission in the following year.

They were what one might have expected: The existing law of murder was satisfactory with one exception, the doctrine of "constructive malice". "The supreme crime should carry the supreme penalty." Too many people were being reprieved. He saw no reason for reprieving on the ground of age or insanity. The age of liability to the death penalty should not be raised from eighteen to twenty-one. The Home Secretary should not be bound to carry out a jury's recommendation to mercy. It was not a catalogue of weakness. A judge in the reign of Queen Victoria would have found little to disagree with.

The Royal Commission held 63 meetings, heard evidence from a total of 215 witnesses in this country and abroad and finally brought out in September 1953 a monumental Report. It is a prodigious document, supplying a wealth of source-material on the subject, but its actual recommendations—save for detailed suggestions for improvement in the treatment of prisoners awaiting execution and thereafter—were an exercise in typical Royal Commission ineffectualness. They could find no effective way of classifying murder unless the jury was given the power, after finding the prisoner guilty, of hearing evidence and deciding for themselves whether imprisonment should be imposed instead of the death penalty. If this recommendation could not be accepted, then they said the time had come when the question was not of limiting, but of abolishing, capital punishment. The test for insanity should be changed: the jury should consider whether the prisoner not only knew he was doing wrong but whether he was capable of preventing himself from committing murder—a novel doctrine, as was the basic idea of leaving it to the jury to choose whether it should be life or death.

The recommendations met with popular disapproval, and Sir David Maxwell Fyfe, then Home Secretary, declared them unworkable. In a House of Lords debate on the Report in December 1953 Rayner, in a blunt, uncompromising six-minute speech, declared, "I am bound to say—and I say it with all sincerity—that rather than take part in such a performance [leaving the decision on sentence to the jury] I would resign the office I hold, for I think it would be destructive of everything in British law." The Churchill Government formally rejected the recommendations.

But the ground-swell for abolition did not abate. The refusal of a reprieve for Derek Bentley and the execution of Ruth Ellis in 1954 for the murder of her lover David Blakely in a Hampstead street—plus the continuing enigma of the Evans–Christie affair over the murders in 10 Rillington Place—gave the abolitionist campaigners their cue. In November 1955 the late Sydney Silverman, M.P., returned to the attack: with the backing of nine other M.P.s from all three major parties he introduced his private member's Death Penalty (Abolition) Bill. He won over the House of Commons; and in February 1956, on a free vote, a majority of M.P.s resolved, "That this House believes that the death penalty no longer accords with the needs or the true interests of a civilized society."

The Home Secretary, by now Major Gwilym Lloyd George (later Lord Tenby), did not thereupon—as Chuter Ede had done in a similar situation in 1948—incur Lord Goddard's immediate wrath by publicly announcing that all murderers would automatically be reprieved until the issue was decided. He said nothing, but in effect did exactly the same. He reprieved everyone sentenced to death throughout the ensuing thirteen months of Parliamentary debate.

The House of Commons passed Mr Silverman's Bill, and it was

on its Second Reading in the Lords that Rayner rose on 10 July 1956 to address a tense, packed house. Standing at the feet of Viscount Templewood, the sponsor of the Bill in the House of Lords, and with Sydney Silverman at the Bar behind, Rayner began with a reaffirmation of his basic attitude to the whole question of crime and punishment. "I confess to feeling some emotion or sentiment in the matter," he told his enrapt listeners, "but my sentiments are more in favour of the victim than they are of the murderer. There is a tendency nowadays when any matter of criminal law is discussed to think far more of the criminal than his victim.

"If the supporters of this Bill could convince this House that public opinion desires this change, a wholly different set of circumstances would arise," he continued.

"So far as I can see there is no real demand for this Bill in the country, and it has never been submitted to the electorate.

"One gets almost overwhelmed with letters and resolutions begging one to oppose this Bill. I do not say that this is any real gauge of public opinion.

"But I cannot find any indication anywhere that the country is in favour of it."

The police force, he went on, was under strength in every great city.

A county chief constable had told him that he had never known a time when so many of his officers took out life-insurance policies.

"Is this the time to remove what rightly or wrongly the police and the prison service believe to be their main protection against attack?

"We have to remember that our police are armed with a short baton, the only weapon they have against these gunmen and other people who do not hesitate to shoot and take the lives of policemen.

"If this Bill passes I am sure it will encourage resignation from the police forces and make recruitment more difficult."

He agreed that the death penalty did not stop certain crimes. He thought it had little effect, for example, on wife-murders.

But even there he recalled a brutal assault on a wife in which the accused said, "If it was not that I would swing for you, I would do you in."

He went on, "That is the sort of thing the death penalty prevents. I do not want to joke in this matter, but what would be the effect on such people if they knew that they would be sent to a sanatorium or some other comfortable place if they committed murder?

"I believe the fear of the rope, as it is generally called among certain classes, is a very great deterrent.

"If this Bill is passed, judges will not be able to give any greater punishment for deliberate murder than they can give now for burglary, for breaking into a church (sacrilege), or for forging a will."

He spoke of ruffians who used knives, razors, coshes, broken bottles—and of all weapons he thought a broken bottle was about the worst to push in a man's face.

"Why do they always stop short of murder?

"They inflict these horrible wounds which may need twenty or twenty-five stitches in a man's face. They don't stop short of murder from any motive of humanity.

"The people they attack are men they hate and loathe, and want to put out of action."

The Lord Chief Justice recalled the case last year when a bandit caught after a chase in London fired low at a young constable. "He fired low because he knew what the consequences would be if he murdered the policeman.

"When he was arrested his first question was 'Is the copper dead?' That is what he was afraid of."

And then to the accompaniment of many cheers from the Lords, he said gravely, "I do not believe that young policeman would be alive today if the ruffian had not known that the death sentence would inevitably follow if he had killed him.

"These instances make me say with all the earnestness I can command: do not gamble with the lives of the police."

He then recalled a case that had come before the Court of Criminal Appeal: "A little spinster, 4 ft 9 in in height, lived on the edge of some village and was so afraid of being attacked that she had all the windows of her cottage screwed up. A young brute of twenty-three broke into that house and battered that poor little creature to death. All her ribs were broken, and then he cut her throat, and all he got was some trivial jewellery.

"Are these people to be kept alive?" Rayner asked, in his level voice.

There were murmurs of indignation from many peers. One of them exclaimed, "That man was reprieved."

"Yes," said Rayner, "he was reprieved after I had seen the report of the medical men sent by the Home Secretary to examine him. The report was that neither on legal nor medical grounds was there any reason for saying that he was insane.

"And yet he was reprieved!"

He then turned to the Home Secretary's universal reprieving of murderers which was taking place at present. "I do not want on this occasion to get into any conflict with the executive," he said.

"I do not want to discuss how far it is constitutional, merely because one House of Parliament has passed a Bill, for a general dispensation to be given for the crime of murder.

"I will only say that if anybody takes the trouble to read the Bill of Rights he will see it was declared on the motion of the House of Commons that the suspending power and the dispensing power (the reprieve) as it has been exercised recently—that is to say, on every occasion—is contrary to the law."

As for life imprisonment as the alternative to the death penalty, "I say at once that life imprisonment, although passed as a sentence, can never be carried out in fact. To say to a young man of twenty-five that for the rest of his life he is to be kept away from his fellows, except fellow-criminals—it would be terrible. One knows the utter spiritual, mental, and physical deterioration that sets in after a man has suffered a long term of imprisonment. I should shrink from the very idea of saying that the sentence for murder should be life imprisonment in the full sense."

But he did think that the time was ripe to amend the law of murder. No judge liked to pass sentences of death in cases in which he knew the penalty would not be carried out. Many amendments could be made to the law of provocation and implied malice.

Yet he thought the present system as it worked until recently—with reprieves given where mitigation could be found—had worked well. "Your lordships can be assured that the only people hung are those guilty of cruel, deliberate murder without mitigation."

His last words were: "I put my views strongly because, from experience, one gets to feel strong views in these matters and should not be afraid to express them. When a man deliberately murders another he is committing the supreme crime, and should pay the supreme penalty."

Their Lordships were impressed. Despite a speech by the Archbishop of Canterbury saying that he would vote for the Bill and seek to amend some of its details later, the House of Lords rejected Mr Silverman's Bill by an overwhelming majority—238 votes to 95.

The Government—and the nation—were back to 1948, with the Upper Chamber, ranked behind the Lord Chief Justice of England, blocking the path to abolition in the name of public opinion. But there the comparison ends, for the outcome was very different. This time there was no face-saving Royal Commission culminating in

Alice-in-Wonderland recommendations. The Government this time brought in their own abolitionist Bill—a compromise, halfway-house measure, the Homicide Bill cutting back the death penalty to only six categories of murder: murders in the course or furtherance of theft, murders by shooting or causing an explosion, murders in the course of resisting arrest or escaping from custody, murders of policemen or those assisting them in the course of their duty, murders of prison officers in similar circumstances and murders where the same person had killed more than once and been convicted on separate occasions.

On a free vote, this measure passed the House of Commons and came up on Second Reading to the Lords. Everybody wondered, what would happen now? How would the old man take it? For a third time running, would he stand before the guns of what some considered progress waving his defiant sword in the air?

Rayner's performance on 21 February 1957 was a strangely muted affair. He seems to have realized that the tide—at least, in Whitehall and Westminster, if not in the country at large—was no longer with him. He said there was one reason why he thought the judges would welcome the Bill, and that was that they hoped it would put an end to "a perfectly intolerable situation that was causing them considerable embarrassment"—and he went off into a long attack on Home Secretary Lloyd George's continuing habit of reprieving every prisoner sentenced to death. "Is this to go on?" he said. "The judges are feeling now a sense of the greatest embarrassment. They have to administer the law as it is. They will have to administer the law as it is altered. They have had to pass sentence of death in every case of murder where there has been a conviction. Now they will have to pass sentence of death in what is called capital murder.

"I hope the judges may feel now that although these so-called capital murders are being reprieved, in exactly the same way as in what will be called non-capital murders, they may not be put into this position of having to pass sentence of death in these cases only to find that it is a reprieve.

"One virtue in this Bill is that I cannot believe that if it is passed, where there are murders which are declared to be capital murders, that the law will not be allowed to take its course. If the law is not allowed to take its course, then in Heaven's name let us abolish it altogether."

This was Rayner Goddard ceasing to play King Canute and, as a realist, trying to ensure that at least something of what he would have called 'sanity' would return to the law of murder. His manoeuvre was successful. The perplexed Lord Chief Justice got a categoric answer from the Government Front Bench. "I have made inquiries, and I am able to make the following statement," said Lord Salisbury, then Leader of the House and Lord President of the Council. "So far as the future is concerned, there is no doubt at all that once this Bill becomes an Act no difficulties of the sort envisaged by the noble and learned Lord can arise; and this is the determination of the Government."

The House of Lords did not divide. The Bill got its Second Reading, and went on to become law as the Homicide Act of 1957, remaining in effect until Sydney Silverman's final private member's Murder (Abolition of Death Penalty) Act made the scaffold a museum-piece in 1965. In those intervening eight years of uneasy compromise the proportion of reprieves dropped slightly—from 45 per cent of all persons sentenced to death to just under 40 per cent. But such was the sway that Lord Goddard's powerful personality had over even informed persons that the 'pledge' he had obtained from Lord Salisbury in the February 1957 debate was generally considered to have been more effective than in fact it was. "We have no doubt that the small number of reprieves these days stems from Lord Salisbury's firm assurance to Lord Goddard," the Secretary of the Howard League for Penal Reform, then Mr Hugh J. Klare, told me in 1964.[3] It was ironic homage to Rayner's charisma.

But Lord Chief Justices not only concern themselves with great matters of State and fundamental principles of the law or high-flown principles of crime and punishment. They also sit from time to time, just like any other Queen's Bench judge, to hear ordinary, everyday actions for damages for negligence, breach of the Sale of Goods Act, claims for compensation for personal injuries and the like. "I had to spend a lot of time (as Chief)," Rayner once wrote to Sir Arthur Bryant, "trying collisions between two stationary motorcars, each on its proper side of the road, or those in which men and girls in factories would put their fingers into moving machinery."[4]

Two months before the Homicide Bill debate in the House of Lords, on 11 December 1956, Rayner had a civil case before him which brought into sharp focus the two contrasting aspects of the work of his high judicial office. He sat to hear a straightforward, in no way out of

---

[3] Cited in *Reprieve: A Study of a System* at page 81.
[4] Quoted by Sir Arthur Bryant in a letter from Lord Goddard in an article in the *Illustrated London News* in June 1971.

Two Official Secrets Act Cases

Klaus Fuchs (on left of picture) leaving London Airport for East
Berlin after serving the fourteen-year sentence imposed on him by
Lord Goddard
Photo Keystone Press

Paul Thompson (left) and William Miller (right), when young Oxford
University undergraduates at the time of their trial in July 1958
before Lord Goddard and an Old Bailey jury for very different
Official Secrets Act offences

**Lord Goddard's Predecessor and
Successor as Lord Chief Justice**

Lord Caldecote, the lawyer-politician
who preceded him at the time of his
earlier appointment (in 1936) as
Britain's first Minister of Defence
*Photo Radio Times Hulton Picture
Library*

Lord Parker of Waddington, the
Appeal Court judge who succeeded
him, photographed in his robes as a
Lord Justice of Appeal
*Photo Radio Times Hulton Picture
Library*

the ordinary, claim for damages brought by a 25-year-old cinema usherette from South London against her employers for their alleged negligence in having a defective staircase and inadequate lighting at the cinema where she worked. Her name was Bentley—she was Miss Iris Bentley, only sister of Derek Bentley.

"Perhaps she might prefer that another judge should hear this action," Rayner said to her counsel at the start of the proceedings. "The plaintiff has no objection to your hearing the matter," he was told.

Miss Bentley had injured her right knee falling down some stairs at the Astoria Cinema, Streatham, on 2 August 1953, some seven months after her brother's execution. Neil Taylor (later a Q.C.), her counsel, said that because of her nervous state at the time, after the "terrible tragedy" to the family, her recovery was not as quick as it might have been. She had had psychiatric and physiotherapy treatment.

Miss Bentley gave evidence, and so did the house manager. He told Rayner that he regularly used the staircase and did not find it dangerous. Rayner said that he had seen some photographs of the staircase and the lighting supplied to him as part of the ordinary documentation in a case of this sort—but he would prefer to inspect the premises and see for himself exactly what the situation was. John May (later a High Court judge), counsel for the cinema company, gave him directions to enable him to visit the Astoria on the following morning.

This was Rayner, aged seventy-nine, up to his old habit of "going to see for himself". "It isn't very easy to get to unless I go by car," he told counsel, "but Colonel Nasser"—this was at the time of Suez—"has something to say about that. I have a little petrol so I will go in my own car and then it can't be suggested that I have been got at."

So the next morning Reiffer, his loyal chauffeur, drove him out to Streatham and Rayner had a look at the cinema staircase for himself. He came back to court and eventually gave judgment against Miss Bentley. He explained that from the photographs he had expected to see a larger staircase, but in fact it was very small and in a very confined space. The lighting in such a confined space by a 15-watt lamp was sufficient. It was "a perfectly safe and proper staircase".

The old man was functioning in full command of his powers. In February 1957 he received a mock-angry letter from Sir Hartley Shawcross, Q.C. Sir Hartley had been appearing before him on behalf of the County Council of the West Riding of Yorkshire seeking to obtain a ruling that a claim for no less than £258 789 against Huddersfield Corporation for moneys allegedly owing in consequence some twenty years earlier of a rearrangement of administrative responsibilities within the West Riding was not statute-barred under the Limitation Act of 1939 and was still an enforceable debt. In a pithy judgment, Rayner had ruled the claim was statute-barred and sent the County Council away with the proverbial flea in their ear.[5]

"My dear Rayner," wrote Sir Hartley the next day, "I am sorry to say that I have a certain serious complaint to make against you. You have done me out of two well-remunerated briefs in the Court of Appeal and the Lords!

"After yesterday's affair, the Clerk of the West Riding County Council . . . came round to my chambers bursting with enthusiasm—but not for me!

"'The old boy', he said, 'had his finger on the vital points from the word go . . . you could not get a thing past him . . . unless you want to go on, I am perfectly satisfied!'

"So there it was. I had to agree that there was no possibility of upsetting you. And we are all agreed that it was quite obvious you ought not to think of depriving the country of its most distinguished L.C.J."

A charming and one has no doubt well-merited tribute; but for how much longer could Rayner, facing his eightieth birthday, put off the prospect of his retirement?

---

[5] The judgment is reported in (1957) 1 All England Reports at page 669.

19 The Last Summer

No one, not even Rayner, could go on for ever. On 5 April 1957, he
had celebrated his twenty-fifth anniversary as a judge, in all of which
time he had missed only one day from court through illness. It was
an unprecedented record. "It is not necessary for me to say in what
high esteem all those who practise before your Lordship have always
held you," F. W. Beney, Q.C., the senior silk appearing before him
that day, told him on behalf of all the members of the Bar. "We
hope that you will continue for years to come still to occupy the
important position that you hold."

But in five days' time the Lord Chief Justice would be eighty years
of age: for how much longer *could* he go on?

The first rumours of retirement had been heard as far back as
1953, when he had held office for seven years and was said to be
minded to go so that he could be succeeded by Sir Hartley Shawcross or Viscount Monckton, the brilliant lawyer who was then still
a member of Winston Churchill's last Administration. It is indeed
true that at an early stage Rayner wanted first Sir Hartley and then
Lord Monckton to succeed him;[1] but he was never prepared (nor indeed was he ever asked!) to accelerate his own departure so that either
of those two events could come to pass.

The rumours died down. Then two years later, in 1955, they
started up again when word got around the Temple that he had disposed of a large number of his own personal copies of the Law

---

[1] Private information from the late Lord Parker of Waddington, Lord Goddard's
successor, to the author.

Reports; but those fresh rumours were in turn promptly scotched when it became known that Rayner had merely regarded the old copies as dilapidated and had simply replaced them with another complete set. In that same year, as if deliberately to spike any more ill-founded talk about his impending departure from office, Rayner, at the age of seventy-eight, set off and covered two separate Circuits; something, it was said, that no former occupant of his post had ever attempted.

In May 1956, a month after his seventy-ninth birthday, he again left London and conducted Assizes in a barn-storming tour of seven towns so as to speed up the trial of a large number of pending cases. In the month before his twenty-fifth anniversary tribute, in March 1957, he showed he was still up to his normal razor-sharp form: he was sitting in the Court of Appeal with Lord Justice Jenkins and Lord Justice Sellers. They were hearing a tax appeal from a property firm challenging Mr Justice Danckwerts's refusal to set aside a General Commissioners' finding as to their income tax. Two days had been allotted for hearing the case—but that must have been before the authorities realized that Lord Goddard would be the presiding judge. After an hour and a half's hearing the appeal was dismissed: "I do not propose to deliver a reasoned judgment," said Rayner, "because this is a perfectly hopeless appeal. If the Commissioners had not held as they did, it would have been a perverse finding." He said, with a characteristic snort, that he was now in the position of "genuinely seeking work".

These signs of unabated vigour were there for all to see, but there had never yet—at least, in modern times—been an 80-year-old Lord Chief Justice. "He was so loved and respected by his judges," says Lord Parker of Waddington, who was himself for four years one of "his" Queen's Bench judges, "that no one wanted to think about his retiring. But in the last year or two he was beginning to feel very tired, although he didn't show it."

The stories started up again: following his eightieth birthday, several newspapers openly speculated on the Chief's imminent departure. But judges read newspapers too. The author has a newspaper cutting from the *Manchester Guardian* for 1 May 1957 cut out of the paper by Rayner himself and with his own handwriting on it: "Lord Goddard kills retirement rumour", runs the sub-headline. For on the previous day Rayner had taken the opportunity of a formal luncheon to celebrate laying the foundation stone of the new Manchester Courts of Law to say, "In the newspapers I have been told so often that I am about to retire that I sometimes felt I had retired. But you have just drunk my health, and considering my age, it is not too bad. I can still do a pretty good day's work, and I don't see why I should burden the country by making it pay me a pension. The newspapers will have to put up with me for a little longer."

The rebuff was taken in good part. "He knows quite well, of course, that the newspapers are quite happy to put up with him," wrote the "Comment" column in the London *Star*. Rayner had also said, "I have looked up my expectation of life and find that there is an even chance I may be here—I hesitate to say in my present position—when the courts are opened." Commented the *Star* leader-writer: "So long as a man feels and thinks like that he can surely go on doing his job well, whether he is 80 or 90, Lord Chief Justice or court usher. On the question of retirement we may safely trust to the Court's own judgment."

Two months later his old Circuit had the opportunity to pay homage to its most illustrious son. On 17 July 1957 a record attendance of 107 people thronged the long tables in Gray's Inn Hall to do honour to Rayner on a special Circuit congratulatory dinner on his eightieth birthday. Speeches were made, toasts were drunk and the old man rose to his feet to reply. "My memory goes back fifty-eight years and I do not remember a dinner of this nature before," he told the faces turned reverently towards him. "This honour makes me very humble. For a good time, I was a faithful member of the Circuit. I feel that you have paid me a very wonderful compliment."

The words were simple and the emotion patently genuine. Rayner was both embarrassed and warmed by the affection in which he knew he was held. It is permitted to old men at times to be close to tears.

Yet there was still nothing maudlin or soft about the Chief. Six days before the Circuit Dinner, Rayner had been the principal guest at the Lord Mayor's annual dinner to Her Majesty's Judges at the Mansion House. "People are constantly asking what is the cause of crime," he told the vast room, stiff with elegance and the white hairs of distinction. "I do not believe that the psychopaths alone can provide an answer. Personally, I think that human nature remains constant. Those who sit in the criminal courts know that it does not change very much, and must come to the conclusion that the age-old causes of crime are still the desire for easy money, together with greed, passion, lust and cruelty." It was to be one of the most famous assertions of his basic philosophy: Churchillian in its blunt use of simple, ancient words. The strength was still there, in abundant supply.

His eighty-first birthday came and went, with still no indication when the old man might be prepared to stand down. Yet the dates on the calendar were there for all the world to see: 1877 seemed an awfully long time ago for a man to be born who was still in 1958 the Lord Chief Justice of England. The speculation about retirement started up again.

At the Queen's Bench Judges' meeting at the beginning of the Hilary Term in June 1958 his assembled judges felt at last constrained as a body to mention the subject to him. Mr Justice Finnemore, speaking on behalf of them all, urged him not to consider retirement yet and stay on "not only because we respect and admire you but rather because we love you". Rayner was moved, but noncommittal: for he knew that the time could now not be far off. Not because he was aware of any intellectual failing, but because of the brutal physical fact that he was beginning to be worried about his hearing. Courtroom acoustics are not the best in the world, and Rayner Goddard was not the sort of man to wear an artificial hearing aid when performing his duties.

Says Peter Stephenson, his private secretary throughout his years of office, "He thought he ought to go while his hearing was still adequate. He told me that he did not want people to say the silly old dodderer ought to have gone years ago. He wanted to go when still at his best."

He still had not chosen the exact date; as he told a friend, he did not want to retire, but when he went down to the Old Bailey in early July 1958 to preside over the coming session he knew in his heart that it would be the last time he would sit in the world's leading criminal court. Perhaps appropriately, what was to prove 'Goddard's Last Great Case' concerned two young men: both undergraduates at his old university, both passionately sincere and dedicated to what they thought right—and both, as they have since freely admitted to me, terrified and in awe of the powerful old man who was to conduct their trial.

Paul Richard Thompson, twenty-three, of Corpus Christi, and William Miller, twenty-four, of Lincoln, both ex-National Servicemen, were charged with three of the most serious offences possible for an Englishman to commit against his country in time of peace. The first count of the indictment was that, having in their possession secret official information to which they had access as persons who had been employed under Her Majesty, they communicated that information to a named person who was other than one to whom they were authorized to communicate it. The second count was that they had used the same information in a manner prejudicial to the safety and interests of the State, and the third count alleged that they had received secret official information having reasonable grounds for believing that it was communicated to them in contravention of the Official Secrets Act, 1911; all three charges being contrary to Section 2 of the Act.

It was a grave matter, even though the "use of information in a manner prejudicial to the safety of the State" referred, not to a Klaus Fuchs-type operation, but to the publication of an article in the Oxford University magazine *Isis*. Eighteen years after the event, William Miller, now a successful publisher, analysed for me[2] his actions and motives of that time: "Together with a lot of other students I had felt that at a time of heightened cold war, people were not aware of the real danger of nuclear war. This was after Suez and the repression of the Hungarian rising—and I had protested against both. People did not realize that a nuclear war would have been a whole paradigm-shift away from conventional war.

"My family were voting in Gravesend, a constituency where Sir Richard Acland had resigned from Parliament over the issue of nuclear disarmament, and I had been very impressed by his arguments.

"In December 1957 I came back to Oxford after Christmas and talked to some friends. We decided we would try to publish an issue of 'Isis' devoted to nuclear warfare and its effects and make people less complacent about the idea of the cold war being a hot war.

"The article which was the subject of the prosecution was not written by me, but I knew the facts in it were true. I had learnt Russian during my National Service and I was a signatory to the Official Secrets Act. I captioned the article and I was responsible for supplying the illustration. That issue of *Isis* was the only one which, after selling out, was reprinted."

The issue, No. 1316, was dated 26 February 1958. There were signed articles, notably "The Moral Responsibility" by Professor C. A. Coulson, F.R.S., which advocated Great Britain's unilateral rejection of nuclear weapons. Vicky had contributed his famous cartoon showing Macmillan and Eisenhower playing the harp on one cloud and Khrushchev on another, with the caption: "I *told* you that ours is bigger than yours, didn't I?" But a number of articles were co-operatively written, and there was the acknowledgment that the

---

[2] In an interview on 23 March 1976 confirmed by Paul Thompson in a letter of 27 March 1976 as being "perfectly fair".

unsigned articles had been written or commissioned by a group of compilers—including William Miller and Paul Thompson.

An editorial introduction commented, "The articles show how easily war could come, and how nearly disarmament talks could have succeeded with less intransigence on both sides." The article on which the prosecution was based read:[3]

FRONTIER INCIDENTS—EXPOSURE

"The doctrine of Western sincerity and the good fight against Russian wickedness is fostered in many little ways: and not the least of these is the misreporting of news. We wish to expose one variety of this. Frontier incidents are almost invariably reported as ferocious and unjustifiable attacks by Russian fighters on innocent Western aircraft peacefully cruising well within their own frontiers. Sometimes it is conceded that the victim has lost its way. This is British understatement at its best. All along the frontier between east and west, from Iraq to the Baltic, perhaps farther, are monitoring stations manned largely by National Servicemen trained in morse or Russian, avidly recording the last squeak from Russian transmitters—ships, tanks, aeroplanes, troops and control stations. It is believed, perhaps rightly, that this flagrant breach of the Geneva Convention can provide accurate estimates of the size and type of Russian armaments and troops, and the nature of their tactical methods.

"In order to get this information the West has been willing to go to extraordinary lengths of deception. British Embassies usually contain monitoring spies. When the Fleet paid a "goodwill' visit to Danzig in 1955 they were on board. And since the Russians do not always provide the required messages they are sometimes provoked.—A plane 'loses' its way; while behind the frontier tape recorders excitedly read the irritated exchanges of Russian pilots: and when the latter sometimes force the plane to land an international incident is created, and reported in the usual fashion. The famous Lancaster bomber incident near Berlin was deliberately provoked in this way.

"In a moment of crisis irresponsibility of this kind could well frighten the Russians into war. Certainly if Russian planes were to fly over American bases the American reply would be prompt. But there is no controlling the appetite of the statistical analysers at Cheltenham. Perhaps the best example of their activities is in the Baltic. After the war a fleet of half-a-dozen exceedingly fast

---

[3] This is the first time that the article has been reprinted at its full length.

Mercedes-Benz torpedo-type boats were built, and, manned by sailors from Hitler's navy, were sent out under English captains to provoke and listen to the Russians. They would head straight for the Russian Fleet at exercise and circle round a battleship taking photographs. When they had succeeded in concentrating all the guns of the fleet and recorded enough messages they fled. When in Swedish waters, contrary to all international conventions, they flew the Swedish flag. One British captain, who was suitably equipped with a wooden leg which lent a certain glamour to the Quixotic behaviour, so far exceeded the normal practice, which was merely to enter Russian territorial waters, as to go into Leningrad Harbour and on another occasion to land a small party in Russia. It was incredible that this should have been allowed, but the irresponsibility bred and sheltered by the Official Secrets act is uncontrollable. In 1956 the new German Navy took over the full control of these boats and are doubtless happily continuing our own policy."

An accompanying photograph of a naval craft was captioned: Mercedes-Benz spy boat.

The article certainly made its impact in Oxford, where *Isis* was organizing a voluntary referendum on nuclear disarmament to which 5 000 signatories responded. But there was a lull while the authorities absorbed it. After three weeks Special Branch action became apparent, and C.I.D. men from the Oxford Police were ordered to question students in order to discover the authorship of the article "Frontier Incidents". Since four names had been published as the compilers of the issue, the investigation was not difficult. The interrogation was continued, however, by the Press. Paul Thompson told *The Times*, "I don't think it was a possible breach of the Official Secrets Act because the article doesn't reveal secrets to the enemy. There is no strategic reason why these facts shouldn't be known. The Russians, for obvious reasons, know already."

The activities of other sections of the Press were not so decorous. A *Daily Sketch* Reporter asked William Miller, "Are you a Communist?" He replied, "No, I am a Socialist." The exchange was printed as: "I asked Bill Miller if he was a Communist. He fingered his red tie. No, he said."

Throughout that Easter the first Aldermaston March—from Trafalgar Square to the atomic base in Berkshire—was organized, and the volume of support for it astonished the nuclear disarmers as much as the authorities. A few weeks later Thompson and Miller were charged at Bow Street. "The trial proceedings", Miller says, "were arranged to be held in London rather than at Oxford because of feeling among the students." *Isis* began to organize a defence fund, which reached £541, but this was estimated to cover only the cost of the preliminary hearings. The defendants were committed for trial at the Old Bailey on 17 July 1958. The university's Long Vacation had started, and Miller and Thompson had had time to sit for their final examinations.

For the Crown the Solicitor-General, Sir Harry Hylton-Foster, Q.C., led Mervyn Griffiths-Jones (later the Common Serjeant) and Christmas Humphreys. For both defendants appeared the young and able junior barrister, Peter Rawlinson, then already an M.P. and later to be knighted and Attorney-General in a Tory Government. William Miller recalls: "When I eventually appeared at the Old Bailey I was very frightened. I was almost certain that my letters had been opened and my telephone calls tapped. The prosecuting counsel who made most impression on me was Mervyn Griffiths-Jones. He presented a picture of myself that I could not recognize. With eloquence, he confirmed my paranoia, my sense of being persecuted. I still thought—I still think—I had done the right thing, although the article was misinterpreted and many people thought I was a Communist."

The Solicitor-General in opening told the jury that Thompson and Miller did their National Service in the Royal Navy in a branch of Intelligence. He claimed that they published their article in total disregard of the law, if not in defiance of it, and furthermore in breach—the jury might think in dishonourable breach—of undertakings they had given to maintain reticence. He read out the article "Frontier Incidents". He said that the printers had asked Miller if the contents were true and he had replied, "Perfectly." When questioned by detectives Miller had said, "The information in the article is true; there are at least a hundred people in Oxford who are familiar with the facts printed. I myself was doing this sort of job. The man who wrote it has a far better knowledge than I. We discussed it before we handed it in. We knew of the possible implications, in fact a prosecution would do a great deal to our cause."

The Court spent the rest of the day in secret session. On the next day Paul Thompson, giving evidence, said he was a practising member of the Church of England and had never associated with the Communist Party. Earlier in the year he had become seriously interested in the issue of nuclear disarmament. "I already had several friends at Oxford who also felt very strongly about the matter and I was in sympathy with them. It was not on a political basis at all." A special issue of *Isis* dealing with nuclear disarmament was discussed "and I felt it was my moral duty to support it". Describing to Peter Rawlinson how the article came about, he said, "It was part of the plan. We wanted to produce a completely rational argument. We felt two things, first that Russian attacks on Western aircraft had been used as evidence suggesting that nuclear disarmament was impossible, and secondly that the idea of an instant deterrent is not in my opinion consistent with any continuous activity along the frontiers." He had no dishonourable intention with regard to matters of secrecy, and until the Press reaction he had not thought that the article was dangerous.

William Miller, giving evidence, described the campaign within the university regarding nuclear disarmament. "Did you feel strongly about it?" asked Rawlinson. "I still do," he replied. He said that he had not received any secret information from anybody which helped him to prepare the article, and he had had no wish or desire to damage the safety of the State. "I was questioned by Lord Goddard," Miller recalls, "and I think he saw I was a very frightened young man." Rawlinson asked him, "What do you say if you have made an error of judgment? What is your view?" He answered, "I should feel I had done something really very terrible, and I should be very sorry."

"I dare say", the Solicitor-General told the jury, "you accept that they are very sorry, but I am afraid it does not alter the fact that in my submission they are guilty under the first count of unlawfully communicating secret official information which came into their possession by reason of their service under the Crown." The Court again went into session in camera.

Then on the third day of the trial, unexpectedly, except to those privy to the lawyers' secrets, Peter Rawlinson rose to tell the Lord Chief Justice that the defendants now wished to change their plea to guilty on the first count. Sir Harry Hylton-Foster said that the Crown would be prepared to accept this, and Rayner told the jury that they were discharged from returning verdicts on the two remaining counts in the indictment. Miller comments today, "All cases of this sort have a certain amount of stage management; perhaps this is right. Lord Goddard was a very good stage manager."

What does Mr Miller mean by that remark? Now for the first time the true story of the *Isis* trial can be revealed. Sir Peter Rawlinson, freed from his obligation of confidentiality by his two ex-clients, has written to me:[4] "It was obvious that there was, in law, no defence to the charge. But it was my judgment that the case could not be properly comprehended without the L.C.J. hearing the evidence. I knew that Thompson and Miller could not be understood unless there was a plea of 'Not Guilty' and thus the offence put into its true perspective. So I told Harry Hylton-Foster of what we intended and of our intention to change the plea to Guilty at the appropriate moment. The L.C.J. was also informed.

"As a result we were able to shew that the offence was not basically serious and to indicate the two defendants' motivations and sincerity, and Rayner Goddard listened patiently and with understanding."

Sir Peter makes the point that this was *not* plea-bargaining. "Rayner gave me no assurances whatsoever on the sentences he might impose. I simply did not know. As you know yourself, defence counsel does from time to time find himself in a position where the best way to get over his client's case to a court is for him to be advised to plead Not Guilty, for the evidence then to be heard in its entirety and only then for the plea to be changed to Guilty when all the facts as to the offence itself are before the court."[5]

Says William Miller, "When Lord Goddard was asking me questions in the witness-box he tried to put me at my ease by asking about my college and college life. This could be seen in two ways, either that he would not have been so sympathetic to someone who was not a student at an Establishment foundation—or that he genuinely understood that I was a young student terrified by the panoply of the law." Those who knew Rayner Goddard will have no doubt that the second alternative is the more truthful.

Peter Rawlinson proceeded to call various witnesses as to the character of the two men in the dock. After a number of almost embarrassingly flattering words of praise from university tutors, Rayner observed, "The more it is emphasized to me that these are unusually intelligent young men, the harder it is for me to take the view that what they did was not done deliberately." This was still not going to be a walk-over for the defence.

Rawlinson carefully phrased his question to the next witness, the chaplain and modern history tutor at Lincoln College who was to speak for William Miller. "Is he," he asked, "a sincere person in a

---

[4] In letter of 26 March 1976.
[5] In conversation 28 March 1976.

religious and Christian sense and a man of great enthusiasm but perhaps of a woolly, if enthusiastic, mind?" "I think that would be a correct statement," the chaplain agreed.

Rawlinson made a speech in mitigation, and hush fell as the Lord Chief Justice prepared to speak. The two men in the dock stood silently in front of him. Everyone turned towards the stocky, powerful figure hunched on the Bench. "A tremendous feeling of apprehension came over the court," says a young man present throughout the trial and closely identified with the defence. "Lord Goddard gave them a tremendous dressing-down, like a policeman administering a 'frightener' to someone. Or a stern headmaster. We all thought they were going to go down for far longer than they did because of his manner of delivering judgment."

Said Rayner: "It is not for young men employed in these matters, either at university or elsewhere, to decide for themselves what is vital to the security of this country and what secrets may be maintained and what secrets are of less value than others. You had all the provisions of the Official Secrets Act made clear to you, and it is to your credit that you did not deny that the work you were engaged upon was secret, and I have no doubt in some respects of high secrecy.

"But you published to the world your experiences as men engaged in this high secrecy. I am afraid I have got to sentence you."

There was a deep silence in court. The Lord Chief Justice paused: "I feel it my duty," he said, "to pass a sentence upon you of a very lenient character, but it must not be thought that if there is a repetition of this offence it will be treated so lightly. I am communicating with the Secretary of State to ensure that your short sentence will be served in the most favourable conditions and away from criminals. You will both go to prison for three months, the sentence to start from the first day of the last session, that is, the 17th of June."

The effect of the sentence was that, with remission for good conduct, Paul Thompson and William Miller would serve one month, and serve it from the start in an open prison. It seemed unprecedented. "It was certainly regarded by our fellow-prisoners," says Miller, "as something unusual, perhaps unjust." While he was serving his sentence Paul Thompson, eighteen years later Professor of Sociology at Essex University, received the news that he had got a First Class honours in his examinations.

The backdating of the prisoners' sentence and their going straight to an open prison was entirely due to Rayner. Sir Peter Rawlinson explains: "He himself sent for the prison authorities and personally authorized and arranged that the two should go forthwith to an Open Prison and not first to an ordinary prison. Rayner G. wrote to me after the case: he was v. kind and complimentary about the judgment shown in handling the defence, and on his own initiative told me of what he had personally directed should be done with the two, since he wanted them to get straight off to an open prison and not be put in contact with the ordinary prison processes. This was solely his doing."

What was never realized by any of the principals concerned, except perhaps by Rayner himself, was that in the issue of *Isis* dated the very week before the issue on nuclear disarmament he had been attacked in print in a way which, if only half the things his traducers were saying about him were true, could have led to his being prejudiced against the two young men he was trying to such an extent that they *really* would have cause to call him the modern Judge Jeffreys. In an anti-Establishment article entitled "TOP PEOPLE: The Men in Scarlet" the author, David Cocks, had launched himself at Her Majesty's Judges. The article began:

"'Her Majesty's Judges are satisfied with the almost universal esteem in which they are held,' said Lord Chief Justice Hewart in one of his splendid moments. Of course people who make remarks like that really lay themselves open. And generally speaking they get the bucket thrown at them. Judges are a sitting target if you're out Establishment-baiting. It's easy to point to our learned Lord Chief Justice eyes shut, chin set, mouth buttoned down in a Maughamish arc, and quote his own words at him: 'Then did you ever see such a more shocking thing *than that?* . . . The sight of a Travers Humphreys or a Goddard makes you want to do your nut. . . .'"

By his conduct of the trial of Paul Thompson and William Miller Rayner showed that this intemperate judgment was not only lacking in charm but ungrounded in fact. Most people will be more interested in Mr Miller's own subsequent comment, "I think that Lord Goddard did give some assurance of fairness. . . . There was a sort of coolness and calmness there, although as a judge he stood for almost everything I was opposed to . . . I actually rather took to him!"

Yet for a completely balanced picture of the 81-year-old Rayner Goddard in this, his last great case, justice demands that the words be quoted at some length of the young supporter of the defence whose views have already been cited earlier: "He was a little hard of hearing, but his voice was gruff. I was nineteen then, had not yet gone up to Cambridge; it seemed to me inconceivable that he could have been at University over sixty years ago.

"He struck me as remarkably courteous to everyone—particularly to the two young men in the dock. They looked so young and terrified. He wrote everything down with great care—at times interrupting the cut and thrust of what counsel were saying by writing everything down with a gold pencil. He called each defendant 'Mr' and the whole thing appeared an upper-class exercise. I remember the interminable discussions about whether *Isis* was still sold on the street as it had been when Lord Goddard was there in the late nineties. I remember thinking: 'Christ, that man cannot be that old!'

"I don't ever remember thinking he was not fair. I did have the feeling it was a privileged exercise. It was not justice with the popular touch. It was all very much removed from the actual crime—'Now you naughty boys, go back to your studies at College!' That sort of air.

"Undoubtedly, by the climate of the times, they got a very light sentence. There was a feeling that they had committed an undergraduate prank, and Goddard seemed to be treating it as such—but in fact these were two young men who had deliberately committed a crime in passion and out of a sincere conviction of their cause. That aspect, the old man on the Bench, I do not think appreciated at all. That two young scholars of their college should commit such a crime could only be explicable on the basis of its being an undergraduate prank."

That judgment, from an intelligent, young non-lawyer, sums up with clarity the strength—and the limitations—of Rayner Goddard in his eighty-second year, and thirteenth as Lord Chief Justice of England.

20 The Last Great Decision—Retirement

The *Isis* Trial ended on 18 July 1958. Rayner was then left to grapple with a trial far more difficult to control: the trial within himself to summon up the will irrevocably and definitively to resign from office. He had no other interests, apart from his family and his friends, outside his work: no long-put-off yearning to paint or listen to music or read books at large, or embrace any other kind of life. His life was his work, and now he must end that work—and in so doing impose upon himself a sentence of death in its own way as grim and final as any he had pronounced in court, black cap upon his head. " 'I shan't stay much longer'," Mrs Prue Clayton, his youngest daughter, says he had told her some months earlier, "but the thought was anathema to him. He dreaded the thought of retirement."

But it had to come. On 26 July Rayner wrote a formal letter of resignation to Harold Macmillan, then the Prime Minister: he said he would like his resignation to take effect during the Long Vacation, soon to start, so that his successor could take over in time for the beginning of the new Legal Year on 1 October. He also wrote as a courtesy, informing them of his decision, to the Queen and to Lord Kilmuir, the Lord Chancellor (who, as Sir David Maxwell Fyfe, had been the Home Secretary who failed to reprieve Derek Bentley).

The die was cast, the decision made and carried into effect. The Trinity Law Term, and the old Legal Year, ended on 31 July; it was arranged with the Prime Minister that Rayner's resignation would become effective on 29 September so he would have the pleasure of presiding over one last session of the Court of Criminal Appeal: the habitual one-day Vacation session in August at which, unlike many other holders of his office in that holiday month, he always liked to attend.

Although renewed speculation about possible retirement now appeared with heightened urgency in the newspapers, there was as yet no official announcement. Rayner's Queen Bench judges dispersed for their summer vacation, knowing that their Chief had it in his mind to retire fairly shortly, but, as Mr Justice Donovan later wrote to him, "putting off the moment of your departure and the emptiness it will leave, by saying 'Well, it won't happen till Christmas'." Only to a very few close friends, and within his immediate family, did Rayner let his decision be known. His ex-pupil (now a Law Lord), James Tucker, then aged seventy, wrote to him, "I have never heard even a whisper that you were losing grip or not at your best. Nonetheless, I think you are wise to go. People are always remembered by what they were like at the end and there is always a risk at your age." Chill but true.

Wednesday, 20 August 1958, was the day fixed for the Long Vacation sitting of the Court of Criminal Appeal, held as usual in the vast, impressive courtroom of the Lord Chief Justice of England. It was to be Rayner Goddard's last day on the Bench as Lord Chief Justice. The Press had somehow been tipped off and were present in some numbers, but the Bar itself did not know. "The formal announcement came in the evening newspapers," recalls Quintin Iwi, now an established junior barrister but then a young man of only two years' Call. "I appeared in front of Goddard that day, but at the time I did not know that would be the last time he would be there. I think he must have kept it quiet deliberately. He would not have wanted any courtroom tributes, or anything like that. No, he wasn't any different in the way he handled the court that day—just the same as usual!"

Punctual as ever, on the stroke of ten-thirty Rayner strode into court, accompanied by fellow-octogenarian Mr Justice Cassels, and Mr Justice Ashworth, a mere stripling in his early fifties. His movements were brisk, his manner grave. Those who looked for any signs of emotion looked in vain. The first case of the day was the appeal of a man convicted on a capital murder charge at Leeds Assizes. The hearing lasted just over an hour. "On the evidence of this case," said Rayner, "no jury could have returned a verdict other than they did." The appeal was dismissed.

Five other appeals and twenty-seven applications for leave to appeal followed. To a young barrister who was plainly not succeeding with a plea based on the so-called good character of his client, he said sharply, "You are not asking us to increase the sentence, are you?"—then, when dismissing the appeal a few minutes later, adding to the unsuccessful youngster, "I'm sorry to be unsympathetic". Speaking about approved schools, he remarked with a shake of the head, "They don't seem to be able to give them a pat on the place . . . the place it was meant for." Looking at the documents in another case, he read out the phrase "Living carelessly and drinks heavily," and added, "He won't get any drink at Borstal, will he? Appeal refused." To a widowed mother, standing before him in the well of the court, whose 17-year-old son was appealing against a sentence of Borstal training for office-breaking and larceny, he said, "What would happen if the Court took a very lenient view and allowed your son to go home tomorrow?" The woman, near tears, whispered, "Oh, thank you, sir." "But what would you *do*?" persisted Rayner. "I shall promise to do my very best to see he becomes a good citizen," she replied. Judgment of the Court: In view of the youth's previous good character, a sentence would be substituted allowing him to be released on the following day.

Finally, when the day reached its end, it was unspectacular. At 3.29 p.m. Rayner rose, a splendid figure in his crimson robes, his tight grey wig, as always by this time of the day, slightly atilt, and gathered up his papers with what a *Manchester Guardian* reporter thought was "perhaps just a shade too much briskness". In an instant the Registrar of the Court was on his feet, and said in a quick whisper—audible only to the Press bench—"Goodbye, m'Lord." Rayner was already bowing to the Court. As he straightened up he spoke his last words from the Lord Chief Justice's bench: "Goodbye, Thompson," with the faintest of smiles, and he was gone. A newspaper photograph of Rayner crossing the pedestrian crossing outside the Law Courts on that last day before his retirement shows a man still alert and spruce in his summer-weight light-grey suit and black bowler with furled umbrella jauntily hanging from one arm with his hand in his trouser pocket—but the eyes are downcast and the expression is sad. (See photograph opposite p. 306.)

After the official announcement the letters and tributes poured in. From his judges from all over the world wherever they might be at that time: "My dear Chief, It is 7.30 a.m. and the ship has just anchored in Palma Bay," wrote Mr Justice Hinchliffe on board the Royal Mail liner *Andes*. "In *The World's News* pushed under the cabin door I read of your retirement. It makes me feel sad." "My dear

Chief," wrote Mr Justice (later Lord) Edmund Davies, "Today's *Times* announcement of that which we had been fearing is saddening news for a great number of people both in and out of the legal profession. It induces in me (almost your Junior Judge) feelings of the greatest regret that someone who has so consistently helped me will soon no longer be 'the Chief'."

From closer at home, in the United Kingdom, the members of his 'team' expressed themselves in terms not merely of regret but of deep affection, if not love: "Dear Chief," wrote one, "So the melancholy truth is out. I knew you would go but there is a grim finality about the official announcement which makes me feel as a man feels who is told that he is to lose his best friend." "My dear Lord Chief," wrote another, "You will be getting scores of letters and I hesitate to add to them, but I would not like this occasion to pass without my sending you every good wish for a happy time in retirement. Almost equally strong is the urge to say how very grateful I am, and always will be, for the continued kindness which you have shown me in so many ways. Believe me, I know how much I owe to you, and I am truly grateful." "My dear Rayner," wrote Mr Justice Hilbery, "It was with a heavy heart that I read the announcement in *The Times* of today . . . The moment is not inappropriate for me to try to express to you all my gratitude for the help and support you have always given to me—I shall ever remember all your kindnesses to me and I am proud to think that I have had your confidence . . . Ever yours in affectionate regards, Malcolm."

Retired judges wrote to him; one remembering his "many kindnesses to me personally . . . but for nothing more than the consideration you showed me by securing for me the Old Bailey for my last appearance, another grateful for the memory of "your unforgettable and unforgotten help" when he was ill. Even Lady Croom-Johnson, the widow of a dead judge, wrote to tell him, "Reggie and I used to speak of you often, and we were full of admiration for the revolutionary reforms you managed to get through in the administration of the Law Courts. He was very fond of you, and valued your friendship more than perhaps anyone else's on the Bench."

Q.C.s wrote their private letters of homage and good wishes: including John Widgery, present Lord Chief Justice—"I hope that you will not think me presumptuous in writing to say how much I personally shall miss you. I am only one of many who remember with gratitude your unfailing kindness and consideration when we were struggling beginners"—junior barristers, the President of the

Law Society, the Lord Mayor Locum Tenens on behalf of the City and Corporation of London, the Justices' Clerks' Society, the Judges' Clerks' Association, the Society of Chairmen and Deputy-Chairmen of Quarter Sessions in England and Wales. And there were letters from outside the law: from Winston Churchill, at Cap d'Ail in the South of France—"I saw in the newspapers the news of your resignation. I should like to record to you my regret that you should be relinquishing your great office, to which you have added lustre, and my congratulations on the long and great services you have rendered to us all", from Dr Geoffrey Fisher, the Archbishop of Canterbury—"I need not say with what unstinted admiration I have observed you in your public capacity"—and from his own housekeeper, the faithful Mrs Nellie Walpole, who sat down and wrote to her employer, "My Lord, Now that you are away from all the hustle and rush, which was suddenly thrust upon you this week, may I say how much I hope you will find as much contentment in your new life as you must be feeling in the knowledge that the old has been such a great success."

Polite and well-turned letters are a commonplace—though not necessarily from one's housekeeper—at time of retirement, but Rayner must surely have been quite an extraordinary personality to receive such warm letters as these: unlike most of his other private papers, he kept them carefully preserved to the very end of his life.

"Lord Goddard," said *The Times* on the day following the announcement of his resignation, "has been one of the greatest judicial figures of the common law. It may be said of a judicial system which has survived for centuries and has proved, indeed, ever growing in strength that no one is indispensable to its proper functioning. Equally, however, it may be said no one has been more indispensable to it than Lord Goddard. By reason of his position as first Judge a Lord Chief Justice can exercise great influence on the working of the Courts throughout the country; but whether he does or not depends on the largeness of his character and the will of other Judges and magistrates to emulate his example.

"Criticisms in plenty have been made of the 'Lord Chief' from time to time. . . . His zeal in the dispatch of judicial business has sometimes been interpreted as impatience or unwillingness to listen to a man's case against which he has turned his mind. No one could say, however, that his strong feelings on some subjects do not come straight from the heart, and those who have watched him in Court over the years have become ever more impressed by his readiness to listen to anything if he was not convinced that it was a mere waste of time of everyone concerned. His greatest quality perhaps has been his humility. Never has he hesitated to acknowledge that he was wrong on a point of law at the first opportunity if that is what he had come to believe. His jest, 'I am prepared to put on a white sheet,' sums up the one part of his armour that no critic could pierce.

". . . It has been his vast humanity on almost any topic—his complete lack of any kind of pomposity—that has given his views on each and every subject such appeal to all; but dignity he has in full measure and whenever the majesty of the law or the freedom of the subject has been in danger he has not failed. Lord Goddard is a man loved by many. . . ."

It was a glowing tribute, albeit sadly at variance with the article by Bernard Levin that the same newspaper saw fit to print thirteen years later within ten days of his death.[1] But who was to succeed this "loved" Lord Chief Justice? That was now proving a matter of considerable perturbation in both Temple and Fleet Street alike.

"There are certain indications," *The Times* had commented as far back as 29 July, three days after Rayner had in fact written his private formal letter of resignation to the Prime Minister, "that the Lord Chief Justice may be intending to retire at the end of September. A straw in the wind is that he has been refusing certain invitations to functions which he would normally have attended as Lord Chief Justice." After a gracious reference to its being "ungrateful to expect him at the age of 81 to continue much longer to bear the burdens of this heaviest of all judicial offices," the leader-writer got down to the real business of his article: "This will be no ordinary retirement, it will raise an important constitutional issue—that of the principles to be applied in choosing a Chief Justice." Rayner's had, for the first time, not been a political appointment, and *The Times* was concerned that the precedent should be followed: ". . . this great judicial position should not be regarded as some kind of political plum. The fact that it has so been regarded in the past has by common consent led to the appointment of some thoroughly unsatisfactory Chief Justices.

"Still less does acceptance of the principle imply that the present Attorney-General, who has given great service to his country, to the law, and to his profession, is not the best man for the job. If he is, he should be appointed to it. But if he is appointed, it must be made perfectly clear that he is appointed on merit alone, and that this is not a revival of an intolerable practice.

---

[1] See "Aftermath".

". . . It is essential that, whoever is chosen, there should be a clear acceptance of the principle that fitness for the job alone should always govern the appointment."

The London *Evening Standard* had seven days earlier, on 22 July, been the first to break the story of Rayner's decision to go by the end of September, and had confidently asserted, "Lord Goddard will be succeeded by Sir Reginald Manningham-Buller, the Attorney-General."

On 6 September, came the official announcement from Downing Street that the new Lord Chief Justice would be—Lord Justice Parker, a "lawyers' lawyer", a judge for the past eight years with no political connections whatsoever. What had happened to Manningham-Buller's chances?

"I did not raise a finger to assert the Attorney-General's right to the succession," says Lord Dilhorne, as Sir Reginald Manningham-Buller has now become.[2] "I do not believe in such rights of inheritance. The man for the job is the man who will do the job best. I personally think the Lord Chief Justice's job is one of the most awful jobs in the world. I wouldn't go as a volunteer. The incessant work. The mass of papers. Every weekend having to toil through it all. Masses of administration over a wide field. The difficulties of influencing other judges all of equal rank into doing what you think should be done, when in fact you have no power. Primus inter pares. It's a tremendous burden: Rayner discharged it perfectly in the many years he was Lord Chief Justice."

Although he would not have "volunteered" for the office, it was common gossip in the Temple[3] that Manningham-Buller would very much have liked to be asked to take it on—not because of any so-called political 'right' to the job, but because it was, after all, the supreme permanent judicial post, the top of the tree. Rayner himself knew this as well as anyone. Once the Prime Minister's decision had been made he wrote privately to both Sir Reginald and Lord Justice Parker. Manningham-Buller wrote back a charming, somewhat sad letter thanking him for his kindness in writing to him, and admitting frankly that he would have liked to have followed him—although he would have been a difficult man to follow.

"My dear Chief," wrote back the new Lord Chief Justice-designate, on the actual day of the announcement of his appointment, "What a joy it was to get your letter and I did so appreciate all

---

[2] He was created Lord Dilhorne on succeeding Lord Kilmuir as Lord Chancellor four years later, in 1962.
[3] As the author can personally testify.

you said. As I tried to tell you on the last day of term any measure of success I may have is in large measure due to you. That was at a time when I thought that I was completely out of the running. Today I am more than ever conscious of your help and the confidence you have shown in me. I can never repay you unless it be by furthering your example. . . ."

"I knew that in that last year or two he wanted me for the job," the late Lord Parker of Waddington has told me. "But it came as a complete surprise to me when I was in fact appointed. I thought it would be Lord Dilhorne, and it was from him, indeed, that I received my first letter of congratulation.

"I must say that I believe the non-political nature of the appointment, now made clear for all time by Rayner's original selection for the post, my own and that of my successor, is of vital importance for the administration of justice in this country.

"Rayner was there at a time of change from the 'God Almighty' attitude of the judges under Hewart to the days when judges are ordinary, humble human beings. He was at the transitional period. I should have thought, furthermore, that the very fact that he was non-political and a respected judge in his own right helped develop a team spirit among the judges which I doubt existed previously, which is still there and which they could not have had when they rather felt they had a boss foisted upon them by the politicians."

To what extent did Lord Goddard's plumping for Hubert Parker affect Prime Minister Macmillan's eventual choice? It could not have been an easy or quick decision: Macmillan's letter of acceptance of Rayner's resignation was dated 29 July, five and a half weeks before the announcement of his successor. Lord Parker was a sound lawyer, son of a Law Lord and a highly skilled trial and appeal judge, but—and, if he were alive to read these words, Lord Parker would unhesitatingly agree—Manningham-Buller had, especially in the past couple of years, won considerable, if belated, respect for his forensic ability, and there were several other judges equally competent to perform the duties of Lord Chief Justice.

Is it possible that Rayner obstinately stayed on as Chief, not only because of his own fears of the emptiness of retirement, but because he wanted to try to ensure that the man he wanted got the job after him? I have asked Lord Parker that pointed question, and obtained this guarded reply: "Of course, he had a natural interest in who his successor would be. Wasn't it Earl Warren, the American Chief Justice, also aged around the eighty mark, who is supposed to have said, 'Either you appoint X or I hang on?' I don't suggest that would be right—or that it happened in this case—but, human nature being what it is, and with pride in his office, I don't deny you consider the possibilities. That may have delayed his actual moment of going. I went to the Court of Appeal in 1954 and was rather out of touch with him after that; but I do know that he was very anxious that his successor should be a judge and non-political.''

The hour of Rayner's formally handing over office approached. It was customary when, as at that time, hereditary peerages were still being created, for retiring Chiefs to be raised up one rung in the lordly ladder—from Baron to Viscount. On 5 September Harold Macmillan wrote "privately and confidentially" to Rayner: "Before going through the usual procedure of making an informal proposal to The Queen, I would like to consult you privately as to your own feelings regarding a suitable honour to mark the termination of the Office of Lord Chief Justice of England. If it were your wish I would certainly be ready to recommend to Her Majesty the conferring of a Viscountcy upon you. It occurs to me, however, that since you did not wish a hereditary peerage at the time of your appointment, you might take the same view now. In that case, if you were agreeable, I would suggest to Her Majesty some other recognition, for instance, a Grand Cross of one of the Orders of Chivalry—perhaps the G.C.B." And so it proved: the sonless Goddard still did not want a hereditary title. On 29 September, the day when his retirement came into effect, it was formally announced: "The Queen has been pleased to approve that the Right Honourable Lord Goddard has been appointed Knight Grand Cross of the Most Honourable Order of the Bath."

Five days earlier Rayner had attended to his last official business as Lord Chief Justice. Characteristically, the last letter that he wrote in that capacity was to send a friendly message of greetings to a fellow-judge—not even a member of his own Divison—who had been promoted to the Court of Appeal. "My dear Willmer," he wrote to the new Lord Justice Willmer, "My warm congratulations and I am sure you will be glad to get away from dreary divorce. How absurd it is that a man appointed to the Bench because of his Admiralty experience [at the Bar, Gordon Willmer, K.C., had been a leading Admiralty practitioner] should have to spend practically all his time on divorce cases. Your experience however in both branches will be invaluable in the C.A. and I am sure you will enjoy it.—I enjoyed my six years there more than any other of the years I spent on the Bench.

"This is the last letter I shall write in L.C.J.'s room—it could not be on a more welcome subject."

And that was the end. On 1 October the Lord Chancellor, the President of the Probate, Divorce and Admiralty Division, the Master of the Rolls and all the Lord Justices of Appeal and Judges of the High Court of Justice assembled in the Lord Chief Justice's Court for the inauguration of the new Chief. Before addressing himself to welcome Lord Parker to the office, the Lord Chancellor said of his predecessor: "Never since the days of Lord Mansfield has a Chief Justice left such an impression on the whole country, and never has the holder of that high office been looked up to both by those who appeared before him and those who sat with him, with such respect, admiration and warm affection. Lord Goddard has become an institution, and for our institutions we in this Court keep a very special place in our hearts."

By tradition and personal inclination, Rayner was not present to hear those words. But as the strong old man started the long, last winter of his life, they must have given him cause for pride—and, it is hoped, some manner of comfort for the too many sad years that lay ahead.

21 The Long Last Winter

Many of Rayner's letters of farewell had spoken of his "long deserved rest", his "well-merited relaxation from his labours" and the like. It was ironic: the writers should have known their man better. As he had feared, although there were flashes of brilliant sunlight, for much of his retirement Lord Goddard was not, deep in his heart, a happy man—and the retirement was long.

For the first few years things were not too bad. His eldest daughter, Mrs Pamela Maurice, recalls: "One day when he was visiting us at Marlborough—my husband Jim was a doctor in the town—shortly after his retirement, he told us he had had a letter from a woman living near Swindon who said that her old aunt who lived with her, had heard that my father had relations near by, and would so much appreciate a visit as she had been parlourmaid to his old aunt and uncle at Stroud, with whom my father used to stay as a pre-prepschool boy.

"I accordingly drove him over to see the old lady, and he found her in bed, but otherwise very sprightly, and as he walked into the room she exclaimed, 'Why, it's Master Rayner!' As my father said roaring with laughter, as he returned to the car, 'It isn't everybody that can be called Master Rayner at the age of eighty-two!'"

He travelled abroad far more than he had ever done in his years of active office. He went on several cruises to warm and exotic places that he had never visited before; and began soon after leaving office with a ten-week cruise to South America. Returning sun-tanned and fit, he startled the Temple, two weeks after his eighty-second birthday, in April 1959, by coming back to the Law Courts: to sit in

Appeal Court Two, next door to his old Lord Chief Justice's Court, to help clear the heavy arrears of appeal cases.

It was unprecedented. No one could remember any earlier instance where a retired Lord Chief Justice had come back to the courts to sit again in judgment, but Rayner did so in characteristic fashion. At 10.30, on the dot, wearing the plain black robes of a Lord Justice of Appeal, he strode into court, leading Lord Justice Romer and Lord Justice Pearce, placed his rimless glasses firmly on the bridge of his nose, glanced briefly at the spectators—an unusually large number for the normally somnolent Appeal Court Two—and settled briskly down to work.

His first case was an appeal by a litigant in person, a retired businessman from Ascot, who alleged that Mr Justice Havers had gone wrong in rejecting his claim for fraud against the Ministry of Works: he said they had ruined a company of which he had been managing director and principal shareholder. Rayner listened to him as attentively as he could—wig tipped slightly forward, left hand clasped across his mouth with his thumb creasing his cheek, brow furrowed in contemplation: his typical posture—but he could not contain himself for long. "But only your company itself, not you, could possibly have a cause of action—even if you could prove fraud!" he expostulated. Legally, the appellant's case did not even begin to get off the ground: perhaps despairingly, he referred the Court to King John, Edward III and Magna Carta. "I don't think you need bring in Magna Carta!" said Rayner. "The trouble is you have not had any advice in this matter. You have probably run yourself into hundreds of pounds with these transcripts. These proceedings have been misconceived from beginning to end."

The appellant, nothing if not courageous, began to quote from "the White Book", High Court lawyers' white-bound "Annual Practice", their bible setting out the Rules and Orders relating to the conduct of High Court actions. Again Rayner gently but firmly brought him to heel: "The White Book is a very dangerous sea for a non-lawyer to embark upon," he warned.

The appellant argued he had a right in equity to bring the action. "You'll have to write a new book on equity, then!" said Rayner. "The Court has never heard of the equity which you wish to apply." In the end, Rayner, after consulting briefly with his brethren, said the appeal was dismissed: "The appellant's proposition is hopeless". He asked for leave to appeal to the House of Lords. "No," said Rayner. "In mercy to you we will not give you leave to appeal." The Court rose.

The original hearing before Mr Justice Havers had taken five days. The Court authorities had allotted the whole day for the appeal. Rayner and his two colleagues were back in their rooms within half an hour. The old leopard had not changed his spots.

1959—the same year that Parliament in its wisdom passed the Judicial Pensions Act laying down that all newly appointed High Court judges should henceforth automatically have to retire at seventy-five—was a good year for the eighty-two-year-old Rayner. After his stint in the Appeal Court, he went back to his other old haunt, the House of Lords, and sat on several appeals there,[1] he took part in a House of Lords debate on road accidents and, on 30 June he addressed the annual general meeting of "Justice", the British section of the International Commission of Jurists.

At the "Justice" meeting, it was Lord Goddard, the legal reformer, who spoke. His subject was committal proceedings before magistrates. "I suggested changes to the then Home Secretary [Mr Chuter Ede] back in 1948," he said. "A committee was set up as a result of my suggestions and certain proposals were made, but nothing has been done." Predictably, what concerned the ex Lord Chief Justice was the appalling waste of time that most committal proceedings caused, with magistrates having to listen for hours on end to witnesses giving evidence that no one at that stage would seek to challenge; cross-examination of any length, except in the rarest cases, being generally left to the trial court before judge and jury. "I have always wondered why the evidence of these witnesses cannot be put in the form of a statutory declaration," said Rayner.

The impetus that the ex-Chief thus gave to the movement for reform helped bring about an eventual change in the law when, some eight years later, the Criminal Justice Act of 1967 permitted 'paper' committals by examining magistrates, on sight of written statements alone, except where the defendant was not represented or his lawyers specifically requested a full, old-style committal.

1960 continued reasonably active for the indomitable old man. To the end of his days he never left the Temple or the atmosphere

---

[1] As a peer who was also a former holder of high judicial office, Lord Goddard, even after retirement as Lord Chief Justice, remained automatically entitled, without restriction of age, to sit as an *ex officio* Lord of Appeal in Ordinary, although the actual place where he sat as emeritus Law Lord was no longer the chamber of the House of Lords but a Committee Room of the House where, since 1948, all appeals have been heard—so that appeals can be taken throughout the day and not restricted only to the mornings; as they had always been when Rayner had sat as a regular Law Lord and the Chamber was occupied by the non-judicial Lords for their normal non-legal Parliamentary duties in the afternoon.

and company of lawyers. Living in his top-floor flat in Queen Elizabeth Building, tended by a housekeeper and a manservant, with his devoted daughter Peggy Sachs and her husband, Sir Eric, living in a flat on the opposite side of the landing, frequently lunching and dining in Inner Temple Hall, he was a familiar figure to everyone in the law in those days of the early nineteen-sixties; his stocky, well-tailored form was often seen walking sturdily around the Temple or standing on the steps outside the Benchers' entrance to the Inner Temple Hall talking to some crony. "That's Lord Goddard!" 16-year-old solicitors' clerks or junior barristers' clerks just starting in the Temple would be told. Even in his early days of retirement, Rayner's mystique as (in Lord Chancellor Kilmuir's words) "an institution" was still growing.

In June and July 1960 he was sitting again in the House of Lords as part of a remarkably strong Bench of five Law Lords hearing a capital murder appeal. The author has been unable to trace any other case where a current Lord Chief Justice and his predecessor have sat alongside each other in judgment—but that is what happened in *Director of Public Prosecutions* v. *Smith*.

Unfortunately, it did not prove too illustrious a precedent. A policeman had been killed, but no one contended that his death had been deliberate. P.C. Leslie Meehan and Jim Smith had grown up together in the same part of South-East London. They liked each other, and were quite good friends—even though they were on different sides of the law. At about 7.50 on the evening of 2 March 1960 Jim Smith was driving his Ford Prefect car—with some sacks of scaffolding clips he had just stolen lying in the back and ranged in the boot. He was stopped by traffic lights, P.C. Meehan saw him and strolled over—just to have a chat. But, looking through the driving window, he saw at once what was in the back of the car, and told his friend to pull in to the kerb on the other side of the lights.

Smith began to move slowly forward across the junction, with P.C. Meehan walking along beside him; but suddenly he put his foot hard down on the accelerator and began to pull away. His car had no running-board, but the brave policeman sprinted after him, grabbed the side of the car and grimly held on while Smith careered erratically down the road. Finally, after the car had travelled about 130 yards, Meehan lost his grip, fell—and was run over by a bubble car coming from the opposite direction. His skull was crushed, and he died from his injuries.

Smith did not immediately stop, but drove on for some 200 yards to a place where he dumped the stolen clips—and then returned, *of his own free will,* to where a small group had gathered round the stricken police officer. "I am the driver of the car he was hanging on to. I know the man. I would not do that for the world. I only wanted to shake him off," he said.

Killing a police officer in the execution of his duty was, undoubtedly, capital murder under the Homicide Act of 1957. But had Jim Smith 'killed' his friend?

At his trial at the Old Bailey in early April Smith maintained that he had accelerated by mistake and did not know that Meehan was hanging on to his car. He also said that he was scared and frightened, and in effect did not know what he was doing. He claimed that the weight of the clips had possibly affected the steering, and throughout he asserted emphatically that he had no intention either of causing the police constable any severe injury or of killing him.

But it is a time-honoured maxim in the law that "a man must be taken to intend the natural consequences of his acts". If you drive along a road at accelerating speed, with your car proceeding in a zigzag course, and knowing that someone is trying to get you to stop and holding on to the side of your car all the while, are you not to be taken to intend "the natural consequence of your act", if he eventually falls off and into the path of an oncoming car? Mr Justice Donovan summed up to the jury in these bare terms: "The intention with which a man did something can usually be determined by a jury only by inference from the surrounding circumstances including the presumption of law that a man intends the natural and probable consequences of his acts." And that is all he said on that aspect of the case. It was not over-helpful. The jury scratched their heads, and brought in a verdict of guilty. Jim Smith was sentenced to death.

He appealed to the Court of Criminal Appeal, where a Bench consisting of Justices Byrne, Sachs (Rayner's son-in-law) and Winn, quashed the conviction and substituted a verdict of manslaughter, with a ten-year gaol sentence in place of the capital penalty. Mr Justice Byrne, giving the judgment of the Court, relied heavily on an earlier dictum from Rayner Goddard in the 1947 case of *Rex* v. *Steane* to support their decision: "No doubt," Rayner had said, when Lord Chief Justice, "if the prosecution prove an act the natural consequences of which would be a certain result and no evidence or explanation is given, then a jury may, on a proper direction, find that the prisoner is guilty of doing the act with the intent alleged, but if on the totality of the evidence there is room for more than one view as to the intent of the prisoner, the jury should be directed that it is for the prosecution to prove the intent to the jury's satisfaction; and if, on a review of the whole evidence, they either think that the intent did not exist or they are left in doubt as to the intent, the prisoner is entitled to be acquitted."

Something like that much fuller—and fairer—direction is what Jim Smith's jury should have been told in place of the sparse words of guidance from Mr Justice Donovan. That at least was the view of the Court of Criminal Appeal. But the Director of Public Prosecutions, then Sir Theobald Mathew, did not agree. He asked for, and obtained, the Attorney-General (still Sir Reginald Manningham-Buller)'s *fiat* to take the case to the Lords—and so a uniquely impressive array of judicial talent was gathered on 27 June 1960 in the Law Lords' Committee Room to hear Manningham-Buller open, as leading counsel for the D.P.P., the case which, wearing his other hat as Attorney-General, he had solemnly decided it was proper to bring before the Appellate Committee.[2] The assembled judges were Lord Kilmuir, still Lord Chancellor, Lord Goddard, Lord Tucker, Lord Denning—and, most junior in status in that gathering, Lord Parker of Waddington, the new Lord Chief Justice.

"Father was so excited when he was going to take part in the Smith case," says Mrs Prue Clayton: but it must be stated that the old man, then in his eighty-fourth year, did not shine in his contribution to the Appellate Committee's hearing or their eventual decision. The argument of counsel was spread over five days, with Edward (later Judge) Clarke, Q.C., leading for Jim Smith, but in all that time the fairly full report of the case in the "Criminal Appeal Reports"[3] does not record a single intervention by Rayner, although Lords Kilmuir, Tucker and Denning are shown as frequently interrupting to elucidate a point or present a counter-proposition for counsel to deal with: that was most unusual behaviour for the man whose nickname on the Bench had been "Doggie".

In the result Lord Kilmuir gave the sole judgment of the Committee, referred to technically in accordance with House of Lords niceties as an "opinion"; with Rayner merely saying, "My Lords, I agree with the opinion which has just been pronounced." He *could*

---

[2] In fact, this was the last time this much-criticized procedure took place. The need for the Attorney-General's *fiat* to appeal to the House of Lords in criminal cases was abolished by the Administration of Justice Act of the same year.
[3] Vol. 44 of the "Criminal Appeal Reports" (1960) at page 261.

have rendered a separate "opinion", whether assenting or otherwise, but he merely said that: the Ancient Thunderer was muted. One has the uneasy feeling that perhaps Lord Kilmuir only invited Rayner to sit with him on this occasion to make more acceptable the Committee's eventual judgment which certain quarters of the Legal Establishment may have been minded from the start to give:[4] for Rayner's earlier dictum in *Rex* v. *Steane* was "distinguished" out of all application to the present case and the law of murder virtually rewritten in a draconian form with the ruling that henceforth juries were to decide all questions of "intent to kill", not on a subjective basis of what the actual man in the case is to be presumed to have intended from his actions but on the objective basis of what they think a so-called "ordinary reasonable man" would be thought to have intended in those circumstances.

Mr Justice Donovan's laconic direction to the jury was upheld and Jim Smith's conviction of capital murder restored; although mercifully Smith was not hanged. Mr R. A. (later Lord) Butler, then Home Secretary, had already announced prior to the appeal hearing that, no matter what the eventual decision of the Appellate Committee might be, the death penalty would not be carried out and instead Smith would serve a sentence of life imprisonment: the usual practice when the Director of Public Prosecutions succeeded in obtaining the Attorney-General's *fiat* to take to the Lords from the Court of Criminal Appeal a defeat for the Crown in a capital case. Nevertheless, the Appellate Committee's decision was unpopular at the Bar and much criticized in academic circles, and Lord Denning himself subsequently (and particularly on a lecture tour the following summer in Israel) sought to explain away what has been called by at least two distinguished commentators[5] "the unfortunate effect of the decision".

The Smith judgment did not stand the test of time. Some seven years later Parliament, in the Criminal Justice Act of 1967, virtually abrogated it by providing:[6] "A court or jury, in determining whether a person has committed an offence—

"(a) shall not be bound in law to infer that he intended or foresaw a result of his actions by reasons only of its being a natural

---

[4] Undoubtedly, Lord Kilmuir formally read the judgment as the presiding judge "but, on good authority, it is believed that the judgment was written by the Lord Chief Justice, Lord Parker": state Professor Terence Morris and Louis Blom-Cooper, Q.C. in their *A Calendar of Murder* (Michael Joseph, 1963) at page 163.

[5] Morris and Blom-Cooper, *op. cit.*, at page 163.

[6] In Section 8 of the Act.

Lord Goddard leaving court on the last day he sat as Lord Chief Justice of England
Photo Mirrorpic

Lord Goddard on his ninetieth birthday, on 10 April, 1967, at a family celebration at Claridge's Hotel. Only two members of the family were missing: Mrs Prue Clayton, his youngest daughter, was recovering from an operation, and Martin Maurice (grandson) was in the U.S.A. (*Back row, l. to r.*): Mrs Kate Pulay (granddaughter); George Pulay (granddaughter's husband); Sir Eric Sachs (son-in-law); John Clay (granddaughter's husband); Archie Clayton (son-in-law); Richard Sachs (grandson); Christopher Clayton, Stephen Clayton (grandsons); Dr James Maurice (son-in-law) (*Front row: l. to r.*): Mrs Pamela Maurice (daughter); Lord Goddard; Lady Sachs (daughter); Miss Maud Goddard (sister); Miss Rosanagh Clay (granddaughter)

and probable consequence of those actions; but

"(b) shall decide whether he did intend or foresee that result by reference to all the evidence, drawing such inferences from the evidence as appear proper in the circumstances."

Those words, *drawing such inferences from the evidence as appear proper in the circumstances*, in fact bring the law back on to the even keel of Lord Chief Justice Goddard's dictum twenty years earlier in *Rex* v. *Steane*. It is perhaps unfortunate that Rayner ever agreed to sit in the Appellate Committee hearing Jim Smith's appeal. Old men vary from day to day. It was not the happiest incident in his long judicial career; and, so far as my researches have been able to establish, Rayner did not again sit as a judge to hear a case.

But his hour was still not yet over. In December 1960 he presided in the Law Society's Common Room over a debate organized by "Justice" in connexion with their report on "The Preliminary Investigation of Crimes". It posed the question: "Should the suspect and the accused be required to answer questions?" F. H. Lawton, Q.C. (later a Lord Justice of Appeal), who had been chairman of the committee responsible for the report, defended its verdict that the present rule should be maintained that an accused could not be compelled to give evidence in court, and John (later Sir John) Foster, Q.C., M.P., argued that at the committal stages in a magistrates' court before a case got to trial it should be the duty of the accused to go into the witness-box and tell his story.

Both silks were widely respected, and leading members of their profession, but there can be little doubt that the majority in the large turnout came to see and hear the legendary Lord Goddard in the chair. They were not disappointed. He was in splendid form that night.

Summing up the arguments at the end of the debate, Rayner said that he was puzzled as to how, when and why the practice arose of police officers being obliged to caution the man they were going to arrest. "You may get a man bursting to confess," he said, "but he is stopped." It must have been before 1848, he said, but "many hours of study" had failed to find the origin. He had never understood, now that people were much more highly educated and when very few people could not read or write, why if a suspect desired to make a statement the police did not give him paper and a pencil for him to write it out.

"Some years ago I was in touch with someone at the Home Office—an Under-Secretary—on this matter. The Under-Secretary said, 'Of course, you would not suggest that a prisoner should write out his own statement.'

"I said, 'I certainly would suggest it', because an accused person at his trial says, 'I never said that, the policeman put that into my mouth.' If they made out the statement themselves, they could not say that. No doubt the police might have to ask some questions, but you could see what they wrote in. I think that change would be very good."

Of prisoners' ability to write, Rayner said that every weekend he used to get twenty or thirty applications for leave to appeal from prisoners. "I did not find any disinclination on their part to write, and to write at considerable length," he commented wryly.

Finally, this octogenarian, caricatured by so many who still even today do not really know what he stood for, raised a basic objection to John Foster's proposal that it should be the duty of everybody to answer questions that might be put to them by the police. "How are we going to enforce such a rule? If a person is being questioned by the police and he refuses to answer, is he *ipso facto* to be guilty of a crime?" said the ex-Lord Chief Justice in tones of disbelief.

His general health was good, his constitution remarkably robust, his hearing—though perhaps no longer sufficient to pick up with ease all the nuances in court—was still perfectly adequate for ordinary, everyday purposes. But his sight was beginning to fail somewhat. "I have some difficulty in reading your letter. I daresay my sight is not as good as it was," he wrote to me in December 1961 when answering my request for an interview for my book on the reprieve system.

Yet his mind was still as alert as ever: "If you want my ideas on how and why—i.e. the principles on which—reprieves are given in capital cases I can only say I have not the least idea and often wished I knew." He agreed to see me upon his return to London after Christmas, when he confirmed his still continuing remarkable approachability by telephoning my senior clerk out of the blue one morning. The unfortunate Leslie French laconically stretched forward to pick up the phone, then went quite white and turned, drained of colour, to me: "It's Lord Goddard! He wants to speak to you!" Such was the awe in which the old man was held in the Temple during the years of his retirement.

Eventually, as related in the earlier chapter dealing with Craig and Bentley, I visited Lord Goddard in his flat one Thursday morning in early January 1962. I found a courteous, lively old gentleman, tinged with sadness: "I'm a has-been now!"—"No, Chief, you're not."—"Don't you tell me. I know what I am!" His final words as he stood with me by his front door as we waited for the lift to arrive: "We're getting sloppy!"

In 1964 he had a unique honour conferred upon him: he was made an Honorary Bencher of the Middle Temple, of which his son-in-law, Mr Justice Sachs, was also a Bencher. "I believe him to be the first Bencher of one Inn ever to be elected to the Bench of another," says Sir Eric Sachs.

He kept in touch with 'his' old judges. Lord Edmund-Davies, now a Lord of Appeal in Ordinary, was first appointed a Queen's Bench judge in January 1958, the year in which Rayner had retired. So he had only been one of the old man's team for a matter of months and the two had never sat together, but Lord Edmund-Davies had gone on to preside over the murder trial in 1959 of Guenther Fritz Podola, who made legal history by being the first person accused of murder to try to run the defence—in which he failed—that his total amnesia of the circumstances of the crime meant he could not be tried for it, the trial in 1964 of the Great Train Robbers and the Tribunal of Inquiry into the Aberfan Disaster in 1966. "Lord Goddard pursued me with kindness," says Lord Edmund-Davies. "I am sure that I am not an isolated example of that, although I'm the only chap with an autographed signature—"To Edmund Davies, J. from his friend Goddard'. He wrote me over Podola, and the Train Robbers' trial and Aberfan. I am sure my case is not a unique one. He kept in touch with those who administered *and* practised the law, and he most certainly kept in touch with his judges after he had left the scene."

"My dear Edmund-D," Rayner wrote after the Great Train Robbers' trial and Mr Justice Edmund-Davies' controversial thirty-year sentences for the main ringleaders. "May a *very* old ex-Judge send you a line of congratulation and admiration on the way you handled the train robbery case? I was always sure you would be a success on the Bench. . . .

"The case must have been a great strain and I hope you will get a bit of a rest. I don't believe you put a foot wrong from the start to the finish. . . . At my last judges' dinner at the Mansion House I emphasized that the duty of a judge in criminal cases was primarily to punish—reformation is for those who give after-care or worked among prisoners, and I said I was sure you could not reform men while they were in prison, and reformation in most cases was the last thing they would consider. Many no doubt would not fall into crime again, but far more made it their purpose and laughed at reformation.

"I wish I could be sure that you would often sit in the CCA"—the *"very* old ex-Judge" felt there was a certain weakness there— "However, I must not criticise, for I am out of it. You need no criticism. . . ."

Particular friends to Rayner in those last years were Judge Ifor Lloyd, Q.C., and his wife Naomi. "Until the last six months his memory was extremely good," says Judge Lloyd. "My father and I, as a young man, had been dining at Rayner's Lodgings when he was the Assize Judge at Nottingham once on the Midland Circuit and two sisters were there. On one occasion, at some time in the sixties, Rayner turned to me and said, 'Were you there that night? Do you remember one of them falling over the carpet on arrival and saying, 'Damn, this bloody carpet!' and he laughed happily at the recollection. Obviously it had suddenly amused him again after all those years.

"He very rarely used to join us in the Temple Church for Sunday morning Divine Service; but always after lunch I used to go for a drive with him in his car, and his man would take us off somewhere into the country—often to Buckinghamshire.

"On the Inner Temple Bench, if you got him going after dinner, he was a very good talker. He was splendid company then and used to tell a host of excellent stories—generally about his old days on the Western Circuit, and he used to quote a lot about Serjeant Arabin, that old-fashioned judge of Victorian times who was always saying odd things in court.

"He would not accept the 'permissive society': it was against all that he stood for. When he was already in his nineties, we started having waitresses in Hall. Some were young and quite attractive, and dressed in the fashionable mini-skirts of the time. 'Good God, look at that one over there!' he once told me. 'Little trollop! Showing far too much leg!' I told him he was supposed to have bad eyesight."

In the autumn of 1966, aged eighty-nine, he went with his favourite grandson, Richard Sachs, on a cruise up the Baltic to Scandinavia and Russia. By now, according to Mr Sachs, he was in a wheel-chair—but only "occasionally, under considerable protest and when absolutely necessary, such as when going round the vast spaces of the Hermitage Museum in Leningrad". But "Grandfather was fantastic! He was, as always, marvellous company to be with—even if his comments on the paintings in the Hermitage were not profound specimens of artistic criticism."

On 24 May 1965 Rayner went down for the last time to the House of Lords to speak in a debate. As with his first speech in the Lords seventeen years earlier, when he had felt it his duty to speak out against the proposed 'experimental' abolition of capital punishment in the Criminal Justice Bill of 1948, so he felt moved to protest against another piece of proposed reform to which he was unutterably opposed. The occasion was the Second Reading of Lord Arran's private Bill to take homosexual behaviour in private "between consenting adults" out of the ambit of the Criminal Law, a proposal which finally received Parliamentary sanction with the passing of the Sexual Offences Act in 1967.

"It was his last speech in the House of Lords, and I was there," says Lord Dilhorne. "He was listened to with great attention and affection by the House, although—perhaps alas!—his views did not receive the support of the majority. He was in full command of his faculties, although not with quite the fire or voice of his younger days. It was a very great effort on his part, but his physical infirmities never affected the quality of his mind."

Nor his sense of humour. During the course of his speech Rayner had fulminated: "There is not a judge who has to go on Circuit, as I had to go for a good many years, who does not find from time to time in various parts of the country what are generally referred to by members of the Bar as buggers' clubs. They are very careful to keep out young boys because they know there are heavy sentences imposed, but they have these coteries of buggers where horrible things go on, and a judge has to listen to stories which make him feel physically sick."

Naturally enough, the newspapers took up with gusto this talk of "buggers' clubs". It was the kind of thing they expected from the unrepentant old man. Shortly afterwards, Rayner met Lord Arran by chance—"I'm being plagued by letters asking for the addresses of these damned places!" he growled.[7]

In April 1967 Rayner celebrated his ninetieth birthday. It was not an occasion that either his family or the law would allow to go unmarked. Deafness was increasing its hold upon him, his sight was badly deteriorating and he needed now almost continuously the support of a stick and the ever more frequent use of the wheelchair, but there was the delight of a family dinner at Claridge's to enjoy on Monday, 10 April, the actual birthday itself, and on Tuesday and Wednesday the Inner and Middle Temples celebrated with special dinners in their respective Halls. The dinner in Middle Temple Hall,

---

[7] Private information, Lord Arran to the author.

where Lord Justice Sachs (as he now was) presided as Treasurer of the Inn for that year, was a particularly splendid occasion, for the Inn honoured not merely one but three distinguished nonagenarians that night. Sir Kenneth Swan, Q.C. (born 13 March 1877), and Sir James Cassels (born 22 March 1877) joined Rayner as guests of honour in a night of tribute unique in the annals of the Inns of Court.

Reporting in *The Times* the following morning, Philip Howard, the Richard Dimbleby of quality journalism, wrote: "Last night more Middle Temple Benchers than one would care to shake a tipstaff at dined together in their great Hall. It has seldom, if ever, been so full for dinner. From the gloomy gallery the five long tables of black gowns flapped and fluttered over their dishes like a rookery in spring. Torches protruded from the wall high overhead, flammiferous with electricity. From behind the High Table at the top of the Hall portraits of ancient lawyers in ruffs and wigs looked down with approval on their legal posterity. . . .

"Enter the Head Porter, elegant in his impressive gown, bearing before him like a quarter-staff the large and lethal-looking Treasurer's stave tipped with silver. He hammers three mighty blows on the ground like something out of Camelot. The Treasurer, Lord Justice Sachs, says a delightful, and intricate, grace in English—'Glory, Honour and Praise . . . Replenish our hearts with joy and gladness.'

"More thunderous bangs, followed by toasts, and huffing and puffing and lighting of cigars. The Treasurer reads out a message from the Queen Mother, who says she has heard with satisfaction and pleasure about the very special occasion to celebrate the birthdays of three Benchers of the Middle Temple tonight. 'This remarkable hat-trick is a tribute not only to the health and vigour' of the three grand old men, 'but also to the vitality of the whole legal profession'. She sends warm congratulations and good wishes to each of them, and to the Inn which with affection has watched three of its Benchers grow to happy longevity. 'Many happy returns of the day.' The applause makes the dust fly from the sinister suits of armour round the walls.

"The Middle Temple then drink, 'with unstinted admiration, to our illustrious, our indomitable, our irrepressibly gay guests of honour'. Great, gaunt rafters ring with claps and cheers, and 'for they are jolly good fellows'.

"And the High Table file out down a corridor of din behind the Head Porter. At the end the three old embodiments of the Law turn and bow, and wave almost boyishly to the Hall. Overhead in the gallery, assorted wives, daughters and sisters confess to lumps in throats. 'We'd better go down and collect them,' or they'll be swinging on the chandeliers' says some female relation disrespectfully."

A few days later, his old Circuit gathered in Gray's Inn Hall to pay Rayner homage. Ninety-seven members attended. "Rayner's speech was short, not very fluent, his powers were waning," says Sir Joseph Molony, Q.C., then Leader of the Circuit. And yet—"as I was steering him from the table, rather early, to avoid imposing strain unduly, someone from the standing gathering cried out, 'What about Albert?' Rayner stopped, turned round to face the company and recited 'Albert and the Lion' faultlessly."

As the nineties tightened their grip on the old man, so his moments of joy grew less. "I tried to look after him in my year—1968—as Treasurer of the Inner Temple," says Lord Stow Hill, the former Sir Frank Soskice, Q.C. "We became really close friends from then on. He was so frightfully grateful if you were kind to him. So long as he possibly could, he always used to come and dine in Hall, and have Sunday lunches and take part in Grand Nights. Most nights he was there, if now nearly always in his wheelchair. Yet he was still the greatest fun after dinner—when the port circulated."

"There *were* pleasures during that period," says Richard Sachs, "but not very many. His particular friends—Clement Penruddock, who would drop in to see him, Ifor Lloyd and Stow Hill—were a great comfort to him. Lord Stow Hill was especially good: he used to take his work and go and do it in my grandfather's flat—just to keep him company."

"In those last few years, he was very deaf, a sick man feeling very much he had outlived his usefulness," says Lord Shawcross. "The last time he came down to stay with us in the country—it must have been in 1968 or 1969—we had to put him in a ground-floor room because of the wheel-chair. We invited him down next for Easter, but he said he couldn't come. So we invited him out to dine with us in London. He accepted but at the last moment he cried off."

Rayner was entering the last painful stages of an old man's existence. There was little pain in the physical sense, but life was beginning very much to lose its remaining joys, especially for someone who had for so many years possessed such enormous vigour.

"He had always been very much mentally alert," says Judge Ifor Lloyd, "but there was a very marked change in him during the last six months to a year of his life. Victor Russell, Sir Harold Morris and Rayner always used to dine together in Hall on 26 January every year, the anniversary of their Call Night. In latter years, everyone in Hall stood up when they walked out. By the start of 1971 Rayner was the only one of the trio left—Russell and Morris had both died some years earlier. It was becoming painfully evident in recent months that Rayner was failing appreciably, and many people made a special effort to get to Hall to dine on the night of 26 January 1971—but he sent a message at the last moment to say he was not feeling too good. In fact, I think he could not face it. It would have been too emotional for him."

Yet even as late as October 1970, when aged ninety-three, he could still respond to the intellectual challenge of meeting and striking up a friendship with a young solicitor from Liverpool named Edward Birch, whom he encountered on the last cruise he ever took to the Mediterranean on the s.s. *Chusan*. "When I learnt that Lord Goddard was one of the passengers, I determined that I must meet him," writes Mr Birch.[9] "From a distance he gave the impression of ferocity and I can well remember wondering how I was going to pluck up the courage to approach him."

After a couple of false starts, he finally asked Rayner's manservant if he would approach the fearsome-looking old man on his behalf. "The man went over to Lord Goddard, who called me over to him. Lord Goddard asked me my name and I replied adding that I hoped he did not object to me disturbing him, and I explained that I had wanted to introduce myself to him rather earlier but my courage had failed me. To the best of my recollection, his exact words were 'Balls, my boy, balls' and he went on to gently chastise me for my timidity. I was quite staggered at his immediate warmth and friendliness and very quickly lost my awe-struck attitude."

The two became firm shipboard friends, and the young Mr Birch used often to take over from Rayner's manservant and wheel the old man around the deck. "He was very easy to be with and, although there would be long periods of silence, they were not difficult silences . . . I was more than grateful for the opportunity to talk with a man who had been the leader of my profession for so many years."

"He told me that he had not been a worrier, and had gone from case to case without regret—a decision made did not cause him any sleepless nights. But he did add that he did regret the hanging of

---

[9] In a letter dated 14 March 1976.

Ruth Ellis.[10] Not because he thought there was any doubt whatsoever about her guilt or the conduct of her trial but simply because she was a woman."[11]

Literally, to the very end, Rayner preserved his remarkable approachability and his affection for youth.

Some five months after the old man's return from his Mediterranean cruise, Timothy Daniell, a 20-year-old Bar student, a total stranger who had never met Rayner or any member of his family before, rang the front-door bell of his flat in Queen Elizabeth Building. "He was the only man I admired as a judge and embodiment of the law at that time," says Mr Daniell, now in practice at the Bar. "I asked the housekeeper who answered the door if I could see Lord Goddard. I explained who I was, that I was a young Bar student and so on; and she came back to me and said, "Come round next week at tea-time'."

Young Timothy Daniell duly returned at teatime exactly a week later. What happened then and in the following weeks made so profound an impression upon him that he recorded the events in his diary. With his permission, these extracts are now printed. They provide a unique glimpse of Rayner Goddard within weeks of his death:

"Thursday 4th March:

I shall never forget the thrill of entering the drawing room where was Goddard, the man who ruled the Bench in the common mind since the War and who gave England a strong and trusted custodian of the Criminal Law.

G "Who are you?"

"Sir, I am reading for the Bar and have seen you going in and out of the entrance—my pupil-master's chambers are below—and I am most grateful for the honour to meet you. You are the most respected judge for us students and I want you to write the Foreword of my book."

G "What book?"

"A book on the Inns of Court," etc. [Daniell was working on a guide to the history and geography of the Inns of Court.[12]]

---

[10] Executed in 1955 for the murder by shooting of her lover David Blakely after she had been thrown over, and at a time when she was not fully recovered from miscarrying Blakely's child.

[11] Compare Mrs Maurice's statement, quoted at page 89, of Rayner's robust attitude to the hanging of women earlier in his career, when at his prime. To what extent can reliance be placed on views expressed by him in the last year of his life?

[12] *A Literary Excursion to the Inns of Court in London*, described and illustrated by Timothy Daniell (Wildy and Sons, 1971).

G "I never write forewords."

"But this is different. You have lived to a great age, and I think this should be stated for it would be appreciated."

We then remembered to have tea . . . We chatted about the Bar—his premonition of bad times to come and falling standards—and dinners in the Inner Temple. I mentioned old (Sir) Harold Morris and 'Magdalen Punch'. Stirred the memories.

Then told me I could come and have tea and read to him my manuscripts, and he would consider whether he could write a foreword.

Went away as pleased as punch.

Friday 19th March:

Call on the flat and Goddard in spirited form. Welcome relief from swatting for Finals.

G "I would like to hear about the Inner Temple . . . Well, I learnt something but dining there has changed since I knew it. I dine there this Term. I must not be late . . ."

G. tells me about the Elephant & Castle: the cockney derivation: the Infanta of Castille which they could never pronounce. I told him I would include this in my book. G. very cheerful today. We discussed crime—he said that there were too many appeals by bad advocates in his court and this Legal Aid was a step backward for the Bar's standards.

Judges had a duty to stamp out frivolous methods of time-wasting which many defences were nowadays.

I asked about the Craig case. G. was emphatic that an accessory was liable in criminal responsibility as much as the offender and that a lot of gas had leaked over the ages of the two defendants. The law was quite clear in the matter . . .[12]

Saturday 3rd April:

Had tea. Suggested the writing of the Foreword.

G "No. It is not any good. I used to give appeal judgments without hesitation. Now I cannot give you a single paragraph! Old age is a terrible handicap.'

We juggled with a few thoughts and I hid my note-book in the folds of the Bergere's cushions as he talked. Fortunately, his housekeeper came in to remove the tea tray and bucked him up to

---

[12] Compare this view with what he told the author nine years earlier in January 1962, and the view, entirely different in tone, expressed in his tape-recorded interview with David Yallop some months before—as set out in Chapter 17 on the Craig and Bentley case.

write the Foreword, which he did falteringly, and signed it at his desk with her help. (The ink wasn't running).

I was thrilled pink, and he asked:

"Please give me a copy. You won't let me down?"

I replied that I would come in and see him before Easter, and then after my exams.

Saturday 10th April:

Work till 1.30.

Spot Lord Goddard's birthday in the daily paper—a good occasion to take him around my bottle of 1927 Taylor" (a bottle of vintage port that Daniell had, unknown to Rayner, bought him as an eventual 'thank you' for the Foreword) and welcome some hopeful felicities from a young man beginning his legal career for a wise man ending his own.

He was in a sallow mood—there is something I like about him—a positive quality, tainted with a dry humour—which though now parched, finds expression in the atmosphere of his home.

He seemed genuinely pleased that I had delivered myself to him on his birthday. When I asked him how he was—he replied—"Not well, when you get to my age, you don't want to go on living."

I told him that I hoped very much he would keep well and I looked forward to seeing him as soon as my exams were ended when I would come round and spend time with him, and paint his portrait into the bargain."

This is the Foreword that Rayner wrote 'falteringly' with his own hand seven days before his ninety-fourth birthday:

"Starting at the Bar now is very different to what it was. Called to the Bar in 1899, I accepted my first brief in the reign of our Sovereign Queen Victoria. In those days there was no scheme of Legal Aid to which everybody can now turn. Half a century later, in 1948, the Legal Aid Act was introduced. How far that has been an advantage to the Bar may be doubted.

"I have read this book. Mr Daniell is to be congratulated in showing the uninformed layman what the Inns of Court represent in history and in the present day."

The old warrior was in harness to his master, the Law, to the last. But by the time that Timothy Daniell's book appeared in the early summer of 1971 an extra fly-sheet had to be inserted edged in black bearing the simple legend: "To the memory of Lord Goddard in gratitude."

Those who knew and loved Rayner will be happy to know that he drank and enjoyed that last bottle of 1927 Taylor. But then finally late one evening at about 10.00 p.m. on Whit Saturday, 29 May 1971, when the nation was relaxing on a holiday weekend and the Temple was near-deserted, the stalwart, obstinate mechanism of his life-force at last ran down and, quietly and at peace in his own bed, the greatest Lord Chief Justice of this century sank gently into the ultimate darkness.

At his own special request, there was no Memorial Service. "He had been compelled by virtue of his office to attend, with considerable boredom, irritation and hostility, too many memorial services for other people," explains Richard Sachs. They were 'a waste of time', he used to say, 'exercises in hypocrisy'. He was determined that no such exercise would take place in his case."

On Wednesday, 2 June 1971, after a small private funeral service in the Temple Church, Rayner was cremated at Golders Green Crematorium: again at his own special request. The manner of his going was like his life: the very opposite of pomp, hypocrisy and humbug.

I leave the last word to his daughter, Lady Sachs: "I am so very glad that one of the more merciful dispensations of Providence has been to enable all of us to forget the last cruel years of extreme old age with its attendant infirmities and to remember with love an able-bodied, mentally vigorous, contentious, cantankerous, prejudiced, fair-minded, infinitely compassionate and lovable human being."

Aftermath

In his lifetime, Rayner Goddard had never been a believer in the *de mortuis nil nisi bonum* principle. *De mortuis nil nisi bunkum* he used to say to Lord Hodson. But in his own case what happened almost amounted, in some quarters, to *de mortuis nil nisi malum*.

It was the Whitsun Legal Vacation when he died. The courts were closed for some two weeks and there could not be the customary tributes in court on the Monday morning following his death. But the newspapers did him fair honour: "With his death there has passed from the scene a great judicial figure, whose strong personality was made familiar far beyond legal circles by his fearless, independent, and often controversial expressions of opinion," said Monday's *The Times* at the start of a three-column-long obituary. "He was an enlightened, if stern, judge renowned equally for clear-cut views and for forthrightness in expressing them," said the *Daily Telegraph*. And the other national newspapers expressed themselves in much the same way, according to their own particular style.

It was all very pleasant, very English and entirely appropriate for the circumstances where a distinguished judge had died, in extreme old age, well over a decade after he had left the active scene. No doubt when the High Court reconvened on 8 June at the start of the Trinity Term there would be the formal tributes paid by his own profession. In due course there might perhaps be a biography, 'official' or otherwise, to endeavour to put down on paper something of his personality and his life. And that would be the total. The old judge would have gone to the Valhalla of legal worthies, his family and close friends would mourn deeply and sincerely, then the pain—eased by knowledge of his age and ever-increasing infirmities—would soften into a warm glow of remembrance, and Rayner would pass into the grey mists of those who wait for all of us on the other side of Eternity.

But it was not to be. On 8 June, on the very morning that judges, lawyers and friends of Rayner opened their copies of *The Times*, knowing that the Trinity Term was due to start that day and there would be sympathetic words said when the courts sat at 10.30, there staring at them on the left centre page was an article by Bernard Levin—headed "Judgement on Lord Goddard". It was a scathing attack, written with all the verbal brilliance of which Mr Levin is so capable. Taking as its starting-point a mention in "The Times Diary" feature by "PHS" the previous week of David Yallop's forthcoming book on the trial of Craig and Bentley, Levin launched into a passionate denouncement of Rayner's work and ability as a judge. It was a pyrotechnic display of invective towards the recently dead man: "Goddard, as Lord Chief Justice, was a calamity. The obituaries read as though they were written by lawyers, and should therefore be taken with a whole Lot's wife of salt . . . . Goddard's influence on the cause of penal reform was almost un-relievedly malign; with a coarse callousness (his fondness for dirty jokes can hardly have been entirely coincidental) there was not only a desperate ignorance of the springs of human behaviour (including, of course, his own) but what seemed like a positive pride in his ignorance . . ." And so on, and so on.

One has no doubt whatsoever that Mr Levin is kindly man, expressing only views that he sincerely held. He continued: "Not only behaviour like Goddard's, but his attitudes, or at the very least the overt expression of them, are now all but impossible on the Bench. I sat through the Laski libel action, over which Goddard presided, and recall distinctly a very revealing exchange. Sir Patrick Hastings (himself one of the last of a breed of lawyers which has now died out) was cross-examining Laski, sneering at his socialist beliefs and pretending to be shocked by them. At one point he goaded Laski beyond endurance and the gentle professor, remembering that Hastings, before turning his coat, had been Attorney-General in the 1924 Labour Government, began in his most languid drawl. 'Really, Sir Patrick, when you were a member of the Socialist Party . . .' Hastings immediately began to abuse Laski and to bluster about 'impertinence'; and Goddard *therefore* [author's italics] weighed in *on the lawyer's side* [Mr Levin's italics]. I do not believe that could happen today."

Memory can play cruel tricks with us all. The Laski libel action had taken place some twenty-five years earlier. It is rather a shame that Mr Levin does not seem to have checked the transcript to see if his "distinct recollection" of "a very revealing exchange" was in fact right. It was not. The official transcript of the proceedings taken from the shorthand notes of the Association of Official Shorthand Writers Ltd., Royal Courts of Justice, would surely not have been too difficult for him to find. It was published as a hardback book by the *Daily Express* after the action was completed.[1] It shows a somewhat different version of the exchange that Mr Levin remembered so well:

Hastings was cross-examining "the gentle professor" on this passage from one of his writings: "The present weakness of discipline is due, as I have argued, to the fact that men no longer accept the values it was conceived to support. If those values are the best, the antithesis between the governors and the multitude is so great that the restoration of discipline to the plane of the old equilibrium is impossible except by force."

So—" 'That means this, does it not,' said Hastings, 'quite impossible in the struggle between privilege and—are there any privileged in the Socialist Party?' Laski—'Why, indeed Sir Patrick, when you were a member—'

"The Lord Chief Justice: 'No, Mr Laski.'

"Sir Patrick Hastings: 'Do not be rude.' Laski—'It is the last thing I want in the world.'

"Hastings: 'It may be difficult for you to be courteous, but do not be rude.' Laski—'Not in the least'.

"Hastings: 'You are rude to everybody, are you not?' Laski—'I do not think so.' "

Sir Patrick Hastings did *not* immediately begin to abuse Laski. He did *not* bluster about "impertinence". Rayner Goddard did *not* "therefore" weigh in on the lawyer's side. The facts—and the nuances —were entirely different, according to the transcript.

But to return to Mr Levin's article. As quoted so far, it would not justify treatment at length. One may question the tastefulness of writing that kind of article at that particular time, with Rayner only ten days dead. David Yallop's book was due to be published later that year; could not Mr Levin have kept what he wanted to say for just those few months longer and then written an absolutely splen-

---

[1] *"The Laski Libel Action": Verbatim Report* (Daily Express, 1947) at page 94, partly cited earlier in Chapter 12 at page 164.

did review of the book vilifying Rayner as much as he liked? Would that not have been a better thing to do—than to write such a piece when the family and other close mourners were at the peak of their grief?

People can give their own answers to those questions. No one has a monopoly on taste—or on opinion.

But what does need to be dealt with is the amazing allegation with which Mr Levin saw fit to close his article.

"By now," he wrote, "I am aware, many a pen must be twitching, especially in the Temple, to write to *The Times* denouncing this column as, in the traditional phrase, 'a cowardly attack on a dead man'. Let the writers know this: that I wrote and published such sentiments, and stronger ones too, while Goddard was alive, and not merely while he was alive but while he was still Lord Chief Justice. And thereby hangs a tale.

"In the late fifties a 'quickie' biography of Goddard appeared. I took the opportunity to hang on the peg of a long review-article about it my views of its subject. A few days after the article appeared, a messenger from the office of the Director of Public Prosecutions arrived at the offices of the paper in which it had appeared, and bought 50 copies. A few days later still, a lawyer friend telephoned me and asked if I would remain where I was for an hour or so, as he had something urgent and important to tell me which he did not want to commit even to the telephone. When he arrived his news was that a secret meeting of High Court judges (his information was that there were over 20 of them) was going on at that very moment, the judges having been asked for their collective advice on whether I should be prosecuted for criminal libel.

"Either they advised that I should not, or they gave contrary advice and it was not taken, for nothing actually happened. But in view of the fact that, quite apart from the principle involved, there was an overwhelming likelihood that one of the judges at this clandestine gathering would have presided if I had had to stand trial, I could not help feeling that this episode was one of the most disgraceful legal improprieties that had ever taken place in this country. I do not think that that could take place today, either."

But did such a meeting in fact ever take place? Is it conceivable that in the late fifties "over 20" High Court judges could meet together in this grossly improper and clandestine way because of an attacking article, however hard-hitting, in a newspaper or journal? These are far weightier questions than a mere verbal onslaught on a dead man. Rayner Goddard's memory is secure. His achievements and the force of his personality will survive. Indeed, his friends and admirers quickly gathered round. Later on that same morning on 8 June 1971, Lord Denning said at the sitting of Appeal Court One: "He will go down in our annals as one of the greatest of Chief Justices. We who saw him day by day in his court speak from knowledge. We say he was respected as no other judge of our time.

"Some there may be, nay are, who say things about him even at this time. To them I answer: They do greatly err. They do not know the man."

For days the correspondence columns of *The Times* rang with the clatter of contending pens. Lord Parker of Waddington, his successor and himself only just recently resigned from office, wrote from retirement to protest that Mr Levin's "below-the-belt attack on such a hard-working, dedicated and public-spirited man as Rayner Goddard was entirely unwarranted especially at this time". Lord Devlin, Lord Shawcross, Lord Stow Hill, Lord Hodson wrote in defence of their friend. Mr Jeffrey Simmons, managing director of W. H. Allen & Co. Ltd, the publishers of David Yallop's book, wrote to say it would be coming out in November and quoting Mr Yallop's taped interview with the old man. Mr George Greenfield, a literary agent, wrote to tell his anti-Rayner story, already recounted, about the old man's bad taste in recounting as one of his "favourite after-dinner anecdotes" the story of how at Winchester Assizes he had just sentenced three prisoners simultaneously to be hanged for murder when a barrel organ in the street outside started to play the *Eton Boating Song*—"we'll all swing together". Mr Giles Playfair, son of Sir Nigel Playfair (who proposed Rayner's barrister friend of Jewish origin to the Garrick Club in May 1930 but did not, unlike Rayner, resign from the club when his man was black-balled), wrote to ask whether Lord Goddard "wasn't one of the most determined and harmful enemies to penal reform in history". The Hon (later Sir) Kenneth Younger wrote recounting an incident from the debates on a minor clause of the Criminal Justice Act of 1948 which he claimed showed that "Goddard had misrepresented the circumstances which did not support his argument".[2]

---

[2] Sir Kenneth Younger wrote in his letter to *The Times*, appearing on 15 June 1971, "I well remember being required as Under-Secretary to present in the House a rather pointless little Bill to increase the penalty for attempted rape. Goddard had urged this upon a reluctant Home Office on the strength of a single case in which a relative of one of his judicial colleagues had been the victim.

"By an odd chance I had had a dock brief in this case and was able to produce the press reports showing that Goddard had misrepresented the circumstances,

Others joined in, for and against. It was a vigorous debate which made "the Top Paper" very much discussed in "Top" circles at that time. It might even have sold a few extra copies.

On 5 December 1974 I wrote to Bernard Levin a personal note asking if he would agree to see me so that he could give me the benefit of his views on Lord Goddard in some depth and in some detail. I made the point that mine was an "official" biography, but that nevertheless I wanted to make it as full and widely based as possible. By return of post, Mr Levin replied in the most courteous fashion declining the invitation to a meeting because "I really have nothing to say. I made my views known, fairly unambiguously, in the article I wrote after his death, and in the earlier one, which followed the same lines. But I have made no great study of him, and everything I would want to say about him, or indeed could say about him, you therefore have."

On 10 January 1975 I wrote again to Mr Levin stating, "I want to write about Lord Goddard as a man in the round. If in fact a

---

which did not support his argument. The Home Secretary, however, told me that he thought the Bill, which was irrelevant rather than harmful, had better go forward, since he had had to reject Goddard's advice on so many other points of greater importance." In a letter to the author, dated 12 February 1976, the late Sir Kenneth amplified his charge: "On being shown the file, I found that the *only* reason" (for the proposed change) "was pressure from Goddard. While he insisted that judges were constantly complaining about the 2 year limit, he gave only one identifiable instance . . . By an extraordinary fluke I had defended the man on a dock brief. The jury quickly decided to convict and the judge Travers Humphreys . . . gave him 18 months. In doing so, he made no complaint about the maximum but referred to it as follows: (This is from a cutting which I still have.)

"The jury have convicted you upon evidence that could have left no doubt in the mind of any reasonable person who heard it of an abominable outrage . . . A respectable lady walking along the road must be protected from men with passions like yours and such disgusting and horrible behaviour as you were guilty of. If you had not a good character up to the present, I would have sentenced you to the maximum term of imprisonment which the law allows.'"

No doubt Sir Kenneth, as a former Chairman of the Howard League for Penal Reform, disapproved exceedingly of Lord Goddard and most of his views on penalty, but at the time of which he writes Sir Travers Humphreys was still alive, still sitting as a King's Bench judge and often (indeed, whenever possible) sitting with Goddard as his right-hand man in the Court of Criminal Appeal. Whatever Sir Kenneth Younger's yellowing press cutting may say, is it really likely that the Lord Chief Justice of England would deliberately and consciously misrepresent to the Home Secretary of the day what his distinguished judicial colleague's views were? Is it not more likely that Humphreys, then aged eighty-one, and without the benefit of a contemporary record, told Goddard, in perfect good faith, that he would have liked to have been able to give the attempted ravisher of the judge's niece a longer sentence—or something to that effect? It is not necessary to ascribe deliberate deceit to Rayner Goddard's actions.

meeting of the judges was called either at his behest or even on 'a wink is as good as a nod' principle, I want to know about it—and include it in my book." I therefore asked if he had any specific information that could assist me: "Dates, how, when, anything?" Would he be prepared to tell me the name of the anonymous friend he quoted in his article so I could contact him for myself?

On 15 January 1975, Mr Levin replied that he "must clear up one misunderstanding. I never suggested that the meeting was called at Goddard's behest, or even on the 'wink as good as a nod' principle. And I should be astonished to learn that he did anything but disapprove of it. If he had one characteristic above all, it was his indifference to criticism." As for giving me the name of his informant, he would first have to consult him: "Unfortunately, of course, it was a long time ago now, and he may have forgotten all about it, or at any rate the details. There is an additional complication, in that he has since attained a certain eminence, and may well wish not to be in any way involved in reviving the matter." But Mr Levin assured me that he would write to him, and if he authorized him to give me his name, he would of course do so.

I waited, and then within a very few days received Mr Levin's further letter dated 21 January 1975, telling me that, as promised, he had got in touch with his informant, and told him of my wish to talk to him. "I regret, however, that he does not wish, as he puts it, 'to reveal the details of the story'. He adds "actually I am not at all sure that I can recall anything beyond the bare outline of the matter". I am sorry about this; and I hope this somewhat protracted exchange has not delayed your work on the book, which in any case I look forward to reading when it appears."

A civilized, but not over-helpful, correspondence. So what are the facts?

Bernard Levin's article on the "quickie" biography of Rayner (a somewhat ungracious reference to Eric Grimshaw and Glyn Jones's *Lord Goddard, His Career and Cases*) appeared in *The Spectator* for the issue dated 16 May 1958 at page 629. Headed "Brother Savage",[3] it did indeed contain similar sentiments to those in his *Times* article as well as, to use Mr Levin's expression, "stronger ones too". It berated Rayner's "intellectual megalomania", "the girlish

---

[3] Lord Goddard was not, in fact, a member of the Savage Club of long standing. He only joined when specifically invited to do so in 1956. He was never very much of a club man, not having joined any similar gentleman's club since resigning from the Garrick in 1930. He was, however, a member of several select dining clubs, such as "The Other Club" and "Grillions".

emotionalism which seems to be his only reaction to such subjects as capital and corporal punishment", some of his views were described as a "wretched blot on the English legal system", his speech at a Royal Academy Banquet was categorized as of "appallingly indiscreet vulgarity", his "curious liking for . . . dirty jokes" was condemned, on the question of insanity in murder it was written "Lord Goddard walks hand in hand with ignorance on one side of him and barbarism on the other" and there was much more in similar vein—ending with what Rayner's friends still consider the unkindest cut of all: in a reference to another book reviewed by Mr Levin at the same time, a study by an American author, Dr Frederic Wertham, of a Puerto Rican juvenile gang killing in New York, Mr Levin concluded: "As Dr Wertham throws the pebbles of his indictment into the pool of society the circles of guilt spread farther and farther out, till the last ripple laps against the feet of every one of us. And Lord Goddard's are of clay."

Undoubtedly, the article caused great offence. "Rayner was deeply wounded by it—deeply, deeply wounded," says Lord Edmund-Davies. Nevertheless, all the evidence points unswervingly to the conclusion that the meeting of which Bernard Levin complains never took place.

Mr Levin wrote of "over 20" High Court judges attending the meeting. At that time there were (apart from the Lord Chief Justice himself) twenty-six judges in the Queen's Bench Division. It is difficult to understand how, even if the whole bizarre story were true, judges from any other Division could have been included: a Chancery judge or a judge of the Probate, Divorce and Admiralty Division would hardly have had very well-informed views on criminal libel, a somewhat rarified part of the criminal law.

Yet there were not "over 20" Queen's Bench judges in London at that time! If Mr Levin had checked—and it would not have been impossible to do so—to find out how many Queen's Bench judges were out of London on assize in May 1958, he would have discovered that the number was probably not less than eight.[4] Eight from twenty-six leaves eighteen. The meeting of which his anonymous barrister friend "who has since attained a certain eminence" had told him was a physical impossibility.

I have approached Lord Dilhorne, who was Attorney-General at the time, to see if he can assist. If any such prosecution were being

---

[4] One such easy source of reference would have been the "Notices" at page 269 of the bound volume of *The Law Journal* for 1958.

considered—and I can find no record of any actually having been brought relating to an attack on a judge for at least two hundred years—he would have been the prosecutor. It would have been his decision to institute proceedings. I can state authoritatively that, if Lord Dilhorne *had* been minded to take such a course, he might well have asked Rayner himself for his views but the final decision would have been his alone, and he most certainly would not have consulted the Queen's Bench judges, even if only because it would then have been impossible to find a judge to try the case. Indeed, even without the judges being involved in a consultative capacity, it would still have been difficult to find a judge to take the case—which would, in itself, have been enough to make the whole idea of a prosecution a non-starter.

It must be said that I have not approached any of the Queen's Bench judges of that time who are still living, and asked them the specific question: "Did such a meeting take place?" That would seem to be an impertinence and entirely an improper procedure, bringing the judges themselves into the arena of personal controversy; especially in view of the fact that the allegation comes originally from someone not prepared even now to allow his name to be disclosed or even meet me to discuss the matter.

But what about that mysterious messenger from the office of the Director of Public Prosecutions who, Mr Levin wrote, arrived at *The Spectator's* offices and bought 50 copies? What is the story behind that? I wrote to Sir Norman Skelhorn, Q.C., the Director of Public Prosecutions, asking for elucidation, but was met with a polite, albeit not completely unexpected, expression of difficulty in disclosing official records for the purpose of their being quoted in a biography.

Lord Hodson, the retired Law Lord who was one of Rayner's closest friends, would seem to have the truth of the matter. On 15 June 1971 *The Times* printed his letter: "It is . . . difficult to prove, but to me unthinkable, that such a conclave took place". And on 20 March 1972, in an interview, he told me: "Reggie Dilhorne was then Attorney-General and he did take rather a poor view of the article. He wanted to prosecute Levin for it. He thought he was going too far. But Goddard, although upset, pooh-poohed the idea and said it was nonsense, and that was all there was to it! I am convinced in my own mind that there was never any meeting of over 20 Queen's Bench judges to decide whether or not to prosecute—although I accept that Levin, in good faith, may well have thought there to have been."

For my part, I do not for one moment challenge Mr Levin's good faith, but I cannot believe that I am alone in thinking that it was an unfortunate allegation to make in a responsible newspaper and under the imprint of one of the most respected names in contemporary journalism. However, let it not sully the reputation and undying fame of a man on whom, as we have seen, his own daughter has passed the sharpest and fairest judgment: "An able-bodied, mentally vigorous, contentious, cantankerous, prejudiced, fair-minded, infinitely compassionate and lovable human being." How splendid to have that said about one!

Index